Snake's Marble

A Persian Memoir

Mehry M. Reid
and
Thomas R. Reid

VANTAGE PRESS
New York

FIRST EDITION

Published by Vantage Press, Inc.
516 West 34th Street, New York, New York 10001

Manufactured in the United States of America
ISBN: 0-533-11387-3

Library of Congress Catalog Card No.: 94-90835

0 9 8 7 6 5 4 3 2 1

To the millions of Persian people who were forced to flee
their native land after the Moslem fundamentalist coup

Contents

Preface

In this book, I invite the reader to pass through the "wooden gate" and enter the home I knew as a child. Meet the members of my family and those simple, loyal, unforgettable characters who tended to many of our daily needs. We looked upon them more as family than as servants, and in addition to making our lives comfortable, they entertained us with their stories, beliefs, and superstitions. Come in and enjoy the hospitality and warmth that has characterized for thousands of years the way of life of millions of people in that far-off country known as Persia, or Iran. Let me introduce you to the sociocultural customs of a nation that contributed so much to civilization as we know it today.

To many people, the word *Persia* is associated only with Persian carpets, Persian cats, caviar, and, possibly, Persepolis. But to a native-born Persian, it conjures up a variety of different images—majestic snowcapped mountains that seem to harbor hidden mysteries within them; conduits of water that run for miles underground and finally emerge in sparkling purity to give life to the land; lifeless salt deserts that stretch for miles between old caravanserai; forests full of wild flowers, animals, and birds that delight the eye and the ear; old houses with stained-glass windows and unique "fish pond" recreation rooms in the basement; ancient bazaars; cold, swift-running mountain streams; orchards, their trees heavy with fruit; gardens of roses; the lilting songs of nightingales—all beneath a deep blue sky that looks down on a warm and friendly people.

I will try to acquaint you with Persia's rich cultural heritage that extends back to before the dawn of recorded history. Much of the ancient history of the land and its people is chronicled in the works of the ancient poets, who expressed in verse their thoughts and commentary on the current events of their time. In this book, the reader will learn to appreciate the Persian love for poetry and understand how poetry frequently has been used to express the feelings of the people toward the political and social mores of their time. Persian poetry celebrates the courageous deeds of the brave heroes of centuries past, even predating the founding of the ancient Persian Empire by Cyrus the Great and his son Darius from 550 B.C. to 300 B.C. In a different vein, it revels in the beauty of nature and love. At times, poets used their verse like a sword to defend themselves against inequities. On the darker side, poetry has been used to castigate the acts of that group of men, the mullahs, who, in the guise of religion, attempt to brainwash the masses, making them their puppets in order to exploit them and profit from their ignorance.

The Persia in which I lived was in a period of transition from a society fettered by the repressive rules of Islamic religious law to a society governed by a constitutional monarchy that sought to educate the masses and enfranchise the women. For example, I attended one of the first coeducational elementary schools, where the girls were able to compete and learn on an equal basis with the male students. By the same token, I had a cultural bridge to the old way of life through my grandparents, who regaled me with stories of their youth. My childhood was enriched by close contact with the servants, who had served my grandparents and my parents for so many years that they seemed a part of the family. From them, I learned how old superstitions governed in part their everyday lives, just as I learned over the years to appreciate their steadfast loyalty and devotion to our family. As the reader will see in chapter 6, these simple, guileless folk, while for the most part illiterate, had much to impart to one willing to listen and learn. This book will attempt to answer many of the questions that Westerners have concerning the customs and way of life in the Persia that I knew.

I have been told that I am blessed with a photographic memory, and this book is a collection of those memories, a window to the past. However, I would be woefully remiss if I did not express my gratitude to my brothers, my sisters, and all of the friends who filled in many of the details I had forgotten or never knew. Whenever we get together, we enjoy reminiscing about the good old days, and I wish that we could do it more often. I left Persia a few years before the revolution. Thousands of Persians fled the country during and after the revolution, some in fear for their personal safety. Those of the intelligentsia who could, fled because they could not tolerate the barbarism and repression that became the hallmark of the fundamentalist fanatics who now govern the land. These refugees are now scattered around the world. They have intermarried with peoples of diverse cultures, and children are being born who may never see the land of their ancestors.

For many years I thought about writing the memoirs of my childhood, but when my daughter, Mojdeh, told me that she was carrying my first grandchild, this was the catalyst that got me started. I wanted to leave for him and his descendants a family history of sorts and a feeling for the customs, traditions, and way of life of the country where half of his forebears were born. I hope that it will be of interest to the thousands of children born to other expatriates, as well as my own grandson. The history of Persia throughout the millennia is that of conquest and being conquered but always reemerging, perhaps with some change, but basically unchanged. I fervently hope that the same cycle will repeat itself and a new and enlightened government, independent of religious influence, will eventually evolve.

The names of most of my family members have been changed to protect their privacy. The views expressed, especially those concerning religion, are my own and do not necessarily reflect the beliefs of all members of my family. I want to thank my husband, Tom, for his help and encouragement as well as his patient listening to my stories and translating them from my English to the proper English prose. We had a good deal of fun writing this book over the past four years, although some days went by without a word being put to paper while my husband just sat and listened, as so often happens to a married man.

Chapter One
Window to the Past

My heart is like a bird lost from her nest;
It wanders everywhere with no place to rest.
　　　　—Nazemi Shirazi (Grandfather Agha Bozorg)

Often in my dreams I go back to our home in Mashhad where I lived the first eleven years of my life. I wander again along the brick paths through the gardens resplendent with beds of geraniums, roses, petunias, and pansies. I dally beneath the fruit trees in the orchard, and in my mind's eye I see myself pushing my cousin Genoos on the swing hanging from one of the trees, while she sings to me in her sweet voice. From the lower branches of the trees heavy with fruit, I pick an apple, pear, plum, apricot, quince, or cherry, or gorge myself on the sweet white mulberries dripping from the tall tree near the grape arbor. I see the shimmering reflection of the yellow, purple, and white iris planted along the banks of the clear stream that flowed through our property and hear its gentle murmur humming a background for the songs of the many colorful birds.

I sit in the brick-floored gazebo at one end of the garden and revel in the scent of the jasmine and pink damask roses that climb up the sides and cover the roof. I tuck a sprig of jasmine behind one ear so that I can smell its perfume as I wander about. I watch the many butterflies as they flit between the roses in the garden next to the gazebo and try to match their bright colors with those of the flowers. I break off a few leaves of the mint, tarragon, and basil plants growing in the herb garden and rub them between my palms, inhaling their fragrance, which blends so

1

well with the earth scent rising from the freshly watered petunia beds. Today, whenever I smell honeysuckle, I hear the cooing of the doves that used to nest at the top of the honeysuckle-covered roof pillars of our porches.

I can see Gholam, our burly gardener, walking up from the stream with a huge watering can in either hand to water the flowerbeds and then, this chore completed, watch him as he stands barefoot in the stream to open the gate of the irrigation ditch that carried water to the vegetable garden and orchard. I remember the day when I ran breathlessly to tell Grandmother of my discovery of a nest full of baby birds in the hedge next to my father's library window and how she admonished me not to touch them for fear that the mother bird would abandon her brood. I can still hear the singing of the birds at dawn; the chatter and giggling of the maids as they congregated around the pool in the afternoon, relaxing after they had finished their work; and the low, murmuring voices of my grandparents as they sat on the porch of an evening, entertaining each other with anecdotes or reciting poetry.

Our house was situated on a six-acre plot of land located at the intersection of two streets in the residential section of Mashhad. The entire property was surrounded by a high brick wall, with entrance gates on the southern and eastern sides. A brick walkway bordered by hedges led from the east gate into the property. Just inside the east gate and to the right next to the wall, there was a single-story building that was the servant's quarters. To the left there was the shady tunnel of a long grape arbor. Directly ahead and about twenty yards from the gate, several stone steps led down to a lower level.

This lower level was divided into four parts by brick walkways that intersected at a central circular flowerbed with a statue of a girl in the center. The uplifted right hand of the statue held a bouquet of flowers that served as a base for a light. The four sections of land were planted with rows of fruit trees—apple, plum, cherry, quince, pear, and apricot. At the end of the north-south path and next to the south wall there was a gazebo covered with climbing roses and jasmine vines. Flanking the gazebo on both sides were flowerbeds filled with dozens of rose bushes, bearing a variety of multicolored roses.

2

A large courtyard filled the area between the north wing, the connecting center wing, and the south wing of the house. In the center of this courtyard there was an octagonal-shaped pool about five feet in depth. Water was piped to the pool from the well in the *otagh chahee* (well room) inside the house. It spewed into the pool through the open mouth of a carved stone lion's head mounted on the edge of the pool nearest to the house. Four brick walkways radiated from the pool, dividing the courtyard into four sections, each filled with flowerbeds and decorative shrubbery. Next to the walkway surrounding the pool, at the edge of each flowerbed, grew four trees—a large willow, two tall pines, and a poplar tree.

The pool was not a swimming pool in the sense that it could be used for such by adults, but it was large and deep enough for small children to learn to swim. By the same token, it was a hazard for toddlers, and the adults were constantly on guard to prevent any accidents whenever any young children were playing around the courtyard. During the spring, starting just before *Now Ruz*, the Persian New Year, and throughout the summer and early autumn, the pool was drained and refilled with well water weekly. The drained water was not wasted, of course. Gholam, the gardener, would first use it to water the flowerbed around the courtyard, and the rest was channeled off to irrigate the orchards.

After the pool was drained and cleaned, a man who was hired just for this purpose made his weekly visit to fill it. He would go into the well room[1] in the house and sit on a raised platform next to the well. His legs straddled a block of stone shaped like a large bowl, in the center of which there was a hole with an underground pipe leading to the stone lion's head spout at the pool side. With his feet, he operated a treadle-powered windlass that brought the water up from the well in a large leather bucket, the top of which was rimmed with an iron ring to make it sink below the water surface for filling. As each bucket of water was brought up, he would tip it into the hole in the stone between his legs, and the water would flow into the pool. It would take him about five hours to completely fill the pool, and all the while we could hear the distinctive noise of the creaking windlass. My sister Tooran gave up trying to learn to play the

3

violin when she was told that her playing sounded like the pool man's music!

As I mentioned above, the pool was a potential hazard for toddlers and small children. I remember one weekend afternoon in early summer when I was about three years old. I had taken a small basket to the orchard and filled it with sour cherries. We had always been warned to wash any fruit or vegetable before eating them, so I stopped alongside the stream to wash my basket of cherries. My brother Jamshid was in a particularly truculent mood that day, and as soon as I started to wash the fruit, he shouted at me to be off—this part of the stream belonged to him that day! I moved to another area. He followed and again claimed riparian rights over that section. After an unsuccessful attempt to use a third spot, I moved to the courtyard pool. I sat down on the raised edge of the pool and dipped my basket in the water, swinging it back and forth to wash the cherries. A few cherries floated out of the basket and started to sink into the pool.

I leaned forward to retrieve them and promptly fell face first into the water. I began to gasp and swallow water, all the while flailing my arms frantically. Suddenly, I felt a pair of strong arms lifting me out of the pool. It was my father who had been watching me from the porch of the south wing of the house, where he and some guests had been sitting and chatting after lunch. Within seconds he had reached me and pulled me to safety. The guests all wondered how he was able to react so quickly. Father told them that when he saw me sit on the edge of the pool, he knew that I was going to fall in. He did not order me away from the water but rather kept a close watch on me so that he was able to pluck me out before any damage was done. I guess that he felt that a good scare would be the best lesson for me.

Later in the autumn of that same year, I was playing in the sitting-dining room of the north wing, whilst my sister Katayoon prepared the table for dinner. She asked me to cross over to the south wing, where my father was reading in his library, and tell him that dinner was ready. I refused to go since the courtyard was dark and I was afraid. She repeated her request. Rather than comply or stay and possibly be punished, I moved to the next room and continued my play. Katayoon did not notice where I went and assumed that I had gone to call my father for dinner.

4

After ten or fifteen minutes, I heard a commotion out in the courtyard.

I went out and found Katayoon thrashing about in the pool, shouting, "Mehry! Mehry! Where is she?" The pool was ringed by family and servants, all talking and speculating on my whereabouts. I stood in the back of the circle, wondering why there was so much fuss. A few seconds later, someone noticed me. Poor Katayoon was helped out of the pool, wrapped in blankets against the chill, and hustled into the house to change into dry clothes. It turned out that she had heard a splash as something fell into the pool and assumed that I had stumbled into it in the dark on my way across the courtyard. A few minutes later, the family cat slunk into the house, soaking wet. No one knew exactly what happened, but everyone suspected that my brother Jamshid, the prankster, had struck again!

Around the periphery of the courtyard, between the flowerbeds and the house, there was a wide bricked-over space. It was there, under the stars, or on one of the porches, that the family slept during the warm summer nights. At the beginning of summer, the servants would bring from a storage room the wooden beds that we were to use during the summer and set them up wherever we chose to sleep during the warm season. Each fair summer evening they would make up these beds for us with a mattress, sheets, and a light blanket. My grandparents slept on the porch outside their wing of the house. Father did not sleep outdoors but remained inside in a small bedroom next to his library. The rest of the family's beds were scattered all about in the open courtyard.

My favorite spot was beneath the willow tree next to the pool. After everyone was in bed and the lights were out, I would lie there in the darkness, breathing in the cool, moist night air and enjoying the sight of the moonlight filtering through the branches of the row of tall poplar trees on the west border of the orchard. The moonlight reflected from the pool, and once in a while, as a light breeze ruffled the surface of the water, the reflection would dissolve into hundreds of dancing silver butterfly wings. All was silent except for the chirp of the crickets and the occasional faint clatter of horses' hooves on cobblestones as a *doroshkeh* (horse-drawn carriage) passed in some distant street

5

beyond the high walls. I soon drifted off to sleep.

In most of Persia, except in the mountains in the north and west and in those areas near a river, such as the city of Isfahan, there is a scarcity of water due to the low rainfall. In these arid surroundings, any oasis of greenery that can be created is lovingly cherished and tended with care. The Persians are famous for their ability to make beautiful gardens, utilizing as little water as possible. The Persian garden is more than just a showplace; it is a place for relaxation and renewing of the spirit. The many flowerbeds in the courtyards and bordering the walkways in our garden were all beautiful because of Gholam the gardener's tender care; but of all the lovely places in the gardens and the orchard, the *alachegh* (gazebo) was the favorite spot for all the family.

Early every summer morning, my father could be seen walking with hands clasped behind his back in the rose garden next to the gazebo, inspecting each bush. Gholam would watch him from a distance, anxious to detect any sign of disapproval. Grandfather Khan always awoke before sunrise and walked out to the gazebo, where he would pluck a handful of the newly opening jasmine blossoms. These he would carry back to the house and put in a bowl of water next to Grandmother's place at their table. Grandmother always looked forward to this and called it her gift of love that made her day. One day she told me she had overslept that morning and had had such a beautiful dream. She dreamed she was walking down a tunneled arbor covered so thickly with fragrant jasmine that the blossoms touched her face as she walked along. She woke up to find that Grandfather was standing over her dropping his morning gift of jasmine blossoms on her face to gently awaken her.

My brothers and sisters, when they came home from work or school with friends, would usually sit in the gazebo with them and have afternoon tea. Occasionally, on weekends when all my sisters and brothers were home and available to help, we would carry our food to the gazebo and take our dinner there. Several evenings during the summer, Father would gather with some of his friends in the gazebo for a *bazm*, the Persian name for an evening of self-entertainment. Those who could would play musical instruments; all would sing and recite poetry, both original and classical. The musicians would bring their own instruments, usually one of the four stringed instruments unique to Persia: the *tar*, a six-string instrument similar to a mandolin but having a richer tone; the *setar*, a smaller version of the *tar*; the *kamancheh*, played with a bow like a cello; and the *santoor*, a percussion string instrument similar to a zither.

The violin was also popular; my second eldest brother was a virtuoso with this instrument. This type of entertainment *(bazm)* is an old custom in Persia. Music and poetry have been an important part of Persian life for thousands of years. Many historians believe that the ancient Persians were the first to devise musical instruments. In 1966, two archeologists, one from the University of Chicago and the other from the University of California, unearthed a fragment of terra-cotta in southern Persia bearing drawings of a group of musicians playing the harp, drum, and an instrument having the appearance of a ram's horn, along with a singer. This fragment was dated to the year 3400 B.C. In the Louvre Museum, there is a headless terra-cotta sculpture of a person playing a lutelike instrument. This was found in an archeological dig in Persia and has been dated as originating about 6000 B.C. The ancient holy book, *Avesta*, which is a collection of the teachings of Zoroaster, founder of the first official Persian religion, contains a part known as the *Kata* that is believed to be the oldest Persian collection of hymns for worship. Persian classical music, which developed during the Sassanid period before the Islamic conquest, has influenced the music of all of the countries of the Middle East. When Alexander the Great conquered Persia in 330 B.C., he was so impressed with the Persian musical expertise that, when he returned to Greece, he took back with him two thousand Persian musicians.

No true Persian cannot help but feel a spiritual joy and peace that seems divinely inspired when he listens to the old classical melodies, especially when they are played on a single instrument, such as the *tar*, by a skilled musician. My father's brother was a master of the *tar*. Late one summer night, when he was visiting us, he stole off by himself to the gazebo, where he sat and softly played his *tar* by the light of a full moon. As he played, a nightingale from somewhere in the orchard began to sing. My uncle would stop his playing for a few seconds; then the nightingale would sing in answer. This continued for couple of hours, with the bird coming closer and closer to my uncle, until the bird was perched just a few yards away on one of the rose bushes. I and my brothers and sisters lay in our beds around the courtyard pool listening, enthralled by the impromptu concert performed in the moonlit dreamlike setting. Every time the nightingale sang, it was a different melody. That is why the nightingale is called *hezardastan* in Farsi, meaning "thousand stories."

Grandmother and Grandfather Khan lived with us for as long as the family lived in Mashhad. After we moved to Tehran, they continued to live in the Mashhad house until their deaths. They occupied the north wing, where they had their own kitchen, sitting rooms, and bedrooms. The south wing, which we called the *beerooney* (men's quarters), contained my father's library, a formal parlor, a dining room, my parents' bedroom, and a large room that Mother used as a kind of walk-in closet and storage room. The gate in the south wall opened into the *beerooney* courtyard, and it was through this gate that guests were admitted and entertained in the parlor and dining room. There was no direct interior communication between the south wing and the rest of the house. To access these areas from the *beerooney*, one had to go out one of the rear doors and cross the courtyard.

The central and north wings were known as the *andarooney* (female or family quarters). They contained bedrooms, sitting rooms, kitchens, several pantries, and, in the center, the well room. This separation of the men's quarters from the female quarters was a hangover from the old days when male visitors were not allowed to look upon the women of the household and were entertained exclusively by the men of the house. This was not the custom when I was a child, but the traditional nomenclature differentiating the formal reception area from the living quarters still persisted.

The kitchens were the busiest rooms in the house, because it seemed that some sort of food preparation was in progress all day long. There were no food processors, mixers, or other modern appliances to speed up the work, and many of the traditional Persian dishes require prolonged cooking. The food was not hot or spicy but delicately seasoned with fresh or dried herbs, saffron, and a little garlic. There was always a wonderful aroma in the air whenever you opened the kitchen door. As I think back, I am amazed at how such a variety and quantity of delicious food could be produced in such relatively primitive facilities. The old-fashioned Persian housewives were truly creative culinary artists; they worked from no cookbook, and the simple peasants hired as cooks required much training before they achieved sufficient expertise to be allowed on their own in the kitchen. I remember how amazed and happy the cooks, Soltan and Naneh, were when Father brought home the first mechanical food grinder and clamped it to the corner of the large table in Grandmother's kitchen. Now they could grind up meats and nuts rather than laboriously chop them or pound them in the stone mortar with the double-headed wooden pestle. My older sisters carefully supervised them for several days to make sure they did not get their fingers too far in the funnel top while they turned the crank with the other hand.

We had two kitchens, one for Grandmother and one for my mother, located next to each other in the northwest corner of the house and connected by a door. Each had a concrete sink about six feet long, with two cold water taps. At one end of the sink in Grandmother's kitchen, a large, circular, woven wooden tray rested on three edges of the sink. This held a sheepskin bag that contained one of the staples of Persian diet, yogurt. The liquid yogurt, seasoned with thyme and other dried herbs, was put into the skin sack. The liquid gradually seeped through the skin, draining onto the wooden tray and then into the sink. When the yogurt was about the consistency of sour cream, it was ready to eat. Every day or so, additional fresh yogurt would be added and mixed with the thickened remnants by kneading the sack.

Periodically, Grandmother's maid, Naneh, would wash down the outside of the sack and rub the surface with salt to prevent the skin from deteriorating. Almost every day when I came home from school, I would go to the kitchen and beg Naneh for a slice of fresh bread spread with yogurt as a snack to tide me over until dinner. This, I am sure, was better for me than the peanut butter and jelly sandwiches that are so popular with Western children. Persians believe that yogurt is one of the healthiest foods because it contains bacteria and lactic acid that aid the digestive system. A Russian patriarch who lived to be 130 years old attributed his longevity to his thrice-daily consumption of yogurt and black bread!

The kitchen stoves were next to the outer wall of each kitchen and they shared a common chimney. The stoves were made of brick, with an iron grate inset about fifty centimeters above the floor. Wood or charcoal was fed through an iron door in the front and burned on the grate. The ashes fell through the grate and were removed through an opening in the front below the doors. This opening also generated a draught to feed the fire. The top was made of a sheet of cast iron, with four or five circular openings of different sizes on which the copper cooking pots were placed. Removable lids covered the holes not in use. There were no ovens in the stoves; our bread dough was prepared in the kitchen and sent to the local bakery for baking, or bread was purchased ready-made by Gholam on his daily trek to the market.

Our family kitchen had one interesting embellishment: There was a tiled countertop that was the work of a famous architect and artisan named Taherzadeh Behzad, who had become a friend of my father during the construction of the Shahreza Hospital. This talented man supervised the manufacture of the decorative tiles for the hospital and frequently brought small gifts of his work to Father when he came to visit. The countertop was about five feet in length and thirty inches wide. It was inlaid with tiles that were in a pattern similar to that in a Persian carpet: varicolored leaves and flowers interconnected by gracefully curved lines on a white background. Portions of the design were done with twenty-four karat gold paint. Needless to say, this countertop was not used for chopping or any heavy work. A few pieces of Taherzadeh Behzad's artistry are still cherished by several members of the family.

The name Behzad, or Bihzad, has been associated with Persian miniature painting for centuries. The most famous is Kamaladdin Bihzad (1450–1537), who illustrated many important Persian manuscripts, such as the *Gulistan* by Sa'adi, the *Khamesa* by Nizami, and the *Timur Namah*. Persian miniatures are not painted to be viewed as separate works of art, but rather are illustrations prepared for manuscripts. It is an extremely delicate and colorful art form, as well as very complex. They contain a profusion of human and animal forms. The older miniaturists did not use perspective or shadow in their paintings. The viewer seems to be looking down into the picture space from a great height. My husband and I treasure a copy of FitzGerald's translation of Omar Khayyam, illustrated with fifty beautiful paintings by a contemporary Behzad named Hossein Behzad Miniatur.

As children, the pantries held a special fascination for us. It was there that we found stored the many goodies upon which we feasted at every opportunity. One pantry was situated between the dining room in the south wing and the center living quarters. Here were kept the table linens, dishes, silverware, and—more important to the children—a half-dozen or so deep wooden bins with hinged tops. Every autumn these bins were filled with dried apricots, apples, peaches, and nuts. We managed to empty every bin by early springtime, long before the new crop had ripened in our orchard or fresh fruit was available in the market.

Another pantry opened off the rear wall of the kitchen in the central wing. This was a large square room with a narrower extension, whose floor was partially bricks and partially dirt. Embedded in the earth of the dirt-floored portion of the pantry were five huge wide-mouthed ceramic amphora used by Grandmother to make wine vinegar. On two walls, a narrow shelf ran close to the ceiling. On these shelves the quinces, which in Persia are the size of a grapefruit and very sweet, were stored after the fall harvest. Some we ate fresh and others were baked in the embers of the charcoal stove until the outside skin was a deep russet and the inside a delicious steaming pulp. In the ceiling, there were exposed beams embedded with many nails. These were used as hooks on which to hang, in the fall, bunches of nearly ripe grapes that gradually ripened and provided fresh fruit for several months.[2] The beams were quite high and the servants had to bring in a ladder in order to reach the nails and hang the grapes. My brother Jamshid was a prankster who was always concocting practical jokes to bedevil the family and the servants. He made a long wooden pole with a hook on one end with which he was able to reach the grapes. Whilst I stood watch at the doorway, he would sneak into the pantry, take down a bunch of grapes, and then steal off to eat them, sharing with me, of course. The servants were mystified at the gradual disappearance of the fruit since no one ever saw a ladder taken into the room.

Behind the well room, there was a storage room where coal, logs, and the watering buckets were kept. Along two of the walls, there were counters upon which were stored the delicious white Persian melons and watermelons that were brought to the house every summer. The family consumed a prodigious number of these melons throughout the growing season. In the fall of the year, the last of the melons, as well as watermelons, were stored and saved for the celebration of *yalda*,[3] the longest night of the year.

Every week, porters from the local fruit market would lead a train of asses laden with melons through the east gate and proceed along the periphery of the orchard to the courtyard in front of the well room. There, the delivery people would unload their panniers and the servants would carry the melons into the storage room. One day, one of the donkeys wandered off after being unloaded and ambled across the courtyard pursued by two of the men. They were unable to stop him before he got into Grandmother's sitting room in the north wing. Here, he relieved himself of a great quantity of urine, saturating the carpet. Needless to say, the delivery men received a royal tongue-lashing from my irate grandmother. Never again was any donkey allowed to remain unattended.

In addition to the well that we used for drinking water and to fill the courtyard pool, we had a second source of water on our property that was used for irrigation of the orchard and watering the gardens. Without this water, the delicious fruits from our orchard and the lovely flowers in the many beds around the property would not have existed. A clear stream, which branched off from the government-owned Alamdasht Ghanat,[4] which was about two miles from our house, flowed onto our property through an opening in the northeast corner of the wall. Father paid a fee for this service every calendar quarter. This stream passed through many other properties before it reached ours and continued on to others after leaving our land, but it remained clear and free of pollution. In fact, some of our neighbors who did not have wells used this water for drinking after treating it with chlorine. Water is a precious commodity in Persia and great care is taken to preserve its purity.

The stream, after it entered onto our land, was divided into two branches by means of two dug ditches. The wider of the ditches went west then south and east around the periphery of the property. The smaller ditch went from the northeast to the southeast corner of the wall, where it reunited with the other branch before it exited our property. Thus, all four sides of our property had access to fresh water. Culverts conducted the water under the brick walkways that divided the orchard. At intervals, along both streams, irrigation ditches led off into the orchard, which was on a slightly lower level. The larger stream had several deepened areas dug to a depth sufficient enough to allow the gardeners to dip and fill their large sprinkling cans. Along the north wall, between the stream and the orchard, there was a strip of unplanted land about ten yards wide that was used for various domestic tasks too messy to do in the kitchen, such as making tomato paste.

One yearly ritual that I enjoyed was making rosewater. When the fragrant damask roses were in bloom, we children were set to work gathering the petals. A temporary fireplace was made on the north side of the orchard, next to the stream, by simply lining up two rows of bricks. These supported a large copper pot with a conical top, and under the pot a log fire burned between the bricks. The rose petals were boiled in water in the pot and the steam led off through a copper tube to a large glass jar. The distillate of rosewater was then transferred to small glass bottles that were tightly corked and sealed with clay or a paste of flour and water.

Sometimes, when I had no one to play with, I would amuse myself by floating a paper doll erect on the surface of the flowing stream and following it as it drifted from one end of the property to the other. I cut the doll in the shape of a figure with outstretched arms and a full skirt. As it turned and twirled along, it looked like a dancer pirouetting. I would follow it, carrying a long stick to prod it back into motion whenever it became stuck.

Later in life, I sometimes felt that I was like one of my paper dolls caught in a flow over which I had no control. Sometimes I became stuck or stymied by a temporary impasse until something happened to prod me along; but I was always moving forward and usually for the better.

Because we had a well and a stream on our land, we were not dependent upon the public water system. Before the installation of water lines throughout the city, the public received their water from open conduits, called *joobha*, that ran along the sides of the streets from the highest elevation of the city in the south and west to the lowest elevation in Mashhad. The water was brought via *ghanatha* from the mountains and stored in reservoirs prior to distribution throughout the city via the *joobha*. The city was divided into districts and each district received its allocation of water on a certain night of the week. During the day before the scheduled distribution, each *joob* was supposed to be cleaned thoroughly by city workmen, but this was often performed in a haphazard manner.

Each house had its own cistern, which was filled by a pipe running from the *joob*. The cisterns were large, brick-walled structures built underground next to an outside wall of the house. Some of these had a flight of stairs leading from the surface down to the base of the cistern, where there would be a pipe with a faucet to draw off the water as needed. This area was cool in the summer and used for storage of perishable food. The water was also pumped from the cistern by hand pumps and, in the better houses, pumped to a storage tank on the roof and from there piped to the kitchen and bathrooms.

The distribution of water in each district was supervised by a government official who expected to be bribed by those townspeople who wanted more than their allotted share of water. The poor people who did not have their own private cisterns or a well would have to carry their water from the public cisterns called *ab anbars*, which were scattered throughout the city. The *ab anbars* were huge underground structures with brick walls plastered with mortar. The vaulted ceilings were supported by massive brick pillars connected by arches. The water faucets were in the base of the cisterns at the bottom of long stone stairways, which led down from an entrance gate at street level. The entrance gate was often under the supervision of a security guard posted to prevent attacks on unaccompanied women.

The superstitious folk believed that the depths of the stairs were frequented late at night by *jinn*, who looked like humans except for their hooved feet. Zivar, one of our maids, swore that she saw one of these *jinn* one morning before dawn. She told me that a *jinni* would not harm one if you spoke to him pleasantly and did not look at his feet. I never did learn how you could tell if you were in the presence of a *jinni* without looking at his feet!

After the government installed a municipal water supply, which piped pure spring water directly to the houses from reservoirs, the public and private cisterns were no longer necessary. Private cisterns were often converted to underground storage rooms; or, if the cistern happened to be adjacent to a cellar wall, the basement might be expanded to incorporate the cistern. One very large public cistern in Tehran was converted to a restaurant. The process of emptying the water and cleaning the walls and floor took over a year to complete. Several workmen were killed due to asphyxiation by methane gas produced by the slimy residue that had accumulated on the floor over many years. The transformation of the cistern into a restaurant included decorating the brick ceiling and supporting pillars with multicolored tiles. The finished restaurant was large enough to seat several hundred diners but, because the huge pillars broke up the expanse, there was a feeling of intimacy, although the underground location made for a somewhat eerie atmosphere.

A friend of the family told me a story about how he put his private cistern to use during the Russian invasion and occupation of Mashhad in World War II. Our friend had a valuable collection of antique swords. People were advised to hide all valuables so, before the Russians arrived in the city, he wrapped the swords in oiled silk with many layers of outer wrapping and dropped the bundle into his cistern. Years later, the public water system was installed in Mashhad and, after he had connected to the pubic system, he decided to clean out his cistern and retrieve his sunken treasure. He hired laborers to pump out the cistern, and after the water level was down to about one foot, he dismissed them. He aired out the cistern for a few days. Then, with the help of his son, he put down a ladder and climbed down into the muck. He found the wrapped bundle of swords and brought it out. When he opened it, he found the swords in excellent condition.

The house of one of our neighbors, who lived a few blocks down the street, was next to a public cistern. They had their own private water tap into the cistern, which was reached by a flight of stairs leading down from their garden. In the cool landing at the bottom, they built a number of shelves that they used for food storage. I remember one afternoon I was playing hide-and-seek with some neighborhood girls in their garden. I went down the stairs to hide and found two of my playmates, who had had the same idea. We all knew there was food there and we all came for the same reason—to eat. I still remember how delicious the freshly pickled small cucumbers tasted! It may seem strange to the Western ear to hear that a child would consider a cucumber as a treat, especially in these days of fast food when French fries seem to be the staple of the youth. However, as a child, fresh or dried fruit was a coveted sweet and candy was only available on special occasions such as *Now Ruz.*

I remember how delicious the tree-ripened apricots in our orchard were to me as a little girl. One summer afternoon, I dragged a ladder over to one of the apricot trees. With considerable difficulty, I managed to lean it against the tree and inch it up to where I could climb into the lower branches. I went up into the tree and sat there eating one after another of the juicy apricots, oblivious to everything but the enjoyment of stuffing myself. Eventually I had enough and looked down to begin my descent. To my surprise, the ladder had vanished! I never found out who took it. I didn't dare to shout for help because I was supposed to be in bed for my afternoon nap. After what seemed an eternity but was probably no more than an hour, I saw Gholam passing along a nearby row of trees. I called to him; and when he came to the tree, he looked up at me and asked, "What are you doing up there?"

I answered, "I just wanted some fruit, but my ladder vanished before I could get down!"

Gholam found another ladder and helped me down from my perch. "I don't know who took your ladder," he said, "but it was a

16

good punishment for you. You know that you were supposed to be in bed for your nap."

In the twilight of early evening, Jamshid and I used to play in the orchard with some of the neighborhood children. One favorite game was hide-and-seek, and we had a rule that the game would be confined to the orchard. Another rule was that any person who was hiding had to make some sound if he was not found after five or ten minutes. One evening, Jamshid hid himself on top of the grape arbor. Unbeknownst to the rest of us, he had made himself a megaphone out of cardboard and secreted it on top of the grape arbor earlier that day. After he had climbed to his hiding place and was not found, he observed the rules of the game and shouted "Hoo! Hoo!" through the megaphone. We all ran toward the direction of the sound. Jamshid waited a minute or two, then he pointed the megaphone in the opposite direction and repeated his call. Again we ran to where we thought the sound was coming from. Jamshid ran us back and forth all round the orchard for about a half hour. We could not figure out how he could move so fast from place to place. In the meantime, Jamshid was sitting up on the arbor munching on the grapes. Finally, he came down and showed himself, declaring that he was the winner and we were all stupid because we could not find him.

The years I spent growing up with my family in Mashhad were some of the happiest years of my life. Sometimes my memories of certain events make them seem like yesterday to me. Other times, my recollections dim; but, in either case, reminiscing over those days, especially with other family members, is a constant source of pleasure. On those too rare occasions when I along with a few of my brothers and sisters manage to congregate for a couple of days somewhere in the world, our remembrances of days gone by truly open a window to the past.

Notes

1. These were the days before a public water system was installed, and private wells were common in our neighborhood. My aunt once told me a story about one of her neighbors who had two teenage sons. The boys used to hide a small bottle of wine on the end of a string in their well every Thursday

17

morning. That afternoon, which is the day before the weekend in Persia, they would pull it up and secretly drink it. The parents discovered the bottle one Thursday but decided not to say anything to the boys. Rather, the father emptied the wine and replaced it with his urine. No one ever mentioned the incident again, but the boys got the message!

2. A friend told me an interesting story about this custom of hanging grapes for future use. Her teacher once admonished his pupils to enjoy life at every opportunity, less the chance escape them. He illustrated this by the following anecdote. "I hung grapes in my pantry every year to eat in the winter. Whenever I went to pick some for eating, I always chose the grapes that had started to spoil and saved the good ones for future eating. When all of the grapes were gone, I found that I had not eaten one really good grape. Now I know that it is useless to save the good ones for the future, so I enjoy them while they are fresh and throw the spoiled ones away."

3. The celebration of *yalda* is a custom dating back to before the days of Zoroaster, the prophet who founded the original Persian religion. It stems from a belief that following the longest night of the year, the sun is born again, since from that point on, the days grow longer. Family and friends gather to eat fruit saved from the summer, especially pomegranates and melons, along with nuts and sweets. They sit up for a long time that night, reciting poetry, joking, and chatting in celebration of the solar rebirth.

4. *Ghanatha* are a uniquely Persian system for conveying freshwater from underground springs in the mountains to the plains. Deep wells are dug in the foothills. When freshwater is struck, underground conduits are then dug to channel the water downhill. At intervals of about sixty feet, vent holes are dug down to the level of the conduit to provide fresh air for the diggers. The conduits may run for as long as thirty miles, and the initial depth may be as much as much as seven to eight hundred yards. The channel itself is usually nine or ten feet deep and about four feet wide. There are thousands of *ghanatha* throughout the country. Some were installed by the government while others were dug privately and the water sold for profit. One prime minister during the Qajar dynasty named Mirza Aghasi built *ghanatha* more or less as a hobby. He loved to visit the construction sites *incognito*. On one visit, he rode up to a laborer and asked him how the work was progressing. The laborer replied that there was no sign of water and the man who ordered the digging in that area must be a fool. Aghasi retorted, "You are the fool. If the dig does not produce water for him, it does produce bread for you." The first *ghanatha* were probably dug at least one thousand years ago, and new ones are still being constructed today where needed. A *ghanat* in Tehran, called ghanat Mirza Alireza after the man who built it and donated it to the public 170 years ago, still provides a copious supply of fresh water.

Chapter Two
Family Ties

All humanity is one family created from the same essence.
If one member suffers misfortune, all will suffer.

—Sa'adi

The family is a closely knit structure in Persia, and I was fortunate in that I grew up in a large family surrounded by loving brothers and sisters, my father, and my grandparents. But, before I speak of them, I must introduce a woman whom I loved dearly and who had a profound influence on me throughout my infancy and childhood. She was my nanny; and to understand how close was our relationship, we must go back to the time of my birth. My mother's unexpected and, to be truthful, unwanted eighth pregnancy terminated with the birth of fraternal twins. My twin brother was the first to be born, and I followed along in short order at 8 A.M. one sunny morning in early July. My twin brother was a chubby, healthy, and thrifty baby; but I was weak and undersized. The family did not entertain much hope for my survival.

My mother was excessively weakened by the twin birth and was not able to nurse two children. She asked her niece Saleemeh, a young, strong woman who had recently given birth, to nurse me until my parents could find a wet nurse. At that time, there were no prepared baby formulae so, if a mother were not able to nurse her baby, she had to feed the baby cow's milk or find a wet nurse.[1] My parents interviewed a number of women but were not able to find one with all the qualities they were looking for until one day a friend of the family, who knew my

19

future nanny's husband, remembered that this man's wife had been nursing a baby who had just died. The friend introduced Nanny to my parents who, after seeing her and talking to her, were impressed with her demeanor and intelligence and immediately hired her. And so this was how Khorsheed, whom I called Nanny-jon, entered our life, moved into our home, and began nursing me when I was two weeks old.

Nanny-jon lived in our house as long as I had to be nursed. After I was weaned, she moved back to her own home and commuted daily to care for me until she could no longer work for us. My twin brother was nursed by my mother and continued to thrive until tragedy struck. A few weeks after we twins were born, the family went to the country for the summer, as was their custom every year after school let out. My mother, some of the servants, and all the children (except for me and my eldest brother who was studying in England) went to the country resort of Shandeez. I was left at home in the care of Nanny, father, and my grandparents. A few weeks later, my twin brother contracted diphtheria. Before they were able to get back to the city and our doctor, he died. My mother was overwhelmed by grief and guilt, for she was convinced that the boy's death was a divine punishment for separating her twins. The only consolation she had was in finding me healthy and thriving in the care of my nanny when the family returned home. Life sometimes plays games with us; my healthy, strong twin brother was now dead and I, for whom there had been little hope for survival, was still alive and healthy.

Nanny-jon (*jon*, or *joon*, is an affectionate Farsi suffix appended to a person's name, meaning "dear" or "dearest") was of medium height and pleasingly plump. She had long, shining black hair over which she always wore a white scarf that showed a little bit of her hair over her forehead. As was the custom at that time, this scarf was folded in a triangle with one corner hanging down her back. The other two ends were gathered beneath her chin by a pin, from which one corner of the scarf fell over either breast. She was usually dressed in a long-sleeved, brightly colored, flowered cotton blouse with a high collar that buttoned from her neck to her waist. She wore a short, pleated skirt (with two front pockets in which she always kept clean folded handkerchiefs) over ankle-length black pantaloons, the traditional garb of the servant class. Her bare feet were thrust into flat sandals, which made little flapping noises as she moved energetically about. When she looked at you, one could see the love and kindness shining from her large, lively black eyes. Her cherubic red cheeks always had a newly scrubbed look and the fresh, mild scent of essence of rosewater clung to her. Nanny spoke in a low modulated voice and was most respectful to everyone. All of my family admired and loved her, and I cannot recall anyone who did not remark on her kindness, her sincerity, and her good heart.

Nanny, her husband, and her four children lived with her mother-in-law. During the times when Nanny-jon lived at our house, her mother-in-law and her husband looked after her young children. I loved my Nanny-jon with all my heart. She took the place of my mother, who died when I was three years old. I still remember the intense grief and sorrow I felt when it finally became necessary for Nanny-jon to leave our employ because the demands upon her from her growing family outweighed our family's need for her services.

My father's family had lived for generations in Mashhad. Some of the family enjoyed long happy lives: My paternal grandmother, for example, lived to the age of 101; her eldest daughter (Grand Aunt) was 100 years old when she died; and Grand Aunt's son died in 1993 at age 103, following a leg fracture sustained in a fall (possible pulmonary fat embolus?). On the other hand, my paternal great-grandfather's (Khashayar) life came to an untimely and tragic end at the young age of forty. Khashayar, a tall, handsome black-haired man with piercing black eyes and a slim, erect figure, was a career employee in the foreign service, having begun as a clerk when he was about nineteen years old. Because of his intelligence and ambition, he rose rapidly in the ranks and at the age of thirty-nine was appointed ambassador to Afghanistan.

In the later half of the nineteenth century, travel in the Middle East was difficult; and a journey from Mashhad to Kabul, the capital of Afghanistan, was an undertaking that required weeks of preparation and a couple of months' travel time. Khashayar decided to leave his wife and two young sons in the care of his brother until he got settled into his new position and had an

21

opportunity to find suitable housing for them in Kabul. He journeyed to Kabul by caravan accompanied by two assistants and took up temporary residence in the embassy. Afghanistan at that time was in its usual state of turmoil; competing tribal factions carried on intermittent attacks of open rebellion against the British-supported central government as well as covert acts of terrorism.

Several months after taking office, Khashayar was returning to the embassy on foot one evening shortly after sunset when he was set upon by a small band of terrorists. They beat him, stabbed him to death, and then tore out his heart, presumably for ritual consumption later. Thus his promising career was ended at the age of forty. My great-grandmother never remarried and the two boys, who were ages ten and twelve at the time of their father's death, were raised by her and their uncle. The older son, Kayvan, was greatly affected by the horrible nature of his father's death and developed an aversion for anything to do with politics or government service. He later became a merchant.

The other son, Kyomars, who was my paternal grandfather, was much like his father, both in appearance and mental ability. He also was blessed with artistic talent and loved poetry. He followed in his father's footsteps, entering government service at the age of twenty-one. The same year, he married a thirteen-year-old girl from Mashhad. Marriage at that young age was not unusual in those days. One might think that the intellectual and spiritual development of a thirteen-year-old girl would be curtailed by marriage, but this was not the case with Kyomars's wife. This girl, my grandmother, was called Sheereen Banoo, which means "sweet lady," and according to the people who knew her, the name was most appropriate.

Kyomars and Sheereen Banoo were a well-matched couple, each possessing a gentle nature and an even disposition. When Sheereen Banoo was first married, she was a shy, sensitive child, but she soon began to mature into a clever and well-informed lady. She was endowed with an innate curiosity and yen for learning and her husband nurtured her budding intellect. He patiently answered all her questions about the adult world into which she had been so abruptly thrust by marriage and instilled in her a love of poetry and literature. Kyomars, in later years, said of his wife, "I picked a rosebud from the bush and now it has opened into a beautiful flower." Sheereen Banoo was, in fact, a remarkably handsome woman; but her real attractiveness lay in her bubbling personality and keen sense of humor. She was an accomplished conversationalist and everyone loved to sit and talk with her for hours, listening to her stories and hearing her recite poetry.

Kyomars frequently discussed his work with his wife and always consulted with her when a major decision had to be made. This attitude was unusual in an Islamic society wherein women were considered inferior in all respects to men. My grandmother told me a story of how she and Kyomars became involved in a business venture as a sideline. One day Kyomars came home from his office in the government building and as soon as he came in the door, Sheereen Banoo could see that he was excited about something. He sat her down next to him and said to her, "You will never guess in a hundred years what I am going to say to you. Today I learned that there is a business for sale at a good price. The owner wants to move out of town and is in a hurry to sell. It is a clock and watch store located on Arg Avenue and I stopped in to look at it on the way home. I think that it would be a good investment for us. It would give us a little more income even though we would have to hire someone to run it for us."

"You are right," Sheereen answered. "I would never have guessed that you were interested in becoming a businessman. But let's not be hasty. We will sleep on it and decide in the morning."

One week later they were the owners of a store that did not have much in the way of inventory but was located in a prime spot in the best business district in Mashhad. Within a year, the store was well stocked with watches and clocks imported from Switzerland and they had hired a young man as manager along with a salesman and watch repairman. The business flourished over the years, but my grandmother always suspected that the real reason her husband wanted the place was because of what it soon became—a hangout for grandfather's friends. Every afternoon he would meet with some of his cronies in the back room of the store where they would discuss politics, gossip, and recite

23

poetry. Grandmother said that if Kyomars could ever tear himself away from his friends for a few minutes, he might check on the business.

I used to visit the back room of the store as a child and I remember it well. It was a moderately large room containing a desk, a few chairs, and a safe; along the walls there were several benches covered with red Turkoman rugs. A table occupied one corner topped with a samovar, which was kept boiling all day long. I can still hear the bubbling samovar and, in the background, the faint chiming of the grandfather clocks in the front showroom. How can I remember so well the details of this place when Kyomars died before my father was married and my father never took any interest in the store during his lifetime? That is another interesting story that I will tell later on.

Kyomars was very successful in his job with the government of the province of Khorasan. When he was thirty-five years old, he was honored with the title of *Ameen*, which was appended to his surname and means "reliable" or "trustworthy." He was also a gifted artist, renowned in his wide circle of friends for his beautiful calligraphy and talent for illumination, as well as being a scholar and poet. The culmination of this artistic talent was a handwritten book of verse several hundred pages long and lavishly illuminated along the margins. The single copy is a cherished family treasure.

During the nineteen years of his marriage to Sheereen Banoo, Kyomars fathered five children—three boys and two girls. The couple were very happy in their marriage and they were devoted parents. However, fate has a way of playing cruel tricks on those who least deserve it. When Kyomars was forty years old, he retired one night, seemingly in perfect health. He never awakened. He suffered a heart attack during his sleep and quietly passed away. He had been so like his father during life and, like his father who had been assassinated, he died at the same age of forty, but of natural cause. Kyomars's untimely death was a shock to Sheereen Banoo and the children, but Sheereen was a strong woman and she soon fell into the role of a single parent. Fortunately, she was well off financially since she received a pension from the government as well as income from the clock store.

At the time of Kyomars's death, his firstborn child—a girl named Shahrbanoo—was eighteen years old and married. We always called her Grand Aunt and her sister was known as Little Aunt. Shahrbanoo bore five children and, at the time of her death at age one hundred, her descendants numbered about sixty. Grand Aunt was a kind and gentle soul who was always available to me and my sisters and brothers whenever we needed a confidante or advice. Little Aunt, on the other hand, was the antithesis of her sister. My memories of her are all unpleasant and I do not like to dwell upon them. Suffice to say, she was a malicious and hypocritical person. She was intensely jealous of my mother and hurt her at every opportunity. We children always felt that the heartbreak she caused my mother contributed to her early death.

The second eldest child of Kyomars and Sheereen was a boy named Feraydoon. Kyomars loved all his children but this first son was the apple of his eye or, as he put it, "the jewel of his crown." As a child, this lad gave early evidence of budding genius and his inquiring nature was encouraged by Kyomars. The boy often accompanied his father to work where he would stand by Kyomars's desk in the government building absorbing knowledge and astounding the staff with his grasp of facts. Feraydoon was seventeen years old when his father died. Shortly after his father's death, Feraydoon applied for his father's position. He was well known by Kyomars's coworkers and his appointment seemed assured. There was some bureaucratic delay but, after several months, a messenger arrived one morning with a letter confirming his appointment. Again, an ill-natured fate intervened. The night before the letter arrived, Feraydoon died after a short illness, apparently the victim of a ruptured appendix.

My father's only surviving brother, Ardesheer, became a physician and we called him Uncle Doctor. He was tall, slim, handsome, and always impeccably dressed. He was fond of good living and his house was always full of guests whom he entertained in grand style. His gracious and gentle disposition made him beloved by his patients and many friends. We children looked upon him as a second father, and after my father's death he became even closer to me. When he died of a heart attack in 1977 at age seventy-six while attending a patient in his office, I

25

was not in the country. When the news finally reached me, I was heartbroken for a long time.

It is difficult for me to talk about my father, Esfandiar, without resorting to hyperbole. Like his brother, he was a tall man with an erect carriage who enjoyed superb health until his sudden death at age eighty-four following a single massive coronary occlusion. His profound intellect and sharp mental faculties remained undimmed to the end; in fact, he won a chess game from one of my brothers two hours before he died. He was respected by all who knew him and was loved for his generous and compassionate nature. Many of the poor people of Mashhad owed their survival to his anonymous philanthropy; he gave food, clothing, and fuel to the cold and hungry who never knew the identity of their benefactor. My father never became a very wealthy man, but he made enough to support his family in comfort and to educate his children. In addition to being a scholar and a wise person, he had a highly moral character and conducted all of his affairs with honor. His position with the government gave him many opportunities for illicit gain, but he never succumbed to temptation.

Father's main avocations were chess and history. He had an extensive library, which contained antique and modern volumes on history, poetry, philosophy, and Farsi translations of Western classics and novels. He spent many hours reading in his library. We always knew where to find him when he was at home. We children had free use of the library and we could always find something to read no matter what our age level or interests. My father treasured two volumes in particular: One was the book of verse written by his father; and the other was a small antique leather-bound volume on the history of ancient Persia, handwritten and illuminated with Persian miniatures gilded with twenty-four karat gold. Unfortunately, many of his books are not in the family today because the library was ransacked by knowledgeable thieves who selectively stole the most valuable volumes.

My father had little regard for most of the fanatical religious Moslem mullahs although he did respect a select few because they were good people, not because of their religious rank. He used to say that beneath most mullahs' turbans there was a devious and crooked mind. My grandmother told me this story

26

about one of my father's clashes with the mullahs: Once one of the ayatollahs who held a supervisory position at the Shrine of the Imam Reza in Mashhad petitioned Father to change one of the regulations regarding the use of moneys donated to the shrine by pilgrims. My father found out that the change would only serve to line the pockets of the petitioner and refused to grant the request. The ayatollah persisted in his demands and tried to pressure my father, even to the point where he indirectly implied that bodily harm might occur to my father or his family. When this did not succeed in altering Father's position, the ayatollah sent his son to our house one day at a time when the ayatollah knew that my father would not be home.

When he arrived, the son asked for my father and, when informed that he was not at home, requested to see my grandmother. My grandmother went to the door and the son, with eyes piously averted so as not to gaze upon a woman's face, proffered a bag full of money at arm's length, saying that it was a gift to my father from the ayatollah. Grandmother knew the circumstances of the dispute between Father and the ayatollah so she said to the messenger, "You pretend to be a religious person. You do not look into my eyes but here you are trying to bribe my son to do something improper. That is even more sinful. You are lucky that my son is not at home because he would throw you out into the street!" With that said, she threw the money in his face and slammed the door!

Grandmother Sheereen, of course, played the dominant role in arranging my father's marriage; and I was always an eager listener to her stories about his meeting and courting my mother. As Grandmother told it, she met my mother through a friend who knew mother's family, originally from Shiraz, but now resident for some years in Mashhad. Grandmother's friend was very impressed with the youngest girl in this family. She told my grandmother about her and arranged a small tea party in her home to introduce the girl and her mother to Grandmother Sheereen. Grandmother also was impressed by the girl's personality and beauty. One day she took her nineteen-year-old son aside and said to him, "Esfandiar, I have told you this before but you never paid any attention to me. Now I am more serious. You are at an age when you should be married and starting a family. I have met a girl who I think would be perfect for you."

Esfandiar replied, "I hope that you are not talking about some twelve- or thirteen-year-old child."

"No," answered Grandmother, "she is fifteen and a half years old. She is well-bred, as well as pretty with a lovely figure. She is just like a ripe peach on the tree, ready to pick and eat. If you do not move now, I am sure that someone else will soon pluck this fruit."[2] Grandmother continued with the arrangements, and after a number of visits back and forth between the two families to iron out the details, the marriage was arranged. Esfandiar, who by this time was twenty years old, was united with a six-teen-year-old maiden, who spoke with a lyrical Shirazian accent. They were to remain happily married for twenty-two years during which time they had ten children, eight of whom survived. The survivors were equally divided in gender, four boys, Kaveh, Kayvan, Jahan, and Jamshid; and four girls, Katayoon, Tooran, Azar, and me.

My mother's family had been merchants in Shiraz for a number of generations before moving to Mashhad. She was the youngest of the four children born in Shiraz sired by my maternal grandfather and his first wife. My memory of my maternal grandfather is that of a thin old man with a snow-white beard and mustache who walked with a bent back carrying a cane. He was ninety-four years old when I was born; he had sired my mother at age fifty-nine. Following the death of my maternal grandmother he, at age eighty-four, took a second wife who was forty-two years his junior. This marriage produced a third son who was born and still lives in Mashhad, the patriarch of a family of thirty children and grandchildren and their offspring. Grandfather died at age 110, the most long-lived in our family; and he was alert to the end. Everyone, including his wife and even the servants, called him Agha Bozorg (Grand Sire). He was also called Sa'adi since he resembled physically the famous poet from Shiraz and because he was a prolific writer of verse himself, which he would recite in his sweet Shirazian accent to friends and family.

Agha Bozorg used to visit our home about once a month, each time staying for a few days. He insisted upon walking the mile or so from his house to ours which, at his advanced years, was a major undertaking. A small bedroom was always ready for him and the first thing he did upon arrival was to repair to his bedroom where he rested and drank a cup of tea. He always arrived in the morning, and after he had rested, he took his lunch in his room. When he had finished eating, we younger children were allowed to visit with him. We would all gather around his bed and I, being the youngest, was allowed to sit on the bed snuggled up to him. Agha Bozorg would put his arm around my shoulders and stroke my hair while he talked. He never really became reconciled to the early death of my mother at age thirty-eight, and he often remarked on my resemblance to her. He would say to me, "Mehry-jon, when you grow up you will be a copy of your mother. You have her eyes, her expressions, and her tall figure."

After we had all settled down around his bed, the wonderful stories would begin. Agha Bozorg transported us to fabled lands and places, which he had visited in his travels as a merchant or which existed only in his fertile imagination. He told of royal courts in distant countries, sailors and ships, and mountain caves full of treasure protected by *jinn* or huge snakes. We heard of strange people of different colors, some of whom were so tall that if they stretched their arms on high their fingers would be burned by the sun and others so short that one had to lie down to talk to them. He described distant lands where it was so hot that the natives cooked their meals on flat rocks heated only by the sun and lands of perpetual winter where the inhabitants had to tunnel through the snow to enter their homes. He told of flying carpets, King Solomon's mines, *jam-e-jaam,* and *kar-e-dadjal*.[3] Some of these stories smack of Baron Münchhausen's tales and probably were Agha Bozorg's version of the same. However, it did not matter to us children whether or not the stories were true. We were as equally enchanted with his fiction as we were with his factual accounts.

Agha Bozorg was a scholar of history as well as a poet. He wrote a history of the 1904 Japanese-Russian war that was entirely in verse and illustrated with photographs that he had collected in his travels or clipped from newspapers during the war. He also wrote a volume of lyrical poetry that is of particular interest because of one poem he wrote while in his seventies in

29

which he foretold what he would be doing and the status of his health each decade beginning at age eighty. The poem ends with his uncannily accurate prediction of his death at age 110! His poetry was published from time to time in a local newspaper.

My mother, Nazanin, was the youngest of Agha Bozorg's four living children by his first wife. The second eldest son returned to Shiraz, the city of his family's origin, in his early twenties. He studied veterinary medicine and practiced there for the rest of his life, during the course of which he sired four children. Agha Bozorg's oldest child, Aunt Ozra, married a merchant from Mashhad who was a prosperous dealer in imported antiques. The eldest son moved to Nishabur. He founded a transportation company, married a local girl (who produced five children for him), and lived out his days in that city. We called these two uncles "Uncle Shirazy" and "Uncle Nishaburi."

As I mentioned before, my father, Esfandiar, married at age twenty. It was only a few months after his wedding when he was approached by Peerooz Khan, the young man whom my grandfather had hired to manage the clock store on Arg Avenue. Peerooz had been a frequent visitor to our home, especially after the death of my grandfather. He reported to my grandmother on the status of the business and delivered the profits to her. My grandfather had been dead for four years when Peerooz, then a man of about twenty-six, requested a meeting with Esfandiar. They met in the back room of the store.

Peerooz opened the conversation something like this, "Esfandiar, I have known your father and mother for many years, and I loved and respected your father. When he died, I felt that I had lost my best friend. However, life must go on for all of us. Your sisters are married and you are about to have your first child. Your brother, Ardesheer, soon will be leaving home to study at the Polytechnic Institute in Tehran.[4] Your mother is not even forty years old and has a long life ahead of her. She will soon be all alone. I have admired her for a long time and I would like your permission, as the male head of your family, to marry her."

Esfandiar promised to speak with his mother and report back. The proposal was accepted by Sheereen Banoo. A few months later, she and Peerooz Khan were united in a simple ceremony. Peerooz Khan moved in with Grandmother and the rest of the family and continued to manage the clock and watch store. When, a few years later, Father built the house in which I grew up, he made the north wing especially for Grandmother and Grandfather Khan and they occupied it for the rest of their days. The couple became devoted to each other, and their mutual love and affection never wavered. Peerooz Khan, whom we called Grandfather Khan, was the only paternal grandfather I knew, because my father's father died before Father married. Grandfather Khan frequently took me to the clock store as a child, and that is why I remember it so well. I did not discover that he was my step-grandfather until I was nine years old when one of the maids, in the course of telling a bedtime story, disclosed the fact. When I broached the matter to my oldest sister, she answered, "What difference does it make? Do you love him any less?"

The knowledge did not change my love for him in the slightest and Peerooz Khan loved all of his step-children as if they were his own. Peerooz Khan was fluent in both Arabic and Turkish, and he was able to converse in French and Russian. He knew Farsi so well that he could trace the root of every word. All his education was acquired in his youth under various private tutors. Grandfather Khan played chess[5] so well that he was able to beat Father, who was an expert in his own right. However, whenever he played with any of his young grandchildren, his way of teaching was to allow them to win with difficulty, all the while pointing out their mistakes. He and Grandmother never had any children, but they lived happily together for almost sixty-five years. When my grandmother, who was thirteen years older than Peerooz Khan, died at age 101, Peerooz Khan lost all will to live and he passed away a few months later.

This chapter has described the immediate members of my family, but one must remember that my father and mother had aunts and uncles also and they had children and their children had children. Second and third cousins abounded and, like all Persian families in those days, we all knew each other and visited back and forth, especially during the traditional visitation at *Now Ruz* (New Year). There was always something going on in the family: a wedding, a funeral, a dinner invitation, or sometimes unhappy occasions such as a divorce or death of a young child. Most of my mother's relatives lived in Shiraz, and therefore our contact with them was more limited than our contact with Father's relatives, most of whom lived in Mashhad and Tehran. Nonetheless, we were a close-knit family when I was a child. Now, due to emigration for various reasons, we are scattered about the globe and I have some distant cousins I have never met personally.

Notes

1. A friend, who had been raised on cow's milk as a baby, used to say that whenever he was in the country and he heard a cow mooing, he thought that his mother was calling!
2. Persians are fond of using elaborate similes to describe female charms. Expressions such as "her mouth is like a rosebud," "her arms are like rhubarb," "her skin is like porcelain," etc. are commonly heard. This sounds somewhat stilted to the Western ear but is perfectly natural to the poetic Persian. I knew one man who always referred to his wife as his "plum" because, as he put it, every time he looked at her, his mouth watered.
3. According to Shiite belief, the *kar-e-dadjal* is an ass from whose hairs various musical sounds are emitted when he moves. It is said that he will herald the reappearance of the twelfth imam, Mehdi. *Jam-e-jaam* is a bowl that, when looked into it, shows anywhere in the world. After the invention of radio and television, Persians maintained that these inventions were predicted by these ancient tales. Today there is an ethnic Persian television news program called *"Jam-e-jaam."*
4. Before the University of Tehran was founded by the Reza Shah, there was but one institute of higher learning in the country. This had been founded by Amir Kabeer and was called Daralfonoon, which roughly translates to Polytechnical Institute. This school was staffed by French and Austrian teachers and offered courses in mathematics, physics, philosophy, chemistry, and military science. Prior to the founding of Daralfonoon, the only way that a student could matriculate at college level was to study abroad.
5. Chess is believed to have originated in Persia about A.D. 500. The word *chess* comes from the Farsi word for king *(shah)*. From Persia, the game spread east to China. After the Arabs conquered Persia in the 600s, they took the game west to Spain from where it spread to the rest of the Western world.

Chapter Three
Mashhad

Ask not our garden, our lands, or from whence we came;
we were born in a world of love and are happy in our hearts.
— Naziry Nishaboory

For the first eleven years of my life, I lived in the city of Mashhad, the capital of the large, fertile province of Khorasan located in the northeast corner of Persia. Mashhad is situated on a broad green plain that is one of the most productive agricultural regions in Persia. Mountains rise to the northeast, northwest, and southwest. The river Kashaf runs from west to east and is about twenty-two kilometers to the north of the city. Also, to the north and a scant one hundred kilometers distant, is Russia. Afghanistan lies about 150 kilometers to the east, separated from Khorasan province in part by the river Harirud. The Harirud flows from south to north and eventually disappears in Russian Turkestan. The Mashhad of today is inhabited by about a million people and, with its high-rise apartment buildings and traffic-filled streets, is not much different from many other large cities in the world. However, at the time I lived there, Mashhad was one of the most beautiful, quiet, and peaceful cities in Persia and a wonderful place in which to grow up.

Tree-lined streams of water fed by runoff from mountain springs and *ghanatha* ran beside many of the wide cobblestone streets. Small parks filled with flowerbeds were scattered throughout the city. In the outskirts, there were larger parks containing flowing brooks that at intervals widened into pools where people swam. During my childhood, the city was not as large as it is today and the populace was able to walk to most places of business and to the schools, theaters, and parks. *Doroshkehha* (horse-drawn cabs) were plentiful and easily obtained for longer trips; the more affluent drove their own automobiles.

Due to its location in northeast Persia, Khorasan, in the course of history, has been overrun a number of times by invaders from both the north and the east. Its cities have been pillaged and destroyed again and again over the centuries and rebuilt as many times. Despite its turbulent history, the province of Khorasan has been a center of learning since ancient times. Scientists and poet-mathematicians, such as Attar and Khayyam, were born in Khorasan, as well as the famous poets Ferdosi and Ghazaly. The Persian king, Nader Shah Afshar, who conquered Afghanistan and northern India and brought the famous peacock throne to Persia from India, was a native of Khorasan.

Khorasan, because of its temperate climate in the summertime, attracts many vacationers. Mashhad is also a year-round tourist attraction because the Shiitte Moslem religious Shrine of Imam Reza is located in the city; and one of the great Persian poets, Abul Qasim Mansur Ferdosi, was born, lived, and died and is buried in the village of Tus located about fourteen miles to the north of Mashhad. His epic poem of sixty thousand verses called *Shahnameh* (Book of Kings) was composed over a period of thirty years and traces the history of Persia through fifty dynasties from about 3600 B.C. to the time of the Moslem conquest in A.D. 641. The origin of most contemporary Persian folklore is found in Ferdosi's poetry.

Ferdosi was born about A.D. 940 and lived for over eighty years. A story is told that shortly after his birth, his father one night had a dream in which he saw his son standing in a high place from which the boy shouted a single loud cry of greeting. From all points of the compass, there came answering cries and singing. The father sent for an interpreter of dreams named Najibaldeen, who told him that his son would become such a famous orator that his fame would extend all over the world.

As a young man in Tus, Ferdosi became interested in ancient Persian history, and after some years of study, he began to record in verse the legends that had been handed down by word of mouth from ancient times. Another Persian poet and native of Tus, Abu Mansoor Daghighy, had started, some years earlier, a poetical history of Persia but had never finished it due to his death at the hand of one of his slaves. The one thousand verses that he had completed were mainly about the life of Zoroaster. Ferdosi learned that Sultan Mahmood Ghaznavi, then the king of Persia, was seeking a poet to finish the work started by Abu Mansoor Daghighy; and so he journeyed to Ghazneh, the capital, to apply for the job. Three famous poets—Farrokhi, Asjodi, and Onsori—were attached to the sultan's court; and after hearing some of the verses composed by Ferdosi, they conspired to block his access to the sultan for fear of his competition. Finally, a friend introduced Ferdosi to court on the day that the sultan was interviewing a number of aspirants. After hearing some of the verses that Ferdosi had composed, the sultan commissioned him to complete the history and promised to pay him one *dinar* (a gold coin) for each completed verse.

After thirty years' labor, the epic poem was finally finished. Ferdosi presented the manuscript to the sultan and requested his promised payment. The sultan, in the meantime, had had a change in heart. Instead of the gold coins promised, Ferdosi was given sixty thousand *derham* (silver coins). According to contemporary accounts, the payment arrived by messenger while Ferdosi was bathing in the public bath. Ferdosi had spent thirty years completing his epic, during which time he had supported himself by expenditure of his own not inconsiderable wealth. Nonetheless, when he saw that he had been paid in silver instead of gold, he became so incensed at the sultan's perfidy that he immediately gave half of the money to the bath attendant and the other half to the waiter in a nearby tearoom where he lunched.

Ferdosi wrote a letter to the sultan denouncing him for his treachery and, after sealing it, gave it to a messenger with instructions to deliver it after twenty days. Knowing that his letter would provoke the wrath of the sultan, Ferdosi left Ghazneh and went into hiding in the house of a friend in the town of Harri for six months. He then moved to the province of Tabarestan. While there, he composed one hundred additional verses in which he castigated the sultan for his dishonorable behavior, pointing out that no true Persian would so behave and attributing the sultan's lack of honor to his mother's Turkish ancestry. The governor of Tabarestan managed to persuade Ferdosi not to publish these inflammatory verses. After the furor had died down, Ferdosi moved back to Tus, his birthplace.

After some years the sultan, perhaps fearing for his place in history, relented and decided to honor his original commitment. Legend has it that the sultan sent the payment in gold to Ferdosi. But on the day that his messenger bearing the payment arrived at one gate to the city, Ferdosi's body was being carried out through another gate. The sultan tried to give the money to Ferdosi's daughter, but she refused to accept it. Finally, Ferdosi's sister sent word to the sultan that if he truly wished to honor her brother, a fitting memorial would be the construction of a dam in the river Kashaf near Tus. Ferdosi had planned to build this dam himself with the proceeds from the royal commission. The dam was built and the ruins are still visible to this day, as are four miles of the original thousand-year-old city walls. The sultan's efforts to make amends came to naught, however, because after Ferdosi's death the verses that he wrote while in hiding circulated throughout the country and the true story of the sultan's duplicity became known to the public.

In 1928, the Reza Shah ordered a monument to be constructed over Ferdosi's grave. A square marble structure eighteen meters high centered in five acres of gardens was erected and dedicated in 1934, the approximate one-thousand-year anniversary of his birth. Verses of Ferdosi's poetry are carved into the four sides of the monument. Near the base on the south side, there is carved a description of the commissioning of the monument and the dedication ceremony. My father was one of the official hosts of the ceremony, which was attended by the Reza Shah and officials and scholars from all over the world.

A local poet wrote a poem to welcome the Reza Shah to Mashhad and my brother Jahan, age eight at the time, and my sister Azar, age six, were chosen to recite the verses at the ceremony. Grandfather Khan drilled the two of them for weeks before the big day until they were letter-perfect. In preparation for their public appearance, the two children were outfitted with

36

new clothes from head to foot. Alas, something happened to cause a delay in the ceremony; and at the last minute, the recitation of the poem was canceled. Jahan, in relating this story to me, remarked that he didn't mind at all. He had obtained new clothes, which he would not otherwise have gotten, and still remembers the poem to this day! The inscription on the base of the monument describing its commissioning was done one year after the dedication ceremony by a famous calligrapher named Emadalketab, whom my father, after consultation with the prime minister at that time, Mr. Forooghi, brought from Tehran.

The pure rhymes of Ferdosi's poetry live in every Persian's soul; and to this day his verses are recited throughout the land in coffee shops, in schools, and on radio and television. In Ferdosi's time, it was becoming fashionable to write in Arabic or a combination of Farsi (the original Persian language) and Arabic, because of the recent Arab conquest of the country. However, not one Arabic word is found in any of his works. They are all written in Farsi, which, in part, accounts for the special place he occupies in the hearts of all Persians. When the mullahs came to power after the Islamic fundamentalist takeover in 1978, they tried to suppress Ferdosi's poetry and forbade public recitation of his verse. They eventually realized·that they could not purge from the minds of the people their deep feeling for this literary inheritance. The one-thousand-year anniversary of Ferdosi's death was commemorated *publicly* in Mashhad in 1990.

Mashhad is a mecca for both tourists and religious pilgrims because Emam Reza, the eighth of the twelve Shiite Moslem imams, is buried in the city. Emam Reza died suddenly in A.D. 818 in what was then the small town of Sanabad. He was buried next to the tomb of a caliph of the Abbasid dynasty named Harun al-Rashid. The Shiites believe that Emam Reza was poisoned for political reasons, so his tomb became known as Mashhad (the place of martyrdom), hence the derivation of the name of the present city that grew up around the tomb. Over the years, a beautiful shrine was erected around the tomb of Emam Reza. My father wrote a comprehensive work on the history of the province of Khorasan and the city of Mashhad, part of which is dedicated to a description of how each addition was made to the shrine over a period of twelve hundred years under various major dynasties, particularly the Safavid, the Qajar, and the short-lived Pahlavi dynasties. At a central point within the shrine is the tomb itself, surrounded on four sides and on top by lattice work inlaid with silver and gold. Thirty-one meters over the tomb soars a huge dome covered on the outside by copper sheathing overlaid with gold foil and decorated on the inside with mirrored tiles.

The gold overlay was donated by Shah Abbas Safavid I after he traveled on foot as a pilgrim from his capital in Isfahan to Mashhad in 1607. Present-day air travelers to Mashhad see the glittering gold dome as a prominent landmark on the approach to the airport; but before the advent of air service, pilgrims used to come by bus and their first glimpse of the dome was from a hill about ten miles south of the city. The conductor customarily stopped the bus at this point and congratulated the pilgrims on their seeing the dome for the first time while holding out his hand for *gonbad nama*, the special name for the tip given to reward one who guides the devout to the shrine.

The central area containing the lattice-covered tomb is surrounded by large (about four to five hundred square meters) chambers floored with marble slabs that are white, beige, and light green in color. The walls are marble up to a little over a meter from the floor, at which point there is a row of tiles painted with beautiful intricate designs. Above the painted tiles, the walls and the vaulted ceilings are decorated by mirrored mosaic tiles that reflect the light from numerous huge crystal chandeliers, six to eight meters in diameter, hanging by massive chains from the high ceilings. Open-air, marble-floored, walled courtyards surround the shrine on three sides with gates opening out onto a thirty-meter-wide street that encircles the shrine.

The construction of this circular drive was ordered by the Reza Shah in 1929 and completed in 1933. The minutes of the meetings to plan the construction of the road were handwritten by my father and are preserved in the records of the shrine. Scattered about the various courtyards are buildings housing a museum, a library, and a theological seminary, as well as two mausoleums, one containing the body of Sheik Bahaee, a mathematician, astronomer, and philosopher who was a contemporary of Abbas the Great A.D. (1571–1629). Bahaee taught in the seminary of the shrine and was the author of eighty-eight scientific books and treatises. After his death at the age of seventy in the city of Isfahan, his body was returned to Mashhad for burial in a mausoleum that is said to be in the same room where he taught. The other mausoleum, adjacent to the north side of the shrine, contains the body of King Tahmasb, the second king of the Safavid dynasty, which ruled Persia from about A.D. 1505 to 1724.

The courtyard on the north side of the shrine is called *Sahn-e-Kohneh*, or Old Courtyard. In the center of this courtyard, there is a large fountain called *"saghahkhaneh"* ("place to drink"), which is carved from a single block of white marble. A golden dome supported by pillars covers this fountain. Water from the central bowl flows down into a catch basin, to which several dozen cups are attached by chains for the convenience of thirsty pilgrims who wish to imbibe the holy water. The fountain was brought to the shrine by King Nader from the city of Harat in Afghanistan after he had conquered that country in the early eighteenth century.

There is a portico some twenty-one meters in height on the south side of the Old Courtyard leading into the shrine. This is decorated with mosaic tiles, and King Nader later added to the decor by covering the interior walls with gold leaf. On the west side of the Old Courtyard, another tall portico leads out to the city streets. Next to this portico, there is a tall tile-covered clock tower with a clock face on four sides. The clock chimes every fifteen minutes and can be heard from some distance. On the east side of the courtyard, there is a portico some thirty-three meters in height on the roof of which there is a tower called *Naghareh Khaneh* ("House of Drums") where every day at sunrise and sunset trumpets and drums sound out ruffles and flourishes to call the faithful to prayer. In the old days, one could hear this summons throughout the town. Nowadays, the modern city traffic prevents one from hearing it unless one is very near the shrine. The east and west porticos, as well as the one on the north side of the Old Courtyard, were all constructed by Abbas the Great.

A steel lattice-work window is inset into the south wall of the courtyard next to the gold portico. The devout attach pieces of fabric or thread to the lattice, symbolizing their supplication to the imam for cure of illness or various other wishes. Some afflicted pilgrims attach ropes around their necks and tie themselves to the window. Then they sit quietly in meditation in the belief that the power of the imam will be transmitted through the rope to their bodies and effect a cure of their illness. Other pilgrims bring their winding sheets (three meters of white cotton fabric) to the window and rub it thereon in the belief that when they are wrapped in the shroud after death they will be blessed.

There are many stories about the miracles ascribed to the imam: The blind have had their sight restored; the dumb have been made to speak; the lame who tied themselves to the lattice window for three days and nights are said to have departed on their restored limbs. These stories differ little from those ascribed to miraculous cures occurring at other religious shrines throughout the world; for example, those at Lourdes in France. Faith healing is a common practice in many religions. One of our servants was convinced that a large boulder actually rolled unaided to the shrine to worship. When my grandfather chided him and called him a fool for believing such a ridiculous tale, the servant replied that, although he personally had not seen the stone move, people who were in the shrine on that fateful day had sworn to him that they saw the miracle, ergo, it must be true!

On the east side of the shrine, there is another white marble courtyard called the New Courtyard (Sahne-e-No), built during the Qajar dynasty in the nineteenth century. The twenty-meter-high arched entrance (Ayvan-e-Tala) to the shrine from this courtyard is covered with tiles sheathed with gold foil. Another twenty-meter-high portico in the south wall of the New Courtyard provides access to the museum and library, while similar gates on the east and north open onto the city streets. There is one fountain surrounded by flowerbeds in the center of the New Courtyard that is purely decorative and not used for drinking or ritual washing. However, there are always a number of porters wandering about with large leather water bags slung across their chests who offer water to the pilgrims in return for a tip.

To the south of the shrine there is a mosque, the *Masched-e-Gowhar Shad*, named for the queen of King Rokh of the Tymoorian dynasty, who built it in A.D. 1405–18. This is one of the finest and unbelievably beautiful mosques in the world. The large praying chamber is surmounted by a massive dome forty-one meters high covered with turquoise-colored tiles and flanked by two minarets forty-three meters high. The mosque is separated from the shrine by a spacious courtyard paved with green-and-white marble in the center of which there is a shallow rectangular pool. This pool is on the site of a house that was occupied by an old woman at the time King Rokh was acquiring the land to build the mosque.

The old woman refused to sell her home, maintaining that if the queen were to have a mosque built in her memory beside the shrine, she (the woman) wanted to keep her house for the same reason. The queen, being a humane person, requested her husband to build the mosque next to the house rather than force the woman to vacate. When the woman finally died, the house was razed and the site covered with marble. Low marble pillars were erected to mark the periphery of the original building. In recent times, about 1950, the marble paving and pillars were removed and the pool was built. This is now used by worshippers, most of whom are probably unaware of the story of the stubborn old woman, for their ablutions before prayer.

At each entrance to the shrine, there is a small room lined from floor to ceiling on three sides by divided shelves. The worshippers leave their shoes with an attendant, who gives them a claim check and deposits the shoes into one of the numbered pigeon holes. I remember a story about an old man whom my grandparents had brought to Mashhad from a remote country village to work during the summer as a helper to Gholam, our gardener. The old man wanted to become *Mashhadi*[1] from the first day he arrived, but my grandparents put off giving him permission for some time because they were concerned that this ignorant old fellow would have difficulty making his way about the city. Finally, they could no longer resist his supplications. They bought new clothes and shoes for him and sent him off to the public bath to make himself presentable. When he returned, they gave him some money and told him to hire a passing *doroshkeh* in the street outside our courtyard gate and tell the driver to take him to the shrine. They also gave him a paper with our address written on it to show to the driver for his return trip after he had finished his prayers. The old man did not return until some hours after he was expected, and when he finally arrived, he was shoeless and very upset. Upon questioning him, it finally came out that he had removed his shoes outside the courtyard gate and left them in the street. When he returned, the shoes were gone. The poor man in his confusion mistook the street gate to the courtyard for the entrance to the shrine, and as a good Moslem should, he removed his shoes before entering, confident that they would be there when he returned.

In the neighborhood around the shrine, there are a number of bazaars that were built over the years to take advantage of the pilgrim trade. Here one can find almost any commodity for sale. In Persia, the bazaars are similar to the enclosed shopping malls found in the Western world that encompass several blocks. The various shops are accessed by roofed-over streets of varying widths, the ceilings usually being high, vaulted structures with small glassed domes at intervals to admit light and air. Except for the major roadways used for deliveries, no vehicles or animal-drawn carts are allowed in the bazaars. In addition to being a trading center, the bazaars are also a place for the exchange of gossip and sometimes for the expression of political views. The merchant owners of the shops can, when united, exert a powerful political influence. For example, if an official decree is unpopular, the merchants may decide to close their shops in protest, bringing to a halt the commercial lifeblood of the city, until their grievances are redressed.

The largest and most well-known bazaars in Mashhad are the Bazaar Bozorg and the Bazaar Koochek. These contain a variety of shops offering a large assortment of merchandise. There are many smaller bazaars, which are offshoots of the larger ones. Each of these smaller bazaars specializes in one commodity: The gold bazaar has many small shops (some no bigger than a telephone booth), all of which sell gold in one form or another; the carpet bazaar will sell rugs and carpets exclusively; and fabric, shoe, turquoise, etc. bazaars all offer their special items. One of the most interesting is the copper-work bazaar. Here the artisans sit pounding out and shaping copper pots, trays, and bowls. The noise is deafening and the saying goes that one may break wind with impunity in the copper-work bazaar since no one will hear it!

Some bazaars are not so specialized and are more like flea markets. There one can find locally made handicrafts such as embroidered tablecloths and cushion covers; hats and jackets made from karakul lambskins with the fleece inside and the outer leather surface decorated with elaborate needlework designs; necklaces and praying beads of glass, wood, or porcelain; as well as everyday necessities. The shops that sell spices also sell various seeds for planting or for cooking. The best saffron in the world is produced in Persia in the city of Tabas, north of Mashhad. In late summer when the saffron flowers (autumnal crocus) are in bloom, one can smell their sweet scent for miles around the city. Real saffron has a bitter taste but a sweet odor. Approximately four thousand blossoms are required to produce one ounce of commercial saffron. No wonder it is so expensive!

I have heard that, in years past, people in the Tabas area made a drink from a distillate of saffron flowers. Overindulgence in this concoction caused a fatal illness known as the "laughing disease," so named because of the laughing expression found on the faces of the victims at the time of death. This sounds like the rictus associated with strychnine poisoning; and indeed the alkaloid colchicum, from which the drug colchicine (used in the treatment of gout) is made, is extracted from the autumnal crocus. This is a very potent drug and prolonged exposure will lead to toxic levels and death. One of the symptoms of colchicine intoxication is muscular paralysis, which probably accounts for the death rictus and the descriptive term "laughing disease." To this day, it is said that saffron farmers are always smiling.

Other shops sell distillates and extracts of rose and orange blossoms and willow water made from the bark and buds of the tree. These are sold for medicinal purposes as well as for cooking and as a flavoring for the cold *sharbatha* that are a popular summertime drink. These *sharbatha* are prepared from the juice of the pomegranate, sour cherry, orange, quince, peach, rhubarb, and lemon in various blends boiled with sugar. The concentrated syrups are sold by the bottle, or the chilled diluted drink may be purchased by the glass ladled from a leather bucket hanging near the door of the shop. Willow water is purported to be a cure for fever; anisette (nonalcoholic) is prescribed for the relief of flatulence; and a distillate of mint leaves is a favorite cure for upset stomach.

Another shop will be filled with baskets brimming with nuts and seeds for sale—pistachios, walnuts, hazel nuts, peanuts, almonds, cashews, sunflower seeds, and watermelon seeds. Persian pistachio nuts are famous throughout the world for their high quality. They are carefully graded by size, with the largest commanding the highest price. When the pistachio ripens, the green outer skin drops off and the inner shell splits halfway open. The harvested nuts are roasted with salt and a little lemon juice. A kind of preserve or jam is made from unripe nuts picked before the shell hardens. The nuts are soaked in lime water, boiled to remove any bitter taste, and then boiled again in sugared water. The resulting concoction is delicious but quite expensive. Unripe walnuts also are used to make a preserve, the regular ingestion of which is said to ensure male potency.

A bazaar that is peculiar to Mashhad, since the type of soft black stone used is found only in the mountains four kilometers south of Mashhad, is the stonecutters' bazaar. This stone is used to make *harkareh* (a special kind of stone pot). A single block of stone is shaped into a pot form and hollowed out. The sides of the pot after shaping will be no more than one-half centimeter in thickness and the bottom about one centimeter thick. The pots are seasoned by rubbing olive oil on the inside, then boiling water therein. This process is repeated until no more oil is absorbed into the stone. The end result is a cooking utensil that is perfect for preparing dishes that require prolonged slow cooking since the stone, once heated, maintains its temperature for hours. Small stone pots called *deezeeha* are used by coffee shops to prepare individual servings of a hearty soup called *abgoosh*, which is cooked slowly overnight and served at lunch the following day.

The neighborhood around the shrine is highly commercialized. In addition to the bazaars, there are hotels, bed and breakfast inns, restaurants, coffee shops, barber shops, public baths, and public toilets. My brother told me a story about an incident that occurred in one of the public toilets when he was a child. These old-fashioned toilets were built directly over the sewer system, and the facilities were simply a hole in the stone floor emptying through a pipe directly into a sewer. The sewers were deep brick-lined trenches with a narrow catwalk on one side, along which a man could walk to clean out the overhead pipes as necessary. The cleaner walks along the catwalk carrying a lantern and a long stick that he inserts into the pipes to free up any blockage. As he makes his way from toilet to toilet, the cleaner shouts out a warning of his approach to alert anyone overhead who is using the facilities. One day, a cleaner was moving along a sewer thrusting his stick up each pipe and crying out his presence in the usual way. A deaf old man was squatting over one of the toilets, lost in thought, when suddenly his serenity was shattered in a most distressing manner. The poor soul leapt up screaming and promptly fell into a faint, convinced that he had been victimized by an evil *jinni*.

In the days prior to the installation of modern municipal sewer systems in the cities of Persia, each private home disposed of its sewage by means of a cesspool. This was simply a large underground chamber, lined with brick or terra-cotta, dug next to one of the outside walls of the house. The toilet, which was merely a hole in the floor slightly raised by a concrete slab, was connected to the cesspool by a terra-cotta pipe and flushed by emptying a pail of water into the pipe. The waste material drained through the gravel floor of the cesspool into the ground. Needless to say, this arrangement oftentimes failed to provide optimum sanitation, in which case the cesspool would have to be pumped out. A story was reported in the local newspaper about one parsimonious man who had a good deal of trouble with his cesspool not draining properly. One of the public sewer lines passed near his house, and he decided to solve his problem by surreptitiously connecting his drainage pipes directly to the public sewer line instead of emptying them into his cesspool. He, without government approval or professional engineering consultation, had a trench dug from his basement to the public sewer and installed a connecting pipe. Unfortunately, he did not realize that the sewer was on a higher level than his basement and as soon as he breached the wall of the sewer, the malodorous contents of the sewer flooded into his basement, filling it within a few minutes. From that day forth, this man was known as "The S—t Thief."

Modern downtown Mashhad, even in my childhood, was a study in contrast to the area surrounding the shrine. The downtown streets were wider and cleaner, and lined with modern neon-lit shops and office buildings. Here one did not see pilgrims in chador or turbaned mullahs wandering about in their robes; but rather women stylishly dressed in the latest Western fashion were seen doing their shopping, and men in business suits with white shirt and tie went about their daily chores. The main street downtown runs from north to south and is called Arg. On Arg Avenue, one can find all sorts of restaurants, coffee shops, banks, shops, cinemas, etc. A small but beautifully landscaped park called Bagh Melee (national garden) is on the west side of Arg Avenue.

This park has many flowerbeds, sculptures, fountains, and lily ponds, which are fed by small streams flowing from the nearby mountains. Here the people of Mashhad would gather of an evening to promenade with friends and family, and listen to the music played by small bands of musicians. Older people would sit on benches next to the pathways and enjoy the cool, clean evening air while watching the gardeners as they went about their work pruning the shrubbery and attending to the flowerbeds. They would sit in quiet conversation, no doubt commenting on the scandalous behavior of the young people who used the park as a rendezvous. The youngsters would gather in groups segregated by gender and covertly view members of the opposite sex. Although no direct contact was permitted, fleeting eye contact and a half-hidden smile sometimes led to mutual understandings that later evolved into matrimony. No respectable girl was ever seen walking alone, and the young women were always safely home before dark.

About three miles south of downtown Mashhad, there is a barren rock mountain that rises nearly two thousand feet above the surrounding plain. It is called Kooh Sangi (rock mountain). In the foothills on the north side of the mountain facing the city, there is a large three-story building that was built in 1939. It is fronted by a wide verandah extending the width of the structure, and the wall of the building next to the verandah has seven plate glass windows extending from the floor to the ceiling. The roof of the verandah is accessed from the second floor. It is rimmed by a stone balustrade on top of which concrete flower boxes are set at intervals, and every ten yards or so a stone pillar with an electric lamp on top surmounts the balustrade. The flower boxes are planted with flowers that vary according to the season of the year. Wide stone steps bordered by flowerbeds lead up onto the verandah in front and on either side.

When I was a child, the building housed a popular restaurant; and in the summer months the verandahs on both the first and second stories were used for outdoor dining. Sitting at one of the outdoor tables, one could enjoy a pleasant view. Directly ahead, there was a large water reservoir with several decorative fountains in the center and white marble sculptures scattered around its banks. Beyond this reservoir, a straight wide boulevard connecting the area to Mashhad stretched off to the north. Two gravel walkways, separated by a stream of water and bordered by rows of plane trees, ran on both sides of the road. The streams of water were irrigation ditches fed from the reservoir. The reservoir in turn was filled with water from a channel called Gonabad that extended from the town of Gonabad twenty miles northwest of Mashhad. This channel was constructed over a period of six years from 1928 to 1934 by order of the Reza Shah. The project was supervised by my father. Water from five *ghanatha* dug north of Gonabad was combined to feed the channel. Later another five *ghanatha* were dug and their water combined with the original five.

My father was appointed lieutenant governor of the province of Khorasan by the Reza Shah and, thirty years later, served as lieutenant governor of Khorasan and mayor of Mashhad under his son, Mohammed Reza Shah. During his stint as lieutenant governor under Reza Shah, supervision of the landscaping of the park and the roadside areas was one of his responsibilities, along with many other projects. I remember walking with him in his later years along the pathway next to the boulevard over which the trees had grown to form a canopy overhead. I remarked on the beauty of the trees, and he told me of the difficulty he had experienced in obtaining thousands of saplings all of the same size and species. It took him over a year before he could accumulate the entire number of trees necessary to complete the project. He said that the easiest part of the job was the planting—cheap labor was plentiful because unemployment was so high.

Gravel walkways bordered by shrubbery and flowerbeds led to and around the reservoir from the parking areas and, just beyond the reservoir, a grassy meadow stretched off into the distance. This meadow was a favorite picnic spot, especially for picnics under the full moon. I recall one night when about forty members of our family drove out to Kooh Sangi by *doroshkeh* for just such an outing. Everyone brought a dish to share with the others. Cold cuts of meats, fresh herbs, salads, chick pea patties, yogurt with cucumber, and many other delicacies were carried from the *doroshkehha* in the parking lot and arranged on white tablecloths, which covered rugs laid side by side on the grass. The drivers were given plates of food to eat while they waited patiently in the parking area for us to return for the ride home.

Other groups of picnickers were scattered about over the wide meadow and, from time to time, one could hear music and singing as the people entertained themselves. Some people came just to walk in the moonlight, but rarely one saw a young couple sitting alone or walking hand in hand. On this particular night, I remember seeing a handsome young man walking with a group of his friends. The group stopped by our family gathering to talk with some of my young male cousins; and all of the girls were atwitter over one beautiful Adonis named Emad, who was said to be a talented poet in addition to being so good looking. After the visitors had left us, one of my cousins teased the girls about their display and remarked that it was useless for any of the girls to think of snaring this young man since it was a well-known fact that he was in love with the most beautiful girl in Mashhad who returned his affection.

It later turned out, however, that their young love was never to be consummated. The parents of the girl gave her in marriage to the son of a very rich man. The first and last time that I saw this girl was one day when I was playing outdoors with the daughter of a friend of our family who was a neighbor of the girl's family. I glanced over the garden wall and saw a lovely lady playing with a little girl. I stood transfixed by her beauty until my playmate dragged me away. She told me that her family did not associate with their neighbor, because she was known to be a married woman who was in love with someone other than her husband. How narrow-minded and restrictive was the moral code in those days that even the thought of adultery was sufficient reason for ostracism!

The two lovers continued to pine for each other even though it was impossible for them to see one another. Finally, the girl could no longer continue to bear her loveless marriage and she committed suicide. To my knowledge, Emad never married. Many years later when he had become a famous poet, I saw him on television reciting some of his verses. I was shocked to see the difference in his appearance from the handsome young man whom I remembered from that moonlit night of our picnic. He appeared sad and haggard, and his voice was so melancholy. His poetry, which in his younger years had been full of love and optimism, had gradually changed over the years reflecting his broken heart and increasing bitterness with life. Nonetheless, his collected works are beautiful romantic poetry that is treasured by lovers throughout Persia.

The Reza Shah Pahlavi, father of the late Mohammed Reza Shah, became the ruler of Persia in the early 1920s. The country at that time was somewhat primitive, having stagnated for about 135 years under the rule of the Qajar dynasty. The professional class at that time was drawn from those families who could afford to send their sons to one of the few colleges in Persia or to Europe for schooling. The Reza Shah began the modernization of Persia. He established law and order by enacting new criminal and civil legal codes patterned after the French legal system to replace the Islamic so-called legal system administered by the mullahs. He decreed compulsory education for all, built many new schools, and funded the University of Tehran, modeled after the Sorbonne. He established a national bank and encouraged industrialization. He expanded the transportation system and established a central government with a national police force that, for the first time, made travel safe throughout the country. The second year after the Reza Shah came to power, he revived a program of subsidized study abroad that had been started several hundred years before but had not been enthusiastically supported by the Qajar dynasty in recent years. Graduates with the highest grades from high schools throughout the country were sent to various European countries for graduate study.[2]

The first group of students to be sent under the Reza Shah's program were forty in number, and my eldest brother was one of those chosen. He matriculated at the University of London, where he obtained his doctorate degree in economics. It is interesting to note that two of his daughters followed in his footsteps and both graduated from his alma mater with a Ph.D. in economics. I was not yet born when my brother left to begin his studies in England, and I was three and one-half years old before he returned home and saw me for the first time.

Another major project with which my father as lieutenant governor was involved and of which he was most proud was the planning and supervision of the construction of the first modern hospital in the city of Mashhad. Father did this work voluntarily in the evenings after work and on weekends, and never received any compensation for his labors. When the Reza Shah made his first visit to Mashhad in 1926 as a pilgrim, he was reminded that it was a tradition for each shah to contribute something to the shrine as a memorial of his visit. The Reza Shah scoffed at this and replied that he preferred to be remembered by his good works that would benefit all of the people of Khorasan. To this end, he ordered the construction of a hospital to be built on an elevated area called Alamdasht on the western outskirts of the city. This was to be named the Shahreza Hospital.

The architect for the building was a man named Taherzadeh Behzad; and, as I mentioned above, my father was the overall supervisor of the project. It took over five years to complete the building and install the equipment. When it was finally finished in 1933, it was the largest and best-equipped medical facility in the entire country; and to this day it remains one of the best. The official opening of the hospital was in 1934 when the Reza Shah came to Mashhad for the celebration of the one thousand year anniversary of Ferdosi's birth. A state visit such as this required much in the way of preparation, and the first problem was to find a suitable place for the shah, his queen, and the rest of the royal family to stay.

Mohammad Valy Khan Asadi, the governor and good friend of my father, gave up his residence, and he and his family came to our house to stay for the duration of the royal visit. The governor's mansion was redecorated, and the city was scoured to find suitable furnishings. For example, one local merchant owned a large brass bed, formerly the property of a Russian tsar, that he had acquired on one of his business trips to Russia. This was loaned for the use of the shah. However, the shah was in the habit of sleeping on a thin cotton mattress spread directly on the floor, so wooden boards were placed between the bedsprings and the mattress to make him comfortable. The Reza Shah always maintained that since he was a soldier, he would live like a soldier. This philosophy was reflected in his daily life; he was an early riser and consumed only two simple meals a day.

The Reza Shah was very pleased with the new hospital. After the grand tour and the opening ceremonies had been completed, he remarked to the governor, "If I had a few more men like you, I could make Iran into another Switzerland."

The governor replied, "If I had a few more men like Esfandiar [my father], I could make Mashhad into another Rome!"

The Reza Shah ordered the governor to buy at current market value all of the land immediately adjacent to the hospital and keep it in reserve for future expansion of the hospital. My father owned a building lot next to the hospital, and he was one of the first to offer land for this purpose. He received a promissory note from the government guaranteeing payment, but he did not present the note for payment for many years. As a matter of fact, the only member of the family who knew about the note was his brother. Finally, after my father had been retired for a number of years and was residing in Tehran, he yielded to pressure from his brother and presented the note to the current governor of Khorasan for payment.

The land had increased in value considerably during the ensuing forty years, and although the note guaranteed payment at current market value, my father received only a fraction of that. If he had demanded payment while he was lieutenant governor or mayor, he would have received full value; but he felt that to do so would have been an abuse of his position. This was not the only monetary loss sustained by my family in the course of this royal visit. Following his visit to Mashhad, the shah went on to the nearby small town of Fariman to preside at the opening of a new sugar factory. The same fervor of preparation preceded his visit to Fariman, and my father loaned a beautiful crystal chandelier made in Russia that had been hanging in our living room to decorate the shah's temporary residence in Fariman. We never saw it again!

However, this minor loss was more than compensated for by an invitation from the queen to my grandmother, mother, and oldest sister to be received and take tea with Her Majesty and her two daughters while they were in Mashhad. After a flurry of preparation, which included the making of new dresses for the event, they all got into a *doroshkeh* and called upon the queen. That was a long-remembered, wonderful, and exciting day. Grandmother told and retold the story to me many times.

The largest park in Mashhad is on the outskirts of the city and is called Vakile Abad. The park covers over five hundred acres and is densely wooded with a river flowing through it. There is also a smaller sparkling clear brook, originating in the mountains to the north, which feeds a number of natural pools and a waterfall. There are open meadows scattered throughout the woods, chiefly around the pools and on the banks of the river. Here families will come on weekends and pitch their tents to camp. Originally, the land was owned by a rich philanthropist named Malek who allowed the public to use it freely during his lifetime, and he stipulated in his will that the land be donated to the government upon his death to be used as a public park. Malek also donated for public use a library-museum in Tehran that he built to house his collection of over six thousand hand-written antique manuscripts, a stamp collection, pre- and post-Islamic coins of gold and silver, and extensive works of art.

In the park, Malek built a small one-story structure containing several bedrooms and a kitchen, which he used occasionally as a weekend retreat. He allowed his friends and relatives free use of the cottage when he was not there himself. I visited the park many times as a child, and I remember on one occasion we stayed in Malek's cottage for several days. A story is told that an Indian maharajah once visited the park and was so enchanted with its beauty that he decided he would like to buy the land for his own use. He approached Malek with an offer to purchase it at Malek's asking price, to which Malek replied, "I will not charge you anything for the land, the river, the pools, or any of the improvements. However, I will sell you the trees for one *touman*

52

[about twenty cents at that time] each. Go count them and when you have finished, come back to me and we can settle on the price." Needless to say, the maharajah, wealthy as he was and assuming that the trees could be counted, could not afford to buy the park even at the low unit price of one *touman* per tree.

One of my brothers tells an interesting story about a natural phenomenon that occurred near Mashhad when he was a boy. He was playing outdoors in the garden of our home around sunset one day in the autumn of 1935 when suddenly he saw the sky light up with a brilliant red flash that was gone in an instant and was followed by the sound of a distant explosion. Since there was no damage in the city or apparent cause for an explosion, it was conjectured that a large meteor must have fallen. A local photographer named Payman took it upon himself to find the site of impact and, after much searching, finally found a huge crater several hundred feet in diameter with a mass of black stone in the bottom in an isolated area about thirty miles south of the city. He took pictures of the crater, and he displayed them for years in his photography studio. I have been told that it is the second largest meteor crater in the world. Now all that can be seen is a depression in the plain; the crater over the years filled up with soil that eroded from the sides and eventually grassed over.

Over the years, I have visited many beautiful cities throughout the world, but whenever I think of those first eleven years of my life, which I spent growing up in Mashhad, I feel a nostalgia that I have never felt for any other place.

Notes

1. *Mashhadi* is the honorary title given to anyone who has made a pilgrimage to the shrine in Mashhad. Similarly, *Hadji* is the title given to one who has made the *hadj*, or pilgrimage, to Mecca.
2. An old friend, who had been one of the students chosen for study abroad, told me an amusing, albeit somewhat pathetic, anecdote that happened during the time he was studying at a university in Italy along with two other Persian boys. In this university, there were students from a number of different countries. They all frequently got together to discuss life in general and exchange stories. One night, one of the students suggested that it would be interesting if each of the foreign students sang the national anthem of his native country. The Persian boys were the last to perform and they were des-

perately trying to decide what to do because at that time, right after the Qajar dynasty, there was no Persian national anthem. After much discussion back and forth in Farsi, the boys decided that, rather than admit this sad fact and lose face, they would sing a current Persian popular song. They did so and no one was any the wiser, although one student did comment that the tune sounded too sad and was certainly not as majestic as the "Marseillaise."

Chapter Four
Nishabur (Nishapur)

I desire potent wine, with strength to stun me;
To give me a moment's respite from the turmoil of this life.
                                                    —Hafiz

When I was three years old, I underwent an emotionally traumatic experience that is still vivid in my memory: My Nanny-jon,
due to personal problems in her family, was forced to give up her
full-time job caring for me and move back to her house to take
care of her own family. The afternoon of the day that she left she
kissed me good-bye and Grandfather held me in his arms in the
courtyard as we watched Nanny walk away down the path
through the orchard to the east gate. I cried and cried and
Grandfather tried to console me by diverting my attention to a
nest full of baby birds in a nearby rosebush. Finally, I exhausted
myself and fell asleep in Grandfather's arms. I later learned
from Nanny that she had hid herself behind one of the hedges on
the way out of the orchard and sat there crying herself. After she
saw that I had fallen asleep, she continued on her way.

The next day my mother, in an attempt to comfort me and
turn my thoughts away from Nanny, announced that the oldest
daughter of my uncle who lived in Nishabur (Uncle Nishaburi)
was to be married. She told me that the wedding promised to be
a grand affair and since I was now a big girl, I would be allowed
to go, along with my brothers, sisters, and Aunt Ozra's family. So
it came about that, one lovely summer morning, our entourage
departed Mashhad by bus to journey to Nishabur, some one hundred kilometers to the west. My father did not go with us

because he could not be spared from his duties at the government house. I do not remember much from my first trip to Nishabur at age three. One thing that stands out is the sight of the bride as she entered the room for the ceremony. She was clothed all in white and her veil was trimmed with a variety of miniature lights similar to the tiny light bulbs that are used to decorate Christmas trees. These flashed off and on in a most intriguing manner, a source of constant fascination to a three year old.

In my childhood, Nishabur was a small, quiet town of about twenty-five thousand in the province of Khorasan located in the mountains west of Mashhad. Since the town is about fifteen hundred meters above sea level, it enjoys a temperate climate. The fertile valleys surrounding Nishabur have an abundant water supply from mountain streams and produce some of the best fruit, as well some of the best wines, found in Persia. To the north of the town, there is an imposing mountain called Binalood that rises to about thirty thousand meters and provides a spectacular backdrop to the small city.

The sky over Nishabur has a beautiful luminous blue hue that the people say is a reflection of the blue turquoise found in the mountains nearby. Turquoise is the unofficial national gemstone of Persia, and the stones mined in this area are of the best quality, clear blue with a shiny surface. They are frequently combined with diamonds, rubies, or pearls to make lovely jewelry. Inferior grades of turquoise will change color after prolonged exposure to heat and light, but the turquoise from Nishabur retains its clear blue color due to the purity of its crystalline structure. The superstitious believe that wearing an amulet of turquoise will ward off illness and misfortune.

Nishabur is on the main east-west trade route across northern Persia and was the capital city of the country during the Seljug dynasty in the eleventh century. At that time, it had a population of about one million and was known as the gem of all the cities in Persia. It was sacked and burned in A.D. 1220 by Genghis Khan. When all the inhabitants, including the women and children, had been killed, the Mongols went on and slaughtered even the cats and dogs. The son-in-law of Genghis Khan was killed during the battle for the city. Genghis Khan's daughter was even crueler than her father. One captured woman, in an effort to survive, attempted to bribe her way out by offering a precious gemstone to the conquerors. When Genghis Khan's daughter learned that the woman had swallowed the stone for safekeeping, she was too impatient to wait for nature to take its course and ordered that the woman be put to the sword and her stomach slit open. Just to be sure that no stones were left unturned, all of the other women in town were mutilated in the same manner. All of the farms around the city were also put to the torch to ensure that any chance survivors of the massacre would die of starvation. Nishabur boasted one of the largest libraries in the Middle East at that time, and it was destroyed in the sacking. The city never regained its former eminence.

Nishabur is the birthplace of many famous Persians. One of its most renowned native sons is the physician-apothecary and mystical poet Mohammed Farid al-Din Attar. Attar was born into a wealthy family. His father, a physician with a large and flourishing practice, was also interested in spiritual matters and his mother was noted for her piety. As a young man, Attar traveled widely throughout the Middle East and India in search of knowledge. He is reputed to have studied medicine under the tutelage of Shaykh Majd ud-Din in Baghdad. While Attar was the author of numerous works of poetry and prose, he is best known for his "Conference of the Birds," a mystical poem containing some 4,600 rhyming couplets. This portrays the Sufi (see chapter 17) philosophy of the quest for Truth through the symbolism of a story of a group of birds who set out on a journey to find their king, a mythical bird called the *Simurgh*.

Each bird represents a different personality type; and while many aspire to complete the journey (symbolizing the spiritual path to the understanding of God), most fall by the wayside. Finally, only thirty *(si)* birds *(murgh)* attain their goal. The journey involves crossing seven progressively difficult valleys: the first valley that of Seeking; the second that of Love; the third, Knowledge; the fourth, Independence; the fifth, Unification; the sixth, Amazement; and finally, the seventh valley of Annihilation in God.

When Attar was 114 years old, he was caught up in the invasion of Persia by Genghis Khan and beheaded by one of the Mongol soldiers. The legend surrounding his death tells that after being beheaded, he tucked his head under his arm and ran for a mile, all the while composing one of his longer works. At the spot where he finally fell, the awestruck soldier who had killed him built a tomb in which he laid Attar's body. This tomb, to this day, is a shrine where lovers of poetry frequently gather to pay homage to Attar.

Another renowned native son, who was born in Nishabur a century before Attar, was the astronomer, mathematician, physician, philosopher, and poet, Omar Khayyam. Khayyam, whose name means "tentmaker," studied under the Imam Mowaffak of Nishabur, a sage and teacher of great repute whose students almost invariably went on to achieve fame and fortune in later life. While under the imam's tutelage, Khayyam met two fellow students who later attained fame and infamy in their time, Nizam-ul-Mulk and Hassan Sabbah. The three young men made a pact by which they swore that if any one of them, in his lifetime, should attain high office or wealth, he would help the other two.

Nizam-ul-Mulk rose to eminence politically and eventually became vizier to Sultan Alp Arsalan and continued in that office for fifty-five years, serving in the same capacity under the son of Alp Arsalan, Malik Shah. Malik Shah was quite young when he came to power and left the day-to-day governing in the hands of Nizam-ul-Mulk, who was a fanatic Sunni Moslem. The vizier decreed that only Arabic should be spoken in the court and Arabic-style clothing worn. It is said that he never looked in a mirror because he did not want to see his Persian visage. Despite this narrow fanaticism, he did a great deal of good during his tenure in office. He was responsible for the establishment of many schools in Persia, including a renowned center of learning, Nezamiyeh in Baghdad, then a city in Persia.

Hassan Sabbah claimed his rights under the pact and Nizam-ul-Mulk introduced him to Sultan Alp Arslan, who appointed Sabbah to office. Sabbah performed poorly, and after becoming involved in a treacherous plot to take over Nizam-ul-Mulk's position, was dismissed in disgrace. Sabbah went on to found the Persian sect of the Ishmaelians, an evil party of fanatics. The Ishmaelians became powerful enough to seize the castle of Alamut, or Ashianeh-e-Oghab (Eagle's Nest), atop Mount Hoodkan, a part of the Alborz mountain range south of the Caspian Sea. The castle was built on a huge rock three-quarters of a mile long and several hundred yards wide with access only by means of a narrow defile on the north side. From here, for two hundred years, they terrorized what was then the province of Rudbar. These terrorists were users of hashish with which they whipped themselves up to a maddened frenzy before setting out to do their dastardly deeds. The followers of Sabbah became known as *hassussin* because of their use of hashish; and it is believed that the English word *assassin* is derived from this appellation.

According to legend, which is partially substantiated by the writings of Marco Polo, Sabbah constructed a paradise on earth in a remote valley in the Alborz mountains. Here he planted beautiful gardens full of all sorts of fruit and flowers. Water, wine, milk, and sweetened fruit juices were said to flow in unlimited quantities through channels cut in the rocks. Beautiful slave girls were kept there to prepare and serve food and provide amorous services. Sabbah would recruit young men twelve to twenty years old, and these recruits would be rendered unconscious by the administration of hashish and opium. In this state, they were transported to the valley paradise where, upon awakening, they would find themselves surrounded by all the pleasures that they had ever imagined.

After several days of fun and games, they would again be drugged and transported back to the real world. Sabbah would then explain to them that they had been given a glimpse of heaven, courtesy of Sabbah, and if they swore to follow him and obey him without question, they would be rewarded with an instant return to paradise upon their death. In this manner, the fanatic band of assassins grew and flourished. They were sent out by Sabbah to murder selected rulers of neighboring provinces by means of poisoned daggers, which they concealed in their sleeves and with which they tried to commit suicide after they had made the hit. It mattered not if they were caught and killed for they knew that they would return to the paradise they had briefly visited and remembered fondly. As testimony to the evil nature of Sabbah, his former friend and benefactor, Nizam-ul-Mulk, was one of the first victims of Sabbah's assassins.

The Ishmaeli flourished for over two hundred years until disbanded by one of the successors of Genghis Khan, Holakoo Mongol, who captured their stronghold of Alamut. Before Holakoo Mongol burned the castle, a scholar named Atamalek Javini, who was studying in the castle's extensive library, beseeched the conqueror for permission to remove some of the valuable volumes and astronomical instruments. Permission was granted; and Javini saved many of the precious manuscripts, but he left to be destroyed those that detailed the teachings of Sabbah and the history of the Ishmaeli sect. Scattered pockets of Ishmaeli still exist in several areas in the Middle East and Africa but, they no longer practice the role of assassins. The Aga Khan, whose followers annually on his birthday give him as tribute his weight in gold and jewels, is the head of a branch of the Ishmaeli.

Omar Khayyam did not claim his due from the vizier, Nizam-ul-Mulk, as was his right under the pact made in their student days. However, the vizier did grant him a yearly pension, which allowed Khayyam freedom to pursue his scientific and literary work. He was one of eight scholars appointed by Sultan Malik Shah, son of Alp Arslan, to reform the calendar. He compiled a number of astronomical tables and published, in Arabic, a treatise on algebra that was later translated into French and republished. The original handwritten manuscript still exists in the National Library in Paris.

Khayyam's philosophical works were basically hedonistic and at odds with the strict Moslem teachings of his time. He, in fear for his own safety and in an effort to show that he was a devout Moslem, made a *hadj* to Mecca. When he returned, he discussed his philosophical views only with a limited few people whom he felt he could trust. He expressed his views in verse and in short quatrains, which succinctly laid down his philosophy that this life is the only one that exists and one should enjoy it while one can; there is no hereafter to look forward to. His, at times, melancholic verses reflect his feelings of regret for the fleeting sweetness of life and the pleasures of love.

Alas, that Spring should vanish with the Rose!
That Youth's sweet scented manuscript should close!

60

> The Nightingale that in the Branches sang,
> Ah, whence, and whither flown again, who knows?

He poked fun at the world in general. He once remarked that the world, according to old Persian tradition, was carried between the horns of a bull (see chapter 9); and there was also a bull in the sky, the constellation Taurus. In between, he maintained, was a world full of donkeys!

Omar Khayyam is best known in the Western world for his one long poem, the "Rubaiyat." *Rubaiyat* means a collection of quatrains or four-line verses. Khayyam's "Rubaiyat" consists of several hundred quatrains. The midnineteenth-century Englishman, Edward FitzGerald, was a fervent admirer of Khayyam and translated one hundred verses of the "Rubaiyat" into English. For the most part, FitzGerald captured the philosophy of Khayyam, although his work cannot be considered to be a literal translation from the original Farsi. For example, lines from various of the original quatrains were sometimes combined by FitzGerald to make a single verse. But this is not meant to belittle his remarkable achievement, for the FitzGerald translation is beautiful poetry.

An example of the discrepancy between the FitzGerald version and the original Farsi may be found in the following quatrain.

> Indeed the Idols I have loved so long
> Have done my credit in Men's eye much wrong:
> Have drowned my glory in a shallow Cup
>   And sold my reputation for a Song.

My literal line-by-line translation of the same verse, identified as such by Dr. Hossein-Ali Nouri Esfandiary, is as follows.

> I felt that I wanted to start to pray and fast;
> I thought to myself that now I would attain salvation.
> Alas, my ablutions were defiled by my breaking wind
> And my fast was nullified by half a sip of wine.

An example of partial fidelity to the original Farsi is seen in this quatrain.

And, as the Cock crew, those who stood before
The Tavern shouted—Open then the Door!
You know how little while we have to stay,
And, once departed, may return no more.

Again, the literal translation:

It is the dawn—get up my beloved.
Drink little by little and play the harp;
    Those who live will last not long
And those who are gone will not return.

There are hundreds of editions of the several FitzGerald versions, large and small, good and bad. They range from the massive fifteen-pound volume illustrated by the American artist Elihu Vedder to what is purported to be the smallest book in the world measuring one-fourth by three-sixteenths inches. One elaborately bound and jewel-encrusted volume valued at one thousand pounds (in 1912) went down with the *Titanic*.

Khayyam died in 1123 and is buried in Nishabur. One of his pupils wrote of a conversation that he had with Khayyam one day while walking in a garden. Khayyam told him, "My tomb shall be in a spot where the north wind may scatter roses over it." Whether by chance or design, this prediction came to pass. Today, Omar Khayyam's tomb in Nishabur is next to a garden wall over which fruit trees stretch their branches and, in season, shower their blossoms upon the stone sarcophagus. In the 1920s, an umbrella-shaped concrete lattice enclosure was erected over the simple stone tomb. This covering is inlaid with tiles on which quatrains from the "Rubaiyat" are inscribed.

My second visit to Nishabur occurred when I was nine years old. My sisters and I went to visit my Uncle Nishaburi for a few days. By way of entertainment, my uncle arranged for a picnic in the hills outside the town. Early one morning we sisters, along with several cousins and my uncle and aunt, set off on foot for the hike to the picnic area. A servant leading two donkeys loaded down with carpets, utensils, food, and drink trailed along behind us.

On the way we passed through a cemetery on the outskirts of a small village. The graves were marked by stone slabs set into the ground on which were carved the names of the deceased plus an interesting design representing their occupation during life. A carpenter would be represented by a hammer, a tailor by scissors, a barber by a comb, etc. On a number of stones, in addition to the name and occupational symbol, there was carved a snake. We asked my uncle if the snake meant that the person had been a snake catcher. He laughed and said, "No. In this area there are a lot of snakes and the snake carving on the gravestone means that the person buried there died of a snakebite. The superstitious people hereabout believe that if someone is bitten by a snake and the snake is killed immediately, the victim will live. If not, he will die. As a result, what usually happens is that the poor victim is left unattended while everyone rushes about to find the snake and kill it. By the time they get around to taking care of the victim, it is usually too late to save him."

Our party continued on until we reached a cool shady spot by a river. Here, our picnic lunch was unloaded from the donkeys and laid out on white tablecloths spread over carpets. We whiled away several happy hours, eating and playing games, until it was time to return to the city.

My uncle was the father of four daughters before he was blessed by the birth of his only son. This boy became completely spoiled and was the prankster and troublemaker of the family. One story told about him concerns a nasty prank that he played on his mother. My aunt was a fastidious dresser who was overly concerned with her appearance. She was always meticulously made up and always wore perfume. One night, my cousin stole into her room and removed a bottle of cologne from her dressing table. He emptied the contents and substituted an equal amount of his own urine. The next morning his mother liberally splashed herself with the contents of the bottle. She had to spend hours bathing to rid herself of the smell. The boy made the mistake of disappearing for several hours, therefore the finger of guilt obviously pointed to him. However, by the time he was found, tempers had cooled and he went unpunished as usual. Today he is a respected lawyer and the patriarch of a large family with many grandchildren.

Another highlight of this visit to Nishabur was a dinner party given by one of my uncle's friends, who was the owner of one of the turquoise mines for which the area is famous. Our host's wife was from Tabriz, the capital of Persian Azerbaijan, a province renowned for the culinary artistry of its people. The guests assembled in the large living room of the *beerooney*, which was elaborately and beautifully furnished in the European manner. After everyone had arrived and had been served a refreshing drink, we were ushered into the adjacent dining room for dinner. At one end of the dining room, there was a large window overlooking a garden. Around the periphery of the dining room, blankets folded lengthwise had been placed between the carpet and the walls and leaning against the walls were numerous cushions.

There was no table. A snow-white tablecloth covered the carpet; and this tablecloth was covered, except for a bare area next to the hostess's place, with dishes of all manner of delicious foods. There were platters with mounds of rice, tureens full of several varieties of stews and soups, green herbs, several kinds of bread, fresh fruits, and sweetmeats galore. We all sat down on the blankets with our backs supported by cushions against the walls. When all had been seated, two female servants entered carrying between them a huge silver tray on which there was a steaming white hemisphere reposing on a bed of green parsley and partially covered with a rich red sauce.

The whole effect was a delight to the eye as well as the palate. The tray was deposited on the reserved spot next to the hostess. She proceeded to slice into the white mound with a long sharp knife, beginning on one side and working her way around it. We could then see that the white covering was tripe into which had been stuffed a whole boned chicken surrounded by a thick layer of moist savory ground meat. Each guest was served a slice topped with a dollop of the thick red tomato sauce. The dish reminded us of the red, green, and white colors of the Persian flag. We all gorged ourselves; but, as is usual in Persia, there was plenty of food left over to provide a feast for the servants.

My last visit to Nishabur was when I was eleven years old and I, along with my sisters, were moving from Mashhad to Tehran. We stopped off at Nishabur and Uncle Nishaburi met us at the bus depot and took us to lunch at his house. I'll tell about that later.

Chapter Five
A Family Tragedy

Today it is obvious that you are beloved of God
Because he took you and left so many loving hearts
To grieve for you.

—Sa'adi

The reader may wonder why, through this book, I have told so many stories in which my nanny and my grandmother figure so largely. This is because those two persons were the most important people to me throughout my childhood. When I was three and one-half years old, my mother, Nazanin, died at the young age of thirty-eight. My memories of her are not as vivid or complete as those I have of my nanny with whom I spent most of my waking hours every day during infancy and early childhood. I kept in touch with Nanny throughout her life until her death some years after I had become a mother myself. My grandmother was my mentor from whom I learned the social graces, a code of morals, love of poetry, household management, cooking, and all of the other things normally taught by a mother.

I do remember the day my mother was stricken by her final illness. I was sitting in a corner of the family room in the *anda-rooney* with two of my sisters when my mother entered carrying a glass of water in one hand. She shut the door behind her and stood there for a few seconds leaning back against the door. She was extremely pale and before she had a chance to say anything to anyone, the glass of water fell from her hand and she collapsed on the floor. My sisters jumped to her side and one of them ran out of the room calling for help. In a few seconds, the room was full of people—my aunt, my brothers, Grandmother, and several servants. Someone said that Mother was not breathing; someone else called to one of the servants to fetch the doctor. Our family physician arrived a short time later, and one of my sisters led me out of the room. I do not remember anything else about that night, but the next morning I was told that Mother had been taken to the hospital.

Several days later, my oldest sister, Katayoon, took me to the Shahreza Hospital to see our mother. I remember the long corridors and Katayoon holding my hand, pulling me along behind her for what seemed an interminable distance. When we finally got to my mother's room, it looked so large to me and the ceiling seemed so high. A door leading to an adjoining room was partially ajar and through it I glimpsed some furniture, which looked familiar, and many baskets of flowers. Aunt Ozra and my sister Tooran were there, along with a number of people whom I did not recognize. They were all talking together in low whispering voices and I suddenly had a vague uneasy feeling that something tragic was going on. I later learned that my father had arranged that this room adjacent to my mother's would be available so that visitors might be received there by the family. Furniture had been brought from home to furnish it, and friends could call and offer their condolences without disturbing my mother.

My mother was lying on a single bed in the center of the room. It was so high that I could not see over the edge, so Katayoon picked me up and held me in her arms next to the bed. I looked down and saw my mother lying there with her long black hair fanned out on the white pillow. Her face was very pale, and her beautiful black eyes were sunken and looked even larger than usual. We looked at each other for several seconds, and then she smiled at me. We did not say a word to each other, but I have never forgotten the last look that passed between us. It stays imprinted on my mind even to this day; it seemed that I could physically feel the love flowing from her to me. In thinking back on it, I am now sure that she knew she was dying and felt sorry to leave her family and almost apologetic for her illness.

She did not look frightened. Later on, when I was a young adult, I asked my sisters about that night when Mother had collapsed and was taken to the hospital. They told me that when she first opened her eyes a contented smile came over her face and she said, "It was a beautiful trip. If I live, I will tell you where I was and what I saw. If I die, I know where I am going." Mother never had a chance to further elaborate on her experience before she passed away one week later. I am confident that she had never heard or read of what today we call out-of-body experiences, and she was not in the least bit superstitious. Whatever happened to her, it apparently was a great comfort to her and allowed her to face death without fear or foreboding. May we all be so fortunate!

I was not taken to mother's funeral, but the older members of the family told me about it in later years. They said that the New Courtyard of the Imam Reza Shrine was jammed with people, who came to pay their last respects. My father stood in the front row during the ceremony flanked on his left by Agha Bozorg, mother's father, along with my brothers and other close male relatives with their wives in rows behind them. To father's right, the governor and other government officials stood with their wives lined up behind. My sister Tooran told me that to her the ceremony took on a dreamlike quality. She said that she just stood there as if in a trance. She could not believe that someone as young and vibrant as my mother could be taken away so suddenly from her family, who loved and needed her so much, and that she would soon disappear forever down the stairway to the vault beneath the courtyard. Interment in the vaults beneath the shrine or in the vaults beneath the courtyards of the shrine was considered a high honor. My father's father was buried in the vault beneath the *Ayvan Tala*, the golden-arched entrance to the shrine; and, years later, Grandmother and my father were to be buried in the vault beneath the room containing the mausoleum of the Imam Reza.

The days immediately following my mother's death were very disconcerting to me. No one came right out and told me that Mother had died, but with the unerring instincts of a child, I knew that something profound and terrible had happened. My sisters were all dressed in black, my brothers wore black bands of cloth around their upper arms, and Father and Grandfather wore black ties. It was difficult for me at age three to understand why Mother would no longer be with us; the concept of death was beyond my comprehension. During the six months between the time that Nanny moved out of our house and the time of my Mother's death, I had grown very close to her. Fortunately, my nanny came back to work for us on a daily basis as soon as Mother became ill; and since she was there for me when Mother died, I was able to cling to her throughout the mourning period. Our home had always been full of cheerful activity, but after Mother died the atmosphere became quiet and subdued even though friends and relatives were constantly coming and going. There were no sounds of music from my brother's rooms; no giggling chatter from the servants' quarters. The house seemed as lifeless as the half-bare trees outside beneath the cold gray skies of late fall.

There is an old Persian saying, "Grief comes suddenly and overwhelmingly like a sandstorm and disappears slowly as sand trickles from a sand dune." However, as always, life must go on. Mother's death seemed to draw the family closer together as we supported each other in our mutual grief. Grandmother took over the reins of family management; and the children, especially the younger ones, became very close to their grandparents. It was a blessing that those two wonderful people lived with us and were able to help fill the void left by Mother's passing. My eldest brother was studying in London; but the other seven children, ranging in age from twenty-two to me at age three, were all still living at home.

Our house had always been a kind of headquarters for the whole family, because my father was the oldest surviving male progeny in his family and his parents, by custom, made their home with him. Various relatives were always calling to ask advice or help from Father or my grandparents; they were consulted on all sorts of family decisions and problems, especially those related to marriage or business. This custom did not change after my mother's death. Even some thirty years later, after my grandparents had died and Father had moved to Tehran, he still kept his salon Tuesday afternoon and evening. Many relatives and friends would come to call on him regularly every week, except in those winter months when a heavy snowfall made travel difficult. Tuesday dinner was always an open affair; anyone who wanted to stay for dinner was welcome and often twenty or more people would gather round the table.

Chapter Six
My Own Kindergarten

From crib to grave, never cease to search for knowledge.
—Ferdosi

When I was five years old, I began my formal education; but I have always felt that my education really began a year or so before that, in a different and most unique kind of school. Every evening after the family had dined and the dishes had been cleared away, the servants all gathered in Grandmother's kitchen to eat their meal. This was a time of relaxation for them and they would sometimes sit for several hours talking, joking, telling stories, and gossiping in general. My family usually retired to the north wing family room after dinner and occupied their time by reading or doing homework. This room was so quiet that Grandmother often said that it seemed more like a library than a house; and, of course, it was quite boring for me at age three or four. I found my own entertainment by slipping into Grandmother's kitchen every night where I would quietly sit and listen to the servants' dinner conversation. They hardly noticed me, and I was too young to inhibit their good time. It seemed to me that I entered into another world and another time when I took my place on the fringe of their circle.

The permanent staff numbered five and usually there were two additional people, my nanny and my cousin Genoos's nanny. The servants were of diverse background, having come from several different country villages. Their ages ranged from twenty to some forty-odd years. Although virtually illiterate and lacking in proper grammar, they were the salt of the earth. One could not

69

find a more honest, kind, and devoted group of people. They had lively imaginations and a great sense of humor. They were accomplished storytellers and I would sit enthralled for hours listening to their tales. I grew to know each one's innermost thoughts and aspirations, and experienced with them their joys and sorrows.

By listening to their stories, I learned of ghosts, omens, astrology, palm reading, talismans, witches, and all the superstitions common to a simple guileless folk. In later years, I realized how ridiculous and absurd some of the stories were, but I have never forgotten one of them. I still remember with delight how deliciously frightened I was by a ghost story and how I convulsed with laughter over a funny anecdote. Sometimes I would repeat some of the stories to my family, and my brothers would make fun of my gullibility. My sisters, on the other hand, would just smile and say nothing, for they probably had heard the same stories in the same way when they were children. Father and my grandparents never made fun of me, and they would patiently explain to me what was superstition and what was within the realm of credibility. I soon learned to separate the two worlds: I should never repeat the servants' talk to my family and never relate family matters to the servants.

The permanent members of our household staff were Gholam, the gardener who doubled as butler; Soltan, Gholam's wife, was our cook and maid; Naneh was Grandmother's cook and maid; Mashaallah, the son of Naneh, was the assistant gardener and general gofer; and Zivar was our laundress and maid. Additional part-time helpers were hired as necessary when we had houseguests over an extended period of time or during the housecleaning preparatory to Now Ruz (Persian New Year's Day).

Gholam was a strapping man in his early thirties, tall and muscular with broad shoulders. He had twinkling black eyes, short curly black hair, and a sunburned complexion. In addition to his gardening, he also did our everyday shopping, pedaling off on his bicycle each morning to the market, with a large wire basket mounted behind, to pick up the day's supply of milk, meat, bread, and other necessities. Once a week Soltan would prepare the dough for a special delicious bread called *nan-e-roo sangee*, which contained a variety of special spices, onions, and caraway seeds, and Gholam would take it to the local bakery and bring back the baked loaves. This bakery was primarily for the baking of a common flat bread called *sangak*, which is a bread baked on hot pebbles in an huge oven, but during the midmorning or midafternoon when they were not too busy, they would bake Soltan's special dough for us because it too had to be baked directly on hot pebbles.

Soltan was a small thin woman several years older than her husband, Gholam. She had a pale complexion, so she always rouged her bony cheeks. Her long black hair hung down her back, drawn back by a little white bandanna that she knotted in the back of her neck. She and Gholam first met when they both came to work for our family before I was born. Soltan nagged her husband unmercifully, shouting at him to do this or that. It was common gossip among the servants that Gholam had a roving eye and was always looking for an opportunity to fool around with the young single serving girls in the neighborhood. Soltan invariably learned of his dalliances and then the shouting and nagging would start. Gholam would stoically bear up under her abuse and abandon his current affair; but, a few months later, he would find another girlfriend whereupon the cycle would repeat itself. Grandmother always maintained that if the childless couple had had children, their relationship would have been better.

Gholam, because of his daily forays to the market, would bring back stories he had heard that day. One tale that I recall concerned a beggar who had been begging on one particular corner for years. Everyone maintained that he was probably a rich man, but no one had ever seen him go to a bank or buy anything but the bare necessities. One evening, Gholam announced that he had heard that day that the beggar had died on the street and when the authorities came to remove the body, they found that he had sewn hundreds of large denomination bills inside the lining of his clothing.

A story that Naneh told came from the women's gossip in the public bath. It seems that one woman had a husband who was having an affair with another woman and neglecting his connubial duties to his wife. The wife, over a period of time, added sufficient saltpeter to his food that he became impotent. She said that if she could not have him, no other woman would enjoy him

71

either. At the time, I did not understand the full import of the story but I did notice that Gholam, the peripatetic philanderer, listened to it with a worried expression on his face.

Naneh (a slang word for "mother") was the oldest of the servants. She was about forty years old, and since the servants took their meals in "her" kitchen, she was the boss of the group. Years before, she had presented herself on Grandmother's doorstep with a baby in her arms. She told Grandmother that her husband had recently died and she had to find work. Grandmother took her in and she remained; the baby, Mashaallah, grew up in our household and eventually joined his mother in Grandmother's employ. Naneh was a small thin woman who was not particularly pretty but had a sweet open face. Her habitual headgear was a clean white kerchief, which she wore pinned beneath her chin with just a tuft of her black hair showing above her forehead. The long sleeves of her colorful blouses were always rolled above her elbows; and she wore the pleated, knee-length flowered skirt over black pantaloons, which is the traditional garb of the Persian peasant.

It is interesting to trace how this fashion evolved. During the nineteenth century, a Qajar shah named Naseraldeen visited Vienna and attended a performance of the ballet. He was entranced with the ballet costumes of short fluffy skirts worn over tight leotards. When he returned to Persia, he ordered the women in his harem to adopt the same custom; the fashion filtered down to other women in the court and then to the women in the villages. The peasant women, rather than wear the tight leotards, wore loose-fitting black pantaloons with a knee-length skirt. The fashion was soon abandoned by the fashionable ladies about town and in the court, but the black pantaloons and knee-length skirts persisted as peasant garb to this day.

Most of the time Naneh was a kind, placid person, but toward sunset she became withdrawn and short-tempered only to emerge as the happy, lively life of the party after dinner. I later found out that these swings in mood were directly correlated with Naneh's blood level of opium, for she was addicted to the drug, which she took morning and evening in the form of a small pill. Once or twice a week, she would disappear for a couple of hours and return to the house laughing and gay after her visit to one of the local opium dens where she smoked her pipe of dreams. Behind her back, the other servants called her *Naneh-sheerehee,* meaning one who is addicted to opium. Naneh had a pet cat that was very attached to her. The cat would sit with her in the kitchen while she was preparing food, and Naneh would occasionally toss her a scrap of meat. She was so well trained that Naneh could say to her, "I have to leave the kitchen for a few minutes. You watch this plate of meat until I get back." When Naneh returned, the cat would still be sitting in the same spot and the meat would be untouched!

Mashaallah, Naneh's son, was the arbiter of arguments among the servants because he was the only literate of the group. When he was about thirteen years old, Grandmother arranged for him to attend night school where he learned to read and write and finished what would be about the equivalent of the third grade of elementary school. He was a very good-humored young man and everyone liked him. Whenever he had the floor during the after dinner discussions, he would always preface his remarks with "Once I read in a book . . ."; and his opinions therefore were accepted without argument. His portable library consisted of one book, *Mulla Nasreddin,* a joke book from which he would sometimes read to entertain the group. The stories of *Mulla Nasreddin* have been told and retold throughout the Middle East from as far back as the thirteenth century. No one knows the language in which they were originally written or who first recorded them. While the stories are humorous, there is more than mere humor in the tales. There is an underlying philosophy that states that it is not worthwhile to take oneself or anything else in life too seriously. If Mashaallah had to be limited to one book, the choice of *Mulla Nasreddin* was certainly a good one, for therein one can find an appropriate commentary on almost any subject or situation.

I remember one evening when the servants were all sitting around after dinner. Naneh was smoking her hookah and her cat was sitting at her feet, purring contentedly. Mashaallah pulled out his book of stories and read the following.

Once there was a man who was married to a woman who kept a pet cat. The man one day went to the market and purchased a kilo of meat. He brought the meat home and told his wife that he was tired of having a stew of just vegetables and wanted her to prepare a stew with meat as well as vegetables for that evening. The wife was also starved for meat and during the preparation of the stew, she managed to eat the entire kilo of meat herself. That evening, when she served her husband his dinner, there was no meat in the stew. "Woman," he cried, "where is the meat that I gave you this morning?" The wife, frightened to tell the truth, replied that the cat had eaten it. The man thereupon called for the cat and a scale. He weighed the cat and it turned out that the cat weighed one kilogram. "Woman," he said, "if this is the cat, where is the one kilo of meat? If this is the meat, where is the cat?"

Mashaallah was exempt from the compulsory military service at age eighteen, not because of any physical infirmity but because he was an only son. However, when he was about twenty-two years old, he volunteered to enter the army. Before he left, he brought an older friend, Habib, to take his place as assistant to Gholam. Habib was a tall handsome man who turned out to be a fine worker. As time wore on, Habib began to spend more and more of his time in Grandmother's kitchen helping Naneh clean up after dinner. Sometimes, after all the other servants had retired, Habib and Naneh would still be in the kitchen, ostensibly cleaning the pantry.

One summer evening when we were all sleeping outdoors in the courtyard, we were awakened by loud talking and we saw someone come running out of the house toward the servant quarters beyond the orchard. The loud shouting was from Grandmother who had wandered into her kitchen and caught Naneh and Habib *in flagrante delicto*. In the morning, after Grandmother had calmed down, Naneh showed her the marriage certificate uniting her to Habib. She explained that she had been too shy to publicize the marriage for fear that she and Habib would become the butt of joking remarks because of the disparity in their ages. Grandmother was mollified, and now that the secret was out, Naneh and Habib henceforth openly consorted in Habib's room.

Zivar, our laundress and maid, was a strong stocky girl in her late twenties. She came from a small village in the province of Mazandaran near the Caspian Sea, and like many people from this northern region, she had blonde hair and blue eyes. She did not observe the Moslem dress code for females; she never wore a chador and the sleeves of her dresses were short. Zivar was a good-humored, open, and cheerful girl and everyone loved her because of her kind and friendly nature. Grandmother once remarked in a joking manner that Zivar was always anxious to please her; but as soon as she (Grandmother) turned her back, Zivar would have a kiss for Grandfather. I am sure that there was nothing more serious than a mild flirtation between them, because Grandmother was not one to tolerate any hanky-panky.

Zivar was an only child and much loved by her parents. When she was fourteen years old, her parents arranged for her marriage to an eighteen-year-old boy from her village, who came from a good family and seemed assured of a bright future. However, several weeks after the wedding ceremony, Zivar learned a painful secret: Her husband was in love with a distant cousin whom he wanted to marry, but the two families had become estranged and his family forbade the marriage. A few months later, her husband along with his cousin disappeared from the village. Zivar remained with her husband's family for several weeks until she received a message from her husband saying that he had married his cousin and did not intend to return to Zivar.

Zivar went back to her parents and waited patiently for two years in hope that her husband would change his mind. Finally, she gave up hope and went to see the mullah who had performed her marriage. She asked him to grant her a divorce, as a woman is entitled to do under Moslem law if her husband abandons her and she hears nothing from him for one year. Her prospects for remarriage were slim in her own village and life there was a continual embarrassment, so she eventually moved to Mashhad where she wound up in our employ.

Zivar was one of the best storytellers I have ever known. She was a romantic and sensitive person who was able to fabricate with great imagination all sorts of tales. They always began the same way: "Once a long, long time ago," and always ended with "and they lived happily ever after." In retrospect, I can see that her stories were a reflection of her own hopes and aspirations for her future. She was able to change the same story to suit the age and sex of the listener; often I heard her telling a story to my younger cousin that I had heard in a slightly different form. All of her tales featured a good protagonist and an evil antagonist with the good always triumphant, and invariably there was a love story woven into the plot.

Zivar also shared with us some of the superstitions of her native north. One that I remember concerned rainbows. My cousin and I habitually wore our hair braided into two pigtails hanging down either side of our heads. Zivar told us that when we saw a rainbow after a rain shower we should grasp our pigtails in either hand, face the rainbow, and while pulling on our braids sing this song: "I am singing this song just for you, rainbow. Please make my hair as long as your bow."

Fortunately for Zivar, her life took a turn the nature of which could have been the plot of one of her stories. Every year, one of Grandmother's former maids, named Gohar, who years ago had married well and was now a respected matron of some sixty years, came to Mashhad to shop. She always came to see Grandmother and stayed with her for a few days, bringing gifts for which Grandmother never had any use. Grandmother used to complain to Grandfather about the junk that Gohar gave her, and Grandfather would gently chide her with the old proverb: "If the horse is a gift, one does not count the teeth," the Persian counterpart of "Never look a gift horse in the mouth."

Gohar was not educated in a formal sense, but she was a repository of superstitious knowledge. She suffered from arthritis and habitually wore a copper bracelet on either wrist in the belief that this would help alleviate her pain. She also believed that the sting of bees had a similar effect. Grandfather used to kid her about this; he remarked that he was sure that she was right in this belief because the pain of the bee sting would make one forget about any other pain. (It should be noted that the supposed curative power of bee venom for arthritis enjoyed a brief popularity in Western medicine.) Another of her home remedies involved amber; she believed that wearing an amulet of amber about the neck would cause a goiter to shrink. One can speculate that sometime in the distant past, someone suffering from goiter chanced upon an amulet of amber that had become contaminated by a bit of radioactive ore during the process of fossilization and the low-grade radioactive emission had a therapeutic effect.

One day during one of her visits, while she was wandering in our garden, Gohar came upon Zivar and me and stopped to chat. Zivar had been telling me about how if one encountered a good *jinni*[1], one should be careful not to blink lest the *jinni* disappear before granting a wish. Gohar countered with her own story: "If you see the invisible prophet Hazrat-e-Khezr, he will not disappear like a *jinni*. If you see him, you can ask him any wish and he will grant it."

Zivar was immediately entranced and curious; she had great respect for the older woman's so-called knowledge. Zivar asked, "How can one get to see Hazrat-e-Khezr if he is invisible?"

The woman replied, "For forty days, you must get up every morning before dawn, sweep the street in front of your house and sprinkle it with water. On the fortieth morning, the prophet will appear to you and you can ask your wish."

Zivar was fascinated by the story. The next day she swore me to secrecy and then told me that she was going to follow the prescribed procedure. Two months later, she came to Grandmother and my older sisters and told them that she wanted to get married. Grandmother gave her blessing and within a few weeks Zivar married and left with many gifts to start her new life. Seven months later and happily pregnant, she came back to visit. After she had talked to Grandmother and the rest of the household, she took her leave. I followed her to the gate and reminded her that I had kept her secret, and now she should tell me about seeing Hazrat-e-Khezr.

She laughed and said: "I never did finish the forty days of sweeping. In fact, I stopped after a couple weeks because every morning this boy passed the house on his way to work. He finally stopped one morning and we talked. Every morning after that, we met and talked with no one around to bother us. Little by little, we learned about each other and fell in love. So my wish was granted even though I did not see Hazrat-e-Khezr." Thus Zivar's last story ended the way all her others had: "and they lived happily ever after."

Zivar's departure necessitated that a new maid be found to

take over her duties. Grandmother began to inquire around and a friend told her of a young woman who, although she had never worked as a maid, was seeking employment in order to support herself. She had recently moved to Mashhad from the small northern city of Darrehgaz. She was married but had left her soldier husband because she could no longer tolerate living in the same household with her husband's two older sisters and her mother-in-law. Her name was Keshvar, and she was unique with respect to the usual servant in that she was able to read and write at an elementary level. In addition, she was very pretty with jet black hair, brown eyes, and a slim but curvaceous figure. Her demeanor was quite ladylike, and Grandmother and Katayoon decided to quarter her in a small room in the central wing of the house rather than in the servant quarters beyond the orchard. Everyone liked her, and she was treated more like a new family member than as a maid.

Keshvar remained in our employ for a little over two years before her husband found her and, after innumerable visits and much pleading, finally managed to persuade her to return to him. He never bore any animosity toward Keshvar for leaving him; in fact, nine months after she returned to him, she delivered a baby girl with blue eyes just like her father's. Keshvar and her daughter, over the years, remained in contact with our family; every time they came to Mashhad (and later Tehran), they would stay with our family. I discovered that Keshvar had a lovely voice when one day I heard her singing while doing some laundry beside the stream. From that day forth, I followed her around whenever I could and begged her to sing for me the traditional songs of her native Darrehgaz.

Like Zivar, Keshvar was an entertaining storyteller. I particularly remember one tale she told me about how a mountain called Kooh Cheheldokhtar on the border between Persia and Russian Turkmen got its name. *Kooh Cheheldokhtar* means "The Mountain of the Forty Virgins." The meadows on this mountain are quite beautiful in the springtime when they are filled with wild tulips in bloom.

One spring morning, forty young girls from Darrehgaz went to the mountain to picnic and gather the wild flowers. Suddenly, one of the girls screamed and pointed off in the distance to a dust

78

cloud rapidly approaching from the direction of Turkmenistan. It soon became apparent that the dust was due to a band of horsemen who had seen the girls and were galloping toward them. The girls knew that Persian women were much coveted by the Turkoman, and they also knew that there was no chance for them to escape. They fell on their knees, crying and praying to God for deliverance. Suddenly, a wide fissure opened in the side of the mountain near the girls and they heard a deep voice say, "Come to me and I will save you!" The girls leapt into the fissure and it immediately closed over them. When the horsemen arrived, there was no sign of the girls, and after much puzzled searching, they returned to Turkmenistan. The villagers, when they realized that the girls were missing, poured out of the town and began a frantic search, but the forty were never seen again. Exactly one year later, to the day, a spring of pure, cold freshwater appeared at the base of the mountain. The villagers, amazed at the purity and sweet taste of the water, explained the phenomenon by saying that the water came from the tears of the lost maidens. The mountain henceforth was called "The Mountain of the Forty Virgins."

All of the servants believed to some extent in ghosts and the spirit world, but Gholam was the most fervent believer. He was always recounting supposed sightings and encounters with ghosts, which he swore he saw outside his bedroom window late at night wandering about the orchard. He used to advise the other servants on things demonic; for example, a handful of dirt from a grave sprinkled over a sleeping person by a thief would ensure that the victim would not awaken during the robbery. He was very careful to avoid graveyards after dark for fear of being attacked by malevolent spirits. In later years, when I was living in Tehran, I read an account in the newspaper about a gang of thieves who made their headquarters in a local cemetery. They roamed about after dark, covered in white shrouds, attacking and robbing terrified passersby. Perhaps there was some truth to Gholam's warnings.

Another interesting superstition among the servants was their belief in the *bakhtak*, a heavy, bulky invisible creature who comes at night and falls upon the chests of sleeping infants, killing them. It also attacks sleeping old people, who feel it as a heavy pressure on their chests but are unable to move or call out for help. This sounds like an explanation for what we today call crib death and nocturnal coronary occlusion. To ward off the *bakhtak*, it was the practice to attach a talisman called *kosgor-beh* (the female cat's genitalia), a small blue ceramic charm shaped as its name implies, to the left shoulder of the baby's nightdress. This talisman did not work for older people and its use was not considered necessary for infants after they became ten months old. Incidentally, crib death is very rare after the age of six months.

Mashaallah had two pet superstitions that he maintained were absolute fact because he had read of them in a book. He believed that it was dangerous to awaken a sleeping person who was dreaming, because that person's soul left their body during a dream and might not return if the dreamer were suddenly awakened. He also believed that the soul of a dead person remained in his house for three days after death. During this time, it would bring bad luck if the name of the departed were spoken aloud. Any reference to the deceased should only be description: my wife, my father, etc.

In addition to subscribing to the Islamic belief that one's fate was written on one's forehead by an angel at the time of birth and could never be changed, Naneh believed in all the omens and superstitions such as:

If you hear a buzzing or crackling noise in your years, some-one is talking about you.

An itching right palm means you will receive money. An itching left palm means you will be paying out money.

If a crow sitting in a tree calls out three times, good news will come to you.

A sudden feeling of anxiety means something bad will hap-pen.

If one shoe falls on top of the other when you take them off, you will soon be going on a trip.

If, when washing your hands, the soap slips out of your hands, an unexpected guest will arrive.

If you awaken in the morning lying on your right shoulder, all will go well that day and vice versa.

An unexpected sneeze means that one should not start any

contemplated activity. One of the Qajar kings believed so strongly in this last superstition that members of his court took advantage of him by counterfeiting a sneeze whenever the king made a decision with which they did not agree. On one occasion, this shah added a young beautiful girl to his harem. She was so attractive that his first wife was worried that she might be deposed from her position of authority. The first wife ordered a servant to hide outside the bridal chamber door, and when the king went to bed, she was to sneeze loudly. When the shah heard the sneeze, he left the bed without touching the girl. The same procedure was repeated every time the king decided to consummate his marriage until finally he gave up and the girl was dismissed from the harem.

Two very dire omens are dropping salt on the floor and stepping on it, and dropping a piece of bread into a fire or onto lit charcoal. The occurrence of either of these events means that one does not appreciate God's abundance and therefore invites divine punishment. Another bad omen concerns babies born while the moon is in Scorpio (see chapter 22). These unfortunate children are destined to have a nasty disposition throughout their lives.

One of Naneh's strongest superstitions involved the crescent moon that appears after the dark of the moon. She believed the first time one sees this crescent moon, one should look quickly at a green tree, into a mirror, or into water before one looks into the face of another person. If one looked at this moon and then directly at another person, a quarrel would soon ensue. Lunar symbols may be substituted for the green tree or water to avert disaster. For every lunar month, there is a symbol; for example, gold for the month of *Moharram*; a mirror for the month of *Safar;* etc.

Zivar had an interesting superstition involving owls. This superstition, like her stories, was benign and had a happy conclusion if one followed the protocol. If you hear an owl calling out with a high-pitched chuckling sound (laughing), it means that something good will happen to you. If the owl calls out with a mournful hoot (crying), someone will die. To avoid the disaster portended by a crying owl, one should place a cup of water and some candy or sugar cubes on a mirror, and put it beneath the tree in which the owl is perched to make the owl laugh before he flies away.

The Zoroastrian religion considered belief in superstitions to be a cardinal sin, along with polygamy, adultery, lying, suicide, and murder. Most of the superstitious beliefs of the illiterate masses in Persia were fostered and encouraged by the mullahs after the Arab conquest. While belief is inversely proportional to the level of education, as is the case in all societies, some degree of belief rubs off on all classes. For example, one does not see a thirteenth floor or room in many hotels around the world. The popularity of astrology attests to the psychological need of many people to find guidance or help in the management of their lives.

I must confess that I can't help anticipating whenever I feel an itch in my right palm.

Note

1. The belief in the existence of *jinn* started with the Bedouin Arabs, and there are many references to *jinn* in the Koran. They are chiefly portrayed as evil, but the existence of good *jinn* is also recognized. These good *jinn* are invariably Moslem and existed before humans inhabited the earth. Supposedly, they, upon hearing the verses of the Koran, recognized the truth of same and became instant converts. Other *jinn* who did not convert were the evil ones who will be consumed in the fire of hell eventually. According to the Koran, *jinn* live underground or inhabit ruins, and come out only at night, disappearing at sunrise. They can marry other *jinn* and procreate.

Chapter Seven
Snake's Marble

The garden of wisdom is a place of Paradise;
The well of ignorance is an abyss.
—Malekalshoara Bahar

During the long, hot summer afternoons, it was customary for everyone to take a siesta or otherwise occupy themselves with quiet activity in the cool indoors. One afternoon, when I was about nine years old, I was put down for a nap; but, as usual, I wanted to go out and play instead of sleeping. I quietly slipped out of my room and walked across the courtyard toward the orchard. As I passed the south wing of the house, I could hear the scratching noise of my sister Tooran's violin as she practiced her scales. She tried for years to learn to play as well as Kayvan, my second oldest brother, but she was never able to master the instrument. She finally gave it up, much to the relief of the rest of the family.

Just within the past year, we had a small family reunion in Europe. I asked Tooran why she never had continued her study of the violin. She replied, "I never played well and I thought that I should stop trying before I drove everyone in the family crazy with my scratching." Then she told me a funny story about her teacher. It seems that Tooran, along with two of our cousins who were about the same age, would go once a week for a music lesson. Their teacher was a middle-aged man who lived within walking distance from our house. Tooran was trying to learn to play the violin, one other cousin played the accordion, and the other was studying the tambourine. One day when they arrived for their lesson, the teacher was out on an errand. His wife ushered them into the parlor and asked them to await his return. She said that her husband would be back in just a few minutes.

The few minutes elapsed and still he did not come. The girls became bored and decided to play together for their own amusement. They began, with Tooran scratching away on her violin, one cousin pumping enthusiastically on her accordion, and the other banging time with her tambourine. They sounded terrible and the poor wife ran frantically out to the courtyard gate in search of her husband. The so-called music could be heard all over the neighborhood. Finally, the teacher came home and restored order. The girls finished their lesson and went home. A day or so later, the teacher called upon Grandmother, and after the usual polite pleasantries, said to her, "If you don't mind, I would like to come to your house and give Tooran and her cousins their lessons here rather than in my home. I will not charge any more than if they came to me." Grandmother agreed, but later she asked the girls what they had done to make the teacher want to come to our house. Tooran told her that she could not think of any reason except perhaps his wife was tired of listening to music all the time.

All of our family loved art, poetry, and music; and although none of the family members ever became a professional in any of these fields, we all pursued one or more as hobbies all our lives. Kayvan played beautifully and did so all his life. The evening he died, he was playing his violin to entertain some guests after dinner when he suddenly dropped it, collapsed, and died despite an heroic attempt at cardiac-pulmonary resuscitation by his son, who was a medical student at the time.

Now, let's go back to that summer afternoon in my childhood. As I passed through the orchard and approached the servants' quarters, I saw Soltan sitting alone in the shade beside the stream sewing. I sat beside her and saw that she was sewing a tiny felt bag. It looked familiar to me and I asked her, "That looks like the little bag that you always wear around your neck hidden under your blouse. Why do you want another one?"

Soltan was evasive and tried to pass off my questioning by telling me that it was a souvenir of remembrance of her mother. When I persisted in my prying and begged to see what was inside the bag, Soltan finally broke down and confessed saying, "Promise me that you will never speak of this to anyone, but this little bag holds a good luck charm—a snake's marble. The old bag was dirty and worn so I am making a new one." She then opened the incompletely sewn bag to reveal a small egg-shaped ivory-colored object about one centimeter long and half as wide.

"Where did you get this?" I asked.

"From the gypsies," she replied. "There are certain gypsies who know where to look in the mountains for the places where snakes lay their eggs. The snake's nest may contain many eggs, all looking alike, but only one of them will be a snake's marble, an egg without a snake inside. You know how a snake can hypnotize a bird or a mouse, and catch them. When a woman wears a snake's marble around her neck, she will attract and hold the attention of men and it will bring her good luck. I wear this to be sure that I keep my husband's love forever." As we know from a story related previously, Gholam was not entirely faithful; but the snake's marble must have worked somehow, because he and Soltan never divorced.

Then I remembered the day months before when I had accompanied Soltan to the *Chaharshanbeh-bazaar* (Wednesday Market). It had all started when I overheard Soltan asking Katayoon's permission to have time off to go to the bazaar. No one in our family ever went to this flea market, which was held every Wednesday during the summer months. I knew that the only way I would ever get to see it was to go with Soltan. After much pleading, Katayoon finally gave me permission to go with Soltan on the condition that I never leave her side.

That Wednesday was a mild, pleasant spring day. We left early in the morning and walked for about an hour to the outskirts of the city to where the bazaar was located. The ground of an open field was covered with all sorts of merchandise for sale: vegetables, fruit, grains, clothing, cosmetics, wooden furniture, blankets, sewing machines, bicycles, horses, donkeys, sheep, camels, chickens, pigeons, and many other new and used articles. Hundreds of people milled about bargaining back and forth, and the din was such that we had to shout to hear each other.

Soltan and I walked around for some time, hand in hand. I wanted to look at the many articles displayed for sale on the small pieces of rugs spread all over the grounds, but Soltan was not interested in window-shopping, but rather seemed intent on finding one particular item. She pulled me along with her until we finally arrived in an area where several little booths made of thatched straw had been erected along with a few small tents. We entered one of the tents and inside, seated on a low bench, were two tall, thin, black-haired women. Their bony cheeks were sunburned, and their large black eyes glittered from beneath strings of gold bangles that decorated their foreheads. They wore long floral-printed dresses and were bedecked with gold necklaces, earrings, and bracelets. Soltan bought rouge and *sormeh* (kohl), a black powder made from ground antimony from one of the women. *Sormeh* is used as an eyeliner and, according to folklore, it is supposed to strengthen the vision. Then the two of them carried on a whispered conversation that I couldn't hear, but I saw that money and something wrapped in a bit of paper changed hands. When I saw the snake's marble that summer afternoon, I realized what Soltan had bought from the gypsy woman that day in the spring when we visited the Wednesday flea market.

I kept my promise to Soltan, and I have never mentioned this tale of her snake's marble until now. However, within the past few years, I was talking with an old man and his wife at a small party. He was a fairly well-educated former businessman from Persia, the father of five children, all of whom became physicians. During the course of the conversation, probably because the man was so charming, I was reminded of the powers to attract the opposite sex that Soltan attributed to her amulet. I asked the old gentleman if he had ever heard of the superstition regarding a snake's marble.

He answered, "Of course I have. I had one myself and carried it for years in my pocket. It worked like a charm; it seemed that all of my business ventures worked out well and all the women were attracted to me. Unfortunately, it somehow disappeared. I suspect that my wife became jealous of all the attention I was getting from the ladies and managed to get rid of it!"

His wife then interrupted, "Don't talk such nonsense. How could a snake's marble attract women or do anything else? You were young and rich at the time, and women naturally were drawn to you. Now you are old and not so rich, and you have to face up to the fact that the only woman who is attracted to you is me!"

Soltan, in common with the majority of women of her class at that time, was a devout believer in fortune-tellers. Probably a lot of the men believed in them also. The most common and least expensive of the fortune-tellers were the itinerant soothsayers who wandered about the streets calling out their services like the vegetable hawkers. They were usually bearded middle-aged men and wore ankle-length smocks and turbans on their heads. They carried a folded piece of cardboard that, when opened, became a square painted with two concentric circles divided into twelve sections by six lines intersecting in the center. Each of the twelve sections of the outer ring was inscribed with a sign of the zodiac and in the inner circle various symbols such as the sun, the moon, planets, or letters of the Arabic alphabet were painted. This device was called an *ostorlab* (astrolabe), although it bore only a superficial resemblance to that ancient navigational instrument.

The customer would summon the fortune-teller to her doorway where he would squat and, after a prolonged bargaining over the price, unfold his *ostorlab* on the ground. Then he would shut his eyes for several minutes in apparent meditation before producing his *raml*, five or six metal dice strung together by a string that allowed the dice to rotate freely. The *raml* was cast onto the *ostorlab* and the position where it rested noted. After a shrewd evaluation of the customer, the interpretation would begin. These itinerants were accomplished amateur psychologists and managed to tailor their predictions to the perceived needs of the customer. For example, if the customer were a young unmarried woman and the *raml* fell so that one end touched the symbol for Venus and the other end the symbol for Mars, the soothsayer might tell her that he saw a love affair (Venus) in her future but, because of the influence of Mars, the god of war, this affair would be dangerous and best avoided. The numbers showing on the dice would be used to establish a time frame for the predictions or any other purpose that the fortune-teller thought appropriate to the occasion.

Another more upscale type of fortune-teller operated out of

his house and obtained his customers by word-of-mouth advertisement, usually by female gossip in the pubic baths. These oracles, called *mulla-ye-doanevis* (prayer-writing mullahs), specialized in palm reading and also represented themselves as spiritual mediums for contacting the departed. In addition, they sold prayer papers, on which they wrote various imprecations to suit the needs of their clients. The tissue-thin sheet of paper was then folded again and again until it became as small as possible. The customer was warned not to open the paper and was instructed either to sew it into an amulet to be worn around the neck or to sew it into her clothing. Wearing this paper would thus ensure the desired effect—attract a husband, good health, or whatever. If the client had an unfaithful husband, she would be instructed to soak the paper in water and slip the water to the wayward spouse in his tea to ensure his return to the connubial fold. Many recipients of these infusions came down with vomiting and diarrhea, probably because of the ink made from various magical ingredients, which was used to write the mystic charm.

Gypsies also specialized in palm reading. They would appear in town once or twice a year, and stay for a few days. No one knew where they came from or where they were going, but everyone knew that their arrival presaged an increase in pickpocketing and other petty larceny. The gypsy fortune-tellers were usually women, and they plied their trade from door to door, shouting out their services and stopping to perform when called. They would also peddle charms and herbal potions to ward off the evil eye or bring luck or love.

One summer afternoon, when I was supposed to be napping, I, as usual, slipped out of the house and wandered down to the orchard. In one far corner, I saw Soltan, Naneh, and Zivar squatting near the east gate around a pretty gypsy woman, whom they had summoned from the street. The gypsy was reading their palms, and I stood behind the servants and listened. They were not concerned about a little girl, and my intrusion went virtually unnoticed. I was enthralled. How could this gypsy woman know so much about each of the servants just by looking at their hands? I remember that she grasped the left hands of Soltan and Zivar and turned the palms upward. "See," she said, "every person's palm has different lines and mounds. No one is alike and that is why everyone's fate is different. It is written there and you cannot change it. It is there when you are born and it is unchanged until you die." She went on to talk to them about their love life, their health, and their past and future. She said one thing in particular to Naneh that I still wonder about. She said that there was a young man in her life who would be important to her for the rest of her life. At the time, I assumed that she was talking about Naneh's son, Mashaallah. Later on, when she married young Habib, I began to believe that this gypsy knew what she was talking about.

Grandmother, unlike most people of her generation, did not believe in fortune-tellers, the reading of tea leaves or coffee grounds, or any of the other superstitions. She was a very pragmatic and logical person. She scoffed at the custom of opening a holy book at random and allowing one's course of action to be guided by a verse. The only thing that she felt strongly about was the significance of dreams in foretelling the future or understanding present happenings. She cited stories that bore out the validity of dream prognostication, such as the tale of Joseph of biblical fame and that of the father of Ferdosi, the famous poet. She was particularly astute herself at interpreting dreams. Many times I would tell her of my own dreams. Most of the time she would say that a particular dream was of no significance and to forget about it.

I do remember one dream that I had when I was fifteen years old and visiting Grandmother during the summer. I had heard stories from the servants about Hazrat-e-Khezr, the mythical prophet who grants wishes, and I still believed in him. The dream was so vivid and beautiful that when I awakened, I closed my eyes again, hoping that the dream would still be there. That morning I sought out Grandmother and found her sitting alone on a bench on the verandah outside her room, sewing a button on Grandfather's shirt. I sat down next to her and told her that I had had this dream, which was so unusual that I remembered every part of it. I told her that I found myself walking alone in a lovely green parklike place, which extended for as far as one could see in every direction. Clear streams of water flowed through it and there were flowers everywhere. The sky was a gorgeous blue and the sun was shining brightly. I saw other people, mostly walking with another person, but I was alone, enjoying the beauty. It suddenly occurred to me that this place must be the place where one stopped just before entering heaven. Then I saw a group of five or six people running together. As they passed me, I asked, "Where are you going in such a hurry?"

One turned to me and said, "Don't you know? Hazrat-e-Khezr is just over the next hill." I joined with them and soon we came upon Hazrat-e-Khezr, who was pushing by two handles a wooden wheeled cart filled with loaves of flat bread. He was a middle-aged man with a graying beard and pleasant cherubic face.

I said to him, "My wish is that I be one of the guards at the gate of heaven."

He smiled and handed me a loaf of bread, saying, "Your wish is granted. Take this and go on." I continued along, carrying my loaf of bread and rejoicing in my heart; then I awakened.

Grandmother smiled and stared at me in amazement. She sat lost in thought for several minutes and finally said, "This is so interesting; I can't believe that you had such a dream. When I tell you what it means, you won't believe it either. That single loaf of bread you were given by Hazrat-e-Khezr means one year. That wish to guard the gate of heaven means that you are to be married in one year and will be the guardian of your own house, your husband, and your children!"

I looked at her in disbelief. "What are you talking about? I have three older sisters and three brothers who are not married. How is it possible that when I am only sixteen in one year, I will get married before them?"

She laughed and said, "You are right. The older sisters usually marry first, but you asked me to interpret your dream and I did. It is out of our hands." Almost exactly one year later I was married, much to the surprise of myself, my friends, and my relatives!

Among the more modern ladies, it became fashionable to go to those fortune-tellers who foretold the future by reading the patterns left by the grounds in a cup of Turkish coffee. These practitioners of the occult saw their clients only by appointment, and I suspect that the interval between the making of the appointment and the actual reading was spent by the seer in gathering information about his customer. Thus he was able to amaze her by his detailed knowledge of her personal life and instill instant belief in his powers, a ploy calculated to ensure repeated visits and a continuing source of revenue. The reading of coffee dregs became so popular that frequently when a group of ladies gathered for a morning coffee klatch, one of them would perform as an amateur reader for the group.

The only time I visited a professional reader of coffee cups was when I was a young adult living in Tehran. A friend of mine, unhappily married to a wealthy man who abused her both mentally and physically, approached me one day and asked me to accompany her on a visit to one of the most famous fortune-tellers in the city. My friend was a university-trained child psychologist and I was surprised to hear her profess a belief in fortune-telling. She assured me that she really did not believe, but because she was feeling so depressed and frustrated with her marriage, she wanted to go in the hope of hearing something that would cheer her up. She made an appointment for the two us, and a few days later we went to the seer's house located on Kakh Street in an expensive quarter of Tehran. As we entered the large elegantly furnished house, we were greeted by a white-uniformed receptionist, who ushered us into a waiting room resembling that which one would find in the office of a successful physician.

We were served a cup of hot Turkish coffee from a silver tray and instructed to drink it without delay, then cover the cup with the saucer and, holding the covered cup in the left hand, invert the cup by turning it toward the heart. The coffee grounds would thus drain along the sides of the cup, forming a pattern that would be interpreted by the master. While we were drinking our coffee, the door to the inner office opened and a woman wearing dark glasses and a scarf over her head scurried out, averting her face. I thought that I recognized her as a well-known actress and singer but could not be sure.

My friend and I were next and we elected to go in together. We were shown into an inner office, luxuriously carpeted and lined with bookshelves on every wall. The fortune-teller rose from behind his handsome desk and invited us to sit in chairs opposite him. He was a very well-dressed, good-looking, tall, thin man with a serious demeanor.

He first gravely inspected our left palms, then turned over our cups and contemplated each in thoughtful silence for several dramatic minutes. I don't remember what he foretold for me, but he did accurately describe my friend's marital troubles and told her that he saw some light in her future but she would have to be patient for some time before relief would come to her. On the way home, I asked my friend if she felt any better. She answered that she had to feel better because the visit was so expensive that otherwise she would feel cheated. I was reminded of a joke that Grandfather Khan once told me about a man who went to see a palmist, because he was having such bad luck in business as well as in his personal life. The fortune-teller inspected the man's palm and told him, "For seven years you are going to have all these troubles and you are going to suffer."

The man was delighted. "You mean," he said, "after seven years all my troubles will go away?"

"No," replied the soothsayer, "but after seven years you will get used to them!"

I once asked a lady who was reading coffee cups at a party how she did it. She replied, "You must have a good imagination and be able to see shapes in the design made by the grounds. You see symbolic animals, such as a parrot, meaning someone is talking behind your back. You see an airplane or a car and that means a trip in the future; or if you see a jumping tiger, it could mean you are about to take a bold step. Then you interpret what you see according to what you think people want to hear!"

The educated class in general looked upon all fortune-telling as a form of entertainment or, as was the case with my child psychologist friend, a kind of escape valve for frustrations. There were two instances that I remember concerning a different variety of dealers in the supernatural who were not fortune-tellers in any respect but rather what today we call psychics. The first instance concerned a psychic in Tehran named Mansoor. His powers became so well-known that it was difficult to get an appointment with him. His clientele was almost exclusively limited to the wealthy and the highest government officials. I am sure that Nancy Reagan would have consulted with him had she been able. He explained his powers by claiming that we are all surrounded with unseen spirits, just as we are surrounded with unseen radio and television emissions. He believed that certain people, such as himself, had the ability to tune in their minds to these spirits just as a radio tunes in a broadcast.

The story of one of his feats of prescience concerned a good friend of my father's. This man was a wealthy landowner who decided to dispose of one of his holdings. He found the deed to the property among his papers and put it aside in an envelope in a secure place in his house. Several months later, when the time came for settlement on the property, he went to retrieve the deed and found it gone. He and his wife searched their house from top to bottom to no avail. Finally, a friend suggested that he consult Mansoor. The man scoffed at the idea, maintaining that if he could not find the paper after such an exhaustive search, no one could. As the prospect of losing a profitable sale became more and more likely, the man, in desperation, made an appointment with Mansoor. Mansoor listened to the problem then retired to an adjacent room where he sat on the floor and put himself into a trance. After about an hour, he emerged and told the man, "You have a walk-in clothes closet in your home with a high shelf at one end. Look on that shelf and you will find your document."

The man was skeptical of this advice, because both he and his wife had several times looked in the place described by Mansoor. Furthermore, how could Mansoor, having never been in his house, describe such a closet so well? Nonetheless, since he had paid a handsome fee to the psychic and would grasp any straw to avoid the thought of having been cheated, he went home and looked again. There, in plain view on top of the shelf, was the envelope containing the deed!

The other incident relating to a psychic was told to me by my cousin Genoos one time when I had returned to Mashhad for a visit with Grandmother. Genoos and one of her friends got into a friendly argument concerning the supposed powers of a woman living in Mashhad who was supposed to be able to find lost articles, describe happenings of which she had no foreknowledge, etc. Genoos, having been raised by our pragmatic no-nonsense grandmother, maintained that the woman was a fraud. The friend insisted that she was a genuine psychic.

The argument culminated in a bet between the two that hinged on a provable demonstration of the woman's powers. The two went to visit the woman; and the friend asked the psychic to tell them who was in her house at that moment and what, if anything, they were doing. The woman, after five minutes or so of intense silent concentration replied, "Your mother is alone in your house and right now she is frying eggplant for your dinner." The friend asked permission to use the telephone and dialed her house. Her mother answered the phone and after the friend asked her what she was doing, replied, "I am frying eggplant for dinner." Was it just a lucky guess, because at that time of day and season, probably many people in town were frying eggplant for dinner?

I have no explanation for either of the above stories. I only know that they are true, because they were told to me by people who had nothing to gain by making them up and whose veracity was never in question. The only opportunity I had for a firsthand experience was when my sister Tooran decided that she wanted to go to consult with Mansoor. She asked Katayoon and Azar, my two other older sisters, to accompany her; but they both refused, maintaining that they did not believe in such nonsense. Azar, in her usual acerbic way, said, "Do you think that I went to school for sixteen years to get a degree just to squander money on a so-called psychic? Not on your life!"

Then Tooran looked at me and said, "I will take Mehry if you will not go." A couple of days later she called Mansoor's office for an appointment, only to be informed that the man had died the day before. The newspaper reported that the psychic had expired, apparently of a heart attack, while in one of his trances. The superstitious, however, maintained that while he was in a trance, he sent his spirit outside his body and this time it did not come back.

Chapter Eight
School Days

With them the Seed of Wisdom did I sow,
And with my own hand labour'd it to grow.

—Khayyam

One day in early summer, a few days before my fifth birthday, my eldest sister, Katayoon, who was vice-principal of the Hemmat High School in Mashhad, brought home a copy of the first grade primer. She announced that during the summer she was going to teach me to read and write so that I could be admitted to the first grade in the fall. Usually children were not allowed to enroll in the first grade before their sixth birthday; but my sister, through her academic contacts, had learned that if I were able to read and write at the first grade level, I could be accepted at age five. I was not totally illiterate; I could recite and read the Farsi[1] (Persian) alphabet; and I was instantly fascinated with the prospect of learning to put the letters together to form and understand words, for then I might join the rest of the family who nightly buried their noses in various books and magazines. At last I was going to be an adult!

I carried that little primer with me constantly that summer. By the end of August, with Katayoon's patient tutelage, I mastered the simple text and I was ready to take my entrance examination. One morning in early September, with my primer tucked under my arm, Katayoon and I walked hand in hand to the school. We entered the front door and proceeded to the administrator's office where the headmistress and another teacher were awaiting our arrival. Katayoon greeted the ladies, who were old friends of hers, and, after the usual pleasantries, took a seat to one side of the headmistress's desk. I stood next to the desk and put my primer on top in front of the headmistress. She opened it at random and turned it toward me saying, with a smile, "All right, little girl, please read for us. Show us what you have learned."

I began to read at the place she had selected, glancing up from time to time at my sister who was watching me with an encouraging half-smile on her face. The headmistress selected other pages at random for about a half hour, and I read each one perfectly. This was the only examination I took. At its conclusion, Katayoon and I thanked the teachers and made our way back home. Katayoon was happy with my performance and assured me that I would be going to school in a couple of weeks. Sure enough, one week later we received a letter from the school notifying my father that I had been accepted to the first grade. So began my formal education, which, with many fits and starts, has continued to this day.

The school I was to attend was a new private elementary school that had been open only three years. It was unique for that time in that it was a coeducational school, the only one in Mashhad. A year or so later, a second public coeducational school opened in Mashhad and my sister Katayoon became the headmistress. My school was located on Jam Street immediately off Arg Avenue, the main thoroughfare in Mashhad, and about one mile from our house. Although it was a private school, the stimulus for its construction had been the Reza Shah's compulsory elementary school educational program. This program resulted in the opening of many new schools, both public and private, throughout the country. The need for space to accommodate the many children, who hitherto had been allowed to remain illiterate, could not be satisfied by new construction alone and many spacious private houses were either bought outright or rented by the government and converted to public schoolhouses.

Prior to the Reza Shah's educational program, the only schools available to most of the common people were those run by the mullahs. These were called *maktab* and were usually small two-room buildings; the larger room served as a classroom with a smaller walk-in closet in the rear for storage. The *maktab* were usually built next to a mosque. The mullah slept in the classroom and during the day his rolled-up sleeping pallet served as a cushion between his back and the wall as he sat cross-legged on the floor to teach the children or sat on the floor in front of him. The schools were segregated by sex, and the girls' schools were taught by female religious instructors who were the counterpart of the male mullahs. The schools were supported in part by the wealthier mullahs, but the children were expected to bring food and fabric for clothing for the mullah and charcoal to burn in a single brazier that served to heat the room in winter.

The only subjects taught by the mullahs were Arabic grammar and reading, so that the children could read the Koran, and a smattering of Farsi grammar. The beliefs and tenets of the Islamic Shiite sect were strongly emphasized. The children were subject to severe discipline and corporal punishment was routinely administered for any infraction. A favorite form of punishment was to force the child to lie on his back and with his legs elevated and ankles supported on a pole held by two of the other pupils. The mullah then would beat on the offender's bare soles with a switch made from cherry or pomegranate wood. Due to the avarice of the mullahs, the punishment was not always evenhanded. If the son of a rich family made a mistake that called for punishment, a boy from a poor family would receive the flogging while the offender watched, thus assuring that the contributions from the wealthy family would continue. The Reza Shah forced the closing of the *maktab* early in his reign as part of his campaign to lessen the influence of the religious hierarchy.

My school was named Shahdokt (daughter of the shah) Shams after the Reza Shah's eldest daughter, the Princess Shams. It was a single-story brick building containing six classrooms, one for each grade. There was also a library, a gymnasium-auditorium, lavatories, and administrative offices. Later on, one of the offices was converted to a classroom for a kindergarten. My cousin Genoos started her education in this room at age four. A lunchroom provided facilities for heating the lunches of those children who lived too far away to go home during the two-hour lunch break. All the rooms opened off a wide central hallway, which ran the length of the building. Here, each morning, the students would assemble outside their classrooms to sing the national anthem. Then we would file into the auditorium for morning calisthenics led by the physical education teacher and performed to the music of a piano played by the principal. The auditorium was converted to a gymnasium for calisthenics by the simple expedient of stacking the folding chairs against the walls.

Each classroom was spacious and well lit with large windows looking out on a garden and playground to the rear and onto the street in the front. Each room could accommodate twenty-four students seated in individual chairs with arm desks, a more comfortable alternative to the backless benches and long tables found in the public schools. At the time that I started school, there were only twelve to fourteen students in each class, but by the time I finished the sixth grade, the first few grades were completely full. This probably reflected an increasing acceptance of the concept of coeducation on the part of the more conservative elements of society.

Classes began at 8:30 A.M. after we had finished the thirty-minute morning exercise session. The first class lasted until 9:30; then there was a second class until 10:30, followed by a thirty-minute break, during which time we were allowed to play outside or eat a snack brought from home. The third class of the morning began at 11:00 and lasted until noon; then we stopped for lunch. Those of us who lived nearby went home for lunch. The others repaired to the lunchroom, where serving girls, who also doubled as janitors, heated their lunches for them. School reconvened at 2:00 P.M., and the two afternoon classes ran continuously until dismissal at 4:00 P.M.

The afternoon classes were devoted chiefly to handicrafts, painting, music, calligraphy, and sewing for the girls while the boys devoted their time to learning woodworking and other masculine crafts. All students were required to wear the school uniform. For the girls, this was a knee-length dark gray dress with a white collar, white stockings, and black shoes. The boys wore short or long gray trousers, depending upon the season, open-necked white shirts, navy blue jackets, white socks and black shoes. If a girl wanted to wear her hair in braids with a ribbon, the ribbon had to be white. This uniform was more or less the same for schoolchildren throughout the country, both public and private, from the first through the twelfth grade. It was not until college that students were allowed to dress as they pleased.

Madame Dorri was our headmistress. She was a native Russian, the wife of a career diplomat stationed in the French consulate in Mashhad, and had been educated in France. She had one son, a very handsome lad who attended high school in Mashhad. Whenever he came to see his mother at our school, he created quite a stir among the girls, especially those in the sixth grade; but he was very circumspect and never let on that he noticed their glances and giggles. Madame Dorri was a tall slim lady in her late thirties with long blonde hair worn *en chignon*, blue eyes, and a lovely pink and white complexion. She was a chic dresser in the latest Parisian style. All the children loved and admired her as did our parents, especially our fathers. She, of course, spoke fluent Farsi with a slight French accent, which was pleasant and lilting to the ear.

The assistant headmistress was named Mrs. Hamidee. Physically, she was the direct opposite of Madame Dorri. She was quite petite, with short black hair, flashing black eyes, and a hyperactive personality. She was the first to arrive in the morning and the last to leave in the afternoon. In between, she bustled about on her business of running the day-to-day activities of the school. She was the one who rang the bell to summon us in every morning, organized us into orderly lines to file into the auditorium; and she dispersed us to the proper classrooms after the morning exercises. All the while, she checked each child to make sure that faces were clean, fingernails properly trimmed, and hair combed neatly. She made the rounds of the classrooms first thing every morning to check attendance, and if a child was absent without an excuse, she would contact the parents to make sure that all was well. While she was the authority figure in the school with regard to discipline, she never punished anyone physically. We all loved her, although if by chance we happened to show up with dirty fingernails, we did our utmost to avoid her scrutiny.

My first grade teacher was Mrs. Sarabi, a chubby, jovial lady of some thirty-odd years. She taught all the first grade subjects—reading, writing, and arithmetic—as well as painting and handicrafts. After the first grade, we had other teachers for

99

mathematics, history, and geography; but Mrs. Sarabi stayed with us on through the fourth grade, teaching reading and composition on progressive levels. She was not a martinet, but she demanded the best from us. We students felt that we were not sufficiently rewarded for our efforts because one seldom received a perfect twenty, no matter how hard one tried. The marking system in Persian schools is based on a scale of one to twenty, with ten being a barely passing grade and twenty a perfect grade. Mrs. Sarabi rarely gave a mark above nineteen, and even a nineteen was hard to achieve. This was probably a calculated maneuver to encourage us to strive for the seemingly impossible because, toward the end of the school year, she began to become more generous and we started to see more perfect twenties. If a student received a mark between seven and ten in any subject, he or she was required to work with a tutor during the summer and pass a reexamination before starting school in the fall.

My first-grade class was made up of six girls and six boys. We sat four abreast in the first three rows of the classroom. Our families were all well acquainted and several of the girls had been playmates of mine before we started school. All the students came from good families. The father of one boy, who sat next to me for several grades, was Dr. Eghbal, the future chief executive officer (CEO) of the Persian Oil Company and prime minister. Our ranks were slightly diminished in the second grade when the family of one of the boys moved from Mashhad. We became an even dozen again when a girl who had been living in Tehran was accepted as a transfer student. The boys remained outnumbered from then on, and the graduating class at the end of the sixth grade consisted of seven girls and five boys.

I was born in a Persia that was much different than the country into which my grandmother had been born. Fortunately, my father and grandparents insisted on a good education for all family members regardless of sex. This philosophy was not by any means shared by all Persians at that time, and the majority of people still thought that an elementary education was sufficient for a girl since her proper role was to be married off as soon as possible. Growing up side by side with boys, studying, playing, and talking with them in school every day colored my outlook regarding the relationship between men and women. I did not feel that I was inferior to any man as women had been taught to feel for generations in Persia since the Arab conquest. This freedom of thought was the cause, in part, of the failure of my first marriage, because I could not tolerate the attitude toward women by some of my in-laws who had been raised in the traditional Moslem fashion.

We were all good students, but I was near the top of the class each year. This was not due to any particular genius but because I continued the practice that Katayoon and I had began before I started school. Each summer I was tutored by my schoolteacher sister and together we plowed through the textbooks that I would be studying in the upcoming school year. My favorite subjects, however, were not academic but were painting, sewing, and handicrafts, all of which I still enjoy. I recall in particular one handicraft class early in the second grade. One afternoon, Mrs. Sarabi came to class with a supply of crepe paper, scissors, glue, and wire. She proceeded to show us how to cut petals and leaves from the paper and fashion them into roses with green leaves sprouting from wire stems. She was called out of the classroom on some business, and when she returned about forty minutes later, I had finished a bouquet of three roses. She was so surprised to see such a pretty bouquet finished in so short a time by a little second grader that she reached out her arms and hugged me to her chest. She took my roses to the headmistress and to the other teachers to show off my handiwork, and from then on my reputation in arts and crafts was made.

That is one of my pleasant memories of the second grade, but later on that year I had a much less pleasant experience. Right after the thirteen-day break for Now Ruz (New Year's Day) in March, I awakened one morning with a headache, fever, and a painful neck, which quickly became swollen on one side. I had contracted a full-blown case of mumps, which kept me in bed for only one week; but that week seemed like a month. Grandmother nursed me, feeding me *ash* (a hearty soup) three times a day since I could not swallow solid food. I was allowed no visitors unless they had previously been infected with the disease. Grandmother assured me that I would soon recover. She told me that it was fortunate that I was a girl, because boys sometimes had serious complications from the mumps that resulted in their inability to become fathers. I was not sure what she meant by this and she did not elaborate. Grandfather Khan could not understand how I had acquired the infection since no one else in my school was sick. He remarked with a smile that when my uncle had the mumps as a young boy, all the neighborhood girls came down with the disease.

While I was in bed with my neck wrapped in a woolen scarf and feeling miserable, a lady friend came to visit Grandmother. As they sat talking and drinking tea while keeping me company, she remarked that the application of scorpion oil to the swollen glands was a sure cure for mumps. She insisted that she never saw a case where the scorpion oil failed to cause the swelling to disappear within a couple of days. I was frightened because I thought that they were talking about putting a scorpion on my neck, but Grandmother explained that it was not a live scorpion but a salve. She sent a servant to the house of an old man who manufactured the "medicine" with orders to buy some and return immediately. About an hour later, Grandmother brought in a foul-smelling, sticky, black paste that she had smeared on a cloth and wrapped it around my neck, securing it with a woolen scarf. The next morning, she removed the cloth and applied a fresh dressing. The following day, I awoke to find that all the swelling had disappeared and I could eat and swallow without pain. Whether the cure was due to the scorpion oil or due to the infection having run its course, no one could say. In either event, I was well and, after a hot bath, ready to be up and about and back to school.

In later years, I found out how scorpion salve was made. A wide-mouthed jar is filled two-thirds full with equal parts of alcohol and lamp oil. Live scorpions are added to fill the jar and the jar covered tightly. It is then placed in a cool dark place to age for seven years. From time to time, the jar is shaken, and as the alcohol gradually evaporates, the scorpions rot to form the odoriferous paste. Each year a new batch is made to replenish the stock as the fully aged concoction is sold off.

I loved to go to school, and toward the end of each summer vacation, I would count the days until school began. Needless to say, the family and servants also were happy to see the school year begin so that we children would no longer be underfoot all day long. During the school year, my dear old nanny used to come to see me a few times a week, and I would rush home after school on those days to tell her all about my day. One week she did not come to see me and I became very upset. I finally went to my grandmother in tears and asked her why Nanny had abandoned me. My father overheard and tried to reassure me that Nanny had not left me, but rather she could not come because she was ill and confined to bed. I was so unhappy to learn that she was sick that I cried still harder until finally Father, in an effort to console me, told Gholam to take me to visit Nanny. He warned me to make the visit short so as not to overtire Nanny.

Gholam and I walked to Nanny's house, stopping on the way to buy a box of sweet cakes as a gift. When we arrived at the house, Nanny's married daughter greeted us at the door and showed me into the room where Nanny was sleeping on a pallet in one corner. Her eyes were closed, but as soon as she heard me come in, she opened them and gave me a big smile. I wanted to go to her and hug her, but she told me to stay away for fear that she might have some contagious disease. I sat in an opposite corner and chattered away about how much I had missed her and told her all the news of home and school.

While I was talking, Nanny's daughter came into the room with another woman. The daughter said to me, "Someone has put an evil eye on my mother, and we are going to find out who it is and break the spell!"

She and the woman sat themselves down cross-legged on the floor by the side of Nanny's bed facing each other, one at the head and one at the foot. The woman spread a white cloth on the floor between them and placed a round metal tray on the cloth. She then produced an egg with a coin stuck on each end and held it between the thumb and forefinger of her left hand over the tray. In her right hand she held a bit of charcoal and, as the daughter called out various names, she would make a mark for each one on the egg. Finally, after the egg was almost black with the many marks, the daughter named still another person and the egg promptly broke, spilling onto the tray. The daughter jumped up in delight and exclaimed, "That was the name of a neighbor and I always felt that she was jealous of my mother.

Now her evil spell is broken!" I could not understand how a broken egg could make my nanny well, but I privately wished that I had all the eggs in the world so that I might break them and make my nanny's sickness go away! Nanny did eventually recover and lived for many more years.

The girl who joined our class in the fourth grade as a transfer from a school in Tehran was named Parvaneh. We became close friends during the three years we were together in school. Parvaneh was a pretty, friendly girl with long brown hair that she wore in a single long braid that hung down her back, secured with a white ribbon. The boy who sat behind her in school, Mansoor, used to tease her by holding one end of the bow so that as soon as Parvaneh turned her head, the ribbon would pull loose. Parvaneh eventually persuaded Mrs. Sarabi to change her seat, although she was too shy to mention why she wanted the change.

Parvaneh had a beautiful singing voice; and in addition to knowing many of the popular songs of the day, she was able to sing many of the couplets of the classical poem "Mathnawi" by Mawlana Jalaleddin Roomi Mawlavi, a thirteenth-century poet who died in 1238. "Mathnawi" is a long narrative poem consisting of about thirty thousand rhyming couplets in six volumes. It is considered by Persians to be the greatest expression of love and knowledge ever written, even to the point where it is sometimes called the "Koran in Persian," suggesting a divine inspiration. All of the stories and parables in the epic are allegorical and the degree of one's understanding of their meaning depends on the level of one's spirituality. For example, the poem opens with a reed flute lamenting its separation from the bed of reeds from which it was plucked. The reed represents Man who was separated from his divine source and through whom the breath of God is blown.

All textbooks of literature used in Persian schools, beginning with the most elementary primer, contain excerpts from the works of various classical Persian poets. Children are required to memorize these poems in order to pass the course, and this constant exposure to poetry from an early age serves to instill a love of the rich heritage of classical Persian literature. Our fifth grade textbook contained an excerpt from "Mathnawi" called "The Shepherd's Prayer." Parvaneh sang this poem so well that she was asked to perform it at our graduation ceremony at the end of the sixth grade—a sort of musical valedictorian. Her performance was so beautiful that she received a standing ovation from the assembled parents, teachers, and school officials. The following is a translation of "The Shepherd's Prayer" by R. A. Nicholson, a Cambridge scholar who has termed Mathnawi the greatest mystical poet of any age.

The Shepherd's Prayer

Moses saw a shepherd on the way, crying, "O Lord Who chooses as Thou wilt,
Where art Thou, that I may serve Thee and sew Thy shoon and comb Thy hair?
That I may wash Thy clothes and kill Thy lice and bring milk to Thee, O worshipful One;
That I may kiss Thy little hand and rub Thy little feet and sweep Thy little room at bed-time."
On hearing these foolish words, Moses said, "Man, to whom are you speaking?
What babble! What blasphemy and raving! Stuff some cotton into your mouth!
Truly the friendship of a fool is enmity: the High God is not in want of suchlike service."
The shepherd rent his garment, heaved a sigh, and took his way to the wilderness.
Then came to Moses a Revelation: "Thou hast parted My servant from Me.
Wert thou sent as a prophet to unite, or wert thou sent to sever?
I have bestowed on everyone a particular mode of worship, I have given everyone a particular form of expression.
The idiom of Hindustan is excellent for Hindus; the idiom of Sind is excellent for the people of Sind.
I look not at tongue and speech, I look at the spirit and the inward feeling.
I look into the heart to see whether it be lowly, though the words uttered be not lowly.
Enough of phrases and conceits and metaphors! I want burning, burning: become familiar with that burning!
Light up a fire of love in thy soul, burn all thought and expression away!

105

O Moses, they that know the conventions are of one sort,
they whose souls burn are of another."
    The religion of love is apart from all religions.
    The lovers of God have no religion but God alone.

By the time I had finished the third grade, I was able to read children's books and my older sister Katayoon used to bring many of them to me from the city library, as well as loaning me those that she had kept from her own childhood days. One day in the summer between the third and fourth grades, I made my first foray into my father's library to find a book on my own. One low shelf contained a variety of children's books and, after looking them over, I was attracted to one volume that had a picture on the cover. It was entitled *The Blue Rose* and the painting on the cover was that of a nightingale sitting in a leafless rosebush with blood dripping from its breast onto a single rose. A full moon shone in the background. There were no other illustrations in the book but I was entranced by the title and the cover, so I picked it from the shelf and read it.

The story told of a nightingale who lived in a rose garden. All summer long she enjoyed the beautiful flowers and sang her lovely songs every night from dusk to dawn. When the fall came and the cold winds and frost killed off the flowers and all the trees and bushes lost their leaves, the nightingale became sad. One day, the first snowfall came; and that night the moon shone brightly on the garden where the nightingale still perched near her nest, singing a plaintive sad song. A single blue rose was still on the bush near her nest and the bird was so sad that, toward dawn, she pressed her breast against a thorn and died. The blood from her breast dripped onto the blue rose, turning it red. From that day on, no one has ever seen a blue rose because they all turned red in memory of the nightingale.

I loved this story and I read it over and over again to my nanny. She always listened patiently every time as if she were hearing it for the first time. One evening when Nanny was staying over and the servants and I had all gathered in Grandmother's kitchen for the nightly discussions and storytelling, Nanny told the others about the story that I had been reading to her. The servants asked me to bring my book and read it to them—all, that is, except Mashaallah, the only literate in the group. He did not say anything, but I had the feeling that he resented my reading. I was treading upon his territory because for years he had been the only one able to read to the others. Everyone enjoyed the story and after I had finished reading the simple text, Mashaallah asked if he could look at the book. He examined it carefully as if to verify that I had read it correctly. Finally he said, "Yes, it is a nice story. There are so many good stories to read if we could only get our hands on them and find enough time to read them." I was relieved to see that he accepted my intrusion with such good humor but I never again read to the after-dinner group.

My father's library was a never-ending source of pleasure to me because I loved to read. I would hear my older brothers and sisters discuss the books they were reading and I tried to keep up with them, even though I did not always fully understand what I was reading. By the time I had finished the sixth grade, I had read for the first of many times the Farsi translations of many of the Western literary classics. I read *Les Miserables, The Hunchback of Notre Dame, The Count of Monte Cristo,* and *Gone with the Wind,* among many others. Over the ensuing years, I reread them with ever-increasing enjoyment. I also read the classic Persian poets and committed to memory many verses to the extent that I was able to enter into the family *moshaereh*, or poetry contests, and hold my own by the time I was eleven years old.

The *moshaereh* is a uniquely Persian form of entertainment that evolved from the love of poetry so common among the Persian people. Before the days of television and radio, this was a fun way of passing the time among the intelligentsia. The game is played by two or more people. One person starts it by saying the traditional opening line, "I am going to start a *moshaereh* with a wise person [or dummy, depending upon the level of friendship] and perhaps that person is you."

The next person in the circle would then respond with a couplet of verse beginning with the letter *u.* If response is delayed more than a few seconds, that person is out. This exchange can go on for hours, depending upon the number and erudition of the players. If the contest were between a group of poets, original couplets might be composed spontaneously. In our family, Grandmother was a frequent winner because, although she had little formal education, she had memorized a tremendous amount of poetry, chiefly that of Hafiz and Sa'adi. It was fun to listen to the teasing arguments between her and Grandfather Khan, because he always had a proverb to suit any given situation; and whenever he would quote one, Grandmother would respond with an appropriate verse. The *moshaereh* thus served to enrich and supplement our formal education, and the verse that I learned as a child I can still quote verbatim today. Whenever we schoolchildren had a break between classes, we would often organize a spontaneous *moshaereh*.

Sometimes, when I look back on those early school years and our graduation, I am reminded of a flock of pigeons clucking about and feeding on the ground. A sudden noise or stone cast by a mischievous child scatters them and they never return to the same exact spot. So we children, for a few short years, fed upon the seeds of knowledge and, after the sixth grade, we all scattered, never to again assemble as a group. Class reunions are not a Persian custom. However, from time to time in later years I would come across a familiar name in the news and recognize it as one of my schoolmates. For example, one girl who sat near me in class became a famous concert pianist. Two sisters were in classes ahead of me. One, Iran Darroodi, became a famous artist whose works were hung in art galleries in Tehran and Europe. Her sister, Pooran, became a renowned designer and made the coronation robe for Queen Farah in 1967. Another boy, whom I remember as having a constantly runny nose, became a cabinet minister. Apparently he outgrew his childhood affliction!

Note

1. The Persian language had its origin in the Indo-European group of languages, which are the mother tongues of the European countries and part of Asia Minor. As various groups of people began to migrate from Central Europe to Italy, Greece, Russia, England, Persia, and India, the original stock of words remained, but sounds and forms gradually changed. For example, Farsi *madar*, French *mere*, German *mutter*, Latin *mater*, all mean "mother."

Chapter Nine
The New Year *(Now Ruz)*

Awaken and bring the old wine for the New Year;
Let's drink from the cup and renew the vows we made.
Celebrate with me the flowers that greet the spring,
The old year is over and life springs afresh.

—Shahna

No one knows exactly when the Persian custom of celebrating the new year on the day of the vernal equinox, the first day of spring, began. The origin of the custom is lost in antiquity, but it is generally believed that it started during the reign of King Jamshid, the so-called Golden Age, which began about the year 3000 B.C. Legend has it that Jamshid, originally known as King Jam, in an effort to increase his popularity and perhaps ensure himself a niche in history, began a custom of holding public audiences wherein any of his subjects would be allowed to approach the throne to plead a cause or seek remedy of an injustice. The first audience happened to coincide with the day of the vernal equinox that year. This day became known as *Now* (new) *Ruz* (day); and to this day Now Ruz is traditionally a day when clemency may be granted to certain offenders by the authorities. On the morning of the day of the first audience, while waiting for his court to assemble, Jam sat on his throne facing the east. The rising sun reflected off his golden crown and surrounded him with a brilliant aura. When the people saw this wondrous sight, they all began shouting, "Shid! Shid!" meaning "shining"; and henceforth King Jam was known as King Jamshid.

Another charming myth attempts to explain two customs

practiced on Now Ruz. One day Jamshid was being transported through the air on his throne pulled by a flock of swallows. The nest of one of the swallows lay in the path of the king and the bird begged Jamshid to avoid it. The monarch readily obliged the bird, and when the trip was over, the grateful swallow offered the king the leg of a locust sprinkled with water. This gift to the king is said to have been the origin of the custom of giving gifts to relatives and friends on Now Ruz and the Zoroastrian custom of sprinkling a few drops of rosewater on the hands of guests when they come to call during the Now Ruz holidays.

Most of the traditional customs associated with the Now Ruz celebration have their origin in the Zoroastrian religion, which was the official religion of Persia before the Arab conquest in A.D. 632. Zoroaster (circa 628–551 B.C.) was one of the first prophets to preach an ethical monotheistic doctrine which held that the moral law requiring human righteousness came from one good God called Ahura (Lord) Mazda (the Wise, or Full of Light). The symbol of this God is fire (or light), and as such fire is revered by Zoroastrians much as the cross is revered as a symbol of God by Christians. In a slightly different context, Moslems pray toward the Black Stone of Mecca and revere it as "God's House." While fire per se was an object of worship by the ancient Aryans, Zoroaster considered fire to be merely a gift of the Ahura Mazda, and a symbol of the nature and essence of the Wise Lord. The misnomer "fire worshippers" was a Moslem epithet coined to ridicule the ancient Persian religion after the Islamic conquest.

Zoroastrianism is based on three basic tents: good thoughts, good words, and good deeds. The sacred text of Zoroastrianism, the Zand-Avesta, is a compilation of a body of oral tradition and was probably first recorded in written form about A.D. 400. Zoroaster preached compassion for animals and respect for the ecology. Burial or cremation of the dead was forbidden for fear of polluting the earth or the atmosphere. The cardinal sins according to the teachings of Zoroaster are: adultery, lying, killing (or committing suicide), idolatry, polygamy, prostitution, homosexuality, stealing, injustice to others, belief in superstitions, and sloth. Zoroaster was revered in antiquity and his religion, based on high moral standards, left a lasting mark on three other

110

monotheistic faiths: Judaism, Christianity, and Islam.

The Persian calendar year is a solar year of 365 days, 5 hours, 48 minutes, and 46 seconds as opposed to the lunar year (354 days, 8 hours, and 45 minutes) used by neighboring Moslem countries. The Persian calendar year begins on the first day of Spring, the vernal equinox. The first six months are thirty-one days long, the next five months thirty days long, and the last month is twenty-nine days, for a total of 365 days. The odd hours and minutes are made up by adding one day every four years to the final month, corresponding to the leap year of the Gregorian calendar.

The exact time of the vernal equinox was determined with increasing precision over the years. During the reign of Cyrus the Great, about 500 B.C., the minute of the vernal equinox was established with a fair degree of accuracy. The astronomical tables published in the early part of the twelfth century by a group of eight astronomers, which included Omar Khayyam, further refined the calculation to the precise second. The celebration of the New Year is the most cherished tradition in the Persian culture. It belongs to all Persians regardless of their religious affiliation, be it Moslem, Jew, Zoroastrian, or Christian. It is treasured as a symbol of cultural and national identity handed down from their ancestors that has survived foreign conquest and all other trials and tribulations.

The starting year *(Hejrat)* of the Moslem calendar is A.D. 621, the year that Mohammed fled from Mecca to Medina. The starting year of the original Persian calendar was established during the reign of Cyrus the Great. When the Arabs conquered Persia in A.D. 632, they imposed their starting date along with their religion on the people of Persia. However, Persia retained the use of the solar year rather than adopting the lunar year. An abortive attempt was made in the late 1960s by the Mohammed Reza Shah to revert to the old starting date established by Cyrus, but this resulted in so much confusion that it was abandoned after about one year.

Just as the solar year is divided into twelve months, the Persian astrologers, in common with the Chinese, calculate the vicissitudes of time in cycles of twelve years. Each year is named for an animal and the cycle begins with the year of the mouse followed in order by the years of the bull, tiger, rabbit, whale, snake, horse, sheep, monkey, rooster, dog, and pig. Astrological predictions (probably as accurate as the *Farmer's Almanac*) are made every year, and these are influenced by the personality characteristics attributed to the animal of the year. For example, the year of the sheep will see a long harsh winter followed by a pleasant spring and a fruitful summer and fall. Similarly, one's personality will be influenced by the characteristics of the animal of the year of one's birth. Babies born in the year of the sheep will be quiet and thoughtful; those born in the year of the mouse will be cunning and clever; the year of the rooster portends a talkative person who will have a large family; and so on.

Preparation for the Now Ruz celebration begins six to eight weeks before the big day. The house must be cleaned from top to bottom; carpets must be washed; any needed painting should be done; silverware is sent out for thorough cleaning and polishing; gifts should be bought and wrapped; gardens should be cleared of the winter's debris and replanted; a supply of crisp new bank notes and shiny new coins must be obtained from the bank in preparation for the traditional Now Ruz visitations; new clothing for the family and servants must be made or purchased; any worn articles of furniture must be replaced or repaired; cookies and other sweets are baked and stored away, along with nuts and dried fruits bought in the bazaar. All of the above preparations mean additional expense, so it is the custom for employers, including the government, to give their employees a bonus equivalent to at least one month's wage the month before Now Ruz.

Wherever one travels throughout the land during the weeks before Now Ruz, one can see the people from all walks of life preparing for the big day in their own way. People are seen painting their front doors, cleaning windows, repairing roofs and walkways, and cleaning up their gardens. The women from the country villages may be seen lined up along riverbanks washing carpets while in the cities some shop owners will put their carpets face down in the street outside their shops so that the trampling by passersby will pound out the accumulated dust.

Like the Christmas holiday season in the West, the Now Ruz season pulsates with an air of festivity; and as during the Christmas season, there is an infusion of money into the economy. Seasonal employment will be found by various workers, especially those who offer some type of cleaning service. Men can be seen going from house to house carrying wooden poles that they will assemble into a rack over which they will drape carpets and beat them with a wooden slat. Their cries of "We'll shake your carpets! We'll clean your rugs!" blend with the shouts of the wandering cobblers, "Shoes shined! Shoes repaired!"

When I was a child, one could find almost any commodity or service one needed simply by summoning one of the merchants or workers who wandered throughout the city hawking their services or goods. These people were independent entrepreneurs who were without sufficient capital to purchase a shop in which to ply their trade, so the streets became their place of business. In later years, as the economy changed due to the influx of oil money and industrialization, these wandering workers gradually disappeared. Young boys, who in the old days tagged along after their fathers learning the family trade, when they matured were attracted to factory jobs where they found a stable year-round income. Services that had been available at a reasonable cost at the doorstep now were found only in downtown shops.

Another unique service was provided by the itinerant quilt maker. After a winter's hard use, the cotton stuffed into the bed quilts became matted. In the spring the quilt maker came to your home with his fluffing instrument, a wooden bow about eight feet long with a heavy catgut string stretched between the tips of the horns. The bow was placed face down on the floor next to the pile of lumpy matted cotton that had been removed from the quilts. As the quilt maker struck the string with a wooden mallet, the string combed through the matted material. The fluffy renewed material leapt over the string and collected in a mound on the other side. The rhythmic strumming of the string made a pleasant sound, and as a child, I loved to sit and watch the quilt maker at his work. After all the cotton had been processed, the quilt maker reassembled the quilts and they were ready for another winter.

The tin-coated copper pots and pans used for cooking all year long were retinned and repaired by roving coppersmiths who went from one neighborhood to another, setting up their temporary stalls and shouting their availability to all. They made a charcoal furnace by placing charcoal in a slight depression in the ground in the center of which there was the open end of a short length of pipe that led to a hand-operated bellows. The children of the neighborhood loved to gather round and watch the coppersmiths at work; sometimes the children would be allowed to operate the bellows while the smithy held a pot by a pair of tongs over the red-hot coals to melt off the old tin. The utensil would then be scoured by rubbing with sand until the copper surface gleamed, then reheated and a new plating of tin applied. If a large tray were to be scoured, the coppersmith would stand on it with bare feet, working his feet round and round to rub the underside in the abrasive sand. After the coppersmith had finished his work, the utensils would look like new and be ready for another year of use.

New clothing for the children and household servants is considered *de rigueur* for the New Year. The adults may or may not choose to renew their entire wardrobe, but everyone should have at least one new article of clothing. In our household, the first sign of the New Year holidays was the arrival of Mrs. Safeeyeh who came every year about two months before Now Ruz to make the clothing for the women and female children, family and servants alike. She would be ensconced in a room with a sewing machine and a huge pile of fabric, which had been purchased during the year; and one week later, the room would be full of dresses, skirts, and blouses awaiting their final fitting. Grandmother and my older sisters would from time to time help her as well as supervise her work, and my sisters would add the final touches by way of embroidery or other decoration on their own clothing. After she left, the clothing would be carefully folded away until New Year's Day when we would wear it for the first time to ensure good luck for the coming year. In the meantime, the male children were taken to local haberdasheries or to a tailor for their new outfits.

All of this emphasis on refurbishing, cleaning, and new clothing goes back to the Zorastrian belief that the Now Ruz is a time of renewal and a fresh beginning of nature. Man should therefore annually renew himself in spirit, casting out all the sins and animosities of the prior year. Also, the ancients believed that the spirits of the dead returned to visit their homes at Now

Ruz, and the house should therefore be scrupulously clean and filled with a spirit of happiness in order to please the spirits and ensure their blessing for the coming year. The ceremony that begins the Now Ruz season and is symbolic of this renewal is the *Chaharshanbeh Soury*, or Fire Wednesday. On the last Wednesday of the old year, just after sunset, piles of dry thornbushes are ignited; and the people leap back and forth over the flames, all the while calling out imprecations to the fire such as, "My jaundiced complexion is yours and your redness is mine!" meaning all sickness or unhappiness of the past year is dropped into the fire to burn and the energy and glow of the flames are absorbed by the jumper.

The downtown section of any Persian city on the evening of *Chaharshanbeh Soury* is a spectacle of light since those people who do not have room to light their fires inside their property kindle them in the streets. Families will sometimes get together over a common fire in a party atmosphere. It is traditional to build a series of three fires in a row symbolizing the three basic tenets of Zoroastrian faith: good thoughts, good speech, and good deeds. The thornbushes used burn quickly, and after the flames die down, the exhausted jumpers gather round the remaining coals until the last ember dies because it is considered bad luck to extinguish the embers rather than allowing them to burn out by themselves; the bad luck probably being the possibility of unattended embers starting a general conflagration. In ancient times small fires in braziers were sometimes lit on the rooftops of the homes in the belief that they would guide the returning spirits of the dead in their Now Ruz visit.

After all the fires have died out and darkness descends, teenage girls will steal quietly forth, with their heads and faces covered by a shawl or tablecloth, and stand silently in the shadows at the intersection of two streets. They await the passage of people who are conversing as they walk together; and as they pass by, the girls listen to hear their conversation. If the first snatch of conversation that a girl hears is about a cheerful, happy subject, the girl will take this as a good omen for the coming new year. The people who are walking about on the evening of Chaharshanbeh Soury are aware that some girls may be straining to hear their talk and try to keep their conversation in a cheerful, light vein so as not to upset any potential eavesdropper. Another custom, similar to the Halloween custom in the United States, is observed by young girls on this night. With their heads covered and their faces hidden except for the eyes, they will go from door to door carrying a copper bowl upon which they beat with a spoon. When a door is opened, they will silently hold out the bowl to receive gifts of candy or nuts.

Sometimes the neighborhood boys will go about in small groups disguised as begging girls and visit the homes of girls with whom they wish to get acquainted in the hope that the object of their affection will answer the door. If the girl suspects that the caller is a boy with whom she does not want to become involved, she may pull off the boy's head covering and say, "Get lost!" If she is interested in becoming better acquainted, she will go along with the charade and converse with him for a while or until her parents intervene and send the potential swain packing.

In some villages in the province of Azerbaijan, the celebration of Chaharshanbeh Soury begins in the early morning when the people sally forth to find a stream of running water. They will leap back and forth over the stream in the belief that the running water will wash out and carry away all of their problems of the preceding year, thus giving them a fresh start for the new year. This is not a substitute for the traditional jumping over the fire done that evening, but rather an additional symbolic cleansing.

In some villages another traditional game is played on Chaharshanbeh Soury. The lady of the house will hard cook eggs with a vegetable dye to color the shell; that is, red onion for a red color; parsley for green; or tumeric for yellow. The boys of the village will gather that evening in the village square carrying a basket full of eggs in various colors and challenge each other to egg-cracking contests. A boy with an egg of one color will challenge another boy with an egg of the same color, and each will hold their egg with only the tip showing. They then strike the eggs together and the egg that cracks first is forfeit to the opponent. When all the eggs have been fought, the winner is the boy whose basket is most full, although his prize is only a basket of colorful broken eggs.

About two weeks before Now Ruz, the lady of the house prepares the *sabzeh*, a flat dish of sprouted wheat or lentils that is displayed throughout the holiday season as a symbol of spring and the rebirth of nature. In ancient Persia, three weeks before Now Ruz, twelve temporary mud brick pillars were erected in the courtyard of the royal palace. On top of each of the pillars, a different seed was planted—wheat, barley, millet, corn, sesame, lima beans, rice, red beans, peas, peppergrass, chickling vetch, and bastard saffron (a plant that has a flower and color similar to saffron but an inferior aroma). The ancients believed that whichever seed grew well, the coming year would be a good year for that crop. On the sixth day after Now Ruz, the sprouts were plucked and passed out to the people as good luck tokens.

In our house, during the month before Now Ruz, the interior and exterior preparations went on simultaneously. The maids set to work cleaning the house from top to bottom and Gholam, the gardener, with his helper Mashaallah worked diligently on the grounds. A string of donkeys would arrive bearing baskets of manure, which were then dumped into a heap at one end of the garden. After the winter's debris had been cleared away, Gholam would plant hundreds of pansies in all of the flowerbeds and mulch them with the manure.

The greenhouse, which was Gholam's domain and off-limits to us children as well as his fellow servants, was opened and pots of tulips, hyacinths, daffodils, and cineraria, which Gholam had carefully nurtured to bloom, were brought out and placed throughout the house. Huge tubs of jasmine and ornamental orange trees in blossom, which had wintered in the greenhouse, were brought out and placed near the entranceways inside the courtyard where their perfume could be savored by arriving guests. Gholam was exceedingly proud of his work and woe be unto anyone who dared to pick a flower behind his back. "Gholam has opened his magic box" was the expression we all used to describe this annual rite. Father was always careful to be profuse in his compliments to Gholam, as well as generous in tipping him, and this appreciation spurred Gholam on to try harder to please.

About two weeks before Now Ruz, Mrs. Hameedeh, who was an expert pastry chef, arrived to prepare the *reshteh breshteh*, which is special pastry served during the Now Ruz season. This is prepared in two stages; the most difficult part, done by Mrs. Hameedeh, was the preparation of a rice flour batter. Several pounds of rice were soaked overnight, drained, and soaked again. The softened grains were then pounded in a mortar to a starchlike consistency, then the flour was mixed with water to form a thick batter. After the batter was prepared, Mrs. Hameedeh would sit cross-legged on the floor in front of a low kerosene stove on top of which there was a large round metal tray. On her right, there was a large pot filled with the batter and, on her left, several clean towels. She would dip her fingers into the batter, then twirl her dripping fingers over the hot tray dropping a thin stream of batter that congealed into a filigree of adherent strands as it made contact with the heat.

As soon as the batter coalesced, she removed the round clumps, which were about the size of a small tortilla, to the towel and covered them with another cloth. The clumps were then folded while still moist into small rectangles that were dried and stored until the day before Now Ruz. Then Grandmother and my sisters would do the final cooking of the *reshteh breshteh*. Each rectangle of dough was dropped into a cauldron of hot oil. The dough would immediately puff into a translucent pastry, which was removed from the oil when golden brown, placed on a cloth-covered tray to drain, and coated with powdered sugar while still warm. Hundreds of these cookies were made and consumed each year.

After Mrs. Hameedeh had finished her specialized task and departed for another household, Grandmother and my sisters began the baking of other sweets for Now Ruz. Baklava, chickpea cookies, rice flour cookies, window cookies, elephant ears (cookies), candied almonds, and honey almond candy were all made in quantity and stored away for the gala season. Katayoon, the oldest sister, was especially skilled in the preparation of honey almond candy. This confection is made by cooking slivered almonds in a syrup of honey, sugar, and butter flavored with saffron. When the mixture thickens to the proper consistency, it is spooned onto a flat tray where it quickly hardens. Katayoon and two helpers would form an assembly line. Katayoon would sit next to the stove and stir the syrup and nut mixture, which was simmering in a cast iron pot. When it was ready, she dipped the candy out spoonful by spoonful, and one of my other sisters would garnish each piece with ground pistachio nuts. They had to work quickly to get the ground nuts on while the surface of the candy was still sticky enough to hold the nuts.

Another traditional Now Ruz sweet is almond marzipan. Grandmother was the acknowledged marzipan expert, and she had a secret that she carefully guarded. She did not use rosewater, which is the usual flavoring added to the nut and sugar mixture. Instead, she persuaded Gholam, by means of a small tip, to provide her with a basket of jasmine blossoms from the greenhouse. She would cover the bottom of a shallow tin box with a layer of marzipan, then cover it with thin muslin, and on top of that she placed a layer of jasmine blossoms. The box was then tightly sealed and stored away until Now Ruz at which time the marzipan was served in covered glass candy bowls. When the glass top was removed, the delicious scent of the jasmine drifted out to the delightful surprise of everyone.

Another precursor of the Now Ruz season is the appearance on the streets of the *haji firoozha*, or wandering minstrels. Young men blacken their faces with burnt cork or soot and dress in outlandish comic costumes, traditionally red or orange in color, with a conical tasseled fool's cap on their heads. They wander through the streets usually traveling in groups of three; one beating a drum, one playing a kind of recorder, and the third, who does the singing and dancing, shaking a tambourine. People are so glad to see them and welcome them as the harbingers of spring that they tip them generously to show their appreciation of their jolly tomfoolery. The drummer and the piper may or may not blacken their faces, but the singer is always in blackface. He approaches people on the street with a traditional greeting something like this:

"Hello, my master. Look at me, my master,
I am the messenger of Now Ruz.
The wind and rain have gone,
Lord Now Ruz has come.
Friends convey this message:
The new year has come again,

This spring be your good luck,
The tulip fields be your joy."

The *haji firoozha* are seen throughout the whole Now Ruz season. They first make their appearance a few weeks before Now Ruz and disappear the fourteenth day after Now Ruz.

The most important preparation for Now Ruz is the setting up of the *haft seen* table, without which no celebration of the new year would be complete. Every Persian household, regardless of religious affiliation, observes the tradition of the *haft seen* decoration, which has its origin in ancient Zoroastrian times. The literal translation of *haft seen* is seven s's; *haft* being the Farsi word for "seven," and *seen* being the name of the Persian letter corresponding to the English letter *s*. The association of the number seven with good luck probably goes back to the ancient Zoroastrian belief that seven angels (collectively called *Amsshaspands*) descended from heaven to visit earth during the Now Ruz season. As an offering to these celestial visitors, seven trays *(siny)* bearing food were set out. A special bread made from flour composed of seven ingredients (wheat, corn, rice, lentils, lima beans, barley, and millet) was prepared as part of the offering. This bread, along with other food items, a candle, and a fragrant pine bough were placed on each tray. The traditional *haft seen* items are *samanou* (a puddinglike dish made from wheat sprouts and sugar symbolizing sweetness and good fortune); *sabzeh* (green lentil or wheat sprouts symbolizing the springtime rebirth and fertility); *sekkeh* (coins, preferably gold or at least a shiny new coin, symbolizing hope for prosperity); *seer* (garlic for the family's health); *sonbol* or *seeneray* (hyacinth blossoms or cinerroma flowers for beauty); *serkeh* (vinegar to ward off bitterness), and *senjed* (dried berries of the mountain ash, symbolic of the end of winter). Other items can be added or used to replace the above. For example, *seeb* (apple, the fruit symbolic of health and longevity); *sumac* (powdered fruit of another variety of mountain ash used as a spice and symbolic of nature's rebirth); or *sephand* (wild rue to ward off the evil eye and dispel bitterness and grief).

It is tempting to try to relate the custom of the seven items beginning with the letter *seen* traditionally found on the *haft seen* table of today to the seven *siny*; however, before the Arab conquest of Persia the custom was called *haft sheen; sheen* being the Persian letter representing the "sh" sound. Seven basic items used in everyday living beginning with the letter *sheen* were set out: *sharab* (wine), *shekar* (sugar), *shahd* (cane syrup), *sheer* (milk), *sheeriny* (cookies), *shamea* (candles), and *shemshad* (fresh pine boughs). The forced conversion of the Persian people to the Moslem religion did not destroy their observance of Now Ruz with all its traditions. Since one of the *sheen* items, *sharab* (wine) is forbidden to Moslems, a kind of semantic compromise was reached by changing the name to *haft seen* and substituting *serkeh* (vinegar to ward off bitterness), also made from grapes, for *sharab*.

Mithraism is an ancient religion, predating Zoroaster, that originated in Persia and later spread in one form or another to most of Europe and Great Britain. It is a monotheistic religion holding that Mithra, the god of sun and light, was the spiritual path to the ultimate Truth. It was not a religion of the masses, but only for those elite whom the Elders, or Magian Masters, deemed capable of grasping its mystic concepts. Hafiz, the great Persian poet, was basically a Mithraist although he was famous for having memorized the entire Koran. For the followers of Mithra, wine was a very important part of their lives for it symbolized the mysteries of divine love and eternal life. The many references to wine, cup bearers, and taverns found in Persian poetry are, in the main, metaphorical in nature symbolizing the mystery of divine love.

> Hast though forgotten, when as a sojourner
> Within the Tavern gates and drunk with wine,
> I found Love's passionate wisdom lying there,
> Which in the mosque none even now divine.
>
> —Hafiz

Not all references to wine are metaphorical, especially in Khayyam's quatrains. But even there, real wine is often symbolic of a lover as well as praised for its ability to bring joy, free the mind, and bring consolation.

Oh, my Beloved, fill the Cup that clears

Today of past Regrets and future Fears—
Tomorrow? Why, Tomorrow I may be
Myself with Yesterday's Seven Thousand Years.

—Khayyam

Khayyam also rationalized the drinking of wine as a means of adhering to Divine Will.

Since God knew, from the day of eternity
That I would drink wine,
Not to do so would be to render
Null and void the Divine Decrees!

Over the years, the *haft seen* table has been amplified to include other symbolic items associated with the Now Ruz spirit. A bowl of freshwater (the source of life) containing goldfish is found on many tables along with bread (to ensure a prosperous abundance of the necessities of life). The consumption of sweets (*shirini*) or honey is said to assure one of a new year without bitterness. Candles and a mirror were added to symbolize the blessed fire of the Zoroastrian religion and the reflection of the true nature of one's soul. It is customary to place a lit candle for each family member on the table. These are allowed to burn themselves out since it is considered bad luck to blow out one of these candles.

The ancient Zoroastrians believed that the world was balanced on one horn of a gigantic bull and that at the moment of the vernal equinox when the new year begins, the bull would deftly shift the world from one horn to the other. This belief is symbolized by an orange (the world) floating in a bowl of water. With a bit of imagination, the orange, at the exact second of the vernal equinox, will be seen to move ever so slightly.

The *haft seen* table is prepared a day or so before Now Ruz, and is left undisturbed until the arrival of the equinox. The family gathers round the table ahead of time and the countdown begins in the same festive spirit that New Yorkers gather in Times Square to count the seconds until the giant ball drops at the stroke of midnight New Year's Eve. It is customary to begin the new year with the eating of *shirini* (sweets) immediately after the equinox, but the rest of the food is consumed in no particular order.

Now begins the Now Ruz season, which extends to the thirteenth day after Now Ruz. This is the time for a continuous round of parties and visitations. It is traditional to visit the home of each member of the family, and the sequence of visitation is fixed by rigid protocol. The oldest members of the family are always visited first by the younger members beginning on New Year's Day. During the subsequent two weeks, calls are made on the other members of the family and on friends. If, for one reason or another, one wishes to avoid a personal visit with a family member or friend, good manners require one to call when that person is known to be out and leave a card or send one's visiting card by a servant.[1] This almost continuous influx of visitors results in the consumption of a good deal of food, especially if one is a member of a large family. That is why the ladies of the house begin their baking several weeks before Now Ruz.

The Persian custom of calling on family members and close friends is not limited to the Now Ruz season. There are five other occasions when visitation is considered to be a mandatory obligation. These are when someone returns from a long trip, a wedding, the birth of a baby, a serious illness, and a death. Good manners require that a visit for any of the above be reciprocated by a return visit by the person being called upon except, of course, in the case of a death, in which case the return call is made by a surviving family member. The observance of this custom probably contributes in a large part to the close family ties common in Persia. I remember calling on a recently widowed neighbor after I had moved to the United States. When my visit was not returned within a few weeks, I felt somewhat hurt and wondered if I had offended her in any way. Then I realized she had not meant to hurt my feelings. It was just not the custom, in this my adopted country, to feel obligated to return a visit.

The Now Ruz holiday concludes on *Sisdehbedar*, the thirteenth day of the new year. On this day, it is the custom to discard the *sabzeh* that had graced the *haft seen* table. It is considered unlucky to stay at home or work on *Sisdehbedar*, so it is traditionally a day for picnicking outdoors. In early morning families flock to the countryside where they amuse themselves with dancing, singing, games, and feasting all day long. Our family did not go out into the countryside or to the public parks for our *Sisdehbedar* picnic. My father and my grandparents did not want to risk exposing the womenfolk and children to the unruly raucous behavior that was common in the public areas on this day. Public drunkenness resulting in fights between different family groups was not uncommon; and invariably, the unpleasantness would be blamed on the bad luck associated with the thirteenth day of the new year.

It was our custom to take our picnic lunch to the far end of our orchard where we set out the food on the grassy bank of the stream. A temporary brick fireplace was built by the servants and a large pot of the *ash-e-reshteh* (noodle soup), which is traditionally served on *Sisdehbedar*, was prepared early in the morning and kept hot all day to serve to the many relatives who came to join us for the family picnic. The long intertwined noodles of the *ash-e-resteh* symbolize the binding together of the family and friends for the rest of the forthcoming new year, which by custom begins on the fourteenth day following Now Ruz.

Another occasion when noodle *ash* is prepared and served for lunch is on the third day following the departure of a family member on a long journey for a prolonged absence. The long noodles then symbolize a connection between the traveler and the family left behind. If a member of the family is unable to attend the luncheon for some reason, the hostess will send a bowl of the *ash* to them to ensure their continuing connection. The same soup is often used as a welcoming gift to a family on the day they move into the neighborhood.

As many as sixty or seventy members of the family would be present at the *Sisdehbedar* picnic, each family bringing their contribution of food to share. The morning was spent dancing, singing, and playing games, with the children running about here and there while groups of adults sat around playing cards or listening to someone performing on the *tar* (guitarlike instrument) or the *santoor* (dulcimer).

About one o'clock in the afternoon, carriages that had been ordered by Father in advance would begin to arrive and line up in the street outside the east gate. These were hired to take anyone who wished to go on an afternoon ride to Kooh Sangi. Each family would take a carriage, the children sitting on laps or up on the seat next to the driver; and off we would go down the wide tree-lined boulevard leading to the park at the foot of the mountain. The carriages drove slowly along while we looked out upon the throngs of people who were picnicking and making merry all along the road in the grassy meadows. Each family brought along their *sabzeh*, and sometime during the ride it would be discarded along the road. After we reached Kooh Sangi, the carriages turned around and we retraced our route back to the city, the whole ride lasting about two hours. This two hours provided a welcome respite from the tumult for Father and the grandparents who always stayed home. When we got back to town, the carriages would then take each family home in plenty of time for the drivers to hire themselves out again to the revelers who were starting to wend their way homeward.

An amusing custom is performed by young girls on *Sisdehbedar*. They will sit in the tall grass and, without uprooting the blades, knot two blades together all the while repeating to themselves, "I knot this grass today and next year at this time I will be in my husband's house with his baby in my arms."

Since I have been living in the United States, each year as Now Ruz approaches my heart fills with nostalgia for the happy years of my childhood in Persia surrounded by a loving family. The first year of my marriage with my American husband, I felt compelled to make some effort to perform the *Chaharshanbeh Soury* ceremony, but I was too shy and embarrassed to allow anyone in my new family see me jumping over fire; they might think that I was deranged or perhaps performing witchcraft. I stole outside at dusk and crept behind a hedge next to our swimming pool out of sight of anyone in the house. There I set three tiny birthday cake candles in the newly thawed earth and, after lighting them, hopped over each one, crouching all the while so as not to be seen. It was a poor substitute for the roaring thornbush fires surrounded by shouting and laughing friends I had known as a child, but nonetheless I felt better having symbolically burned away the troubles of the past year. After my husband came to appreciate how important the Now Ruz celebration was to me, he began to help me prepare small fires of dried leaves and now we jump together hand in hand. After our aerobic exercise, we have a wonderful Persian dinner.

I still grow the *sabzeh* every year and the green sprouts make an attractive centerpiece for our table, but I do not set out the other six items of the *haft seen*. I do light the candles and turn on all the lights in the house. I will play my tapes of classical Persian music and read the poetry of Hafiz at the moment of the equinox. I think of my family now scattered all over the globe in every hemisphere—north, south, east, and west. I wonder if the departed spirits can find us all when they make their yearly return, separated as we are by thousands of miles of oceans, mountains, and desert.

Note

1. An anecdote is told about one old man who grew tired of the continual visiting back and forth during Now Ruz. He summoned one of his servants and told him to make the rounds of the households that he (the master) felt obliged to visit. Whenever the servant found that the head of the house was not at home, he was instructed to leave a card. When the servant returned that evening, the master asked him how many cards he had left. The servant replied, "Only the jack and queen of diamonds remain, master."

Chapter Ten
Courtship

The act of giving one's heart in love is a noble thing;
For good acts, there is no need to consult the Book.

—Hafiz

Despite the fact that, in the modern Persia that I knew, boys and girls saw each other on a relatively open basis compared to the old days and therefore could pick and choose their prospective mates, the family still played an important part in formalizing the courtship. There was a tacit understanding that observation of the traditional formalities was a way of showing mutual respect between the families of the bride and groom. In days gone by, according to Grandmother, things were much different. The groom never saw his bride before the marriage ceremony. The selection and matching of the two partners, for what would hopefully be for life, was done by the elders of each family and the process proceeded according to a rather rigid formula.

The girl had little or nothing to say concerning the selection of her mate. It was the custom to marry off young girls (eleven to thirteen years old) as soon as possible, because it was the belief that a woman was nothing more than chattel and her only function was to please her husband. Therefore, the earlier she were married, the more time her husband and her in-laws had to mold her character and behavior to suit her husband. This disrespect for the feelings and rights of women was initiated with the infliction of the Islamic religion on Persia. The prophet Mohammed, founder of the Islamic religion, set a prime example. At age fifty-

127

four, he enlarged his already burgeoning harem by marrying a nine-year-old child.

Prior to the Arab invasion, the teachings of Zoroaster governed the relations between the sexes. Monogamy was strictly observed and the women were not forced to be veiled in public. They enjoyed the respect of men and were considered as equals in all respects. In fact, during those days, the Persian Empire was twice governed by women, the queens Poorandokht and Azarmidokht during the Sassanid dynasty. Women were allowed to own property and even run their own businesses.

This all changed with the forced conversion to Islam. The Arabs consider the female as worthless; and women are referred to as *zaifeh*, or the inferior sex. The wife is considered the property of the husband, and he may divorce her, then take her back at his pleasure. The only restriction on his right of disposal is that he cannot sell her. However, if the wife is unfaithful, the husband may kill her without fear of punishment. According to Islamic law, the female offspring of a family are allowed to inherit only half the amount that the male offspring receive. Similarly, in the Islamic court, the evidence given by a woman is accorded one-half the weight as that given by a man. No female is allowed to be an officer of the court, neither as an advocate or a judge. Women are forbidden to initiate divorce proceedings except in the case of abandonment. Then, after a period of one year, she may petition for a divorce, as was the case with our maid Zivar. The female has to have a male protector, either a father, brother, or husband; and all property owned by a woman upon her marriage belongs to her husband, regardless of his ability or inability to manage same. My Aunt Ozra watched helplessly while her second husband frittered away the fortune she inherited from her first husband. Fortunately, her second husband died before she was rendered completely penniless!

When a young man or his family decided that it was time for him to marry, the word was spread that he was looking for a suitable wife. Often all that was required was to drop a hint in the ear of one of the female bath attendants. As soon as the word was out, all the relatives and friends of the prospective groom's family began to talk with his parents about the merits of various eligible girls. The parents would narrow the selection down to several possibilities and send word to the families of these girls that they wished to call upon them and meet the candidate.

According to Grandmother, the typical courtship in the old times proceeded in three stages. The first stage, called *aroos didan* or "seeing the bride," was a formal call upon the prospective bride and her mother by the mother of the groom, who may have been accompanied by other female members of the groom's family. No male members of either family were present during this visit. The purpose of the visit was to view the prospective bride and establish whether or not her physical appearance would be acceptable to their son. If not, the visit was then politely terminated. If the girl appeared acceptable, then they would sit and talk and, by means of oblique questioning, determine her temperament, likes, and dislikes in an effort to ascertain her compatibility with the groom-to-be.

If all went well and the girl appeared to be a likely prospect, the mother would produce a picture of her son and pass it around to the girl and her family before leaving. The mother would then report back to her son on her favorable impression of the girl and attempt to persuade him to consent to the marriage. As mentioned above, in the male-dominated society, in addition to physical looks and charm, if the girl were young and therefore could be molded into the subservient, compliant creature considered the ideal Moslem wife, she was even more qualified.

If it appeared to both sides that the match was a good one, the process proceeded to the next stage called the *khastgari*. This was the formal proposal of marriage by the groom and his parents to the parents of the bride. The bride was not present at this meeting although it was a well-known fact that some girls spied upon the visitors from hidden places, hoping to get some glimpse of the man to whom, hopefully, she would be bound for the rest of her life.

The third and final stage was known as *baleh boroon*, meaning acceptance and agreement. The groom and his parents called upon the family of the bride to discuss the financial agreements to be entered into by the families and to decide the date, time, and place for the ceremony. The financial aspect concerned the amount of money or property which the groom would, by contract, agree to pay to the bride in the event that he divorced her.

Usually the bride's family haggled to ensure that any cash settlement would be paid in gold coins as a hedge against inflation; real property was acceptable for the same reason. This arrangement, in theory, served to stabilize the marriage. However, in practice, the husband could sometimes manage to renege on paying the penalty by making life so miserable for the wife that she would forgo the settlement in return for her freedom. After all the haggling when an apparent agreement had been reached, there was still a way to negate the entire process. If the parents were traditional fundamentalist Moslems, either side could say that they had consulted the Koran by opening it randomly and found that the displayed verse portended a disastrous future for the marriage. Then they would send word to the other family calling off the marriage.

The bride's family agreed to a dowry that was usually about equivalent in value to the groom's (theoretical) obligation. This dowry usually was in the form of the present of a house to the couple and, depending upon the wealth of the family, perhaps its furnishings. It was also traditional for the bride's parents to send to members of the groom's family a variety of gifts, including clothing. These gifts were sent a few days before the day of the wedding and carried to the groom's house on large wooden trays borne on the heads of hired porters.

At the beginning of this chapter, I mentioned that in modern Persia, the Western custom of two people meeting, falling in love, and marrying became the accepted norm. However, in many cases there still lingered a sense of responsibility to one's family to at least attempt to secure the acquiescence of the head of the household to the contemplated marriage. This was the case with my second eldest brother, Kayvan. Unusual for that time, he was still a bachelor at age thirty-five. He chanced to encounter a beautiful girl several times on his way to work. He became smitten with her and finally marshaled the courage to speak to her. After a few conversations over a period of several weeks, he asked her for her address, saying that his sisters would like to meet her.

He asked Katayoon and me (I was married by that time) to visit the girl's family on the appointed day. We all got in his car, and he drove us to within a block of her home. The house was in a miserable neighborhood where all of the houses were of the row house type and fronted directly on the narrow street. As we walked along, from each house a head covered by a *chador* would poke out and watch our progress. We felt that the object of our visit was common knowledge in the neighborhood. We knocked and were admitted to a small parlor by a *chador*-clad mother and introduced to her sister and aunt, who were similarly garbed. The object of Kayvan's affection then entered and her beauty was in stark contrast with her background. We took tea with them and made what conversation we could. The mother, aunt, and sister were obviously illiterate and their ungrammatical speech was that of the lower class. After the shortest time demanded by courtesy, we made our exit and rejoined Kayvan in the car.

On the way home, Katayoon and I both told him that we thought that he was making a mistake in thinking about marriage with a girl with whom he had nothing in common and whose attraction was purely physical. We reported our experience to Father. After we left, Father summoned Kayvan to his study and told him that he had no objection if Kayvan really wanted to marry the girl. "However," he said, "I would not like to see my grandchildren raised in a family so different from ours." This gentle remonstrance was all that was needed. Kayvan did not marry the girl or even mention her name again. In about two years, he met another girl from a good family, married her, fathered two boys, and lived happily with her for the rest of his life.

I remember a story told about a friend of our family who was smitten with a young beauty whom he wanted to make his wife. His parents were deceased, so he approached his older brother and asked him if he would go to the girl's family and present his suit. The older brother refused to go, saying that he would feel obligated to tell the girl's parents all that he knew about his brother, the bad as well as the good. However, the younger man persisted and finally the brother agreed to go. When he visited the girl's parents, he related to them all the good attributes he knew about his brother, but at the conclusion of the visit he felt compelled to say, "My brother is an army officer of some power and influence, but I'm afraid that he uses this power to make money under the table. If, knowing this, you want to give your daughter to him in marriage, do so. If not, forget that I came."

The parents did not hesitate a minute to agree to the marriage. What better mate could be found for their daughter than a powerful man with the potential for great wealth? The last I heard, the couple were still married and living happily together.

Chapter Eleven
The Wedding Ceremony

Happiness is to be face to face with you for life;
This will not happen unless you become my wife.

—Sa'adi

My grandparents were old friends with a Moslem couple who, along with their eighteen-year-old daughter, were frequent visitors in our home. The daughter's betrothal had been arranged in the usual manner, and now it was time for the wedding. Grandfather and Grandmother were, of course, invited to the wedding ceremony, which was to take place one afternoon in the house of the bride's parents. When I learned of the invitation, I became so excited and wanted very much to go to the wedding. I begged Grandmother to take me with her, and while at first she refused, she finally yielded to my persistent entreaties. She said that she would talk to the bride's mother, and if she did not object, I could go. Grandmother said to me, "Mehry, if you were an older girl, there would be no way that I could take you since this is an old-fashioned family who believe that it is bad luck to have unmarried young women present at a wedding ceremony. Since you are only nine years old, perhaps I can arrange it."

After several days, Grandmother told me the good news; permission had been granted and I could go with them. I was a very happy and thrilled little girl; I rushed around to tell everyone in the family the big news. When I told Father, he smiled and said to me, "You are now growing up, so it is time that you have your own jewelry. I will have one of your sisters take you to the jewelry store and buy you a pair of earrings."[1]

The next day Tooran took me to the jewelers, and I picked out a pair of yellow-gold earrings inset with a tiny ruby. Unconsciously, I had chosen my birthstone and I wore those earrings for many years. It seemed to me that the big day would never arrive. Finally it did and Grandfather, Grandmother, and I, dressed in our most elegant clothes, proceeded by hired *doroshkeh* to the bride's home. At exactly one o'clock in the afternoon, we arrived and the *doroshkeh* drew up in front of a wide gate in the courtyard wall flanked by two menservants. After they opened the gate for us, we walked up a long wide brick walkway bordered by flowerbeds full of red geraniums. The walk ended at the steps of a front porch that extended the width of the house. We entered through the front door into a large square reception area brilliantly lit by a massive crystal chandelier and carpeted almost wall to wall with a number of richly colored Persian carpets. Around the periphery of the room, there were chairs and console tables bearing baskets of flowers, each accompanied by a greeting card. In one corner there was a tall grandfather's clock in front of which stood a huge basket of *gole-e-maryam* (polianthes) flowers whose scent perfumed the whole room.

We walked through an open doorway into a spacious parlor carpeted with blue Isfahan rugs and furnished with sofas and chairs upholstered in blue-flowered velvet on a gold background. Through open French doors in the wall on the right as we entered, we could see the dining room. The dining room table had been removed and the chairs relocated to the parlor to provide more seating for the guests. Several long windows in the dining room looked out on flowerbeds surrounding a swimming pool, and beyond that more gardens extended into the distance. These windows, as well as those in the parlor, were hung with gold-colored velvet draperies and off-white lace curtains. Large crystal chandeliers hung from the ceilings of both rooms. A dozen or more dining room chairs were lined up in rows in the parlor, and many small and large coffee tables were scattered about, all laden with silver or china dishes containing cookies, chocolates, nuts, and fruit.

In the center of the dining room, a silver-fringed cashmere cloth *(termeh)* were spread out on the carpet. This cloth was about six by eight feet in size and elaborately embroidered with designs in many shades of red, purple, green, blue, and brown inset with seed pearls. At the left end of the *termeh*, as viewed from the living room, there was a low bench covered with gold velvet just wide enough to seat two people. Facing the bench, on the edge of the *termeh*, there sat a mirror set in a short-legged silver frame. Flanking the mirror on either side, there were silver candelabra, each holding five candles; and in front of the mirror, between it and the bench, there was a copy of the Koran on a low wooden stand. Behind the mirror resting on a silver tray, there was a clear bowl molded from sugar candy.

Large wooden trays, about two by five feet in size, were on either side of the *termeh*. One tray held a huge loaf of flat *sangak* (a type of bread) on which the words "Happy Marriage" were spelled out in red dye made from saffron mixed with a little water. The bread was surrounded by sprigs of fresh green parsley, which completely hid the wooden tray. The tray on the opposite side of the *termeh* was a work of art. It was covered with an elaborate design made from colored *esffandha* (seeds)—red, orange, blue, green, brown, and yellow. This design was surrounded by a wide border of brown seeds upon which was written, in lines of white seeds, poetry appropriate to a nuptial day. Placed on the side of the *termeh* opposite the mirror was a large basket covered with pink and white gauze and full of little gauze sacks tied with ribbon, each containing a gold coin and a few pieces of rock candy.

Silver plates holding different kinds of sweets—baklava, honeyed almonds, marzipan, rice cookies, chickpea flour cookies, and a little bowl of honey along with a bowl full of hard-cooked eggs occupied the center of the *termeh*. To the left of the bench, two loaves of hard sugar *(kaleh ghand)* wrapped in pink gauze and tied with white ribbon rested on a white folded silk cloth to which was attached a needle threaded with colored thread. The final item decorating the *termeh* was a white beribboned cage containing two snow-white pigeons.

In the wall opposite the low bench, there was a doorway that led into the central hallway of the house. In this doorway there was a shoulder-high white silk screen behind which there were six chairs. Seated on these chairs were the groom, the bride's father, the officiating mullah, and two witnesses, along with a notary public who had brought the legal record book to record the marriage and issue the marriage certificate.

The parlor in which we were seated gradually filled up with the wedding guests, ladies and gentlemen, all of whom were middle-aged or older. I was the only child present and, sitting quietly beside Grandmother, I tried very hard to contain my excitement. In the dining room, eight elegantly dressed pretty young ladies stood waiting for the ceremony to begin. About 2:30 P.M., the bride, accompanied by two lady attendants, arrived at the front door, and passing through the parlor past the guests, entered the dining room. She was dressed in a long white satin dress, the sleeves and bodice of which were elaborately embroidered with sequins and pearls. A sheer white veil covered her face to the chin and extended in the back to the floor. Her long brown hair was decorated with orange blossoms; and through the sheer veil, I could glimpse her large beautiful brown eyes and lovely white complexion.

The bride seated herself on the low bench and the ladies, after helping her to arrange her long skirts and veil, took their places around her. One of the ladies opened the Koran and gave it to the bride who held it in her lap with both hands. Another lady picked up the two loaves of gauze-wrapped sugar candy and stood behind the bride. Two other ladies unfolded the silk cloth and, standing on either side of the bride, held it over her head. A fourth attendant held the threaded needle. During this time, the notary public was busy behind the silk screen filling out the marriage documents.

When the paperwork was completed, the mullah began reading the religious service in a loud sonorous voice that easily carried to the guests seated in the other room. While he was reading his liturgy, the lady with the sugar loaves rubbed them together over the bride's head, the crumbs falling on the silk cloth. At the same time, the lady with the needle was busy loosely sewing the colored thread along the border of the silk cloth. The reading by the mullah lasted about ten minutes and during this time the bride sat with her head bent and her eyes fixed on the holy book. The mullah then addressed the bride by name, saying, "Shohreh, do you agree to marry this man?"

The bride remained silent. Again, the mullah repeated his question and, again, the bride said nothing. The mullah asked for the third time and this time the bride answered in a clear, firm voice, "*Baleh* [yes]!"

Now the ladies holding the silk cloth folded it, taking care that the sugar crumbs did not drop on the bride, and put it aside. Another lady relieved the bride of the Koran. The bride's father brought the groom into the room and seated him next to his bride on the bench. The groom took the bride's left hand in his and placed a wedding band on her third finger. The bride then placed her ring on the groom's finger, and the sound of wedding music from a hidden phonograph filled the room. The groom then lifted the bride's veil and together the couple looked into the mirror, smiling at each other's reflection. Each then dipped a forefinger into the pot of honey and touched it to the other's mouth, and the groom chastely kissed the bride's cheek. The notary public entered and placed the record book in front of the couple for their signatures; and after the signing, the mullah and the notary departed.

Next came the groom's parents. They kissed the bride and groom by way of congratulations and fastened a gold and diamond necklace around the bride's neck. They were followed by the bride's parents who, after proffering their congratulatory kisses, presented the bride with a pair of diamond earrings and a gold bracelet. Finally, the bride's father gave the groom a leather wallet containing the deed to a house. After the couple's parents had finished their presentations, the other close relatives trooped into the room clamoring their congratulations and bearing gifts. When all had been received, the couple rose up from the bench and the bride went over to the dining room window that looked out on the garden. One of the attending ladies opened the window and another brought the caged birds to the bride. The bride opened the cage and freed the pigeons through the window, whereupon everyone applauded.

The bride and groom then walked hand in hand into the parlor and shook hands with all the guests. At this time, the bride's old nanny came in carrying a small brazier filled with red glowing charcoal embers. She congratulated the couple and then tossed a pinch of *esffandha* on the coals, whereupon the perfumed smoke billowed up from the brazier. She was rewarded by a gift of a gold coin from the groom. The groom's mother dipped her hand into a bag of sugar candy and threw a handful over the heads of the bride and groom. Finally, one of the ladies handed the basket of gauze-wrapped favors, each containing a piece of candy, a gold coin, and confetti, to the bride and she passed out one to each of the women present.

Perhaps because it was my first, I have always looked back on that wedding ceremony as being the most beautiful of any I have ever attended, including my own. We left the bride's home late in the afternoon, and on the way to our house and for days thereafter, I pestered Grandmother with many questions. Her patience was infinite, and she answered each one as best she could. Our dialogue went something like this:

"Who were those ladies standing around the bride?"

"They were the bride's married sisters, cousins, and other close relatives. As I told you before, no girls eligible to be married are allowed to attend. Also, no divorced ladies or widows are allowed because their presence is thought to bring bad luck on the marriage."

"Why was the mullah behind the silk screen?"

"Because he does not want to look upon any lady who is not wearing *chador* or a veil."

"Why were the ladies rubbing the sugar loaves together over the bride's head?"

"This is to make the marriage sweet."

"Then when the bride and groom touch each other's lips with honey, that is also to make the marriage sweet?"

"Yes, but more importantly, it is to make them sweet to each other."

"Why was that lady pretending to sew the cloth over the bride's head while the other was rubbing the sugar loaves together?"

"That lady was the bride's aunt. She was pretending that she was sewing together the lips of the bride's mother-in-law and her sisters-in-law, so that they will never interfere in the marriage."

"Why did they have that tray covered with those colored seeds that looked like a painting?"

"Many people believe that burning *esffandha* will keep evil spirits away. You saw the bride's nanny burn the seeds in her pot of charcoal and the groom give her a gift of money. In the old days when they were setting up the *sofreh-e-aghde* [arranging the ceremonial dishes on the *termeh*], a bowl of *esffandha* was placed on the *termeh*. Over the years it became a custom to color the seeds and arrange them in designs. Now there are artists who specialize in making beautiful designs with *esffandha* and you can order what you want from them."

"What do they do with it after the wedding?"

"After the wedding, the seeds are dumped together into a bowl and then divided up into little packages. These are given away to any of the family or friends who want them. Whenever they feel that they need to ward off something evil, they can burn the *esffandha*."

"Why were the bread, eggs, and candles on the *termeh*?"

"The bread is to bring prosperity to the couple; the eggs are a symbol of fertility; the candles a wish for a bright and cheerful life together."

"Why was the bride reading the Koran while the mullah was reading the ceremony?"

"She was praying for happiness in her new life. In the old days, before the shah changed the law, brides would pray that their husband would not take other wives as allowed by the Moslem religion."

"Have you ever known a family where there was more than one wife?"

"Yes, I have seen this frequently; but I have never known one where the husband or the wives were really happy. And the children never seemed to get along with each other."

"Why did the bride free the two pigeons?"

"The two birds symbolize the bride and groom starting off to build their own nest and begin a new life together."

"Why were the bride and groom sitting in front of a mirror?"

"In the old days, a marriage was arranged by the parents and, in fact, sometimes a couple would become engaged when they were babies. The bride and groom were not allowed to see each other before the wedding and then the first look is at a reflection in a mirror. Nowadays, boys and girls see and get to know each other before becoming engaged, but the old custom of looking at each other in a mirror during the wedding ceremony is a tradition that is still kept."

"What if they didn't like each other when they met for the first time at the wedding?"

"That was their misfortune; but, somehow, it usually happened that after they lived together over the years, they came to love each other or, at least, learned to respect and depend upon each other."

"But why do they look at each other in a mirror?"

"I guess that this custom started because the couple, especially the bride, were shy about staring directly at each other in front of all the guests."

I said, "So you didn't see Grandfather before you married him?"

Grandmother laughed out loud and patted my cheek. "You are not shy about asking any question, are you?" She thought for a few minutes, then continued, "Well, I'll tell you the truth. I saw him the day that he and his parents came to our house to ask my parents for my hand in marriage. With the help of my nanny, I peeked through a curtain into the room where they were talking; and I want you to know that it was love at first sight. Believe me, a lot of girls did the same thing. But the poor boys were not able to see us, because we were not allowed out of the house unveiled and when we had to travel it was always in a closed *doroshkeh*."

"Are all the wedding ceremonies like the one we saw?" I asked.

She replied, "Oh, no! Not everyone can afford such an elaborate *sofreh-e-aghde* and presents of gold coins to the guests. However the basics, such as rubbing the sugar loaves together over the bride, the sewing of the lips, and the reading of the Koran, are the same. Poor people put the mullah behind a curtain instead of behind a silk screen. Did you ever hear the expression, 'Put the mullah behind the curtain'? This is what people say to a girl who wants to get married, and it means that she should work hard to get a husband. On the other hand, sometimes the girl does not want to marry a certain boy and when the mullah asks the question three times she doesn't say yes when she is supposed to. When the family suspects that this might

140

happen, they arrange with one of the attending ladies to answer for her. The family and guests all clap and shout at the right time, and the mullah behind the curtain is none the wiser."

Since I was only nine years old at that time, Grandmother did not tell me about a custom practiced by some people on the wedding night. To ensure proof that the bride came to her nuptial bed a virgin, it was the practice to station an older female member of the groom's family outside the door of the bridal chamber. After the consummation of the marriage, the groom would cleanse the bride with a special white handkerchief and pass the bloody cloth out to the waiting woman as proof of his wife's virginity. This custom was subject to some cheating if the groom was so much in love that he didn't care or if his sense of honor dictated that he not publicly acknowledge that he had been deceived. Then the groom might prick his own finger to bloody the cloth, and the couple would keep their secret for the rest of their lives. Conversely, the groom who wound up with a clean handkerchief had the option of exiting the bedroom in high dudgeon declaiming that he had been cheated and demand an instant divorce. Needless to say, this catastrophic occurrence would result in a serious rift between the involved families and the bad blood might last for years.

The story is told about a young groom who, on his wedding night after the ritual cleansing of his bride, found the handkerchief to be unstained. His pride would not allow him to denounce his wife as a nonvirgin as was his right. He felt that he and his family would be humiliated if it became known that they had been bilked. He swallowed his pride and accepted the girl as his wife. A few weeks later, he came home one evening to find his wife rubbing her ears, obviously in some pain. He asked her what was bothering her, and she replied that she had had her ears pierced that afternoon. "So," he replied, "that part that should have been pierced when you were a child living in your father's house, you had pierced after you became my wife. That part that should have been pierced for the first time when you became my wife, you had pierced elsewhere!"

Divorce was not common when I was a child. It was taken for granted that when two people entered into marriage, it would last for life. The parents of the bride would admonish her on her wedding day with such expressions as, "You are going to this marriage in a white veil and you leave it only in a white shroud"; or "You will live with your husband until your hair is as white as your teeth". The Persian writer of folklore, Mullanasreddin, tells the story of a recently married girl who ran back home to her father in tears, complaining that her husband beat her. The father chastised his daughter and sent her back to her husband with a note reading, "You have beaten my daughter and now I have beaten your wife."

It is the custom for the bride's parents to host a dinner party the evening of the wedding day. The wedding that I described was followed by a large party in the Sheer va Khorsheed, the best private club in the city. My grandparents did not attend, but my father and older sisters did; and they told me that it was a lovely affair with food, music, dancing, and entertainment for over five hundred people. After the honeymoon, the newlyweds begin a round of entertainment given by various members of both families to welcome them into the family circle. These parties usually start with dinner followed by dancing and singing; and depending upon the size of the families, the parties can continue for months. If other family members happen to marry during this time, the socializing can stretch on and on.

The natural result of the honeymoon was often manifested during the year following the wedding. I remember my grandmother coming home one afternoon from a tea klatch she had attended that morning. When I asked her if she had had a good time, she answered, "Oh, yes, and I wish that I had taken you with me. You remember the wedding that I took you to last year. That girl is going to become a mother. When a girl becomes pregnant for the first time, her parents send her all the necessary things for the new baby—clothes, furniture for the nursery, toys, and so forth. Many of the clothes have been handmade or embroidered by the relatives. Sometimes a net for over the baby's crib is made from the bridal veil. The clothing is enough to cloth the baby for the first two years. When all of the gifts have been delivered to their daughter, the mother gives a party for lady relatives and close friends to show off the *sisimooni* [layette]."

I considered this for a moment, then I asked, "No one knows if the baby will be a boy or a girl, so how do they know what to give?"

Grandmother answered, "They give clothing suitable for both sexes and the things that are not used for the firstborn are saved for the next one to come along."

I thought to myself how nice it would be if there were only some way of knowing ahead of time the sex of an unborn baby. In my childish mind, I arrived at a solution: What if the mother's voice became unnaturally deep if she were carrying a male child? When I broached this amusing fantasy to Grandmother, she replied in all her wisdom, "If God wanted us to know, he would find a way to tell us. It is a good lesson in patience to wait for nine months and then be surprised."

The family always hoped that the firstborn would be a boy. I remember the grandfather of one of my friends asking after she had given birth to her first baby, "Did she have a child or a girl?"; meaning, Was there a man to carry on the family name or a mere female who would be given away in marriage to another family?

The naming of a baby is always a matter for much discussion throughout the pregnancy between the parents and both pairs of grandparents, and all should agree on a male and a female name before the child is born. The baby is given his or her name at a family party called *shab-e-sheesh*, which takes place on the sixth day following the birth. In former days, it was the custom, in the event that the parents could not agree on a single male and female name, to write down three choices for each sex on separate scraps of paper. If a decision still had not been made before the *shab-e-sheesh*, one of the grandparents would take the three papers bearing the names for the appropriate sex and place them in three places in the Holy Book. The book would then be opened at random by the father, and he would page forward from that place. The first name to be uncovered would be the name given to the baby.

If the family is blessed with a male child, the next important party to look forward to is the circumcision celebration. This was an especially important affair in the days when most of the babies were born at home. In modern times, when most babies are born in a hospital, the circumcision is performed there shortly after birth. However, in the old days, the surgery was usually postponed until the child had survived the rigors of infancy and was five years of age or older. The family would bring in a barber or an attendant from a public bath, called a *dallak*, who was skilled in the procedure. After the operation, there would be a party (*khatneh suroon*) held the same day or the following day. The boy, of course, was the guest of honor. He would be dressed in a white robe, which hung loosely from his neck so as not to touch his tender member, and he would be seated in the center of the room. At his feet were heaped the many gifts that the guests had brought, and he would be surrounded by feasting adults.

I remember one circumcision party that was held for three boys, all cousins, who were all circumcised the same afternoon. One of the boys was my brother Jamshid, who was eight years old; the others were eight and eleven. The ceremony took place in the home of the eleven year old. Before the operation, his parents had talked to him explaining the procedure and cautioned him not to mention any details to his younger cousins so as not to frighten them. The three boys along with the men of the families were gathered in one room waiting the arrival of the *dallak* while the ladies sat chatting in the living room. I was playing outside with several other girls. Two *dallak* arrived carrying their small satchels containing their instruments and were shown into the room full of men folk. A few minutes later I heard a loud scream and crying, and suddenly the door burst open. The eleven-year-old boy came dashing out and ran across the courtyard to a large mulberry tree. He leapt into its branches and scrambled to the very top where he sat sobbing. Three of the men came out of the house and gathered at the foot of the tree. They begged and cajoled the boy to come down, promising to buy him whatever gifts his heart desired. Finally, they managed to persuade him to come down; and he was carried, still sniffling back into the house where he became a proper male.

While all this was going on, we heard one of the younger boys crying inside the house and screaming bad things about Mr. Eftekhar, one of the friends of his family. At the time we did not know why he was so upset with Mr. Eftekhar, but later on we found out what had happened. Mr. Eftekhar, while waiting for the *dallak* to arrive, had busied himself by sharpening a pencil with his penknife. One of the other men, in an attempt to reassure the boy, had told him that he need not be afraid of the circumcision; all that was going to happen was the *dallak* would draw a line around his penis with Mr. Eftekhar's pencil. The boy's turn came, and he was held down on the table by one man while another held his head with hands over the boy's eyes. When the boy felt the burning pain of the knife, he screamed, "Mr. Eftekhar, why did you make your pencil so sharp?" This story was repeated over and over in the family for years, and it became a jesting warning whenever someone was in danger of being cheated to say to them, "Be careful; Mr. Eftekhar is sharpening his pencil!"

After the *dallak* completed their surgery, they departed, grinning with delight over the substantial tip that they had received over and above their fee to compensate them for the delay caused by the flight of the one boy. I went into the house, found Grandmother, and, holding her hand, went to offer congratulations to the boys. They were each seated on a pallet in the center of a large room, robed in white and trying bravely to smile. Each was surrounded by piles of presents to which we added our own offerings. That evening there was a family dinner party.

The next morning there was a buzz of activity throughout the house. Workmen arrived bringing tables, chairs, carpets, lanterns, and a number of heavy wooden planks. The tables and chairs were arranged around the periphery of the walled courtyard. The raised edges of the central decorative pool (*hoze*) were spanned by the wooden planks and covered with carpets to make a stage. Japanese lanterns were strung up, crisscrossing the courtyard. Three large thronelike chairs were brought out of the house and placed side by side on the verandah facing the courtyard.

By about 4 P.M. the courtyard was filled with guests, and servants bearing trays circulated among them offering tea, sweets, and nuts. About this time the *motreb roo hozi* (musicians who play over the pool) arrived and took their places on the platform that had been erected over the pool. The musicians were accompanied by two men who were comedy actors and dancers. The younger of the two was in blackface and dressed in red clothes and a red fool's cap. He was called Mobarak and played the part of a servant, and the older man played the part of the master. The two exchanged comic verses, the master ordering the servant about and the servant in turn making fun of his master, all the while dancing to the music played by the three musicians. One played a *tar*, an instrument similar to a guitar; one played a cellolike instrument; and the third pounded out the rhythm with a tambourine.

The gaiety went on for several hours presided over by the three initiates who sat on their thrones, again surrounded by more gifts brought by the guests. Finally, the musicians packed up and left, the sleepy boys retired, and the guests all took their leave, abandoning the courtyard to the servants who busied themselves taking down the decorations and cleaning up.

Note

1. The first jewelry bought for a girl is traditionally a pair of earrings. Shortly after birth, female babies have their ears pierced, and the hole is kept open by a fine silver wire ring. As the child grows older, this first wire is replaced by thicker and thicker silver rings and, finally, a gold ring.

Chapter Twelve
Summer Holidays

Our hearts were like brightly polished mirrors
Reflecting back and forth the love we felt for each other
Our lives undulated together as the waves of the ocean
But we were safe from all storms or calamity.

—Ghasem Rasa

By the time I was eight or nine years old, my brothers and sisters were all in college or the last year of high school. My brother Jamshid, who was the closest in age to me, was now a teenager. The custom of spending the summer months *en famille* in the country (except for Father and Grandfather, who had to remain at work in the city) had been abandoned a year or so after Mother died. Grandmother, however, loved the old tradition of yearly family reunions, and she would organize short excursions of four to five days to Shandeez, the place where our family had traditionally summered, for as many of the family as she could bring together. The family had grown so large and so dispersed that it was difficult to assemble them in one place at the same time.

Shandeez, in those days, was a tiny village nestled in the mountains about twenty kilometers north of Mashhad.[1] A narrow, rutted dirt road connected this country village to the outside world, and twice a week a bus went to Shandeez from Mashhad and returned the next day. This was the mode of transportation that we used to get there; and the journey, because of the bad road and the ancient buses, took two or three hours. It was a jolting, shaking ride and Grandmother did not enjoy it at all. She would sit in the seat directly behind the driver and nervously watch the road and the driver, all the while silently praying. If we children, who were in the back, became too raucous, she would turn and shout to us to be quiet. She feared that the disturbance would distract the driver, and she was in mortal fear that the bus would overturn or the driver would miss one of the sharp turns.

Grandmother was not a good traveler; she would never think of flying and hated long bus or train trips. In later years, after we had moved to Tehran, she never came to visit us; we always had to go to her. She had made only one long journey in her whole life. As a young bride, she traveled with her husband from Mashhad to Herat and Qandehar in Afghanistan. For several weeks she jolted along in a canopied howdah on the back of a camel or a mule. This experience probably soured her on travel for the rest of her life. It was on this trip that she acquired a tiny, blue, paisley-shaped tattoo about one centimeter in length on the inside of her left wrist. She always called this her souvenir of Herat.

The road from Mashhad to Shandeez terminated in the village square which, in addition to residences, had a bakery, a butcher shop, and stalls with fresh fruits and vegetables for sale. On one corner, there was a fabric shop with bolts of colorful cotton cloth lining one wall; and on the other side of the shop, a man sat with a foot-operated Singer sewing machine making shirts and trousers to order and for sale off the rack. The man from whom we rented our summer cottage had a small woodworking shop there where he manufactured doors, windows, tables, and other simple furniture to supplement his income from farming. He was called Amjad Najjar—Amjad, the carpenter. He was a kind, polite, warmhearted individual who did his best not to intrude on our privacy when he came to tend his orchards. He was the one who volunteered to bury my twin brother when he died of diphtheria at age three months. This was not unusual since there were no professional undertakers at that time to serve the remote villages.

There was a tea shop in the square that was a favorite meeting place for the men of the village at the end of the day when they would gather to sit on wooden benches outside and smoke their *chopogh*,[2] a long-stemmed wooden pipe, while sipping tea from tiny glasses. Here, the day-to-day problems of the village would be discussed and solutions offered. Every day, for a few hours, the local barber set up for business by standing a chair outdoors in front of the tea shop along with a small portable table on which he placed his scissors, razors, comb, and towels, along with a Primus stove with a kettle to make the cinnamon tea that he served to each customer as partial consolation for his somewhat inept work.

The arrival of the bus in the village square was the signal for a burst of activity in the village. Families were waiting to meet relatives returning from the city, where they had gone to sell their produce and purchase items not available in the village. Amjad was on hand to meet us, accompanied by a train of five or six horses and donkeys with their drivers. Our bundles of bedding, linens, clothes, and food staples, which had been carried on top of the bus, were off-loaded by the servants and the drivers and transferred to the backs of the donkeys. Grandmother and any of the older aunts who may have been with us were helped onto the backs of horses, and our entourage started off caravan-style with the animals walking single file, nose to rump. We children skipped and played alongside, now able to give vent to the excitement that had been building up since the journey began that morning.

Surrounding the village, there were orchards and small farms that were accessible only by paths wide enough for a horse or donkey. Farmhouses available for rent to summer visitors were scattered throughout the area. While their homes were rented out, the owners moved in with one of their many relatives. The whole village was interrelated by generations of intermarriage, and the headman of the village was the head of the family. Our family rented Amjad Najjar's flat-roofed two-room house, which was a few kilometers from the village and about a one-hour walk. The house had a narrow center hall with one large room on either side and behind these there was a tiny kitchen on one side and a pantry on the other. There was no electricity and the sanitary facility was a privy a short distance behind the house, identified at night by a kerosene lantern hung near the door.

The front of the house had a wide brick-paved verandah; and this is where most of the family slept, ate, and gathered to chat. At night the servants occupied one corner of the verandah and the old folks slept inside. The verandah faced south, and since our house was at a slight elevation on the west side of the valley, we enjoyed a panoramic view across the wide valley to the east and south and of the nearby mountains to the west. A small river, fed by melting snows in the mountains to the north, entered the head of the valley, and as it wound its way south through the valley, it became wider and shallower and eventually found its way to the Kashaf Rood, the river that provided water for most of the villages north of Mashhad. At the head of the valley, a series of dams had been built across the stream; and from these dams, irrigation ditches provided water to the orchards and fields of the valley. The irrigation ditch that served the orchards near our rented cottage was larger than the rest and eventually became the sluiceway that turned the water wheel of the village mill. The water was clear and sparkling, but so cold that we were not able to bathe in it or even wade for more than a few minutes at a time.

The orchards throughout the valley were separated by low mud brick walls surmounted by mounds of thornbushes that provided some protection from the erosion of the elements. The orchard that surrounded our summerhouse was about ten acres in size and planted with peach and apricot trees. The fruit was large, juicy, and delicious in flavor. The owner of the property used the flat roof of the house as a drying platform for the fruit, which he boxed up and sent to the city for sale. During the season, his whole family was involved with the picking, sorting, and drying of the crop; even the smallest children were employed to crack open the apricot seeds and extract the sweet inner meat, which was then dried and roasted.

Beyond the orchards to the southwest, there was a small cemetery; and it was here that my twin brother was buried. Every time we were playing near the cemetery, I used to go and look at the small stone that marked his grave and think how nice it would be if he were still alive and I could have a playmate my own age. I consoled myself by thinking about the old Persian belief related to me by Grandmother. She told me that in heaven there is a tree called *tooba* that nurses all the babies who die. I used to imagine this tree with its spreading branches covered with contented suckling babies hanging like blossoms.

The remaining hours of that first day in Shandeez were spent in getting settled. After we had walked for about an hour, we arrived at the farmhouse. The animals were unloaded and the drivers paid off and dismissed. The servants set to work building cooking fires in the outdoor kitchen area and laying carpets over the verandah and over the straw mats that covered the floors of the bedrooms. The kerosene lanterns were filled with fuel and hung ready for the night. Soon the smell of wood smoke mingled with cooking food filled the air. The adults rested cross-legged on the carpeted verandah and sipped tea while waiting for the dinner to be prepared. When it was time to eat, Soltan and Zivar spread white tablecloths over the carpets and served the meal. We all sat around on the floor and ravenously attacked the food, our appetites whetted by the cool mountain air and exercise.

After dinner, the plates were cleared; and the family sat around talking and telling stories while the servants had their dinner. As twilight gradually turned to night, the kerosene lamps were lit and the servants began to prepare our beds. Thick cotton pallets were unrolled on the verandah and covered with sheets, a blanket, and a pillow. Beds were prepared indoors for Grandmother and any of the older relatives who wanted to sleep inside. I, along with my brothers, sisters, and cousins, bedded down on the verandah. It seldom rained in the summer in Shandeez, but when it did, we all crowded into the two bedrooms with the servants sleeping in the hallway between.

The weather in Shandeez was never hot in the summer, but rather mild as in late spring. There was almost always a light breeze stirring that carried the perfume of wildflowers and moisture from the river and the numerous springs scattered throughout the valley. The sky was a deep blue turquoise during the day and at night looked like a black velvet cloth covered with the sparkling diamonds of millions of stars. There was no light pollution to mask the view of the heavens; and lying in bed at night, I would pick out the constellations that I had learned from Grandmother and Grandfather. If one looked out over the valley, one could see an occasional pinpoint of light shining from a lantern in one of the distant houses, otherwise all was black unless the moon happened to be shining.

In the morning, I awakened at sunrise to the sounds of roosters crowing, cows lowing, and sheep bleating as the farm birds and animals greeted the new day. The villagers kept the same hours as the animals; they were early to bed and up and working before sunrise. My young cousins and I, along with brother Jamshid, played all day long. We would go hiking in the mountains to collect wildflowers and interesting rocks. We played in the shallow river until our feet were as white and cold as marble. Sometimes we went with Gholam and Soltan to the village square where they did the morning shopping for food for the day; other days we helped Amjad and his family in their harvesting of the apricot and peach trees, and carried the fruit to the roof to be laid out for drying. While we helped pick the fruit, we, along with Amjad's children, gorged ourselves to the extent that we had no appetite for lunch. Amjad didn't mind because he was grateful for our help.

On windy days we would walk to a nearby meadow and fly kites that we had made from paper, split cane, and thread held together with *serish* (a special kind of glue), which Jamshid would prepare from the ground root of the asphodel plant. This glue is very strong for bonding paper, if it is not exposed to moisture, and is commonly used throughout Persia. It is prepared by adding cold water to the ground dried root, which has the consistency of sawdust, until a paste is formed. When I think of *serish*, I am reminded of a practical joke that someone, no doubt Jamshid, played on one of our servants.

Naneh, Grandmother's maid and cook, was in the habit of mixing her henna powder with water the night before she went to the public bath. The next morning she would apply the henna to her hair and cover it with a kerchief. A couple hours later, after she had completed her morning work and the henna had set, she would go to the bath and wash her hair. One night, someone put a spoonful of *serish* powder in her bowl of soaking henna. The next day Naneh went through her usual ritual, but when she tried to wash her hair at the bath she found that it was bound together in one mass. It was only after prolonged soaking and with the help of other women that she managed to wash it. Needless to say, she was very irate when she came home. She thought that she had purchased a bad batch of henna until she noticed a few grains of *serish* powder on the table where she kept her henna bowl. Then it dawned on her what had happened and she really exploded. She ran to Grandmother and demanded that the culprit be found. He or she never was exposed.

Our days in Shandeez were filled with endless games, but we also learned about things that were never taught in school or experienced in the city. We learned how to milk a cow; we watched bread making; we collected eggs from the henhouses and watched baby chicks hatching and cows calving. We watched the women of the village make butter in the skin churns. The women would fill an elongated sheepskin bag with fresh cream from cow or goat milk. The bag would then be suspended between two poles and swung back and forth by a woman on either side until the cream turned to butter.

Those few days in the country, which we enjoyed so much, passed so quickly that they seemed like a brief happy dream; but we also had a lot of fun the rest of the summer at home in Mashhad. My brother Jamshid, who was four years older than I, was a very inventive and mischievous boy and I was his loyal accomplice. He was always playing practical jokes on everyone, except Father and Grandfather, but he was never punished because everyone loved him, especially my grandparents. Gholam was Jamshid's favorite target, although none of the servants, his brothers or sisters, or our neighbors were immune from his pranks.

Gholam wore a pair of shoes called *geeveh*, a style popular with peasants. These were simply a flat sole made from a single piece of leather to which there is sewn a cotton crochet upper decorated by embroidery. These shoes are very serviceable but have one drawback: If the upper should get wet, it shrinks and draws up the sole in a crescent shape, making it difficult to insert one's foot. After the cotton crochet dries out, the shoe returns to its original shape.

When Gholam did his daily watering of the garden, he removed his *geeveh* and placed them off to one side so they would not get splashed by water. Jamshid would slip through the shrubbery out of Gholam's sight and moisten the uppers of Gholam's shoes. When the poor man finished his work and retrieved his shoes, he would find the toes turned up for no apparent reason. This happened again and again before Gholam finally caught Jamshid in the act, thus ending the fun. The torment of Gholam did not end, however. His bicycle, which he used to ride to market every morning, would never be in the same place where he left it the night before or he would find one of the tires flat.

Some of Jamshid's pranks required elaborate preparation accomplished in secret. One time during the summer when we all slept outdoors on the porches or scattered around the courtyard, Jamshid and I, during the afternoon siesta time, strung a strong black string from the roof of the center wing of the house over the courtyard pool to the top of one of the trees. That summer, Jamshid and I slept on the porch of the north wing of the house opposite the pool. After dark, he managed to drape another string over the one we had stretched that afternoon. This string, attached to an egg-sized stone, he led over a nail high up on one of the porch pillars and then down to his bed on the porch. After everyone was asleep, he pulled the stone up to the water surface and, by jerking it up and down, made the stone splash noisily in the water.

Grandmother and Grandfather, instead of sleeping in their usual place on the north porch, were sleeping that summer in a bed covered with mosquito netting not far from the pool. Soon we heard Grandmother talking to Grandfather, saying, "Get up! There is a strange noise coming from the pool. See what it is!" Grandfather got up to investigate, and Jamshid allowed the stone to sink below the surface of the water. Grandfather could not seek the black string in the dark, and after looking around returned to bed telling Grandmother that she was imagining things. After a few minutes, Jamshid pulled the string and resumed splashing the stone up and down. Soon we heard Grandmother again. "Get up! There it is again. You never really look carefully at anything!"

This time both of them got up, turned on one of the porch lights, and then walked around the pool. Again Jamshid allowed the stone to sink and the suspending string remained invisible in the poor light. Grandfather grumbled to Grandmother, "You see, there is nothing there. Are you satisfied now?"

They returned to bed and Jamshid repeated the performance. This time the rest of the family (except for Father, who slept inside the south wing and heard nothing) got up and began searching around the pool and the courtyard. More lights were turned on, but still no one saw the string. Finally, everyone gave up and went back to bed and decided to ignore any further noise. Jamshid cut the string and the stone sank to the bottom of the pool pulling the string with it. Jamshid got up early the next morning and retrieved the overhead string, erasing all evidence of his mischief. No one thought to question why Jamshid and I had not awakened with all the disturbance going on about us. It was not until years later when we were all adults that Jamshid confessed. Grandmother's only comment was, "I should have known!"

Jamshid's imaginative use of string to play practical jokes was not limited to the story recounted above. I recall another occasion when the two of us banded together in devilment; but, to describe this escapade, I must first tell about our neighbors. The area in which we lived in Mashhad was not overdeveloped, and the houses were all situated on spacious lots several acres in size. Everyone had their own courtyard, garden, and orchard. The water necessary for irrigation was precious and was carried by an ingenious system of ditches and culverts to each property. Disputes over water rights were common; and although my father and grandparents were not involved in any such disagreements, a feud between Gholam, our gardener, and his counterpart who worked for our neighbor across the street was the reason for Jamshid's prank.

Mr. Golkani, a wealthy banker, lived across the street from our house. His property was enclosed by a high brick wall, as usual. There was a double wooden door in the wall facing our house. His home, a beautiful two-story mansion, was set back from the wall and separated from it by a macadam paved area interspersed with flowerbeds, which was a playground for his children. He had four daughters and each one of them corresponded in age to one of the girls in our family, so we all played with each other in our childhood and, later on, visited back and forth as close friends. The macadam area was a favorite place for roller skating; and his daughter Iran, who was a schoolmate of mine, and I used to skate there frequently.

Mr. Golkani was one of the kindest, most gentle, and generous persons I have ever known. He contributed monthly to numerous charitable organizations, and in addition, he was the anonymous benefactor of many of the poor people in the city. His gardener, Hassan, however, was a horse of a different color. He was an ill-tempered man who continually complained to our Gholam that he (Gholam) muddied the water in the stream that, after leaving our property, passed under the street through a culvert to supply Mr. Golkani's garden. His nagging provided a victim and an excuse to my brother Jamshid to perpetrate one of his pranks.

The wooden doors in Mr. Golkani's courtyard wall opposite our property had a fist-shaped brass knocker with a brass striking plate affixed to the door frame next to the doors. The buildings housing our servants were adjacent to the east wall around our property, and the roofs projected about eight feet above the wall. One evening at dusk, Jamshid carried a ladder down to the servants' quarters and helped me up to the roof. He then went across the street and tied a black string to the brass knocker outside Mr. Golkani's courtyard door, and running back to where I was waiting, tossed the spool up to me. We then secured the string, which stretched high above the street from the roof down to the knocker. After it was fully dark, we went back to the rooftop and lay down, peering over the edge to watch the fun. It was one of Hassan the gardener's duties to answer the front gate whenever the knocker sounded; so after we pulled the string several times and the knocker sounded, the gardener opened the door. Seeing no one, he closed the door. After a few minutes to allow time for him to get back to the house, we again knocked with the same results. This continued a few more times until, finally, the gardener shut the door and stood behind it in an effort to catch whoever was knocking. As soon as we knocked, he whipped the door open, and you can imagine his surprise when he still saw no one there.

Hassan shut the door again and just then a young man came walking down the street, whistling in a carefree way. Jamshid waited until he was opposite the door. He pulled the string; the knocker sounded; the young man jumped and, startled by a knocker moving of its own accord, ran off. At the same time, Hassan, who had been waiting behind the door, flung it open and, seeing the fleeing man, he ran off in pursuit. Hassan never caught the young man; and before Hassan returned, Jamshid pulled hard on the string, breaking it off. The next morning Hassan found a piece of the string hanging from the knocker and, knowing Jamshid, immediately made the connection. He came across to our house and told Gholam that he wanted to talk to my father about Jamshid, who was making trouble for the whole neighborhood according to Hassan. Gholam put him off by saying that my father was not at home, but he would inform him of Hassan's complaint. Gholam never did tell Father, but he told Jamshid that although he had saved his skin this time, if Jamshid ever played any more jokes on him, he would tell my father the whole story.

Sleeping outdoors during the summertime was a common custom throughout Persia. Those people fortunate enough to have a pleasant garden, such as we had, slept there. Others, less fortunate, would sleep on the flat rooftops. While outdoor sleeping was done primarily for comfort in southern Persia before the days of air-conditioning, in Mashhad the summer nights were never so uncomfortable that we had to find relief from the heat by sleeping outdoors. We slept outside because we loved the fresh air and freedom from being cooped up indoors after a long winter.

As I mentioned before, Father always slept inside in his own room in the *beerooney* with his windows open to the gardens. Grandmother and Grandfather had their bed on the patio near the pool or on the porch of the north wing, and the bed was enclosed with mosquito netting. The rest of the family slept on the portable wooden beds that were set up each evening.

We had no mosquito netting but used a bug repellent that was prepared daily by Soltan or Zivar. The citronella grass is native to the Middle East and can be purchased very cheaply in the bazaar. During the day, a generous handful of the grass was soaked in a bowl of water; and by nightfall, the infusion had turned the water yellow and was ready for use. Every night, before retiring, we would dip our hands into the bowl and smear the liquid over our arms and face, being careful not to get any on our lips because of its bitter taste. We were seldom bothered by insects during the night.

All of this leads to another story about the irrepressible Jamshid. My father's younger sister, Little Aunt, came to visit frequently, usually every other day. If she missed a day, the next day she would come and then she would stay overnight with three or four of her children or grandchildren. She was an overbearing woman and not well liked by me or my brothers and sisters. One afternoon, when she came to visit along with her daughter and two sons, she announced her intention to stay overnight. When Jamshid heard this, he decided to have some fun. Soltan had prepared the citronella infusion as usual, and the bowl was in its usual place on the porch next to the kitchen. Jamshid slipped into the kitchen and brought out a half-cup of sugar, which he added to the bowl. He told me what he had done and instructed me to stir the mixture off and on during the afternoon when no one was looking. He told me to be sure not to use it on my skin that night.

The servants laid out pallets on the south wing porch for the guests and set up our beds in the courtyard in the usual manner that evening. Everyone, except for Jamshid and me, doused themselves with the citronella water and retired. The next morning, the faces of the visitors as well as those of my brothers and sisters (except for Jamshid) were covered with red bumps. One of Little Aunt's boys complained to Jamshid about the large number of mosquitoes that we had that year. Jamshid innocently replied that he had not noticed any problem and suggested that perhaps the guests had brought the insects with them. No one noticed that only Jamshid and I were free of bites; I had slept all night with a sheet pulled over my head!

Sometimes Jamshid's curiosity and scheming backfired and he became his own victim. The story of the crows is a good example. Our neighbor Mr. Kasraie, whose property was adjacent to ours on the north side, cultivated a number of English walnut trees in his orchard. Some of these were planted next to the wall dividing our properties and the branches overhung onto our side. Jamshid and I used to pick all the walnuts we could reach as they ripened. There were numerous crows in our neighborhood and they also liked to eat walnuts. They would pluck a ripe walnut from one of Mr. Kasraie's trees and fly to the edge of the roof of our house. Perching there above the courtyard, they would drop the whole walnut onto the brick courtyard and then swoop down to pick up one of the halves of the cracked nut. They would then fly back to the roof and peck out the meat. Jamshid and I used to watch for the birds and when we saw one alight on the roof with a walnut in his beak, we would wait until he dropped it and then rub and grab the nut before the crow could retrieve it. Needless to say, the crows did not appreciate our behavior and, after a while, they began to recognize us and whenever they saw us would set up a clamor. This was only a minor annoyance compared to what happened next.

Near the pool in the center of our courtyard there was a tall pine tree. Close to the top of this tree, a pair of crows had built their nest. Jamshid decided that he wanted to find out how many eggs or fledglings were in the nest. Knowing that the crows would recognize him, he persuaded one of the neighborhood boys to climb up the tree and investigate the nest one summer afternoon. The boy climbed up the tree but when he was about halfway up, the crows started to screech and flutter around him. He came down but Jamshid persisted. He brought a copper bowl from the kitchen and put it on his friend's head, securing it by a scarf under his chin. He sent him back up the tree telling him that he should not be a sissy and not to worry about being hurt by the birds. Jamshid stood at the base of the tree with a long stick that he waved in the air to shoo off the crows. The boy again went up the tree, but by this time a dozen or so birds had congregated. As the boy progressed up the tree, they sounded the alarm; within a few minutes, hundreds of crows had gathered. By the time he approached the nest, there must have been over a thousand birds wheeling and swooping around the tree and their cawing could be heard for blocks away.

The crows were so numerous that the sunlight was obscured in our house. My grandmother, who had been cowering in the house, came to the door. She shouted to Jamshid to come in and leave the birds alone. The hapless friend managed to scramble down from the tree and, with Jamshid, beat a hasty retreat to the house. My sister, who was walking home from a visit to a friend's house, said that she could see the black cloud of birds from a half-mile away and wondered what was going on. By this time, the whole household was all cringing in the house looking

159

through closed windows at the frenzied birds. Finally, the crows began to disperse; but for some time a large number remained perched on the roof and in the trees, watching and guarding against any further threat. When in later years I saw the Alfred Hitchcock movie *The Birds*, I was instantly reminded of that day. By the way, the boys never did get close enough to the nest to see if there were eggs or chicks inside.

From that day on and for several months, Jamshid and I had to carry a stick attached to a length of cord with us whenever we went out of the house. We would whirl the stick in a circle over our heads whenever we saw a crow in order to keep them from pecking at our heads. Grandmother was the most frightened member of the family that day. She stayed behind the closed door of her bedroom and prayed and prayed for the crows to go and leave us in peace. The next morning, she confided to my older sisters that she had to get out of the house and told them that she was going to spend a quiet day with her daughter. She cautioned them not to tell Jamshid where she was going and slipped out of the house through the gate in the *beerooney* court-yard. She walked to her daughter's house and, when she got there a half hour later, found the family and servants gathered in the courtyard at the foot of a tall mulberry tree staring up into its branches. When she asked the reason for the excitement, they told her that Jamshid had climbed to the top of the tree and now he couldn't get down.

Grandmother asked, "Which Jamshid?" When they told her that it was her grandson who had arrived fifteen minutes earlier, she announced, "If he is here, I am not staying." With that, she turned around and walked back home hoping that Jamshid would remain in the tree for the rest of the day.

There was no television when I was a child, and home entertainment was limited to the few children's programs on radio, reading, and listening to records played on our hand-wound RCA gramophone with the picture of a dog listening to his master's voice. However, several times during the summer months, Jamshid and I were given a special treat. One of our adult brothers or sisters would take us to the cinema. Grandmother never went with us because she welcomed the peace and quiet around the house for the few hours that Jamshid and I were gone. The first film that I ever saw was *Bambi*, and I remember how I cried in sympathy for that innocent little fawn when his mother was shot by the hunter and how terrified I was when the forest fire threatened to destroy all of the forest animals.

There were several movie theaters on Arg Avenue within walking distance of our house. I remember one in particular that was in a courtyard next to a one-story building. The courtyard was filled with rows of wooden benches and on the south side, sheltered from the light of the moon, there was a narrow stage with a screen. This outdoor theater was used in the summertime; and when the wind was in the right direction and we were in our beds in the courtyard, we could sometimes hear music from the film faintly in the distance over the noise of the crickets and croaking of the frogs. Matinee showings, of course, were given indoors in the adjacent building.

Another summertime entertainment were the street shows given by the itinerant *Shahr-e-Farang* man. *Shahr-Farang* means "Western city." This man would walk up and down the streets of the city shouting for the children to come out and, for a *shahi* (penny), view his show. His theater was a rectangular black box that he carried slung over his shoulder or wheeled along on wheels attached to one end like a wheelbarrow. The box had three or four round portholes about five inches in diameter spaced along one side. These were covered with glass and backed by a magnifying lens. The children would squat with their faces pressed against the glass and watch as the *Shahr-e-Farang* man turned a crank that wound a scroll-like tapestry covered with scenes from European cities opposite the viewing ports. All the while the man would give a running commentary describing what they were seeing.

When the scroll had completely wound in one direction, he would announce that time was up and another group would pay their penny to him and the show would start again in the opposite direction. The *Shahr-e-Farang* man did not come to our neighborhood because the houses were few and far apart. He strolled the downtown streets where there were many more potential customers. One day when our family was visiting one of our relatives who lived downtown, we heard the *Shahr-e-Farang* man calling outside. All the children immediately became

161

excited and pleaded to see the show. One of the adults called him into the house. He set his box in one corner and all of the younger children were given pennies to see the show. This was how Jamshid and I were able to experience the cinema of the masses for the first time.

The fertile imagination of Jamshid was inspired by the *Shahr-e-Farang* man's apparatus. He saw the possibility of having some fun and at the same time making some money. Grandfather had given Jamshid a magnifying glass some time before, and he used to entertain himself by reflecting thirty-five millimeter slides through the magnifying glass onto a piece of white paper. He would also amaze Gholam and Mashaallah by using the magnifying glass to focus the sunlight and apparently make paper ignite spontaneously. At that time, it was possible to buy strips of thirty-five millimeter film two or three feet long that were fragments from old movies made by Laurel and Hardy or Charles Chaplin, as well as color strips containing animal pictures. Jamshid decided to make his own theater at home.

Next to the servants' quarters there was a room that was used to store things, chiefly the wooden beds we used outdoors in the summer and a few old chairs. The room was about twelve-by-twelve feet and had a single window on the west side next to a solid wooden door. Jamshid and I set about cleaning out the room, and for one week we scrubbed and whitewashed the walls. We also whitewashed the window except for one central pane that Jamshid removed. He covered the empty space with a piece of cardboard with a hole about two centimeters in diameter in the center. On the wall opposite the window, we hung a white bedsheet for a screen and arranged the few old chairs to the rear and empty wooden boxes for seats nearer the screen.

Jamshid constructed his projection equipment from a cardboard shoe box. He made small round holes in the center of each end of the box and mounted his magnifying glass in front of the rear hole. Between the glass and the rear hole, he was able to pull strips of film up and down through slits cut in the top and bottom of the box. This projection apparatus was set on a table with the rear hole next to the hole in the cardboard covering the window. My job was most important for I was (indirectly) the light source. As I mentioned above, the window was on the west side of the room. I was stationed outside sitting on the grass; holding a large mirror that caught the rays of the sun as it rose in the east, I reflected the sunlight through the hole in the cardboard that replaced the windowpane. The light passed through the hole in the back of the shoe box, then through the film and magnifying glass, and the image was projected through the front hole in the box to the bedsheet screen on the wall. Needless to say, our performances were limited to about two morning hours, only on fair days, before the sun reached the zenith.

The grand opening of our cinema was held on a Friday. We did one show for Grandmother, Grandfather, Father, and the rest of the family followed by a second performance for the servants. The next day we had our public opening for the neighborhood children who had been advised of our project by word-of-mouth advertising. We were an instant success. Jamshid and I had invested all of the savings that we had accumulated in our piggy banks for film strips. In order to recoup our investment and turn a profit, we charged the equivalent of about four pennies for the loge (the chairs in the back row) and two pennies for the wooden box seats in the orchestra. After a few days, it occurred to Jamshid that we could make an additional profit by hawking refreshments before each performance. We bought raisins and chickpeas that we packaged mixed in paper cones and sold for three pennies each.

The actual show lasted only about thirty minutes. Jamshid had spliced together enough film strips to last that long, but this might vary according to how fast he pulled the film through. Like the *Shahr-e-Farang* man, Jamshid provided a running narrative whenever appropriate. Occasional comic relief was also provided because sometimes Jamshid inadvertently spliced a section of film in upside down. This part was always greeted with laughter. Some of the children would spend thirty minutes or more getting to our house to see the show, so we had one inflexible rule: Everyone had to visit the bathroom before the performance began. We could not open the door to allow the children out one by one as necessary during the show, and we wanted to avoid any embarrassing accidents.

Our venture into show business lasted about three weeks before we became bored with the project. We could have stayed in business all summer and even raised the price of admission, because all of the parents were happy to get their offspring out from underfoot for a couple of hours. They would have gladly given their children the price of admission in return for knowing that they would be safe and entertained away from home for a little while. Some of our customers came every day that we had a show, even though the program did not change very often. Grandmother and Gholam were especially unhappy when we decided to go out of business, because now Jamshid and I would have more time for devilment.

Although Jamshid was the most ingenious and the chief offender when it came to practical jokes and pranks, he was not the only one in the family to do so. Mashaallah was the victim of a practical joke instigated by two of my older brothers. Mashaallah was a gullible young man, and his imagination was fed by the stories told in the kitchen gatherings of the servants, especially the stories of ghosts and *jinn* told by Gholam and others. Gholam often reported seeing ghosts in the garden during the night when he awakened from sleep and looked out his bedroom window. Mashaallah wanted to sleep outdoors during the summer in the cool fresh air but for years he did not do so, probably because deep down he believed Gholam's stories.

As Mashaallah got older, he gradually became braver. One year he announced that he would henceforth sleep outside in the yard in front of the servants' quarters. He moved his wooden bed out into the yard one afternoon and carefully oriented it so that the head and foot were north and south. He did this because he had once overheard Grandfather Khan say that one should always sleep with the head to the north so that one would be in harmony with the earth's electromagnetic field and therefore sleep well. That night Mashaallah fell asleep under the stars, breathing the fresh night air. Mashaallah was a very sound sleeper. His mother used to say that, once asleep, he would not wake up even if a cannon were discharged next to his ear.

Two of my brothers decided to play a joke on the poor boy. They waited until they were sure that Mashaallah was sound asleep, then slipped quietly through the orchard to the servants' quarters. They picked up Mashaallah's bed and carried their snoring victim several yards away and put his bed down after turning it to the east-west direction. The next day Mashaallah did not say anything, but we noticed that all day long he was very quiet and apparently lost in thought. That evening, he moved his bed back to the original spot. Again that night, my brothers picked up his bed and moved him to the same place they had placed him the previous night. The next day Mashaallah was even more puzzled, but still did not say anything to anybody for fear of ridicule. My brothers also kept their secret to themselves, so no one else in the family knew what was going on.

The third night, Mashaallah decided that he would not move his bed back but would sleep where he had awakened that morning. That night, my brothers picked him up and put him back in his original spot. Poor Mashaallah had had enough. He moved back indoors and slept there.

Grandmother noticed that Mashaallah was no longer sleeping outdoors so she asked him, "What happened, Mashaallah, that you are sleeping inside? Did you catch cold or is it that you don't like fresh air?"

Mashaallah did not say anything about his strange nocturnal transporting but merely replied, "I decided that I prefer to sleep inside behind a locked door with the window open."

Later on, my brothers told the rest of the family about what they had done to Mashaallah, but we never told the story to the victim so as to spare him any embarrassment.

The same two brothers were involved in another more subtle joke that victimized two unrelated persons. Mrs. Farkhondeh was a widow of about fifty-five years of age whose husband had died early in their marriage, leaving her well off financially. Later on, her only son also died and she lived alone except for her servants. She was a rather plump short woman, well dressed and sociable. She occupied her days by visiting all around the city, and she knew everybody who was anybody in town. She could recite the genealogy of all the prominent families and played the role of matchmaker in many marriages. She was also an inveterate gossip, and people said that news traveled faster by her than over the radio. However, she was a pleasant person and she was welcomed in almost every home, especially the households where there were marriageable daughters and sons. She prided herself on being the first person to know any social news in town, and this was the weakness that my brothers exploited in their prank.

One day, they came home and smelled the distinctive strong perfume that Mrs. Farkhondeh wore and knew that she was visiting. They came into the room where she and Grandmother were sitting deep in conversation. The boys greeted her and took seats in a distant corner of the room where they began their own conversation. They talked in a low voice but loud enough to be barely heard across the room.

One brother said to the other, "Have you heard that Abolfazl is getting married? I heard this when I was in the barber shop this morning."

The other replied, "Yes, I heard the same news; everyone in town is talking about it."

While they were talking, there was a sudden break in Mrs. Farkhondeh's stream of chatter. She called over to the boys saying, "Did you say that Abolfazl is getting married? I wonder why I didn't hear about it. Who is the lucky girl?"

"We don't know," answered the boys, "but surely it will come out soon."

Mrs. Farkhondeh mumbled an excuse about a previous engagement and hurriedly terminated her visit. Abolfazl was one of the most eligible bachelors in the city; he was a rich, handsome *bon vivant* and the object of many a girl's fantasies. Nothing more was said after Mrs. Farkhondeh left; but that night when Grandfather came home from his shop, he remarked to Grandmother, "Have you heard the news? Abolfazl is getting married!"

The next day the news was all over town, and poor Abolfazl was besieged all day long with telephone calls congratulating him on his pending nuptials. So it was not only Mrs. Farkhondeh who was victimized but also Abolfazl, who had to spend considerable time denying the news. My brothers enjoyed their joke in private for a long while before, months later, they shared it with the rest of the family. Mrs. Farkhondeh's reputation was not in the least diminished by the incident, and she continued to play her valuable role as matchmaker for many years.

Later on, after we moved to Tehran, these same two brothers were involved in another escapade. Our next-door neighbor had only one child, a girl whom they spoiled outrageously. At the time of this story, she was about sixteen years with a fair complexion but rather short and fat. She owned a lovely pure white Persian cat, which she loved very much. The cat was very friendly and, as cats do, roamed the neighborhood. Whenever the cat came into our yard, we would pet her and feed her and generally fuss over her.

One summer day, my brothers decided to have some fun. When the cat came to our house on her daily visit, one of them fed her a treat and stroked her ears and head. At the same time, the other brother took a cotton ball soaked in Mercurochrome and painted the cat all over from the back of the head to her tail. They released the cat, which returned home.

Soon they heard anguished screams from the other side of the wall between our house and the neighbors. "Mama! Mama! Look what someone has done to my cat! When I find out who did this, I'll kill him!" The mother and daughter proceeded to try to wash the cat clean, but only succeeded in turning the bright red to a bright pink. It was several weeks before the cat regained its pristine white coat. For several days, the girl checked all the hands of the boys in the neighborhood to try to find telltale traces of Mercurochrome. My brothers walked around with their hands in their pockets whenever they went out and were never found out.

My brothers, sisters, and I all had our individual pets. We had dogs, cats, and birds; one older brother even managed to tame a deer brought as a fawn from one of the mountain villages. It followed him around whenever he walked outdoors. One of my sisters wanted a peacock, so one was bought for her; and it strutted around the garden displaying its beautiful fan. It was also a nuisance in that its screeching would awaken the household at the break of day. About the same time, someone else decided she wanted a turkey for a pet and we acquired a pair of them. The peacock and the turkeys did not get along; the turkeys beat up on the peacock so much that it was finally given away to save its life.

The turkeys had free run of the gardens and orchard, and were a constant source of irritation to Gholam, the gardener, because they would get in his flowerbeds and scratch up the young plants. Gholam complained but no one paid any attention to him. He used to go around with a long stick in his hand, and whenever he saw the turkeys in the flowerbeds, he would run at them shouting and striking at them with the stick. The turkeys would beat a reluctant retreat, all the while gobbling furiously at him. It got to the point where the mere sight of Gholam would set the turkeys to gobbling.

One afternoon, Gholam was squatting at the edge of the pool in the courtyard with his head in his hands, resting from his labors and daydreaming. The turkeys walked quietly up behind him unnoticed and suddenly emitted a loud deep gobble-gobble. Poor Gholam started, lost his balance, and fell headfirst into the pool. This was the last straw as far as Gholam was concerned. He pulled himself out of the pool and, dripping water with each step, went to find Grandmother. When he found her in her kitchen, he said to her, "Those turkeys and I cannot stay here together. Either they go or I leave!" Needless to say, the turkeys were given away the next day and Gholam stayed on in peace.

Grandfather and Father were very dignified gentlemen but they were not without a sense of humor. One time they had a little fun with Grandmother, the by-product of which was some pleasure for them and other men of the family. Grandmother, every summer, made wine vinegar for use in cooking, pickling, etc. We had a copious supply of white grapes from our arbors that were ideal for preparing vinegar, as well as other varieties of grapes for eating. A narrow dirt-floored room led off the pantry next to Grandmother's kitchen, and partially embedded in the dirt, there were five enormous wide mouthed ceramic jars. These Grandmother used to ferment the grapes for her vinegar. She was very exciting about using the correct amount of yeast and careful to allow the grapes to ferment undisturbed for the proper length of time to ensure the production of vinegar rather than wine.

One year, when Grandmother opened the jars to decant the vinegar, she found that one of the jars contained wine rather than vinegar. She was puzzled and upset because she prided herself on her vinegar making and this had never happened before. The mystery was soon solved, however, when she noticed that the men of the family, who came for lunch along with their families every weekend, seemed unusually jovial and lively. Somehow,

168

Grandfather and Father had managed to decant several gallons of wine at the right time, and they enjoyed a glass or two with the other male members of the family before lunch. They had apparently added an equal amount of grape juice to the jars in the hope that their thievery would go undetected. From that day forth, Grandmother kept the door to her fermenting room locked and no one but her had a key.

When the summer holiday was over, the energy that we had spent on pranks and mischievous behavior was rechanneled to concentration on our schoolwork. Father was the role model for the entire family, and his love of literature and knowledge was emulated by all his children. Jamshid was always well behaved in school, and his grades were usually the highest in his class. When, as a young man in his early twenties, he left the country to continue his education abroad, he already had two college degrees, one in meteorology and the other in French. He knew French and English well enough to be able to enter a university in any French- or English-speaking country. He decided to go to the United States and, predictably, soon earned a degree in civil engineering.

Jamshid decided to make his permanent residence in the United States. He met and married a lovely girl from Switzerland, took a position with a state government, and raised a family. Years later, when I came to the U.S. to visit him, we sat in his garden in the shade of poplar trees admiring his forty-eight varieties of roses. His garden reminded us of the rose garden near the gazebo that we both had known as children in Mashhad, and as we sat there silently, we both knew that the other was thinking and remembering the happy days we had enjoyed years before. Jamshid was no longer the mischievous boy with whom I had grown up but was now a mature man with a quiet and gentle nature. While we were sitting there, his two young children came running out of the house. The boy was teasing his younger sister and she was screaming in protest.

Jamshid sighed and said, "I don't know why that boy is always teasing and getting in trouble."

I laughed and replied, "You have no right to complain. Don't you remember how you tormented me and the rest of the family, as well as the servants and neighbors when you were a boy?"

Notes

1. Shandeez acquired some distinction in 1930 when a particularly fine vein of marble was discovered near the village. This marble is light lemon in color. One slab of this marble was used to cover the tomb of Emam Reza. The slab was 2.1 meters long, 1.06 meters wide, and 4 centimeters thick. The marble is so fine that the 4-centimeter-thick slab is translucent.

2. This wooden pipe is commonly used by the peasantry in modern times but, in the old days, it was used by all levels of society. Sir John Chardin, in his seventeenth-century travel book about Persia, tells an amusing story about how Shah Abbas the Great, a nonsmoker, tried to discourage the then excessive and almost universal use of tobacco. Abbas ordered the jars of tobacco that were served at one of his state dinners to be filled with dry, shredded horse manure. After the assembled grandees had fired up their pipes, Abbas announced that the tobacco had been a gift to him from his vizier of Hamadan who maintained that it was the most excellent tobacco in the world. He then asked his guests their opinion of the weed, and they all swore that it was the most exquisite tobacco that they had ever smoked. Abbas then turned and, looking on them all with indignation, (sic) "Cursed be that drug that cannot be discerned from the dung of horses."

Chapter Thirteen
Wartime Recollections

A country to ascend to the sun must first seek peace and purity;
To do otherwise is to turn the harvest of human lives to smoke.
—Raady Azarakhshy

I was still a child living in Mashhad when World War II came to Persia. However, my memories of those days are still quite vivid, and to this day, I still do not like to watch war movies with their sounds of low-flying aircraft and bursting bombs. Only those who have lived through an air raid can appreciate the terror of anticipation one feels when an attacking plane roars overhead followed by a nearby explosion. My older sisters and brothers, with the exception of Jamshid, were all young men and women at that time, and they have told me many stories of how the Persian people reacted to the news of the outbreak of war in Europe. There was one universal reaction that reflected the mind-set of a people who had been subject to centuries of alternating conquest and liberation, expressed by the age-old question, "Who will it be this time?"

To understand this thinking, one must remember that Persia has been invaded, fought over, and occupied by various nations many times since the breakup of the ancient Persian Empire founded by Cyrus the Great and his son Darius from 550 to 530 B.C. Due to its geographical situation between the riches of India and China on the east and the Western cultures of Greece and Rome, Persia was overrun by various conquerors from both directions who were seeking world domination. The first significant invasion of Persia occurred about 330 B.C. when

171

the Greeks under Alexander the Great invaded and conquered all of Persia. Later, Persia barely managed to forestall incorporation into the Roman Empire by defeating the invading Roman armies in 260 B.C.

The Arabs invaded from the west in A.D. 641 and forced the Islamic religion on a people who had been followers of Zoroaster for several hundred years, long before Darius made Zoroastrianism the official religion of Persia. The country was again overrun in 1221 by the Mongols under Genghis Khan, followed later by another invasion in 1369 led by the Mongol Turk, Tamerlane. Shah Abbas the Great successfully turned back attacks by the Uzbek tribes from Turkestan on the northeast and the Ottoman Turks from Turkey on the west who tried to invade in the 1500s. The Afghans were the next to invade and conquer in the early 1700s but were driven out after a short time by Nadir Shah Afshar in 1736, who not only removed the Afghans but went on to conquer Afghanistan and northern India. He withdrew from India and restored the local sultans to power but, by way of reparation for the attack on Persia, he obtained the famous peacock throne and the Koh-i-noor diamond.

After Nadir Shah's death, civil war broke out between two rival Persian dynasties, the Qajars and the Zandieh. The Qajar dynasty finally prevailed and ruled for about 130 years until the 1920s, but the country was so weakened that the British and the Russians virtually controlled the government throughout most of the nineteenth century. Persia was a neutral country during World War I, but this did not save it from becoming a battlefield again. The Russians fought the Turks in northwestern Persia in order to defend the Baku oil fields near the Caspian Sea. The British fought rebel Qashqai tribes led by German agents in the south in defense of the oil fields in Khuzistan.

In 1923, the neighboring country of Turkey became a republic and the National Assembly elected Mustafa Kemel as the first president, with the title of Ataturk. Under the direction of the Ataturk, Turkey became the first Moslem country to separate the church from the state, emulating the examples of Western nations that had gone through a similar process.

At the same time (1923) an army officer named Reza, who had become war minister as a result of a military coup in

1921, became prime minister of Persia. Reza admired the work of the Ataturk in his efforts to modernize Turkey, and the Ataturk in turn respected Reza as a fellow progressive Moslem. Reza wanted Persia to become a republic similar to Turkey, with an elected president. However, the mullahs who were the majority in the *Majles* (Persian parliament) feared that the country would become fragmented without a strong royal figure in control. More to the point, however, the mullahs feared that if the country became a republic with an elected president they would lose the power that they had enjoyed for so many years under the previous dynasties, just as the clergy in Turkey lost their influence after the Ataturk became president. As a result, the *Majles* urged Reza to become the shah of Persia. This convoluted reasoning came to naught, however, because under the Reza Shah the political power of the mullahs was eventually virtually nullified. In 1925 Reza became the shah of Persia and the founder of the Pahlavi dynasty that ruled until the takeover by the Islamic fundamentalists led by Khomeini in 1979. It is interesting to note that as soon as the mullahs regained their power in 1979, they called for a republic rather than a monarchy, secure in the knowledge that they could control the vote.

The succession of conquests and the intermittent intramural tribal wars over the years had so conditioned the thinking of the people that one can understand the concern and apprehension that griped the country when war broke out in Europe in 1939 and appreciate the reason for the universal question, "Who will it be this time?" The adults spent many hours with their ears glued to the radio listening to the news from the BBC and the Russian radio station in Baku, relayed through the radio station in Tehran. My only recollection of these broadcasts is that of a deep bass voice speaking in very formal manner and every other word seemed to be Hitler or war. During the phony war period in 1939, in the calm before the storm, families began to hoard foodstuffs in anticipation of future shortages. I remember seeing bag after bag of flour, beans, and rice being delivered to our house and stored in a huge wooden chest located in the well room. Large five-gallon tins of cooking oil filled all available space in the pantries. Even candles and lamp chimneys became scarce as people hoarded them for use in the event of power outages.

Persia again tried to remain neutral during World War II, but as so many times in the past, its geographical location and oil resources worked against it. The Allies needed her oil, and the railroad between the Persian Gulf in the south to the Russian border in the north became a vital link in the chain of supply of war materiel from the U.S. and Britain to Russia. Russia and Britain asked the Reza Shah for permission to transport supplies through the country, but he refused to abandon his declared neutrality. This was not sufficient guarantee to Churchill and Stalin that the southern supply route to Russia would remain open.

The end result, late in August 1941, was invasion by Russian troops from the north and British troops from the south. There was virtually no resistance by the Persian army, and in the Persian Gulf, the minuscule Persian navy was destroyed by the British. In September, the Reza Shah was forced to abdicate and was exiled to Johannesburg where he died in 1944. His son, Mohammed Reza Shah, was installed as king. The new shah signed an agreement allowing the Russians and British troops to remain in the country until the end of hostilities. In 1942, United States troops came to Persia to aid the British in the transport of supplies to Russia. The U.S. troops were based in Tehran and occupied the central portion of the country. Persia finally declared war on Germany in 1943 and on Japan in 1945, but never actually engaged in combat. Probably the most significant direct contribution made by Persia to the Allied cause was to provide the site for the Tehran conference between Roosevelt, Churchill, and Stalin held late in November of 1943. In 1945, Persia became a member of the United Nations.

After the war was over, the United States and Great Britain withdrew all of their troops from Persia; but the Russians remained and continued to occupy Persian Azerbaijan in the hope of exploiting the oil fields in that area. In 1946, Ahmad Qavam, the prime minister at that time, signed, ostensibly in good faith, an agreement with the Russians allowing them to develop the oil fields in the north. However, he cleverly left a loophole in that this agreement was conditional upon the approval of the Persian parliament. The Russians withdrew in 1946 under pressure of a United Nations mandate. They left behind a number of communist cells that eventually evolved into the Tudeh, the communist party of Persia. In 1947, the Persian parliament refused to ratify the agreement made by Qavam and the agreement never went into effect.

Our family innocently and unknowingly gave aid to a future member of the Tudeh during the Russian occupation. It was at the time when my uncle was a young bachelor serving his internship and residency in the Shahreza Hospital and living with us. An orphanage had just been opened next to the hospital, and the government hired a Russian lady named Shermany to run it. My uncle was asked to help the woman and her family get settled. He asked my father to allow the family to stay in the south wing of our house temporarily until they could find other accommodations. Madame Shermany was a widow with four children, two boys and two girls. The oldest was a girl of eighteen, and the oldest boy was seventeen when they came to stay with us.

Over the course of the next several weeks, both the mother and the eighteen-year-old daughter fell in love with my uncle. Madame Shermany was, of course, much older than my uncle and her affection for him was not returned. However, he did fool around a bit with the daughter; one of my sisters came upon them one day lying in bed (fully clothed) and kissing. The mother became so frustrated by her unrequited passion that she once tried to commit suicide by eating an overdose of opium. She came home blue in the face and gasping, and had to be rushed to the hospital to have the drug pumped out of her stomach. Nothing came of the affair my uncle had with the daughter; and after two years, he moved to Torbat to open his practice.

Madame Shermany and her family stayed in our house for a few months, then they moved to another house in Mashhad, and finally, to Tehran. While in Tehran, Madame Shermany along with three of her children became overtly involved with the communist party. Servat, the oldest boy, went to Russia for training and then returned to Tehran. He became one of the national leaders of the Tudeh and was later imprisoned by the Mohammed Reza Shah during his crackdown on communism after the war. I have only a dim memory of Servat, but my sisters have told me that he was a most unpleasant and cruel boy while he was living in our house in Mashhad. He once locked one of my sisters in a small pantry where she was imprisoned for several hours before one of the family heard her cries for help. He was also fond of torturing animals and bullied the smaller children. The oldest daughter, Zola, never embraced the communist doctrine. She met an American physician serving in the occupation forces in Tehran; and after he was sent back to the U.S. following the war, he sent her a one-way ticket to join him, and they were married.

One joyful occasion befell our family during those days before the Russian invasion in 1941: My oldest brother, Kaveh, returned from England. He had completed his studies and came home safely with his doctorate degree in hand. Kaveh visited the family briefly, then left Mashhad to report in Tehran for his compulsory military service. He trained for six months in officer candidate school in Tehran and was then assigned to the military barracks in Mashhad in an administrative capacity. He lived at home during this time and walked to work every day. I remember how handsome he looked in his officer's uniform and how proud Father and my grandparents were of him. They were so happy that he had come home safely, but there was always an undercurrent of concern because of the war.

No one knew how long the proclaimed neutrality would last and it was obvious to all that the country would not be able to ward off any attack. The sense of impending doom, which had been felt by everyone since 1939, grew more and more as the war continued into its third year. Family and friends flocked to our house to see Kaveh, who had been away for so many years, and to congratulate my father and the rest of the family on his success; but, somehow, the congratulations seemed perfunctory because almost immediately conversation gravitated to talk about the war. The latest news was discussed at length and the latest rumors repeated.

My brother's service in Mashhad was brief. He had been home only about one week when the news of the ultimatum issued by Russia and Great Britain was broadcast over the radio. Within a few hours, the city streets were deserted and the stores closed as the people retreated to their homes in anticipation of attack. Blackout regulations were broadcast and antiaircraft artillery batteries were set up in the streets around the army garrison in Mashhad. Our family retreated to the north wing of the house, where we all slept in two rooms with the windows covered with blankets at night.

The Russian army was no stranger to the people of Persia. Following the invasion and annexation of Georgia by Russia in 1800, the Persians under Fath Ali Shah, the first king of the Qajar dynasty, went to war with Russia in 1804. This culminated in the treaty of Gulistan in 1813, by which Persia was forced to give up all rights to Georgia and the right to maintain a naval presence in the Caspian Sea. In 1825, Russia invaded and conquered Persia. This occupation ended following the treaty of Turkmanchai in 1828 that established the boundary between the two countries at the Arak River. All of the land north of the river (present-day Russian Azerbaijan) was lost and never regained. In 1912, tsarist Russia invaded northern Iran and occupied Mashhad. During the fighting, some of the people took refuge in the Imam Reza Shrine in the belief that the invaders would not dare to attack such a sacred place. However, this was not the case and much damage was done by Russian cannonade. The golden dome was partly destroyed and some civilians were killed. This blasphemy created much distress. When, later on in 1917, the tsar was overthrown and executed, some people insisted that this was divine retribution for his desecration of the shrine. The courtyard walls of the Imam Reza Shrine still bear the marks made by the Russian shells.

So it was no great surprise to the people of Mashhad when, on September 7, 1941, eight Russian bombers came over in the morning and attacked the airport and several military supply depots. The next day, another flight of thirty-three planes again struck the airport and the military barracks. The residential areas were not attacked, but at our house the noise was so deafening and terrifying that we all clung together in one room. I remember how I was shaking and crying, as were my sisters. I covered my ears with both hands and pressed against my oldest sister. One particular explosion was so great that we felt the walls of the house shake. We later found out that one of the bombs had struck the fuel depot at the airport, setting off a tremendous blast. After the second attack, the family, except for one brother, moved to my aunt's house, which was farther away from the airport and the military bases.

Father and Grandfather stayed only one night at my aunt's house and then left to rejoin my brother at home. The rest of us stayed there for five days. There was no further bombing, but the skies were still filled with low-flying aircraft that continued to terrorize the people. Finally, on September 9, Russian tanks and trucks full of soldiers entered Mashhad and martial law was proclaimed by their commander, General Shapken. He ordered all the shops and businesses, except for the bakeries, closed. The citizens were ordered to turn in all arms. We had a rifle and two revolvers in our house and rather than give them to the Russians, my father dropped them down our well. They were never retrieved. Our family, as did many other people in town, took another precautionary measure. All of the silverware, sterling hollowware, and valuable jewelry were put together in a large bag that in turn was wrapped in many layers of burlap. This large bundle was buried in the center of one of the flower gardens, and flowers replanted over the freshly turned earth. When it became apparent after a few weeks of Russian occupation that there would be no looting or confiscation of private property, the treasure was dug up and put back to use.

The Russians commandeered the large Bakhtar Hotel on Arg Avenue for their headquarters. Soon after their arrival, the Russians began to round up all of the Persian army officers from the army garrison and any officer they saw in uniform in the city. Enlisted personnel were disarmed but otherwise ignored. The Russians brought the captured officers to the Bakhtar Hotel where they were kept under guard overnight and the next day sent to the city of Ashkhabad, the capital of Turkmenistan in southern Russia, as prisoners of war. Despite the martial law restrictions, families of the captured men gathered in the street in front of the hotel hoping for a last glimpse of a loved one. Mothers and sweethearts sat for hours on the sidewalk in tears, pleading for the release of sons and brothers, but to no avail. Less than half of these unfortunate men returned to their homes after the war. No one knows what happened to the others, but they presumably died of starvation, disease, or execution. Of those who did return, many had been brainwashed and embraced the communist doctrine. These became active in the Tudeh.

My brother Kaveh was captured at his post in the military barracks. While he was being marched with twenty or so of his fellow officers to the Bakhtar Hotel, a close friend of my father accompanied him. He fell into step alongside my brother and whispered to him that he was going to take him to his house and hide him. Kaveh was frightened and, at first, refused to go for fear of being shot. Our friend, however, was not to be deterred. As the loosely guarded group marched down a busy section of Arg Avenue, he suddenly grabbed my brother's arm and pulled him down one of the intersecting narrow streets that was near his home. They ran to our friend's house where Kaveh was outfitted with civilian clothes and kept hidden for two days. A messenger was sent to my father to tell him that his son was safe and would soon be home.

We children never greeted our parents with a kiss on the face. Proper manners called for the son or daughter to first kiss the hand of the parent, who responded with a brief hug or pat on the back to the boys and a kiss on the forehead and a hug to the girls. This custom, a way of showing filial respect, was always observed no matter what the age. My father always greeted his mother in this fashion whenever he returned from an absence and on occasions such as Now Ruz. There is an old Persian saying, "Heaven is beneath the mother's foot," meaning that if you respect your mother and keep her happy, you will go to heaven. My father had always treated his sons in this somewhat formal although kindly manner; but when my brother finally returned home after his narrow escape from captivity, Father clasped him to his breast, hugging and kissing him in relief. It was then that we all realized how worried and grief-stricken my father had been when he learned of my brother's capture.

After four days, the martial law was partially lifted and the stores and other businesses were allowed to reopen. Within a week or ten days, life in Mashhad returned to a semblance of normalcy. Russian troops still filled the streets, but they were very punctilious in their behavior to the civilian populace. There was no looting or brutality, and the soldiers were polite and respectful to the women. Grandfather Khan told us that his store was frequently visited by Russian soldiers who would admire the watches on display. They would stare longingly at the timepieces, but always left empty-handed since they had no money to buy and they were under strict orders not to plunder.

It was obvious that the long-term plan of the Russians was to try to win over the Persian people in the hope that they might gain a foothold and eventually take over all or part of the country after the war. They began publication of a newspaper called *Afkar Khalgh* (Thoughts of the People) that propagated communist doctrine. They started free night classes for adults to encourage them to learn the Russian language and toured the streets with projectors and screens that they used to show Russian propaganda movies. Not far from our house, there was a small unpaved square bounded on four sides by streets. This was called Bicycle Square because one of the streets had a number of shops devoted to the sale and repair of bicycles and the customers used to try out the bicycles in the square. One afternoon, we heard a radio announcement that a movie would be shown in Bicycle Square that evening. All of the servants decided to go see the movie and Jamshid and I tagged along.

When we got to the square, we saw a huge screen set up on one side with a military truck bearing a projector positioned in front of it. The square was jammed with people, all standing. The film was devoted to showing how advanced the Russians were. Factories equipped with modern machinery operated by men and bareheaded women side by side; schools with mixed male and female students and farms with modern tractors driven by men and women were all shown with a commentary in Russian. The audience, which consisted mainly of working-class people who were traditional Moslems, greeted this commingling of the sexes with murmurs of disapproval. I don't believe that anyone was convinced that there was any merit in such a godless society!

About a month after they had occupied northern Persia, the Russians began to bring in refugees from Eastern European countries who had fled to Russia in advance of the invading Nazi armies. The refugees were men, women, and children of all ages. Of the thousands of refugees, a hundred or so Poles were brought to Mashhad. A leather factory that had been closed down before the invasion due to a shortage of supplies was converted to a barracks to house them. As the war wore on, Persian households gradually adopted many of these Poles since they were not considered to be the enemy. They were treated with the traditional Persian courtesy and generosity afforded guests, and many of them intermarried with Persians and stayed on in the country after the war.

The winter of 1941–42 was one of the coldest on record, with heavy snowfalls that fell and accumulated. People joked that the Russians had brought the weather with them from Siberia. The flat roofs of traditional Persian houses require that snow be shoveled off so that the weight will not damage the roof. This chore gave rise to a Persian proverb that reflects the problems associated with an excess of anything: "The more roof you have, the more snow you must shovel." I remember that the shoveled snow was piled so high in our courtyard that my brothers were able to mound it up over the walkway to the north wing and make a tunnel through it to the door. When a thaw came and the snow melted, the walkway was covered with slush and no one was able to use it. Father became very irate with my brothers and ordered them to clean it up themselves. He told them that since they were the ones who had the fun, they should clean up the mess they had made rather than make Gholam and Mashaallah do it.

The long, cold winter of 1941–42 eventually passed and, once again, the Now Ruz season was upon us. The people did their best to observe the traditional customs despite the shortage of food and the inflation in the cost of clothing and other necessities. The traditional Now Ruz visitations continued although the tables laden with food and sweets for family and guests, which we had enjoyed in the past, were now replaced with more spartan fare. Still, the people maintained a cheerful countenance and exchanged the smiled greetings that have always been a part of the New Year celebration. In the summer, the weekly family gatherings for lunch at our house continued as in the past. After lunch, we children played as usual while the adults conversed, recited poetry, listened to music, or played backgammon, the national Persian pastime.

On the surface, life seemed to go on in the normal way, but

we were constantly reminded of the plight of the country by the sight of Russian troops everywhere in the streets of the city. I remember walking home from school when I was in the first grade and seeing soldiers walking about in pairs or groups of three or four. They would smile and wave at us, and we would respond with the only Russian phrase we knew, *"Evdrazny tovarish"*—"Hello, friend." The Russians were delighted by the apparent friendliness of the schoolchildren, which I am sure that they took as a sign that the Russian propaganda was influencing the younger generation. However, they were wrong. When the Russian army finally left in 1946, the withdrawal was a signal for national rejoicing and celebration. The seeds of communism that they had planted germinated to some extent in the Tudeh, the Persian communist party. This party, however, never became a serious threat and eventually was forced underground when formally abolished by the Mohammed Reza Shah.

As I mentioned above, the behavior of the Russian troops toward the Persian populace as a rule was courteous and respectful. But there were a few exceptions. My second-oldest sister, Tooran, was a teacher at an elementary school. One of her fellow teachers was a young woman who was quite beautiful with long blonde hair and a fair complexion unusual for a Persian woman. One day, this woman was walking back to the school after the lunch break. Two Russian officers on horseback, who appeared to be well into their cups, saw her and followed her as she walked along. They tried to pick her up, telling her in broken Farsi that she must be a Russian girl because of her blonde good looks. The woman walked faster and faster in an effort to escape, but the Russians followed her to the schoolyard gate and into the courtyard of the school.

All of the children were playing in the yard, waiting for the afternoon classes to begin. When the principal saw what was going on, she called the office of the superintendent of schools who in turn called the local police and the Russian headquarters. The police arrived along with the Russian military police, and the officers were arrested and taken away in the Russians' jeep. In the meantime, the frightened children took advantage of the distraction and they all slipped out a hole in the courtyard wall behind the school and made their way home. The Russian officers were never seen again. People who lived near the Russian barracks reported that the next morning they heard a volley of rifle shots, so presumably the two were executed after a speedy trial.

In Mashhad we saw only Russian troops, but in Tehran there were British and American troops in addition to the Russians. They commandeered some of the best residencies for their use; and the influx of money, especially by the Americans, was a boost to the economy. The behavior of the American troops was not as circumspect as that of the Russians. Public drunkenness and harmless rowdyism was a not infrequent sight; but, on the whole, the people were more attracted to the Americans because of their friendly openhanded manner and generosity. This feeling of goodwill toward the United States was further bolstered after the war when Persia received financial aid to help the country recover from the war. The prompt withdrawal of the American forces after hostility ceased was interpreted as a sign that the U.S. respected the sovereignty of the nation and had no ulterior designs with regard to territorial expansion, as did the Russians, and no desire to exploit the country's chief natural resource (oil), as did the British.

The first few years of the 1950s were a period of social and political unrest. Street demonstrations and rioting between various political factions became a common sight in Tehran. The young shah did not have the iron hand for ruling that his father had. The mullahs, who had been repressed under Reza Shah, tried to exploit this weakness in an attempt to regain their former power. A religious party financed by the mullahs sprung up. It periodically took to the streets, fomenting antishah demonstrations. The communist cells, left behind when the Russians finally withdrew from the country, evolved into a militant communist party, the Tudeh. It had an underground printing press, which produced single-sheet broadsides full of communist propaganda that they posted on hoardings all over Tehran. Walls of buildings would be painted during the night with slogans such as "Death to the Shah" or "Long live the Tudeh." Occasionally, one would hear of terrorist bombing of public buildings.

Another party called the National Front led by Mossadegh, a cousin of the last king of the Qajar dynasty, became more and more powerful. Mossadegh was a vociferous proponent of the nationalization of the oil industry and the ejection of the British oil company, which so long had influenced the internal affairs of Persia. In March 1951, General Razmara, the prime minister appointed by the shah, was assassinated by a right-wing religious fanatic. In April 1951, the shah appointed Mossadegh prime minister. Mossadegh promptly persuaded the parliament to pass a bill nationalizing the Anglo-Iranian Oil Company (AIOC) and signed it into law on May 2, 1951. Attempts to negotiate an equitable agreement with the AIOC were unsuccessful due to the insistence by the British on keeping all control and marketing of oil in British hands. Finally, in September, Persian troops were ordered to the Abadan refinery to take over; and the British technicians were expelled from the country in 1952. The British responded with an embargo on all Persian oil, confident that the Persians were incapable of running the production and refining facilities. All oil production ceased in 1953 because of the lack of trained Persian personnel to run the drilling rigs and refineries, resulting in great financial loss to the country that year. The impasse was finally resolved with the help of the United States and the United Nations, and a new agreement was reached in 1954 by which eight international oil companies from the United States, Great Britain, France, and the Netherlands were given the right to produce and market Persian oil with a fair share of the profits paid to the Persian government.

During these years, the young shah was gradually asserting himself as a monarch. He succeeded in disbanding and outlawing the communist party, and the repression of the influence of the mullahs on civil government began by his father was again enforced. The popularity and power of Mossadegh reached its zenith following the nationalization of the oil industry. He aspired to overthrow the shah, who was forced to flee the country briefly in 1953. With the help of the American Central Intelligence Agency (CIA) and supported by British interests, the shah returned, ordered Mossadegh's arrest, and replaced him with a less radical prime minister. During all this time, thinking people such as my father, lived in constant fear that civil war would break out and the country would be plunged into further turmoil and fragmented. I remember the day that the shah returned. All that morning, paid demonstrators roamed the city shouting, "Death to the shah and long life to Mossadegh." (I could never understand the wish for a long life to Mossadegh because everyone knew that he was a bedridden, sick old man who habitually wore pajamas, even on state occasions, and frequently wept when he talked for no apparent reason.) Suddenly, at noon, the chant changed to "Long life to the shah and down with Mossadegh."

I was in school in Tehran during this period of political upheaval. There was a legitimate theater, the Sadi Theater, across the street from my school. My sisters Katayoon and Tooran obtained tickets to the opening performance of a play some weeks in advance, and they decided to take me with them. The play featured several famous performers, among whom were Kheyrkhan, Asemi, Khashe, Jafari, and Loreta. When we arrived at the theater opening night shortly before the 8 P.M. curtain time, we found the theater in darkness and the street in front of it filled with angry ticket holders, all demanding admission. A line of armed soldiers stood in front of the theater to keep the crowd from entering.

After a few minutes, a truck with a loudspeaker mounted on the roof of the cab appeared. A police officer announced to the crowd that the theater had been closed indefinitely by order of the shah because most of the theatrical group had been identified as belonging to the communist party and the play contained overtones of communist propaganda. All ticket holders would have their money refunded if they called at the box office the next day or could keep their tickets for a future performance. The theater remained closed for several weeks, and when it finally reopened, the play had been purged of all allusions to communism, but none of the actors were arrested.

By 1956, the flow of revenue from oil was such that the programs of social and economic reform envisioned by the shah were now economically feasible and the country entered into a golden age of prosperity. New factories, subsidized in whole or in part by the government and manufacturing a variety of products, sprung up all over the country. These provided jobs for the people, resulting in a broader tax base for the government as well as improvement in the standard of living for the workers and their families. The system of free compulsory elementary school education began under the shah's father was expanded; more schools were built and more teachers trained. Universities were founded in the major cities, opening up for the first time opportunity for the masses to receive higher education without leaving the country. More government scholarships were provided for study abroad to train the teachers for the new universities. The rail transportation system was expanded to link together the major cities along with a new highway system. Health services were expanded extending care to villages by government-paid nurses and doctors, who operated out of portable trailer clinics; or if the village was large enough, they practiced in clinics built by the local villages with the help of the central government.

Compulsory military service for two years had been a requirement for all males for many years. The shah extended this service requirement to include females; but instead of military training in the conventional sense, he established what was called the Army of Education, the Army of Health, and the Army of Development. Under these programs, the conscripts were trained and then sent out to the rural areas to teach the illiterate reading and writing, assist the medical personnel (especially in matters of public health), and train the villagers in the use of modern agricultural equipment, the building of irrigation systems, etc. The conscripts went out in teams of three and were in many instances met with some antipathy or downright hostility by the village headman and particularly by the local mullahs, who had been controlling the affairs of the villages for years and profiting from the ignorance of the people.

A story is told about one team who went to a remote village. They were met by the village headman and mullah, and they explained to them that they were there to build a school and teach the people to read and write as well as to introduce modern agricultural methods and basic hygiene. The headman and the local mullah had been forewarned of the arrival of the development team, and they connived together a scenario to discourage them. The headman called a meeting of the villagers in the village square. He told the young teachers that it was no use for them to try to teach the people, because they only understood his way of talking. To illustrate this, he smoothed a place in the dirt and told the teacher, "Write down the word snake in the dirt with a stick."

The young man wrote in the dirt the Farsi word for snake, whereupon the headman took the stick and drew a picture of snake next to the word. He then turned to the villagers and asked them which of the two drawings looked more like a snake. Of course, the illiterate villagers said that the headman's drawing looked more like a snake. The original scenario called for the matter to end with this point made. However, the mullah, who most of the time was at odds with the headman, stepped to the center of the crowd and emptied a real snake from a sack onto the ground. "Which of these looks more like a snake?" he asked. "I am the one who speaks the truth to you and you should believe in me!"

Of all the social reforms initiated by the shah, the most significant to me, along with millions of other women, was the granting of women's rights. Under the old Islamic law, which for so many years had kept women under the heels of the males, basic human rights enjoyed by Western women were an unobtainable dream. For example, a man could divorce his wife without her knowledge and custody of any children was always given to the father and his family. Men were allowed to have four wives so long as they were all treated equally. In actuality, equal treatment was practically nonexistent in these households. In addition, a man could have as many concubines as he could afford, as well as enjoy the dalliance provided by *sigheh*, or temporary marriage. Three categories of people were not allowed to vote: males under age eighteen, patients in mental hospitals, and women.

The shah changed all of this. Plural marriage was made illegal; divorce *in absentia* was forbidden; women were allowed to sue for divorce and custody of children; and women were granted suffrage. Women, who during the reign of Reza Shah were able to go on to higher education, now were allowed to put their talents to work outside the home and occupy high positions in the fields of education and politics as well as the professions. When I left Persia in 1976, there were many female physicians, lawyers, college professors, members of parliament, as well as business entrepreneurs. High-ranking government positions, such as minister of education, and ambassadorial posts were held by women.

I knew from the stories told to me by my grandparents what life had been like for women in Persia before the Reza Shah and his son came to power, but fortunately, I grew up during the reign of Mohammed Reza Shah and enjoyed the emancipation and opportunities for women that he instigated. It was also my good fortune to be out of the country and married to a citizen of the United States when the revolution took place in 1979 and the shah was forced to flee the country and the Islamic Fundamentalists took over. Nonetheless, my heart bled for what was happening to my native country; and I felt sick with pity and sorrow for the members of my family, my friends, and all the educated, enlightened people who now had to live in Persia under the new regime. The accounts of the summary trials, and the imprisonment and execution of former leaders filled me with horror.

The shah, who had given so much to the country, ultimately failed because he had gone too far and too fast in his efforts to make Persia a modern, enlightened country able to take its place as an equal among the advanced nations of the world. The mullahs, whom the Reza Shah and his son had gradually eased out of their positions of influence, were now back in power and exercising their vengeance upon all who had the slightest connection to the shah. The education and judiciary systems, which he had established as separate entities from the old fundamentalist Islamic law, were now back under the control of the mullahs. Their control spread like a dark cloud over the land, and the old laws with their barbaric punishments were reinstituted. The mullahs were free to again preach in the mosques to the illiterate masses who had not had sufficient time to be educated under the shah's compulsory educational system. The mullahs understood how to appeal to the masses by promising free rent, electricity, fuel, and all of the other essentials for a supposedly utopian society. They were able to inflame the masses to stage the riots and street demonstrations that were so graphically portrayed by the television coverage during the shameful takeover of the American embassy.

Alas, the utopia promised never came. Instead, the country was plunged into an eight-year war with Iraq that brought more suffering and heartbreak to the people. Fourteen-year-old children were sent into battle and died or were maimed along with thousands of other conscripts. This fruitless and inconclusive war ruined the economy and rampant inflation, which continues to this day, began.

I pray and hope with all my heart that my beloved Persia will someday emerge from the depths of the darkness into which it has been plunged by the fundamentalists. There is an old Persian saying, "Happy is the bird who is free; but happier is the bird who escapes from his cage." I wonder how long the women, who have been forced back into the cage symbolized by the all-enveloping black *chador*, will tolerate their loss of freedom. Perhaps they will be the avant-garde who will lead the country to establish a new regime. Perhaps, someday, Persia will regain the respect of the civilized world, and all Persians will again walk everywhere with their heads held high.

Chapter Fourteen
Beyond the Wooden Gate

I saw a bird, caught in a trap
I thought to myself: he, like I,
Is probably heartbroken and anxious.
I tried to free him from the snare
To no avail—he was used to his hunter.

—Emad Khorasani

As I mentioned before, my mother had only one sister. She was the eldest child of my maternal grandfather, Agha Bozorg. She married, in her early teens, a merchant who had inherited a business dealing in imported antiques, which, through hard work and intelligent investment, he expanded several times. He became very wealthy over the years and their house, which was about two miles from our house in Mashhad, was a showplace. It was an older house, built in the style of yesteryear when large rooms with high ceilings and elaborately carved crown moldings were a mark of elegance and a practical substitute for air-conditioning. The windows, which were not very large as was customary in older houses to conserve heat, contained stained-glass panes in part. A center hallway led from the front door straight through to a pillared verandah in the rear that overlooked a large peach orchard. This was a sight to behold in the spring when the trees bloomed with their gorgeous pink blossoms.

My favorite room in the house was in the basement. It was called a *hozkhaneh*—a room *(khaneh)* containing a decorative pool *(hoz)*. The pool was rectangular, about eight-by-ten feet by two feet deep, and occupied the center of the room. At one end, there was a small marble statue of a girl holding a pitcher directed toward the pool. The pitcher was the spout through which the water to fill the pool was pumped. A tiled channel about six inches wide and slightly below floor level ran around the base of the pool. This channel caught the overflow of water when the pool water was changed. The dark and light blue tiles in the channel matched the row of tiles that lined the rim of the pool. A row of the same blue color tiles decorated the top and bottom of the walls all around the room. The inside of the pool was covered with tiles decorated with various colored designs on a light blue background.

Wooden benches almost as wide as a single bed were placed around the pool next to the walls. These were covered with Turkoman rugs, and elegant velvet or thick brocade cushions. The brick floor was covered with golden-colored straw mats woven in a diamond design. In one corner there was a round table with two beautiful antique china oil lamps and two hookahs with clear crystal bases.[1] In another corner there was a second table with a samovar surrounded by small tea glasses and sugar bowls. My aunt used to entertain her lady friends in this room, especially in the summer since it was always cool in the *hozkhaneh*. They would sit on the wooden benches with legs crossed, leaning back on cushions, talking and sharing the hookahs. Each lady who smoked brought her own personal wooden mouthpiece. Aunt Ozra was fond of putting flower blossoms in the water in the crystal base of her hookah. As she drew on the tube, the water would bubble and the blossoms dance up and down. I loved to sit next to her listening to her stories, mesmerized by the gyrating petals and the bubbling of the hookah and the samovar.

My memories of Aunt Ozra date from the time when she was in her midfifties and living with her second husband, who was to die within a year. Her first husband, who had accumulated their considerable wealth, had died before I was born. My brother Jahan told me that he remembers well the fine carriages and horses that they had and especially one pure white Arabian horse with a beautiful long mane and tail called *Eghbal* (Lucky). This horse was reserved for riding and never used as a carriage horse.

Aunt Ozra had two children by her first husband, a girl and

a boy. The eldest was the girl, cousin Saleemeh, who had been my temporary wet nurse before my parents found my nanny. This was probably why Aunt Ozra felt a special attachment to me, more like a grandmother to a grandchild than an aunt to a niece. Aunt Ozra was a short and slightly chubby woman with a light complexion and long, black, wavy hair. She had a wonderful sense of humor and a plain, simple, easygoing manner. She always was joking and telling funny stories in her sweet Shirazian accent.

She was the soul of generosity with no thought for her own personal welfare. Unfortunately, this worked to her disadvantage. Her second husband turned out to be a ne'er-do-well who never worked and loved to party and drink. Over the years, he gradually dissipated the fortune that her first husband had worked so hard to accumulate. Wonderful antiques, chiefly from tsarist Russia, which had furnished their large house, were gradually sold off to pay for his good times. My sister Katayoon told me how shocked she was to find a floor-to-ceiling mirror with an elaborate brass frame that had belonged to one of the tsars missing when she visited Aunt Ozra one day.

Katayoon also told me of a large wooden chest full of antique silver coins from various countries that was in one of their walk-in closets. Aunt Ozra's second husband sold these off by the bowlful for their silver content rather than their antique value. Fortunately, he died before Aunt Ozra was completely beggared. By the time that I was a child of ten she lived alone, except for her maid and gardener, in her large house with what furnishings and wealth that remained. The yearly sale of the peaches from her large orchard also provided some income. Her two grown children were married and lived in Tehran. She had a wide circle of friends, and she was constantly entertaining her lady friends at home or out visiting them. Everyone enjoyed her company because of her cheerful, fun-loving personality.

Whenever I went to visit Aunt Ozra, she always taught me something of her two special skills—cooking and sewing. She was a good cook, and she believed strongly in the old Persian concept of matching *garm* (hot) and *sard* (cold) foods with the hot or cold nature of people. *Garm* and *sard* do not refer to the actual temperature of the food, but rather to its supposed effect on the metabolism of the consumer. Honey, pistachio nuts, dates, and figs are examples of hot foods; and these are believed to speed the metabolism and "thicken" the blood. Plums, peaches, oranges, and yogurt are considered cold foods that slow the metabolism and "thin" the blood. She insisted that it was important to balance the intake of hot and cold foods according to the hot or cold nature of the individual. An imbalance could lead to illness or dire changes in personality.

Although I was fond of good food, I did not learn too much about cooking from Aunt Ozra, because at that age I did not have the patience to watch her for the hours it took to prepare a gourmet Persian meal. However, she did teach me sewing, which I enjoyed so much and still do. She taught me how to make rag dolls and the clothing with which to dress them. The way she showed me how to make the dolls was to first make a rectangular torso. Then four tubular shaped forms for the arms and legs. Finally, a round head with a long neck would be made and all the parts stuffed with cotton. The arms and legs were attached first to the torso. Then, a stick about the thickness of a pencil was inserted through the neck to the head and the other end into the torso. The neck, partially inserted into the torso, was then sewn to it. The hair was made from woolen yarn and the eyes, eyebrows, nose, and mouth embroidered on with colored cotton thread. The cheeks were painted red with a red pencil.

From the time that I first learned to make these dolls at about age seven until we moved to Tehran when I was eleven, I had made at least fifty of them. When we moved, I felt that I was too grown-up to play with dolls, so I gave them all away to my cousin and other family members and friends. I regretted this later on in Tehran, because at times I felt lonely and I was still not grown-up enough to find companionship in adult circles. My handmade dolls were all sizes and had hair of various colors. Each had a wardrobe of several dresses made from scraps of fabric left over from the adult dressmaking or discarded clothing. My cousin Genoos and I spent many hours together playing house with the dolls. The smaller dolls would be the children and the larger ones the parents. I kept the dolls in a large wooden chest in the bedroom that I shared with Tooran, one of my adult sisters.

One day, I opened the chest to bring out some dolls for play, and I was shocked and dismayed to find that the top layer of dolls all had broken necks. Their poor heads lolled forward or to one side or the other, and they looked so sad. I did not know what had happened and thought that perhaps I had tried to jam too many into the chest and they had broken when the lid closed. I spent hours that day patiently replacing the sticks and reattaching the heads. Then, several days later, the same thing happened. I now became suspicious that someone was deliberately breaking them and I knew that it could not be my sister Tooran. I accused my younger cousin Genoos. She denied having anything to do with it, and we had a fight that ended in tears for both of us. However, our spat did not last. After she had been comforted by Grandmother, the two of us made up within a few hours.

The mystery of the broken dolls continued for the whole summer. Periodically, I would find several of the dolls with broken necks, and each time, I would have to repair them. It was not until I was an adult, married and living in America that I learned who was the culprit. My brother Jamshid confessed to me when he was visiting a few years ago that he had been the one. He said that he felt that I was spending too much time with my dolls and my cousin and not enough time with him, helping him with his devilish pranks.

One afternoon in late spring, shortly after school had let out for summer vacation, Aunt Ozra came to visit. I was ten years old at the time and had just finished the fifth grade. She visited with my sisters and Grandmother for a couple of hours. Just before she left to go home, she said to me, "Mehry, would you like to come with me and stay with me at my house for a few days?"

I was delighted at the invitation and immediately accepted. We set out for the two-mile walk to her house, hand in hand, talking as we walked. Aunt Ozra moved along in her slow deliberate way, but I didn't mind because I was so interested in her stories. After a while, we arrived at her house. I immediately asked her if I could go down to the *hozkhaneh*, because I loved this room and liked to play by the little pool.

Aunt Ozra replied, "Certainly you can go down and play in the *hozkhaneh*; and since you are so fond of pools, I am going to take you to our next-door neighbor's garden and show you their pool. It is one of the loveliest lily ponds in the city. I will send my maid with a message to tell her that we will come over tomorrow morning if it is all right with her."

The next morning about ten o'clock we went next door and sounded the knocker on the wooden door in the front wall of the neighbor's courtyard. A pretty black-haired maid with rosy red cheeks opened the door and conducted us into the center hall of the house where Mrs. Tahery, the lady of the house, greeted us. She was a most attractive woman who appeared to be about ten years younger than Aunt Ozra. Her most striking feature was her beautiful amber-colored eyes. I could not keep myself from staring at them; and later on when we went back to Aunt Ozra's house, I remarked to her about them.

Aunt Ozra replied, "Yes, she has beautiful and peculiar eyes. Some of her lady friends say that her eyes change according to the color of the clothes she is wearing. I personally believe that they reflect her emotions like the four seasons of the year. When she is happy, they are greenish like springtime; when she is mad, they are hot and fiery like summer; when she is sad, they look dark as a gloomy autumn day; and when she feels empty and helpless, they appear cold and frozen as in winter."

We didn't stop in Mrs. Tahery's house, but continued on through to the garden in the rear. After a short walk down a flower-bordered brick walk, we came to a large circular bricked area. Damask rosebushes in full bloom surrounded the area, and in the center there was a shallow, round pool with lily pads floating on the surface. Red and white carp swam around between the lilies. Four large earthenware pots containing jasmine were spaced around the border of the pool. Four wooden benches, each about the size of a single bed, occupied the periphery of the circular area. Two were covered with rugs and were shaded by poplar trees. On one other bench, there was a bubbling samovar with tea glasses.

My aunt and Mrs. Tahery sat on one of the rug-covered benches that was next to the draping branches of a large willow tree growing just behind the rosebushes. The maid went back and forth to the house bringing out various dishes of fruit and cookies. Finally, she produced a hookah for my aunt and her mistress to share and began to whirl the *ateshgardan*[2] to kindle a live coal to light it. I wandered about, intoxicated by the perfume of the roses blended with that of the jasmine. All was so still and calm except for the singing of the birds, who flew back and forth between the surrounding trees and the rosebushes. I sat by the pool watching the flashes of color made by the carp and the reflection of the willow tree on the water. I felt that I had been transported to an earthly paradise.[3]

Aunt Ozra and Mrs. Tahery, even while deep in their own private conversation, must have been watching me out of the corners of their eyes. I must have had an enraptured expression on my face as I sat there. Suddenly I became aware that they had been watching my reaction to the charm and enchantment of the garden when I heard my aunt say to Mrs. Tahery, "That child has a remarkably romantic nature for her age. Look how she sits there drinking in the beauty of your garden and lost in her own thoughts!"

It was around noon that day when we returned home. We had lunch and retired to our rooms for our afternoon naps. As usual, I was not able to sleep, so I quietly slipped out of the house, so as not to disturb Aunt Ozra's nap, and walked around the peach tree orchard. I wandered toward the mud brick wall that separated Aunt Ozra's property from the Taherys' garden. I could not see over the wall, even though it was not very high, but I wanted to look again at the lovely place where we had spent the morning. There were a few wooden crates used for packing peaches scattered among the trees, left over from the previous year's harvest. I carried one of the crates over to the wall, and after moving along the wall to several positions, I finally found a spot that overlooked the rose garden, although I could not see the pool or the benches.

I stood there on the peach crate with my chin resting on my crossed forearms, inhaling the fragrance of the damask roses. After a few minutes, I saw the pretty young maid who had served us that morning emerge from the house and walk down the path to the pool. I could only see her upper body over the rosebushes. She turned and faced the house, and seemed to be waiting for something. A few minutes later, Mr. Tahery came down the path and as soon as he reached the maid, he put his arms around her, pulled off her kerchief, and started to kiss and hug her. The girl seemed to enjoy this very much, because all the while she was laughing and giggling. Soon Mr. Tahery started to open the buttons on her blouse and his kissing progressed downward from her mouth and neck. Then the two torsos disappeared from my view. I assumed that they were now sitting down on one of the benches to continue their kissing. My knowledge of sex at that age was practically nil, in common with all well-bred Persian girls. All that we knew came from snatches of overheard conversation between the servant girls; there were no cable TV, *Playboy* magazines, or other clandestine sources of information. The only movies we saw were Laurel and Hardy, Charles Chaplin, or Disney films.

Despite my limited knowledge, I knew that what I had witnessed was something improper. Mr. Tahery was married and should be kissing his wife, not some serving girl, because that was how I believed that babies were conceived. I rushed to the house and found my aunt sitting in the *hozkhaneh* drinking a glass of tea. I blurted out to her what I had seen.

My aunt did not react in any way but sat there with a serious expression on her face for several minutes. Finally, she turned to me and said, "Come sit next to me. I want to tell you something that you should remember always. First, you should never talk about something that you were not supposed to see in the first place. I know that you did not intend to spy on Mr. Tahery or anyone else, but to talk about what you saw makes it seem that you were spying. Second, Mrs. Tahery knows more than you or I what is going on in her house and her husband's appetite for women. Those young maids come and go almost once a year, but Mrs. Tahery is Mrs. Tahery and the lady of the house. She made up her mind a long time ago that there were certain things that she had to overlook if she were to survive and maintain a strong position in her household. If she did not overlook occasional infidelities, her husband might decide to divorce her or take another wife. She would rather keep her secure position. She was married when she was thirteen years old, and she grew up herself while she was raising her own children. She has no education, skills, or other qualifications that would be of any use outside her four walls. In her home she is a wife, a mother, and the lady

197

of the house with authority; but beyond that wooden gate, she is just a lonely, helpless woman. This is true of thousands of women of my generation."

Aunt Ozra looked very pensive and sad as she spoke to me. I could see in her eyes that she was thinking back on her own life and had left unsaid many other things.

I said to her, "Aunt Ozra, every woman can go to school now and learn. My sisters teach school and make enough money to support themselves, and some of my cousins are nurses working in hospitals."

Aunt Ozra replied, "You are right. The opportunities for your generation are great, but for my generation they came too late." Then she added a verse of poetry:

> They broke our wings and opened the cage door.
> What is the difference if we are out or in,
> We still cannot fly.

I had never seen Aunt Ozra so serious and sad as she was that day; and I never saw her in that mood afterward, even on her deathbed years later. When I grew up, I wondered if the joking, cheerful countenance Aunt Ozra presented to the world really was a mask hiding an inner disappointment with her lot as a woman in the society in which she lived in those days. After all, she was a native of Shiraz, the city of roses, nightingales, and poets, and a sensitive, romantic woman who was the daughter of a poet. She certainly was affected by the changes in her lifestyle brought about by her disastrous second marriage, in which she had been entrapped with an irresponsible man who, according to the law at that time, became the master of her and her wealth. For a woman to ask for a divorce was virtually unheard of then.

The last time that I saw Aunt Ozra was years later when we were both living in Tehran. She was seventy-six years old and died shortly after her last visit to my home. I was married by then, and I remember Aunt Ozra sitting in a chair in my parlor, holding my three-year-old daughter on her lap. It was so wonderful and heartwarming to hear her tell my daughter the exact same stories that she had told me in my childhood, complete with the same gestures and sound effects.

One story was about a lion who lived in a forest lording over all the other animals. Every day he captured one of the other creatures and ate it. The other animals all got together and discussed how they could get rid of the lion. They finally settled on a plan. They dug a large deep hole in the ground and filled it half-full of water. Then they approached the lion and told him, "Sir, we know that you have to eat and understand that you have to kill one of us every day to do so. However, there is another lion now in the forest and we are afraid that none of us will be left if you both have to feed on us."

The lion asked where the other beast could be, because he had never seen him. The fox answered him, "He hides by day in a hole in the ground and comes out at night to feed. Come, we will show you where he is." They took the lion to the hole and the lion looked in, saw his reflection in the water, and leapt in to kill his rival. He drowned and never again were the animals to live in fear. The moral of the story is, by working together all obstacles may be overcome.

The admonition of not talking about another person's misdeeds given to me by Aunt Ozra remained with me for the rest of my life. I have regretted following this advice only in one instance. When I was a girl of thirteen and going to school in Tehran, I walked home one day with one of my classmates who lived close to us to borrow a book that she had at home. When we reached the door to her courtyard, she opened it and we started to enter. Then she hurriedly turned and pushed me out, saying that I could not come in at that time. In the brief time the gate was opened, I had caught a glimpse inside the courtyard and was horrified by what I saw. The girl's young stepmother was tied to a thick tree with her back and buttocks partially exposed. Her father was lashing his wife with a leather belt, and the poor woman was groaning and writhing in her bonds.

I stood outside the courtyard door for a few minutes, frightened and shocked, unsure as to what I should do. I looked around and saw people moving about normally in the street as if nothing unusual were happening. I was not sure that the scene I had glimpsed behind the wooden gate was real or an imagined nightmare. I slowly walked home, trembling and crying softly. No one was home but the servants, and I went to my room where

I sat alone thinking until dinner. That evening, I did not say anything to my family about what I had witnessed.

The next morning I went to school and found my classmate. I pulled her aside and asked her what was going on in her house and what I could do to help her. I told her that I could tell my brother about it, and he would go to the police.

She replied, "There is nothing that you can do. Please do not tell anyone about what you saw. My father often gets drunk and when he does he thinks that my stepmother is unfaithful to him. Then he beats her as you saw yesterday. If the police find out about this, they will put him in jail. Then who will be left to feed us and pay the rent?"

Over the years, many memories grow dim with time. However, that horror I saw remains clear and vivid in my mind to this day. As a young girl, I had nightmares in which I relived it. I have always felt guilty that I misunderstood Aunt Ozra's advice. She meant that one should not invade other people's privacy but never intended that I should not report a crime when I saw one committed. As I grew up, I learned that there were millions of women, uneducated and untrained except for domestic work, who, like Mrs. Tahery and my classmate's stepmother, were the helpless victims of an unhappy marriage but could not go beyond their wooden gates because a worse fate might await them on the other side.

Notes

1. A hookah is the water pipe smoked in parts of the Middle East. The bowl of the hookah is perforated and a tube from the bottom of the bowl leads down to a round base that is partially filled with water. A second tube leads off from the top of the base to the smoker. After the tobacco bowl on the top is filled, the tobacco is lit with a fragment of glowing charcoal. When the smoker sucks on the wooden mouthpiece, the smoke is pulled down the tube to below the water level and then through the water into the smoker's tube. The whole system must be completely airtight in order to function properly. Hookahs are usually elaborately decorated with colored designs and make quite beautiful and interesting ornaments.
2. An *ateshgardan* is a bowl made of loosely woven wire with a yard-long wire chain attached. Charcoal is placed in the bowl and lit. The servant then swings it in a gradually increasing arc until a full circular motion is obtained. The charcoal kindles to a glowing ember that is placed on top of

the tobacco in the hookah. Much practice is necessary to acquire the skill to whirl an *ateshgardan* without spewing out the hot coals. At night, an accidentally released *ateshgardan* may sail off in the air and look like a shooting star!

3. The English word "paradise" is derived from the Greek *paradeisos*. The Greeks in turn borrowed the word from the Persian *pardees* when Alexander the Great conquered the country.

Chapter Fifteen
Thorn Garden

Human beings are each a separate glass
Through which the sun of being's light is passed;
Each tinted fragment sparkles in the sun:
A thousand colors, but the light is one.

—Jami

My father's only living brother, Ardesheer, was twelve years younger than Father. He was a graduate of the medical school of Daralfonoon (Polytechnic Institute) in Tehran and, after his internship and a year of residency in the Shahreza Hospital in Mashhad, he moved to Torbat and practiced general medicine there. Some years later, he returned to Mashhad where he lived and worked for the rest of his life. Torbat is situated in the foothills of the mountains about thirteen hundred meters above sea level. At that time, the population was only about ten thousand. The river Kalsalar runs through the town providing water to nourish the abundant greenery in the town and the surrounding farms where wheat, cotton, and barley are grown.

As is the case in small towns throughout the world, it had a social strata in which my uncle, as a young bachelor physician, circulated at the highest level. One evening, shortly after he had opened his office, he attended a party where he met a man from Tehran who had been appointed temporary mayor of Kashmar, a small city southwest of Mashhad. This man had a beautiful unmarried daughter, the eldest of four children. He was impressed with my uncle's intelligence and charm so, with an eye to arranging a fine match for his daughter, he invited Ardesheer to visit him at his home in Kashmar.

My uncle fell in love with the charming girl at first sight. Her most striking features were her lovely black eyes and beautiful singing voice. This especially captivated my uncle, who was a talented musician himself. After the usual ritual of interfamily visitation, the marriage was arranged within several months. It was decided that the ceremony would be held in our house in Mashhad since it was about midway between Torbat to the southeast and Kashmar to the southwest. Those friends and relatives of the bride in Tehran who wished to attend could make the journey without too much difficulty. I was only about two and a half years old at the time, so my memories of the event are vague and somewhat fragmented.

The south wing of our house was always used for housing visitors, especially when they arrived in quantity. This time, I do recall that the entire south wing of our house was turned over to the bride's family; my mother and father moved to a small bedroom in the north wing. I also remember seeing the shining new four-poster brass bed with silk sheets and coverlets that had been installed in a bedroom in the north wing that was to serve as the bridal chamber for the two nights that the couple stayed after the wedding. I have a photo of myself dressed in a beautiful ruffled turquoise blue silk dress that Katayoon made for me especially for the occasion and, although the photo is in black and white, every time I look at it, I see that lovely blue color. The rest is all a mixed jumble of vague impressions of what seemed to be crowds of people, all in a festive mood. The kitchens were a hive of activity; two male chefs with their helpers were hired to augment our own staff and feed the many guests and visitors. For the party following the wedding ceremony, a group of musicians and a pretty young dancing girl were hired to entertain.

Two days after the wedding, the guests departed; the bride's parents returned to Kashmar, her other relatives to Tehran and the newlyweds went to Torbat. The house returned to its normal routine but the respite was brief. Nine months later, again the south wing was occupied: this time by my uncle and his very pregnant wife and her parents. They all came so that the new baby could be born in the Shahreza Hospital in Mashhad. My uncle, as a physician, did not believe in home delivery if modern hospital facilities were available. A few days after they arrived, my uncle's wife went into labor and my cousin Genoos was born. I remember clearly the day when my uncle brought his wife home from the hospital, carrying this sweet little baby girl in his arms.

The next afternoon there was a party in our house to celebrate the birth of the new baby. The parlor was filled with people, and the dining room table held all sorts of cakes, cookies, and other sweets. Among the guests there was a famous poet named Malek al-Shoara Bahar. He composed a poem in honor of the baby and recited it at the party. This poem is published in one of his volumes of verse, and I have often wondered how many of his many readers know that this poem was composed to honor his friend, my uncle, and his newborn daughter. The first verse of the poem translates something like this:

> To our doctor God gave the gift of a daughter,
> May Homa[1] be her guardian angel throughout her life.

My uncle and his family stayed with us for another few days and then returned to Torbat. The mother never regained her strength after the birth of Genoos, and her health continued to decline over the ensuing months. It came to light that she suffered from rheumatic heart disease contracted as a child. My uncle traveled back and forth with her to Tehran to consult with the heart specialists in the capital until her condition became too grave to permit travel. He had his practice in Torbat to attend to, so he left his wife and baby girl with her parents, who had since moved back to Tehran from Kashmar, in order that she could receive the constant medical care that she required. It was all to no avail: Within two years, she died of heart failure. In the meantime, my own mother had died a year and a half earlier.

My uncle had gone to Tehran, accompanied by his faithful manservant Baba, to be with his wife during her last few days; and they stayed on for a few days after the funeral. Knowing that his wife was terminally ill, he had already made arrangements with Grandmother to bring the child to our house and leave her in her care. His in-laws wanted to keep the child in Tehran, but he knew that he would be unable to see her very often and still keep up his practice in Torbat if he agreed to this. They, however, were quite adamant that the girl be raised by them.

My uncle did not wish to enter into a protracted argument with them; and he also feared that if the situation became too acrimonious, the grandparents might hide the child with other relatives in the city. He could not afford to spend the time it might take to recover his own baby if that happened.

He maintained an outwardly friendly posture with his in-laws, but secretly arranged a method to spirit the baby away. He contacted his nephew who was a student in the University of Agriculture in Karaj near Tehran and arranged for him to hire a car and driver, and stock it with the necessary items for the care of a two year old on a trip. He told him to have the driver park the car a block away from his in-laws' house on a certain day and at a certain time. On the appointed day, he told the baby's nanny to take the child with Baba to the car while he was sitting and talking to the grandparents. After he was sure that they had had time to get to the car, he excused himself on the pretext of going out to attend to some shopping and left to join them. The car and driver with my uncle, Genoos, her nanny, and Baba then swiftly departed Tehran and the next day were in Mashhad. Ardesheer stayed overnight and then left for Torbat to devote his full atten-tion to his practice that he had neglected for over two years due to his wife's illness. However, he returned every weekend there-after to stay overnight and visit with his daughter.

Genoos was a pretty, delightful little girl. She was somewhat shy at first since the only one in the house that she knew was her nanny. Little by little, she became at home and attached to our family. I was especially captivated with her because, for the first time, I had a companion younger than I. Her coming to stay with us was the best thing that had happened to me since my own mother died. Over the next six years, we became inseparable companions; I taught her all the children's games and shared my dolls and other toys with her.

Genoos's nanny was another story altogether. There was something about her that I did not like from the day I first met her; and as time went on, this dislike grew. She seemed to believe that the only way to teach children was to instill in them a fear of punishment, a concept that was completely different from the loving care that I had received from my own nanny. From time to time, she would shout at me to get away from Genoos, and I began to suspect that she wanted to be alone with Genoos in order to punish her.

This suspicion was confirmed in my mind when, a few months after Genoos arrived, I heard her screaming one morning in Grandmother's kitchen. No one was in the kitchen except Genoos and her nanny. I ran to the door and saw the nanny force Genoos's mouth open and put a pinch of red pepper on her tongue, all the while shouting at her, "This is what happens when you do not listen to me!" The nanny then turned to me and said, "It will happen to you too if you are naughty!" Then she washed out Genoos's mouth with a wet rag and cleaned her tearstained face, holding her and telling her that now that she had learned her lesson, she loved her. I thought that this was a strange way of showing love but being only a five year old, I said nothing.

One week later, another shocking experience occurred. It was a lovely summer morning, and Genoos and I were playing in the courtyard when the nanny came out with Zivar, our maid. She said to Zivar, "Will you watch Genoos for a while until I finish my business in the orchard?"

She had a peculiar look on her face and I was suspicious that something unusual was going on. After ten minutes or so, when Zivar's back was turned, I whispered to Genoos, "Would you like to go find your nanny?" Genoos, of course, agreed and we sped off together into the orchard. We heard sounds of distant voices toward the north end of the orchard and ran in that direction. Soon we came upon her nanny, who was squatting down behind one of the trees with her bare back turned to another strange woman who was dressed like a gypsy. The nanny's back was bleeding from several deep cuts, and the gypsy was holding the large end of a ram's horn over the cuts while she sucked on the other end, filling her mouth with blood, then spitting it into a bowl beside her on the ground. I stood there, transfixed with horror at the sight of all that blood running down the nanny's back and smeared on the dirty face of the gypsy. The first thing I thought was that this gypsy must be one of those who lived in a *khandagh*.[2]

Suddenly Genoos, who was standing next to me, screamed hysterically in fright. Zivar by that time had caught up with us. She grabbed Genoos and held her head against her bosom, shielding her eyes from the sight,. The nanny was angry. She leapt up, threw a shawl about her bloody back, and began to berate Zivar for not watching us more carefully. Fortunately Grandmother, who had been away from the house as had the rest of the family, suddenly appeared, like a guardian angel. She saw at a glance what was happening and angrily scolded the nanny, saying, "If you must have that done, go to the public bath or somewhere away from here. Never do it again anywhere near this house!" She then ordered Zivar to take us back to the house. The rest of the day Genoos and I were still somewhat shaken by our experience and we stayed close to Grandmother.

I later found out that we had witnessed a practice common in those days among the lower classes. It was a form of bloodletting that was believed to be a cure for high blood pressure. This service was offered in special rooms set aside for this purpose in the public baths but also was performed by itinerant practitioners, usually gypsies, such as we had seen. The only attempt at control of sepsis was the application of a bit of charred cotton over the cuts after the job was done. The patient was also advised to eat a diet rich in calories for one week and avoid sour foods. Another form of bloodletting was the application of leeches. This was a common therapy for adolescent acne, the leech being applied over the skin eruption until it gorged itself and fell off.

A few weeks later, another episode happened that was the final straw that broke the camel's back insofar as Genoos's nanny's tenure was concerned. It was another summer morning, and Genoos and I were playing in the courtyard. Again all the family were away from the house, and we were alone save for the servants and Genoos's nanny. I don't know what Genoos did or did not do to provoke her nanny's anger, but suddenly she picked up the little girl and carried her down the path from the courtyard toward the rose garden next to the gazebo. She had a malevolent expression on her face, and I was frightened and worried about what she might do to my little cousin. I followed along at a distance, keeping my head below the level of a hedge bordering the path.

I saw the nanny sit down on a wooden bench in the rose garden near the gazebo. She put Genoos on her left thigh with the girl's legs between her own and then crossed her right leg over the girl's legs, immobilizing her. She held Genoos's left hand in her own left hand, then removed a pin that she wore to secure her scarf beneath her chin. She then proceeded to prick the back of Genoos's hand with the pin repeatedly, all the while talking to her angrily. I could not hear what she was saying, but I could hear the heartrending screams from the little girl. I was terrified, and the sight was so painful to me that I felt as if it were happening to me. Finally the nanny stopped, wiped the tears from Genoos's face, and held her until she quieted down.

I ran bent over behind the hedge to the house and went to my bedroom until Grandmother came home. As soon as she came in, I ran to her and told her that there was something that I must tell her. She was busy, but I followed her about until we were finally alone in her room. Then she devoted her full attention to me and asked, "What is it that you want to tell me?"

I started to cry and between sobs I said, "Genoos's nanny punished her this morning by sticking a pin into her hand. A few weeks ago she punished her by putting hot pepper in her mouth!"

Grandmother looked stunned and asked me, "Where were the rest of the servants when this happened?"

I told her about how the nanny had carried Genoos far away from the house to the rose garden where no one could see them.

Grandmother looked grim and said, "That is not a rose garden to that poor child but rather a garden of thorns. I suspected all along that something was wrong because Genoos always seemed afraid of her nanny. I could not put my finger on what it was, but now I know. Sometimes you only learn the truth from the lips of a child. Don't say anything to anyone about this, and especially don't let on to the nanny what you saw. I will take care of this in my own way."

For the next week or so, Grandmother seemed to do nothing, but she did not absent herself from the house. Her attitude to the nanny seemed unchanged, but I noticed that there was always a family member at home. Genoos and I were not left alone again. My sister Katayoon paid special attention to Genoos; she played with her, held her in her arms, and entertained her with stories. I know now that Grandmother feared that the nanny would kidnap Genoos and take her back to the in-laws in Tehran if any precipitous action were taken. Finally, after my uncle had been apprised of the situation and agreed that the nanny must go, Grandmother took her aside one day and told her that Genoos was old enough now that she did not require a nanny. She pointed out that my nanny had been dismissed when I was about Genoos's age and that there were plenty of adults in the household to look after the child.

The next morning, the nanny was taken to the bus depot and given a one-way ticket to Tehran along with a generous sum of money and clothing. Grandmother did not want the woman to depart unhappy and go back to Tehran spreading malicious gossip about our family.

Grandfather Khan knew the reason for Grandmother's apparent generosity. He remarked to her, "I know how you feel about this woman, but remember the old saying, 'A scorpion bites, not because he hates you, but rather because that is his nature.'"

After the nanny departed, the whole family bent over backwards to shower Genoos with attention and love. Even my father, who seldom was demonstrative in his affection to his own children, would call to her when he came home from work, pick her up, and carry her to the house, all the while kissing her and talking affectionately to her. It is normal for the youngest child of the family to feel displaced when a younger sibling arrives, but I was never jealous of Genoos because I loved her as a dear friend. I enjoyed seeing her happiness over the attention she was receiving. Also, I guess that I felt sorry for this sweet little girl who had no mother, brothers, or sisters of her own.

Before my uncle Ardesheer remarried, he came to Mashhad every weekend to visit his daughter. One week, when Genoos was about four years old, he invited Grandmother, Katayoon, Genoos, and me to Torbat to stay with him for a week. We had a good time playing together and exploring the town with Grandmother and Katayoon. Every afternoon, we would go to a pretty little park at the foot of a nearby mountain called Peeshkooh and walk about enjoying the gardens.

The highlight of our visit to Torbat occurred when a recently widowed friend of the family, Mrs. Noor, invited us all to come to dinner and stay overnight and the following day. Grandmother declined to go to dinner since she preferred to sleep at home, so she promised to come the next day with Genoos. My uncle, Katayoon, and I went to Mrs. Noor's house and enjoyed a sumptuous dinner. She had three children: a boy of about seventeen and two younger girls. Her husband, who had died one year previously, had been a physician colleague of my uncle. She was a warm, pretty lady and I was immediately attracted to her. Little did I know that four years later she would become my stepmother.

The Noor residence was a large old-fashioned house surrounded by several acres of orchards and truck gardens that were rented to some local farmers. The house had a large verandah that faced a courtyard pool with a large table on the far side. That evening, after dinner, the adults retired to the pool side table and played a popular card game called *pasoor* by the light of two oil lamps at either end of the table. I sat on the rug-covered verandah and played with the youngest daughter until she became tired and went to bed. I stayed on the verandah paging through some of her children's books and from time to time glanced at the full moon as it gradually rose in the southeastern sky. The night was so still, and I could hear faint snatches of conversation from the adults playing cards. After a while, two of the household maids came out on the verandah, each carrying a copper bowl and a copper spoon. They turned off the lights on the verandah, sat down facing the moon, and began to beat the spoons on the bowls. I was mystified and asked them what was the reason for all the racket. The older maid pointed to the moon and said, "See what is happening to the moon. A dragon is swallowing it and we must frighten the beast away!"

I looked up and, sure enough, there was a border of the moon that was missing. My heart leapt and I was suddenly fearful because I loved to watch the moon and the thought that it would disappear forever terrified me. "Are you sure that you will be able to frighten the dragon away?" I asked.

"Never fear," they replied. "Everyone in town is beating on their copper bowl right now and as soon as the noise is loud enough, the dragon will spit out the moon and everything will be all right."

I still was not convinced. I ran to the table where the adults were playing their card game, unconcerned about the catastrophe. I tugged on Katayoon's skirt to get her attention and whispered, "Do you know that a dragon is swallowing the moon?"

She looked at me and asked, "Who told you that ridiculous story?" She told the rest of the players what I had said and they all laughed.

"Don't be afraid," one of them said, "it is just a shadow and it will go away."

I returned to the verandah and told the maids what I had been told.

"Don't believe a word of it," one of them replied with a scornful gesture at the card players. "As soon as they read a couple of books, they no longer believe in anything!"

I was still confused and didn't know whom to believe. Just to be on the safe side, I asked one of the maids to give me a bowl and spoon. I sat there with them and beat upon my bowl. Somehow, this made me feel better even though it did not appear to have any result because the dark part of the moon was still becoming larger. Finally, I became so sleepy that I had to go to bed. I went to sleep, but all night I had nightmares about dragons chasing moons, one after another. The next morning as soon as I awaked, I went and found the young maid. "What happened to the moon?" I asked.

She replied, "Everything is fine. We frightened the dragon away and he spit out the moon."

That night, after we returned to my uncle's house, I sat in the garden and waited for the moon to rise. I was much relieved when it appeared shining in full glory, apparently unaffected by its narrow escape.

The next day about midmorning, Grandmother arrived as promised followed by Baba carrying Genoos in his burly arms.

Baba was an imposing figure of a man. He never married but served my uncle faithfully all his life. For some reason, all the children of the family obeyed Baba without question, not because we feared him for he never punished us in any way or even raised his voice. It was more because he seemed like a grandfather figure to us and we all loved him. It was rumored among the servants that Baba caught snakes in the mountains and brought them home to make into a soup for himself. That was why he was so strong and lived so long. He finally died in his late nineties, the last few years retired but still living with and cared for by my uncle and his second wife.

Soon after Grandmother and Genoos arrived, we all walked over to one of the truck farms that Mrs. Noor rented out to a local farmer. This particular plot was planted in melons, the long green Persian melons that grow so well in Khorasan. Mrs. Noor greeted the farmer and his family, who were working in the melon patch. They invited us to sit in the shade of the trees bordering the garden and insisted that we have one of the melons. The farmer picked a large ripe melon almost three feet long and sent one of his children to his nearby house for a tray and knife. He sliced the melon on the tray, and we all sat there feasting on the fruit that was still cool from the morning dew. The pearly white meat was crunchy, and the sweet juice ran down our chins. When we had finally gorged ourselves, we rose and took leave of our unpretentious but gracious and friendly hosts. Mrs. Noor distributed a few coins to the farmer's children, and we all walked back to her house, working up an appetite for lunch.

Two years after the death of his first wife, Uncle Ardesheer met and married a wonderful girl from a good family living in Torbat. Over the following years, they became the parents of three boys and one girl. Genoos, because of the better schools in Mashhad, continued to stay with my grandparents until she married after finishing high school. All of my uncle's children are now married, and they all have children of their own; many of them I have never met.

Genoos, as she grew up, showed much promise and she did well in school. Early on, it became apparent that she had inherited her mother's singing ability, because she developed a beautiful voice. I loved to hear her sing. We used to play on a swing hung from one of the trees in the orchard, and I would push her back and forth as long as she would sing for me. She started kindergarten in the same school that I attended and soon became the star soloist due to her fast grasp of the school songs as well as the popular songs of the time. The quality of Genoos's voice was so good that she easily could have become a professional singer. She never did. Whether this was by her own choice or because her husband forbade her to do so, I never learned.

Many years later, when we were both adults, I went to Mashhad to visit my uncle who had decided to practice there rather than in Torbat. He and his family lived in the south and west wings of our former house, and he took care of Grandmother and Grandfather Khan for the rest of their lives. During that visit, my uncle's wife arranged a large dinner party, and after the dinner, we all gathered in the parlor. Genoos and her husband were present, of course, and everyone begged her to sing. After a while, she gave in and sang a song made popular by the famous Persian vocalist, Hideh. It was a song that started on a high note and gradually sank to a low mournful ending. I remember the first few lines went something like this: "Drunkenness does not cure my pain anymore. Sadness has been born in me and never leaves me."

Her voice filled the room, and everyone was transfixed with the beauty of the moment. The high notes seemed to vibrate my heart and the low notes seemed to caress my soul. I was lost in time and thought that this was not the little bird who had sung for me in the orchard but was now a mature nightingale. The little girl was gone as was our childhood together, and I was swept with nostalgia. When she finished, everyone applauded and words of admiration filled the room. I could not say anything. I rose with eyes filled with tears and hugged her and kissed her. Words could not express my feelings.

Genoos and I never talked about her nanny again as we grew up together. Many years later, I went to Mashhad from Tehran to visit with my uncle. Genoos was also living in Mashhad, married and with two children of her own. She called her father one day and told him that her old nanny was at her house and sick. She asked him if she could bring her to him for medical attention. My uncle agreed and that day Genoos arrived with the woman. She was old, fat, and wrinkled; and as soon as I saw her, the unpleasant memories of my childhood came flooding back to me. It then occurred to me that Genoos probably did not remember anything about the treatment she had endured as a child from this woman. If she had, she certainly would not have helped her and treated her so well when she fell ill. How wonderful it is that God gave the human mind the ability to blot out unpleasant memories.

Notes

1. The osprey; according to Persian fable, a bird of good omen.
2. The *khandagh* are fragments of the ancient moat that used to surround the city of Mashhad. Most of the deep moat had been filled in and built upon but, when I was a child, a few segments survived and some parts of these were inhabited by thieves and other outlaws, as well as some gypsies. These renegades would hollow out cave dwellings in the sides of the dirt moat. From earliest childhood, I had been warned to stay away from any gypsy that I might see on the street. I was told that they would tear the gold earrings from the ears of little girls and sometimes would kidnap them. Even though our neighborhood was seldom invaded by any gypsies, the first year of elementary school I was escorted to and from school by Gholam or Mashaallah.

Chapter Sixteen
Around Town

You are gone from my sight but my heart still yearns for you;
The image of you still reflects in the mirror of my heart.

—Abolhasan Varzy

Although I lived in Mashhad for only eleven years, I saw many changes in the city during the busy expansionism of the postwar years. For example, when I was a girl of three or four years, the horse-drawn *doroshkeh* was a common means of transportation, but gradually they disappeared as more and more motorcars filled the streets. Later on, when I was living in Tehran and returned to Mashhad to spend the summer holiday with my grandparents, I was further amazed at how the city had changed from year to year. All of the old familiar sights, which I remembered from my childhood when I explored the city with my sisters or Grandmother or Aunt Ozra, seemed to be vanishing as quickly as the morning fog disappears with the rising sun. While all of the changes were for the most part for the better, I missed the picturesque old buildings, which were being replaced with multistoried modern structures, and the cobblestoned streets, which were now covered with asphalt.

The little lunchrooms with their rug-covered wooden benches in front on which men sat smoking the *hookah* and sipping tea were now modern restaurants. The outdoor stands with their charcoal braziers, where a man would stand fanning the coals with one hand as he prepared delicious kabob with the other, were now kiosks with electric grills without the aromatic smoke that titillated the palate.

215

Another institution that gradually was phased out with the advent of modern plumbing was the *hammam omumi,* or public bath. These baths were much like what are known in the West as Turkish baths. Every neighborhood in the city had one or more public baths, and these varied in their decor and size depending on the affluence of the clientele served. One could always recognize a *hammam omumi* by two distinctive characteristics of the building. One was the entrance, a double wooden door bordered on both sides and the top by decorative tiles with a blue or white background on which were painted various designs. Sometimes there would be a tile inscribed with a line of poetry surrounded by other tiles illustrating it. The other unique characteristic was the roof. It was not flat as were the roofs of most buildings, but rather covered by numerous large and small domes with central or multiple glass portholes, which provided light for the windowless building. The portholes could also be opened (from the roof) for ventilation when the interior became too hot and steamy. Some of the baths built a hundred years ago were huge and are preserved to this day as architectural masterpieces, both for their design and beauty of decor. In these baths, there was a large central chamber with a domed ceiling containing numerous glass portholes supported by elaborately decorated pillars between which Gothic arches led off to a number of smaller bathing areas, each with its own domed ceiling. The walls and pillars were covered with beautifully painted tiles and the floors were marble or tile-covered stone.

Some of the baths contained separate sections for the female and male customers; others did not and a separate time of the day was reserved for each sex. The women, who presumably had more time to spare during the day, were allowed in from about eight in the morning to five in the afternoon. The men were given access from sunset until about six in the morning, so that they could bathe before or after work. In our house, for some years, we had a single shower that was used by the adults; but the hot water supply was not sufficient to allow our large family to bathe every day at home. The adults visited the public bath, which was about a mile from our house, several times a week.

At least once a week, the entire female members of our family would go together and spend most of the day there. Gholam would be sent to the bath the day before bearing small suitcases containing clean clothing to don after our bath, copper trays on which to sit while being bathed, and towels and small rugs that we sat on while dressing and undressing. This paraphernalia was left overnight with the supervisor of the bath. Gholam made reservations for several of the private baths for our use the next day.

The public bath that we patronized was one of the best in Mashhad. One entered from the street through the wooden doors and descended down a flight of seven or eight steps into a corridor at the end of which were two long wooden benches where the *dallakha* (bath attendants) were allowed to sit for their lunch break or to have a cigarette or *hookah*. A door about midway down this corridor led into a large dressing room with a high vaulted domed ceiling. The bath keeper, a middle-aged woman, sat cross-legged on a concrete platform just inside the door to the right. She had a short-legged desk with one drawer where she kept the money she collected from the customers and dispensed the pitifully small wages to the *dallakha*, who worked on a piecework basis. They relied upon tips for most of their income. The bath keeper knew all of the customers and would greet them by name on arrival, inquiring about their health and that of their families as well as any news of births, impending marriages, and any other trivia. As a result, she was the repository of all of the current gossip in the neighborhood.

On the wall behind her head, there was a sign advising all customers that the management was not responsible for any valuables that were not left with the bath keeper. This notice, in typical Persian fashion, was written in the form of a rhyming couplet. The stone platform in the dressing room was about four feet wide and ran around the entire periphery of the room. The platform was used for dressing and undressing and, distributed about next to the wall, were the customer's suitcases containing their change of clothing, loincloths, scrubbing mitts, and other impedimenta necessary for bathing, as well as cosmetics. The platform was covered with a straw mat, but everyone laid their own rug or cloth on top of the mat to sit on while dressing. In the center of the room, directly beneath the glass dome, there was a round shallow pool fed by a central fountain and surrounded by a

217

sunken gutter with drain holes to carry off the cool water that ran continuously over the edge of the pool. Bottles of lemonade were kept in the gutter and were for sale to the thirsty.

A door in the far corner of the dressing room led into the common bath chamber. This room was large with a high vaulted ceiling through which shafts of light filtered down weakly from the glass-topped dome through clouds of steam. The floor was made of closely fitted blocks of stone and heated by fires that were kept burning beneath it. Around the periphery ran a gutter with drain holes that continuously drained off the water that spilled onto the floor. The room was usually filled with naked women of every shape and size, dimly seen through the steam, all talking and laughing. *Dallakha,* wearing short skirts that covered them from the top of their breasts to midthigh, would be drawing water from the hot and cold water faucets that lined the walls and filling the large tin-plated copper pots scattered about the room from which the bathers would dip the water to rinse themselves as they sat on their inverted copper trays on the floor.

It was the custom for women to sit on the inverted copper trays because this raised them slightly off the floor, and they thus could avoid contamination from the water draining from others. There was a story told that at one time a virgin got pregnant because she sat on the floor in the same bath that had been used by men earlier that day! Some women would be applying henna to palms, fingernails, and toenails or dying their hair with madder root dye or henna following which they would apply a conditioner made from a pasty mixture of ground coffee and egg yolks. Others would be immersing themselves in a large concrete hot tub that rested on an elevated platform in one corner, while some would be standing under the spray of showers jutting from the wall next to the tub.

In later years, the shah decreed that the common hot tubs were unsanitary and ordered their removal from all public baths. This was not popular with some of the old traditional Moslems who felt that the only proper way to perform the cleansing ablutions that ensured that their prayers would be heard by God was by total immersion. A mere shower bath was considered inadequate.

The steam-filled room had a festive atmosphere. People brought light lunches and spent hours talking, eating, bathing, and, for those who could afford it, being scrubbed and massaged by the busy *dallakha*. Regular customers had their own favorite *dallak*, and the *dallakha* were an encyclopedic source of social knowledge since they overheard all the gossip and rumors that passed back and forth every day. They also performed another important function. If they were approached by a mother with the news that she had a daughter ready for marriage, the *dallakha* would pass this information along to a mother who had a son considering matrimony. Thus, many marriages were initiated by this introduction of interested parties by a *dallak*. If the subsequent marriage negotiations culminated in a successful match, the role of the *dallak* was not forgotten. She would be rewarded with a generous tip and sometimes invited to the wedding.

An anecdote is told about a mother who had a son eligible for marriage, and she told her *dallak* that she would be interested in hearing about any eligible girls. However, she said that her son was quite particular and insisted that any wife of his must have three traits: She must be a lady in society, a housewife in the kitchen, and sexy in the bedroom. The *dallak* found what she thought was a girl with all these features, and after a short time, the two young people were married. Several months later, the *dallak* inquired of the woman as to whether her son was happy with his wife. The woman replied, "She has the three traits we asked for but my son says that they are in the wrong order. She is sexy in society, a housewife in the bedroom, and a lady in the kitchen, never lifting her hand to do any work!"

Another practical and useful function of the pubic bath was as an informal employment agency. If a family needed a maid or other servant, a word in the ear of a favorite *dallak* was usually all that was needed to find a suitable employee. *Dallakha* also acted as confidants and counselors as they became more and more acquainted with their steady customers. They also prescribed home herbal remedies for various complaints. For example, if a woman complained that her husband was too passionate, the *dallak* might advise increasing the amount of yogurt in his diet and the use of rooster's meat instead of hen's meat. One time a woman complained to her *dallak* that her husband was impotent. The *dallak* prescribed the use of a drug made by grinding the nuts of a certain tree. The woman slipped some of the drug in her husband's food, and the next morning he awakened with a painful priapism that refused to go down. Finally, after enduring it for a couple of days, he went to his doctor who admitted him to a hospital for surgery!

The male *dallakha* were usually accomplished masseurs; many men went to the public baths just to lie on the warm stone platform and luxuriate in their skilled hands. In addition, the male *dallakha* practiced other skills on a part-time basis outside the baths. They were skilled at bloodletting and performing circumcisions; many were barbers and/or tattoo artists. This moonlighting helped to supplement the meager wages they received as bath attendants.

Another door in the far corner of the public bath led to a corridor lined on one side with about a half-dozen private baths. At the far end of the corridor, there was a small cubicle where women could go to apply a depilatory paste before bathing. This little room, in the old days, was also used for bloodletting by *dallakha* skilled in that procedure. The private baths were fairly large rooms entered by a door off the corridor and separated from each other by a concrete partition about seven feet high. Each bath had its own glassed dome set high in the ceiling and a shower, along with hot and cold water faucets. These were the baths that Gholam reserved for our use; and our family, along with one or two maids and perhaps a visiting relative or two, would fill the entire six baths.

After undressing and donning the loincloths brought from home and the wooden sandals provided by the bath keeper, we would all file through the public bath and, two by two, enter our private bathing rooms. We would sit on our copper trays on the warm floor and wait for our favorite *dallak*, Raana. She flitted from one bath to the other, washing the hair of one person, scrubbing another with their own individual rough scrubbing glove, applying henna mixed with madder root to Grandmother's hair, and in general attending to all our needs. The bath usually lasted two or three hours. From time to time I would go to the other cubicles to visit with my sisters or Soltan, Zivar, and

Naneh. The maids would core fresh pomegranate that had been brought from home and serve it to us in small bowls with a spoon. The juicy meat was so cool and tasty.

Years later, although I did not frequent public baths since we had modern facilities at home, I paid a visit out of curiosity to a bath in Tehran called Brelian, which had been recommended as being the best bath in the city. The layout of this bath was different from the one we used in Mashhad. It was the modern type that did not have a common bathing room, but rather had only private bathing cubicles. From the street, one entered a large waiting room furnished with chairs and sofas with magazines and newspapers on small tables for the entertainment of the customers while they waited. An elegant chandelier hung from the ceiling and the floor was marble, deep red in color. In one corner sat a cashier who accepted your money on the way out and wrote down your number when you arrived.

When your number was called, you were escorted through a door into a huge round chamber with the usual glass-domed ceiling. The floor was white marble with a design in red marble. About thirty doors lined the walls all round the chamber, each with a light over the door that was turned on when the bath was occupied. The attendant led you to the bath assigned and wrote down the time on a ticket, which he hung on the door. The charge for the use of the bath was based on how long you used it. If you wanted a *dallak* or any refreshments to be served, you gave him your order before entering the bathing cubicle.

The individual private baths had a dressing room about two meters square separated from the bath by another door, next to which there was a high glass window. A light bulb hung from the ceiling in front of the window providing light for the dressing room and the adjacent bath. A dressing platform with hooks on the wall for hanging clothing ran along one wall. Clean folded towels that one could spread out and sit upon while dressing were stacked at one end. A mirror hung from the opposite wall. The day that I went, the attendant told me that there would be about a thirty-minute wait for a *dallak*. I latched the outer door, undressed, and entered the cozy glass-domed bathing room. A platform made from a single white marble slab about four feet wide ran along one wall. Hot and cold water taps were in the wall

221

at the end of the platform and, next to them, a showerhead jutted out. To the left of the entrance door, there was a bucket filled with permanganate solution, which one could slosh over the marble platform to sterilize the surface. I dipped some of the solution from the bucket, tossed it all over the platform (although it was already clean), filled a copper bowl from the hot water tap, and then rinsed it off. I then turned on the hot water of the shower and let it run until the room was filled with steam. I turned off the shower and lay down on the heated marble platform to await the knock of the *dallak*.

It was so peaceful and quiet. Through the steam-filled room, I could barely see the light filtering through the glass in the domed ceiling. It looked as far away as it did in my childhood visits to the bath in Mashhad. In my mind, I returned to those days. I could hear my grandmother talking with our *dallak*, Raana, and the chattering and giggling of Zivar and Soltan with the tumult of the public bathing room in the background. My nostalgic ruminations were suddenly interrupted by the knock of my *dallak* on the door, and I got up to let her in. When I got home that afternoon I immediately called Grandmother in Mashhad. She was alarmed that I called, because I had talked with her only a few days before. She asked me what was wrong, convinced that I or my child were ill or worse. I reassured her that all was well and told her that I just missed her; I could not put into words the longing that I felt for the happy days of my childhood.

There was an amusing story printed in a newspaper in Tehran about an incident that occurred in a public bath in another city, the name of which I have forgotten. It seems that somehow a man managed to get employment as a *dallak* in the women's section of a public bath. He managed to disguise himself as a woman for several years before he was found out. All of the husbands in the town were enraged that this man had been massaging and washing their wives for years and were ready to form a lynch mob. The man managed to escape from the city and was never caught. The newspaper account editorialized on the advisability of hiring female attendants only after they had been interviewed in the nude. It is said that husbands in that town advised their wives always to lift the skirts of their *dallakha* before submitting to their administrations.

Parenthetically, it should be noted that some males are allowed in female baths; boys up to the age of four or five may accompany their mothers to the bath. A friend of Aunt Ozra once tried to take her six-year-old son to the bath with her. The bath attendant eyed the boy and said, "This boy is certainly over five years old. You cannot bring him to the bath with you. If I allow it, next time you will probably try to bring his father!"

I mentioned above about how the female bath was also a kind of beauty shop for some ladies, who used their time there to apply henna and madder root to their hair and hands. This reminds me of a story concerning another friend of my Aunt Ozra. It seems that this friend planned to invite a group of ladies to her house for an afternoon tea party. She knew that some of the women would bring along their daughters with their small children, and she tried to think of a way to keep the children occupied while the ladies chatted and smoked their hookahs. She had two teenage daughters; and she told them that if they would baby-sit the children in the basement for two hours, she would pay them. After a whispered consultation, the girls agreed on one condition: Their mother had to tell her guests not to come to the basement to check on their offspring during the party.

When the children arrived, the girls took them to the basement and, after first sending them to the bathroom, sat them down in a circle on the floor. In the center of the circle, they placed trays of cookies and other sweets. Before the guests arrived, the girls had secretly prepared a bowl of henna. When the children were all seated, they told them that they were going to make their hands beautiful, just like their mothers. However, the children must sit still with their palms on their laps facing upward until the henna dried. While they were waiting for the henna to dry, the girls promised to tell them stories, and if anyone wanted a sweet, they would feed it to them. Everything went as planned; the children did not interrupt the party and there was no noisy ruckus from the basement.

After two hours, the girls washed the children's hands, allowed them to finish off the cookies and candy, and sent them to their mothers. The mothers were all surprised to see the dozen or so children all with red hands, but everyone was delighted that they had been able to enjoy an uninterrupted afternoon.

Henna was also used by some men of the older generation to dye their beards, and color their palms and the soles of their feet. In addition to its decorative properties, henna was believed to act as a deodorant and a conditioner for the skin and hair. An old man named Haji Khateeb used to pass by our house every day riding on his donkey. His white beard was always reddened with henna, as were his palms. In addition, his donkey's tail and lower legs were frequently dyed with henna. This aroused Grandfather's curiosity, as well as giving him an opportunity for some gentle teasing.

One day, Grandfather stopped the man and, using the respectful title reserved for one who has made a *hadj*, asked him, *"Haj Agha* [Mister Haji], I know that you love your donkey and he has been serving you faithfully for many years, but why do you put henna on his tail and legs? Is there some secret reason for this that you learned through your religious studies?"

"Not at all," replied Haji Khateeb. "The reason is that whenever I prepare a pot of henna to use on myself, there is always some left over. Rather than waste it, I use it on my friend!"

Our wealthy neighbor, Mr. Golkani, had a private bath erected in the courtyard near his carriage house. This was a miniature copy of the public bath, except for the traditional domed ceiling. Instead, there was a small window high up on one wall that could be opened when necessary for ventilation. The building was constructed of blocks of stone and the bathing room, which had a heated floor, was about four-by-four meters. In one corner there was the usual tank for complete immersion and two showers, along with several hot and cold water faucets lining the walls. A small dressing room connected to the bath, and there was a window between it and the bath with a light bulb hanging in front of it, similar to the arrangement in the modern bath I visited in Tehran.

One weekend day in December, which happened to be the day preceding *yalda*, the longest night of the year, Iran Golkani and I were playing in our house. Just before lunch she announced that she had to go home. She and her sisters had to take a bath because the family was having company that night to celebrate *yalda*.

The celebration of *yalda* is a custom that goes back to ancient times and is rooted in the belief that on that night the sun is reborn, because the days begin to grow longer the following day. It is the custom for families to get together and sit around telling happy stories (no sad songs allowed), all the while consuming melons set aside especially for that night, along with nuts and sweets. The superstitious believe that Hazrat-e-Khezr, a mythical prophet who enjoys eternal life, comes to visit the sad and lonely on that night to grant their wishes. Unmarried boys and girls consume salty nuts in quantity without drinking so that they will go to bed thirsty. Since a thirsty person usually dreams of water, superstition has it that if a person of the opposite sex appears in a dream, and proffers the dreamer a bowl of water, that will be the one he or she marries.

Iran Golkani left, but in a few minutes she returned and told me that her mother said that I could join the sisters in the bath if I wanted to. Of course I did, so I went to my sister Tooran to ask permission. She agreed and helped me to bundle up my towels, clean clothes, scrubbing glove, lava footstone, and comb. She admonished me not to come home with soap in my hair; she knew that the *dallak* who usually came to bath the Golkanis would not be there that day because the public baths would be very busy in preparation for the celebration of *yalda*.

Iran and I ran across the street and went directly to the dressing room of the bath. It was a cold, gray afternoon with the threat of snow hanging in the air, and I looked forward to spending a few hours in the warm bath. Soon the other Golkani girls arrived, and we all began to scrub each other. I was only nine years old, and I wanted to show everyone that I could take care of myself. I washed my hair again and again, each time rinsing carefully by pouring water over myself from a bowl filled from the faucets. Sometimes Iran did the rinsing for me, and I rinsed her. We were in that bath for close to three hours when a maid arrived carrying a tray of delicious cold melon slices with forks. I knew that the melon came from the dark of the Golkanis' basement, where it had been hanging from the ceiling in a cotton net sack waiting to be eaten in celebration of *yalda*. The maid said to us, "Mrs. Golkani says that you girls better get out of the bath before you become fish!"

We all dried ourselves and dressed. I walked home with my scalp burning from the repeated washing. My skin felt raw from the scrubbing, and the skin on my hands was all puckered from the prolonged soaking. However, my sister Tooran was pleased: I did not have any soap in my hair, and she would not have to take me to the public bath the next day to get it out.

As I grew older, the family stopped going to the public bath en masse, and usually Tooran took me to the baths and generally supervised my personal needs. I remember one time when the two of us went to a bath that was not the one we usually patronized. Each bathing room had its own water tank on a platform in one corner. While Tooran sat on her inverted copper tray on the floor next to the water faucets attending to her own bathing and waiting for a *dallak*, I walked up the steps to the open hot water tank in the corner and sat on the edge, playing in the water. Suddenly a thunderous clap resounded through the room and I started, almost falling into the deep rank. Tooran had broken wind and the sound, amplified by the copper tray, reverberated off the stone walls and domed ceiling. Tooran looked up and saw me teetering on the edge of the tank. She shouted at me, "What are you doing up there? Get down here and sit quietly! What if you fell in and I could not get you out in time? Should I tell everyone that you died because I farted?"

Scattered here and there around the city there were a number of buildings of various sizes, the external facades of which were similar to that of the public baths: double wooden doors surrounded by turquoise blue tiles with colorful decorative designs. Behind the doors there was a large chamber with a high domed roof. These were the gymnasiums for men and were called *zoorkhaneh*, meaning "House of Strength." Here men gathered to perform gymnastics, wrestling, and weight lifting. These gymnasiums used to be quite numerous in every city in the old days. Mohammed Reza Shah, who had been educated in Europe where he had learned to love sports, early in his reign encouraged the introduction of Western sports, such as soccer, volleyball, basketball, tennis, and swimming for both sexes. Many of the *zoorkhaneh* then closed due to lack of customers. I was not able to visit any of the *zoorkhaneh*, because when I was a child, women were not allowed entrance. I did see my uncle working out at home with some of the traditional Persian-style weights and Indian clubs.

My curiosity about what was going on inside the *zoorkhaneh* was satisfied later on when, as an adult, I had the opportunity to see the interior of one of the *zoorkhaneh* in Tehran. Queen Farah encouraged the preservation of the old Persian customs, and this particular *zoorkhaneh* had been built recently but in the traditional style. The entrance door was surrounded by the usual decorative tiles, and the door was only about five feet high, forcing all who entered to bow as a gesture of respect. The gymnasium was not particularly large, but the ceiling was quite high and domed. Padded benches for spectators lined two walls, and in the center of the room there was a slightly depressed circular arena where the men performed their exercises.

I saw the men performing the ritualistic Persian exercises, stripped to the waist and wearing their elaborately embroidered knee-length tight pants. The exercises were performed to the rhythm of a *zarb*, a large bottle-shaped drum, beaten by a man called the *morshed* who, while drumming, recited verses of Ferdosi's poetry. The *morshed* sat on an elevated wooden platform at one end of the room where he could command a view of the whole arena. The men who regularly worked out at the House of Strength were classified in a hierarchy according to their strength and experience similar to the belt status of karate students. The beginners were known as *nocheh*; and the highest ranking were called *pahlavan* and *peeshkesvat*, men who had not only achieved superior strength and courage but also a high level of spirituality.

In the old days, *pahlavanha* were noted for their honesty, gentle nature, and trustworthiness. Often, when the man of the house was to be away for a prolonged time, he would approach the neighborhood *pahlavan* and ask him to look after his family and guard his savings until he returned. A true story is told about one *pahlavan* who was asked to look after the family of a man leaving on *hadj*. While the man was away, the wife engaged in several acts of infidelity. When the *pahlavan* learned of this, he was so ashamed at what he perceived as his dereliction of duty that he committed suicide.

The day that I visited the *zoorkhaneh*, I was accompanied by two other lady friends. This particular *zoorkhaneh* had been built primarily as a tourist attraction to demonstrate the traditional Persian exercise routine. There were a number of foreign tourists in the audience that day. We watched the men file into the arena, each greeted with a drum roll by the *morshed* that varied in loudness according to the rank of the entrant. The men formed in circles of ten or twelve, and each group went through a series of exercises together in perfect coordination, beginning with push-ups as a warm-up and progressing through synchronous twirling of Persian-style Indian clubs of various weights; the heaviest club was about three feet long and had a short handle attached to a wooden body having the diameter of a medium-sized watermelon. This exercise was followed by a chain-twirling demonstration using a weighted chain attached to an iron bow. Each man in turn performed in the center of the circle for this exercise. The grand finale was a fifteen-minute session of body twirling, each man leaping and spinning as fast as he could but still keeping time to the progressively faster beat of the drummer. The entire performance lasted about one hour and was most impressive.

Another Persian establishment that is a male-only province is the *ghahveh khaneh*, or coffee shop. These are places where men go to be entertained by professional narrators of epic poetry, to hear and dispense gossip, and to partake in political and economic discussions. In previous years, they were much like the London coffee houses in the days of Samuel Johnson, patronized by the upper-class gentlemen who met for the interchange of ideas. Later on, they degenerated (?) into meeting places for men of all classes. My father and my brothers never frequented the *ghahveh khaneh* when I was a child.

The coffee houses were large rooms with a rug-covered raised platform along each wall where the men could sit cross-legged in the Persian fashion and drink their coffee or tea while smoking a hookah or pipe. They could also play backgammon while listening to the recitation of poetry. In former years, the decor in these establishments was most elegant.

One author describes a coffee house that Shah Abbas, four hundred years ago in Isfahan, used to use often as a place of entertainment for foreign dignitaries. It had mirrored walls and a massive central chandelier, which reflected in a pool in the center of the room. The peripheral sitting platform was divided into rows of individual rooms where the shah and his guests would sit while being served by lithesome young boys who also entertained them with dancing in drag. Nowadays, the *ghahveh khaneh* still serve as a gathering place for men, but their function is more like a pub or neighborhood bar sans alcoholic beverages.

When I was a very young child, we did not have an electric refrigerator in our house. We had a wooden ice chest that was filled daily with ice by the iceman who went from door to door, except during the coldest winter months, servicing his regular customers. During the winter, we made our own ice by putting out a few copper bowls of water to freeze overnight. The ice chest was about five feet long, three feet wide, and stood about three feet high. The walls were several inches thick: two layers of wood with sawdust insulation between and lined on the inside with zinc. Along the back of the chest and separated from the front compartments by a zinc-lined partition, there was a foot-wide compartment to hold the ice. Heavy insulated hinged doors provided access to the ice and food compartments from above. It was so cold inside that if one put a container of liquid next to the zinc wall of the ice compartment, it would freeze.

I remember seeing on walks with Grandmother in the northern outskirts of the city several high long mud brick walls, some straight and others conical in shape, standing alone and not part of any building. I asked what they were for and Grandmother told me that these walls were there to provide shade for the ice-making fields on the north side of the walls. Later on, I found out how the ice was made in the old days. The field on the north side of the wall was divided into many squares, each about twenty by twenty inches and about a foot deep. At the northern end of the field, a deep underground chamber was dug for storage of the ice.

When the temperature dropped to freezing in the evening, the squares in the field were filled with water. Early the next morning, while the field was still shaded from the sun by the wall, the ice was removed from the squares and put into the underground chamber. It was then broken up into bits and sprinkled with water so it would freeze into large blocks of ice. This process was repeated every night until the chamber was filled with blocks of ice each about six feet square. The ice was remarkably clear and free from any particles of dirt.

In the old days, ice-making fields were scattered around the outskirts of all of the cities and villages of northern Persia as far south as Isfahan. Ice making was a community project and, in the larger cities, each neighborhood had its own factory. In the spring, when the ice house was opened for the summer, this was the occasion for a neighborhood festival. I never witnessed any of this because by the time I was born, most ice was made by modern refrigeration methods, even though household refrigerators were not in common use until some years later.

Scattered around Mashhad, as is the case in virtually every city in Persia, there are carpet factories that produce the majority of the beautiful carpets for which Persia is famous. Of course, many are made in remote villages where the women of a household will have their own individual loom on which they will weave rugs and carpets for their own use as well as for sale in the local bazaars. Many of these home-produced carpets are beautifully made and of a design that has been handed down from one generation to the next over hundreds of years, each generation perhaps adding a personal touch. My father knew a man[1] who owned a carpet factory in Mashhad, and he arranged for the girls in our family to visit it when I was about ten years old. Tooran, Azar, and I, along with several cousins, went one morning. The factory building was a single-story structure partly underground, probably to keep it cooler in the summer and warmer in the winter. We entered by walking down a short flight of steps and entered a large concrete-floored room containing about forty looms of varying sizes.

Each loom was made of two horizontal wooden beams between which the warp (vertical) cotton threads were strung;

230

the threads were wound around the upper beam and slowly unraveled as the weaving progressed. Above the top beam, there were mounted rolls of woolen yarn in various colors with the threads of yarn hanging down within easy reach of the weavers who sat on a wooden bench in front of the loom. The weavers in this factory were all adults, chiefly women. However, in the not-too-distant past, the workers were mainly children between the ages of eight to fourteen who spent twelve hours or more each day hunched before a loom, never seeing the light of day. This exploitation of child labor was abolished by a decree of the Mohammed Reza Shah that forbade employment of anyone under sixteen in any carpet factory.

Each loom had a *salim*, or director, who told the workers which color yarn to use for each knot in the particular design. He did this by reading from a scroll on which the design had been drawn, and his reading and instructions to the workers was so rapid that his words were unintelligible to anyone except the weavers. A carpet was started by threading a horizontal cotton string (the weft) in and out between the strings of the warp. A horizontal row of knots was then tied around the warp and another weft string threaded on top of the row of knots. As each row was completed, it was compressed firmly into the preceding row by the *salim*, forming the pile, and the completed carpet gradually appeared under the bench beneath the feet of the workers. The downward compression of the pile gives the hand-knotted rugs a characteristic direction similar to that seen in velvet with the down direction pointing toward the end where the rug was begun.

Two basic knots are employed in the construction of the pile; the Ghiordes, or Turkish whole knot, that is used mainly in the Near East and the Senneh, or Persian half-knot, used primarily in Central Asia and the Far East. In Persia, both types of knots are used, depending upon the town or the origin of the tribe producing the rug. A good quality woolen carpet will have three to four hundred knots per square inch; a carpet woven with silk may have fifteen hundred or more. Regardless of the material used for the pile, hand-knotted carpet weaving is hard, time-consuming work. An expert worker can tie as many as ten thousand knots per day, but even with several weavers working on a single carpet, the largest and most intricate carpets may take months or years to complete.

A carpet kept in the palace in Ctesiphon, the ancient capital of the Sassanid dynasty measured 140 by 28 meters. This carpet was called the *baharestan* meaning "field of spring," and it had emeralds, pearls, and rubies threaded into the pile to highlight its intricate floral design. It, rightly so, was considered a national treasure. The savage bedouin tribesmen sacked Ctesiphon in A.D. 637 during the Arab conquest; and when they entered the palace, they were overwhelmed by its beauty. The *tallar kasra* (throne room) was a huge marble-floored room, the walls of which were covered with gold-threaded brocade. The ceiling was supported by twelve marble pillars and decorated by a planetariumlike depiction of the twelve constellations of the zodiac, each star done in gold leaf. Eight smaller rooms with arched ceilings surrounded the throne room. The *baharestan* was kept in the center of the throne room; and when the tribesmen realized that they could not easily transport the huge carpet, they cut it up into portable fragments that they carted off as one of the spoils of war along with the throne made of gold.

The art of hand-knotted carpet weaving began several thousand years ago, probably originating among the nomadic tribes of central Asia, who had both the necessary material (wool) and the need to keep warm in a bitterly cold winter climate. The rugs produced by these nomads were made on horizontal looms that could be easily transported from place to place. Therefore, they were limited to producing relatively small rugs. The factory that we visited had vertical looms capable of producing carpets of any practical size.

The discovery of the Altai (Pazyryk) carpet in 1949 by the Russian archeologist S. J. Rudenko in the grave mound of a prince of Altai in southern Siberia who lived in the fifth century B.C. showed that the art had evolved to a high level of skill by that time. It was only by chance that this woolen rug measuring six feet three inches-by-six feet four inches was preserved in good condition. Grave robbers had invaded the burial mound soon after the burial and left holes through which water entered and froze, thus preserving the rug in ice. The rug is knotted with the Ghiordes knot and shows a mixture of Scythian, Assyrian, and Achaemenian motifs; some scholars maintain that it is of Persian origin while others regard it as Scythian. It has a double border surrounding a red center containing rows of rosettes arranged in squares. The outer border is a row of horses, some with riders, and the inner border is a row of elk.

Persian carpet design, as it evolved over the centuries, progressed from the simple geometric designs of the nomads to the intricate patterns we see today. The earliest designs probably were simply stylized attempts to copy what the rug maker saw in nature. Some people, over the years, have tried to interject a symbolic meaning to the various geometric rug designs handed down from generation to generation. While it is possible that hundreds of years ago some designs may have had a symbolic meaning, it is more likely that certain patterns have become traditional simply because the artist liked them and they expressed his artistic nature. Flowers and leaves, reflecting a love of greenery by a people living in a mainly arid land, have always been a favorite theme in Persian rug design: chrysanthemums, lotus flowers, iris, and palm trees are all seen, stylized in various manner to express the individuality of the artist. A wide variety of animals and birds are also incorporated in Persian rug designs. Some carpets, especially those from the Kirman area, portray famous people such as the shahs of Persia or wealthy patrons. Certain basic patterns have been ascribed to Persian carpets, but over the years all of the so-called basic patterns have become so modified by various artists that, in effect, there is no basic pattern that has been repeated without change.

There were some businessmen around town who did not have a permanent shop nor were they street hawkers. They simply set up their businesses on the sidewalks. Among these entrepreneurs were shoe repairers, scissors grinders, puppeteers, organ grinders with dancing monkeys or bears, china menders, and street photographers. The street photographers would produce a photo while you waited, similar to the self-photo booths seen today in arcades. They set up a backdrop on the wall of a building with a small bench in front of it on which the subject posed. One of my brothers told me about one photographer who had a backdrop that depicted a life-sized white horse standing in a bucolic setting. A leather rein was attached to the horse's painted bridle and the customer would pose holding the rein in hand. Many city dwellers who never rode a horse in their lives had pictures of themselves that looked as if they had just dismounted.

A friend of our family told an amusing story about an experience with a street photographer. It seemed that the school where she had enrolled her son required that he present several pictures upon enrollment. She had these done in a conventional studio; but after the second day of school, her son came home and told her that he must have two more pictures no later than the next day. Since she had no more studio photos and it would take several days to get additional ones, she sent her son with a servant to have his picture taken by a street photographer. When they returned with the photos, the mother was surprised to see that the servant was in the picture, sitting on the bench with her son standing by his side. She said to the servant, "Why are you in the picture? This is supposed to be a photo ID of my son for his school."

The servant replied, "I thought that the price was too high so I tried to bargain with the photographer. I told him that this was only a child and he should not charge as much. He said that the price was the same for a child or adult, or for one person or two. I thought that you should get your money's worth so I posed with the boy!" Needless to say, the mother sent them back with instructions to the servant to stay out of the picture.

Another street business was the china mender. These men were most skilled artisans and usually quite elderly men. If one had an antique porcelain bowl or plate that was broken, they could restore it. Poor people who had broken pottery that they could not replace would bring the broken vessel to the china mender, and when he was finished with it, they could expect to get many more years of use out of the mended article. The method that the menders used is most interesting. The broken edges of the piece were first coated with a mixture of egg white and lime, then joined together and allowed to dry for several minutes to form a temporary bond. Then the mender would drill a series of parallel holes along each side of the crack on the back side using a hand drill with a bit finer than a sewing needle, if the article happened to be a fine piece of porcelain, or a slightly larger bit, if he were mending a ceramic bowl.

The holes were slightly angled toward the crack and did not go through the full thickness of the china so the front surface was not marred in any way. Fine tin wires were then cut to the proper length, heated one by one and threaded from hole to hole across the crack. The angled hole formed the wire into a hook shape and the wire as it cooled formed a tight bond similar to a series of surgical staples. The artist was so precise in his estimation of the required length of wire that the finished repair formed a seal that was watertight and the crack was barely visible from the inside.

The final step in the process was the application of a coat of the egg white-lime mixture over the row of wire staples to fill any minute space that might be between the wires and their holes. I always marveled at the skill of these old men. They were so deft and precise; and all of this expertise did not command high prices, especially when they were mending a cooking bowl for one of the poor. Of course, if the broken article happened to be a valuable antique requiring many fine holes, the price was higher but, as always the case in Persia, subject to bargaining. Unfortunately, these artisans have gradually died off and no one has been trained to carry on the art form.

The scissors and knife sharpeners also doubled as key makers. They would set up their treadle-operated grindstones on the sidewalk along a busy street or sometimes walk through a neighborhood with the grinder slung over their back, crying out their services. Long strings of keys of varying sizes hung from the wooden sides of the grindstone apparatus. These were not blanks such as are used today in the modern key-duplicating machines, but actual keys that the man had found and collected over the years. If one wanted a key made, the scissors grinder would select a key similar to the one to be made and then, by hand grinding and filing, produce a duplicate in a few minutes. As a child, I loved to watch them as they sharpened knives and scissors. I was fascinated by the showers of sparks given off as they held the scissors against the grindstone.

Outdoor food vendors operated much like the hot dog stands that we see today on the streets of New York. They did not move about but had more or less permanent locations from which they sold various dishes, depending upon the season of the year. In the winter they would sell bowls of hot *ash* (a hearty barley, bean, and meat soup) and in the summer cool bowls of cucumber mixed with yogurt. Kabobs of various meats and vegetables were generally available all year round. One particular dish, a concoction of heart, liver, kidney, and onion with a tomato sauce smelled especially delicious. This dish was known in the old days as *hasratalmolook*, or "prince's envy." The reason for this peculiar name is when royalty passed by a vendor on the street and smelled the delicious fragrance, they could not in all propriety stop and partake of it.

One Persian institution that has survived with little change for hundreds of years is the unique Persian bakery. More properly, I should say bakeries because each bakery specializes in one of the five most common types of bread consumed in Persia. Almost every street around town has several bakeries; and these are crowded every day, especially just before lunch and dinner, because Persians like to eat their bread fresh from the oven. Persian breads are flat and vary in thickness from *lavash*, a parchment-thin, round bread baked on a copper plate, to *shirmal*, a sweet thick bread similar to a light coffee cake. In between there is *taftoon*, a round flat bread a little thicker than *lavash; sangak*, an oval-shaped loaf that is baked directly on hot stones and is about as thick as a finger; and *barbari*, a slightly sweet rectangular-shaped loaf a little less than an inch thick.

Sangak is a very popular bread and one of the most interesting to watch in preparation. The stone oven used is about five feet in width and depth and arches over a flat bed of stones, each about the size of an almond. The stones are heated by a fire beneath the floor of the oven. One man will stand on either side of the oven. One of them shapes the dough into an oval shape and makes a few perforations in the top, then sprinkles it with poppy or sesame seeds. His fellow workman slips the loaf onto a long-handled oiled spatula, then slides the dough onto the hot stones. When the bread is baked, after about ten minutes, one of the men will take a long-handled pitchforklike tool and remove it from the oven. Any few stones that may stick to the bottom are brushed off. The loaf is then impaled on a board through which nails have been driven and set upright on a table for display and sale. All of this preparation, baking, and selling goes on at a rapid pace and is accompanied by the steady din of conversation of the customers as they mill about waiting to be served. The bakery is another great repository for gossip, because servants from various houses in the neighborhood see each other every day there and many tales are told.

A clever and amusing street business is the fortune-telling bird. The proprietor has a small booth with a counter on which there is a narrow rectangular box containing several dozen small envelopes stacked on end. A small bird, probably one of the sparrow family, sits perched on one end of the box and tethered to it by a light cord. The customer pays whatever fee agreed upon after the usual haggling, and the owner claps his hands sharply one time. The trained bird hops along the edge of the box and, apparently at random, seizes the edges of one of the sealed envelopes in his beak and pulls it out. On opening it, the customer finds inside a slip of paper telling his fortune much like one finds on opening a Chinese fortune cookie, only somewhat more detailed and written in verse! I never have been able to determine if the trained bird really picks out the envelope at random or if the trainer gives him some hidden signal!

Note

1. On a recent trip to Vienna, I had the honor of meeting and talking with an elderly Persian gentleman and scholar who was an old friend of my father. He told me an interesting story about the owner of the carpet factory. It seemed that when the Reza Shah went to Mashhad in 1934 for the dedication of the monument at Ferdosi's tomb (see chapter 3), the shah declared that it was inappropriate for him to be driven to the tomb of such a revered Persian poet and announced that he would walk the final kilometer to the tomb as a gesture of his respect for the poet. When the owner of the carpet factory heard of this, he ordered that red carpet runners be made and laid the entire route. The crowds of people who lined both sides of the road were moved to tears and cheers as they watched the militarily erect figure of their king striding along clad in his flowing cape.

Chapter Seventeen
Untold Stories

Out of ignorance I chose a narrow path to follow;
Little did I know it would lead to a well of darkness.
—Baba Taher Oryan

I did not grow up in a particular religious family. Everyone in my immediate family believed strongly in one God and the basic tenets governing social behavior as laid down by the ancient Persian religion, which had its foundation in Mithraism and later in the teachings of Zoroaster. No one in our family really embraced the Shiite Islamic faith or observed the formal customs promulgated by the Shiite mullahs known in Persia as the *akhondha*. Grandmother prayed three times a day, but she never tried to impose her faith on any of the other members of the family. The *akhondha* over the centuries corrupted the basic dogma of the Islamic faith as laid down in the Koran with thousands of superstitions and fabrications that became *akhondi*, or doctrine. They preached these elaborations from their pulpits in the mosques to the ignorant and illiterate masses and, in effect, set themselves up as personal spokesmen for God and the final authority on all religious matters. The religion that they teach is not a spiritual faith in God but is more a stylized ritualistic approach to sermonizing designed to create a mass frenzy, then direct that energy to enhance the power of the mullahs over the minds and hearts of the ignorant (see *rowzeh* ceremony later in this chapter).

As a result of this perversion of pure Islamic doctrine by the *akhondha*, many Persian intellectuals, especially scientists and poets such as Omar Khayyam, Avicenna, Attar, Sa'adi, and

238

Hafiz, as well as many of the educated Persian people of today who were born into the Islamic faith, abandoned the Shiite concept of Islam or lost their faith completely. Avicenna[1] was accused of heresy by the mullahs of his time for his philosophical writings and critiques of the Shiite mullahs' teaching. He answered them with a quatrain that, loosely translated, is as follows.

> To accuse me of heresy is gross nonsense,
> No one believes more strongly in God than I;
> Therefore, in my belief, I am unique in this world.
> If I am a heretic, there is no Islam.

Another backlash against the domination of the mullahs was the emergence in the eighth century of the Sufi, a monastic order who believed in the personal unity of man with God as described in the Koran. Through study and meditation they attempted to achieve an understanding of man's relationship to the Divine. The famous Persian poets Mawlana and Attar embraced Sufism and established their own sects within this philosophy. Omar Khayyam, in his poetry, reflects a philosophy that is basically agnostic. Other intellectuals, such as Sa'adi and Jami, converted from Shiite to Sunni in protest against the proselytizing of the mullahs. The famous poet Hafiz remained a Shiite, but in his poetry he ridiculed the hypocrisy and dissimulation of the *akhondha*.

> Ecclesiastics, who don a cloak of piety in the pulpit,
> Abandon this garment when in private and do otherwise.

Again:

> They closed the doors of the wine shops. Oh, God,
> Do not allow them to open the doors of deception.

Not all Persian intellectuals were as outspoken against the Arab conquerors as those mentioned above. Some devoted their skills to promoting themselves in the new Islamic world. They learned Arabic so well that they were able to correct grammatical errors in that language as spoken by the bedouin. They wrote literature and scientific treatises in Arabic and some changed their names to the Arabic equivalent. They welcomed Arabs into their families by marriage with their daughters and became more fanatical Moslems than the Arabs themselves. They found a place in the rapidly expanding Islamic Empire and contributed much to the building of such Islamic architectural masterpieces as the Alhambra in Grenada, Spain, and the Taj Mahal in India.

The characteristic dress affected by the mullahs is a white, green, or black turban (the *ammameh*), sometimes containing as much as six meters of fabric, and a *ghaba*, a loose-fitting ankle-length robe with a sash about the waist. The robe has deep pockets on either side that reach to the knees. These pockets, in the old days, served as carryalls for gifts of money, food, or other things that the mullahs received for officiating at weddings, funerals, and other ceremonies. There is an old Persian homily, "A mullah's pocket can never be filled." This has a dual meaning: The size of the pocket is very large; and secondly, a mullah's appetite for wealth is insatiable.

This reputation for avarice reminds me of another story about a mullah who fell into a deep stream and managed to save himself from drowning by clinging to a large rock near the shoreline. However, he was too weakened to pull himself to safety and so he just clung there, shouting for help. A man passing by heard him and made his way to within reaching distance of the exhausted mullah. "Give me your hand," the man shouted, "and I will pull you out!" The mullah did not budge from his precarious position. "Give me your hand," the man shouted again. Again there was no movement on the part of the mullah. Then the rescuer remembered the old saying about mullahs, "A mullah never gives but only takes." "Take my hand," the man yelled; and the mullah promptly grabbed it and was pulled to the shore.

The wearing of a black turban signifies that the mullah believes that he is Arabic in ancestry and a lineal descendant of the prophet Mohammed. The green turban is worn by those who believe that they are direct descendants of Ali, Mohammed's son-in-law. The outfit is completed with a loose-fitting sleeveless cloak *(abba)* worn over the *ghaba*. One sees these strangely garbed figures shuffling about the streets, clutching a string of prayer beads in their hands, with their lips in constant motion, ostensibly immersed in silent prayer.

Mullahs never wear conventional shoes; their feet are clad in socks and *nalain*, sandals of soft leather that slip off easily when entering a mosque or a private home. These sandals allow the mullah to walk noiselessly. There is an amusing story told about one mullah who was a notorious crook. He tried to counter his reputation by assuming an air of great piety, so much so that he attached small bells around his ankles so that ants could hear him coming and get out of the way before being stepped on inadvertently. He became known as "Mullah Bell-foot," and to this day, thieving mullahs are called "bell-foot mullahs."

Akhondha are unique to the Shiite sect of the Islamic religion. This sect arose out of a schism in the ranks of the followers of Mohammed, which was both politically and religiously motivated, in the early days of Islam. The Arabs by the year 680 had conquered the Middle East, and their empire extended from India to Spain. Mohammed had not designated anyone to succeed him upon his death in 632 A.D.; and during the early years of this period of conquest and expansion of the Islamic Empire, it was ruled by a succession of caliphs who governed by mutual agreement. The fifth one following the death of Mohammed was Muawiyah Ummayad, who was succeeded by his son Yazeed. A group of dissidents, later known as Shiites, formed and attempted to overthrow the Ummayad dynasty on the basis that only the direct descendants of Mohammed, specifically Ali, the husband of Fatima, Mohammed's daughter, and Ali's sons al-Husayn and al-Hasan were entitled to assume the title of caliph.

Ali had become the fourth caliph but was supplanted after a brief term of office by Ummayad. His eldest son, al-Hasan, renounced all claim to the caliphate succession; but Ali's younger son, al-Husayn, gathered a group of followers and continued the movement to overthrow the Ummayad dynasty. This culminated in the battle at Karbala where Yazeed Ummayad prevailed and slaughtered al-Husayn along with most of his family. Ali himself was assassinated prior to the battle at Karbala. Muawiyah Ummayad, followed by his son Yazeed, and the rest of the Ummayad dynasty continued to rule the Arab Empire from the capital in Damascus for almost a hundred years.

A few years after the battle at Karbala, a group of Arabs moved from Syria to southern Persia. Some say that this move was necessary since the group was hated by the general populace because they had taken part in the slaughter of al-Husayn and his family. Others say that the move was the result of dissatisfaction with the Ummayad rule. In either event, these Arabs established themselves in Persia and began to circulate about the land telling their firsthand account of the slaughter at Karbala.

The Persian people, still for the main part newly converted to Islam by force or for economic reasons (the Arabs imposed a head tax on those who did not convert to Islam) and confused as to the precepts of that religion, welcomed them and accepted their teaching. Over the years these Arabs became assimilated with the native Persians, and they and their descendants became the religious authorities known as mullahs. At the same time, patriotic Persian leaders were trying to find a way to shake off the Sunni Arab domination, so the Shiite sect evolved as a form of a national expression of independence.

Dissatisfaction with the Arab rule was also expressed by a resistance movement that attempted to foment open rebellion. The Ummayad dynasty was terminated in 750 by a coup led by Abulabbas, the founder of the Abbassid dynasty. Abulabbas was aided by a Persian folk hero named Abumoslem Khorasani, who had gathered a group of Persian followers called *Javanmardan*. This group had started in the province of Khorasan and had successfully deposed the provincial Arab governor. Over several years, the *Javanmardan* led by Abumoslem managed to gain control over all the provinces in Persia.

Abumoslem secretly offered his help to Abulabbas to overthrow the Ummayads on the conditions that the capital be moved from Damascus to Baghdad, then a city in Persia, and that each province of Persia should continue to be governed by a Persian approved by Abumoslem. Thus, through the political process initiated by Abumoslem and the religious schism brought about by the Shiite sect, Persia achieved a measure of independence from Arab domination. Complete independence and unity were not to be had until some hundreds of years later and following a series of invasions by, among others, the Mongols under Genghis Khan. In the first decade of the sixteenth century, Shah Ismail, founder of the Safavid dynasty, united Persia and made Shiism the official religion of Persia.

By this time, the *akhondha*, while still relatively few in number, had become deeply entrenched in Persia; the common people, who had suffered the most during the turbulent years of conquest after conquest, flocked to them for spiritual solace. There is a saying in Persia that one will flee from a viper to find refuge with a rattlesnake. And so the people, who hated the Arabs, chose the mullahs whom they thought to be the lesser of two evils. The mullahs established schools—not to educate the people, but to propagate their philosophy. They formed a religious hierarchy that played a major role in the justice system of the country based on their interpretation of ecclesiastical law. The influence of the mullahs on Persian politics waxed and waned under succeeding dynasties. Nadar Shah, founder of the Afshar dynasty that succeeded the Safavids, was a Sunni. He despised the superstitious teachings of the Shiite mullahs and virtually stripped them of all power and revenues.

The next dynasty to come to power, the Zandih dynasty, was Shiite—but not fanatically so—and assumed a neutral attitude toward the mullahs. The mullahs achieved their greatest power and influence under the succeeding Qajar dynasty, which ruled for over 130 years. The mullahs became virtually a government within the government.

The Reza Shah, founder of the Pahlavi dynasty, firmly believed in the separation of church and state. Under his and his son's rule, the mullahs lost most of what they had gained under the Qajars. Of course, the fundamentalist movement led by the Ayatollah Khomeini resulted in the mullahs achieving complete power. The wave of executions that swept over the country following their takeover inspired a number of black-humored stories. One story I remember tells of one man telling another that all of the people in a certain city who had six fingers would be executed by the Revolutionary Guard.

"That's not so bad," his friend replied. "Not very many people have six fingers."

"That's true," answered the other man. "The problem is that

first the people are killed, then the number of fingers are counted!"

Most mullahs possess a sonorous well-pitched voice that has been trained from childhood. However, their education is limited, for the most part, to the study of Islamic law as set forth in the Koran plus the elaborations promulgated by the *akhondha* over the years. They are usually quite eloquent and are able to speak for hours using their voice like an organ, raising and lowering the pitch, creating an almost hypnotic effect on their audiences. The usual forum for the mullahs is a ceremony called *rowzeh*, a gathering for the recital of the tragedies that befell Hossein, grandson of Mohammad, at the city of Karbala. A *rowzeh* can take place in a mosque or in a private home. While listening to the mullah's feigned tearful recital complete with wiping of his eyes, the audience is expected to beat their chests and cry in mourning. During the months of *moharam* and *saffar*, the months according to the Islamic calendar when the tragedies at Karbala took place, *rowzehha* are held more frequently. One can walk along the streets and see black flags hanging out in front of various houses signifying that a *rowzeh* will be held there every day for two weeks or even a month. Anyone is welcome to walk in and listen. Of course, the sexes are not allowed to mingle; most of the *rowzehha* held in the homes are for women and those held in the mosques are chiefly for men.

Another forum for the mullahs is the *tekyeh*, a circular amphitheater with a central raised stage, where passion plays are staged to reenact in detail the slaying of al-Husayn and his family. At one side of the stage there is a pulpit from which a succession of mullahs each recite a *rowzeh*, and the audience is encouraged to participate in the usual manner by wailing and singing mournful songs. This goes on for hours. Then the black-clad actors will enter singing songs of mourning while beating their chests. They proceed to the stage and act out the deaths of al-Husayn and each member of his family, all the while accompanied by the wailing and singing of the audience.

In addition to attendance at *rowzehha* and the performances at the *tekyehha*, the mullahs prescribe other public acts of mourning that purportedly will bring people closer to God and ensure their passage into heaven. These include *seeneh zani*, wherein a group of men will walk through the streets beating their breasts in rhythm to the singing of one of the men and repeating the song in unison. They will walk along and be joined by others, all headed for a mosque where they will sit for hours and continue their ritualistic mourning.

Other more horrible and revolting acts are the *zangeer zani* and the *ghameh zani*. The former is self-flagellation. A group of men wearing long-sleeved black shirts with the back cut out will walk through the streets and beat themselves on their bare backs with a heavy metal chain until the flesh is purple with bruises and bleeding. The *ghameh zani* is another act of self-torture. A band of men with shaven heads sit in the street or walk along together, wailing and singing, all the while slashing their heads with sharp knives or razors until the blood runs down, covering their faces and soaking their clothing. These men wear white clothing instead of the traditional black of mourning so as to better show the blood they are shedding.

The Reza Shah forbade all of these disgusting public displays and also banned the practice of holding *rowzeh*. The police were ordered to watch carefully for any infractions, but some of the pious Moslems still managed to carry on private *rowzehha* in secret. One of my brothers told me that one time three of our servants wanted to fulfill a *nazr* (promise to God) by attending a *rowzeh*. They found a willing mullah and walked all the way to Kooh Sangi, the mountain south of Mashhad, where the mullah performed his preaching for them in an isolated spot. On the way back home, two policemen on horseback stopped them and questioned them at length as to what they were doing in the area. They managed to convince the police that they were merely out for a walk.

Mohammed Reza Shah, early in his reign and while still inexperienced, made a grave political error. He did not heed the warning expressed in the Persian proverb, "If you unleash a mad dog, he will not only bite strangers but will also attack the family." The young shah allowed the mullahs to again wear their traditional robes and conduct many of the previously forbidden religious ceremonies, including *rowzehha*. He also made the wearing of *chador* by women a personal option. The practices of self-flagellation and mutilation described above were still forbidden, but gradually groups of men began to be seen again on the streets performing *seeneh zani*. During the high days of the months of *moharam* and *saffar* when most of the public religious practices took place, our family stayed at home and avoided the streets.

Other more benign forms of public mourning that were tolerated by the son of Reza Shah were the *shabeeh* and the *tazieh*. These were street performances where religious people, who were not mullahs but rather the equivalent of the deacons in the Christian churches, would preach to the people while showing painted scenes illustrating the events at Karbala or scenes of hell showing the fate that would befall the unfaithful (the *shabeeh*) or put on a passion play *(tazieh)* in the street.

All of the above are group activities, but the mullahs also prescribed many acts of a personal nature that should be performed by the faithful. Among these is the *nazr*, a personal contract with God in which the supplicant, in return for the divine granting of a wish, promises to perform an *ash nazri* or other penance. The petitioner performing an *ash nazri* places a tray on top of an empty pot in front of his house to solicit donations of money from others who wish to participate in his spiritual agreement. The money is supposed to be used to buy the ingredients to prepare *ash*, a thick soup, for distribution to the poor. Often the money remains in the pocket of the solicitor and the *ash* pot remains empty. In all fairness, before one condemns this practice as a fraud encouraged by the religious hierarchy, one should consider the numerous charitable organizations in the United States who solicit money with the tacit approval of the government in the form of their being granted nonprofit tax exempt status by the Internal Revenue Service. Too often these charities turn out to be simply schemes to defraud the public, with 95 percent or more of the money being used for "administrative costs." A scam is a scam is a scam the world over!

While there is some merit in the performance of an *ash nazri* if it is carried through as intended to provide food for the poor, there is another form of *nazr* called *sofreh nazri*, literally "tablecloth vow," that only serves to line the pockets of the presiding mullah(s) and fill the bellies of the guests. This ceremony is performed only by women and is held in the home of the hostess. I, shortly after my first marriage in order to avoid offending my new family, reluctantly attended one at the house of a distant relative of my in-laws. The ceremony was held in the large parlor of our hostess's house. I arrived a little late, because I had to drive cross-town in Tehran through heavy traffic. I entered and saw a large group of women sitting shoulder to shoulder on folded blankets around the periphery of a room from which all the furniture had been removed.

In the center of the room, overlapping white tablecloths covered the carpet and there were all sorts of cold dishes: cheeses, yogurt, halvah, etc., spread around on the tablecloths. Before each lady there was a plate with a spoon and a fork. On one side of the room a female mullah in *chador,* flanked by two assistants, sat cross-legged in haughty silence. No one touched any of the food, and after I and one or two other latecomers had been seated, the mullah began her preaching.

The mullah started out with the usual narration of the tragedy at Karbala, embellishing the facts with her own interpretation of them as well as the superstitions that had been preached so many times over the years they came to be believed factual. One particular absurdity stands out in my memory. She was telling of the death of Ali Asghar, the six-month-old son of al-Husayn. During the fighting, the baby was crying because there was no water to slake his thirst. Al-Husayn held up the infant in his arms and shouted to his enemies, "You are fighting with me and my men. Why do you make this baby suffer? Let him have some water." Thereupon, one of the archers in Yazeed's army let loose an arrow that pierced the baby's mouth, silencing him. The mullah said that the baby's blood did not drop on the ground but rose to the sky. "That is why the sky is red at sunset every evening! It is the blood of Ali Asghar we are seeing. Remember this!"

When I had first entered the room and saw the mullah sitting there looking so regal and all-wise, I thought that perhaps I would hear something profound and worthwhile during the course of her preaching. But as soon as she began and I heard one nonsensical story after another, I changed my mind. I was reminded of a verse of poetry from one of the old-time Persian poets, whose name I have forgotten, that goes something like

247

this, "Do not be fooled by a head beneath a turban [a mullah]. An empty dome will echo any noise."

After the sermon had ended, servants brought in a variety of hot dishes and the assembly fell to, especially the mullah and her assistants who gorged themselves. The *sofreh nazri* finally ended with dessert and I excused myself. Once outside, I took off the obligatory black scarf that I had worn inside; some of the other women had worn a black *chador* that they had brought with them in defiance of the edict of the Reza Shah. I drove home in the sunset, and as I gazed at the red sky, I thought of the ridiculous story I had heard. I turned my thoughts to the accomplishments of the ancient Persian scientists such as Khayyam and his colleagues, who had determined the time of the vernal equinox to the second, and wondered what their reaction would have been if they had listened to the diatribe to which I had been subjected. It made me sad and frustrated to think that the descendants of these geniuses had become so gullible and easily influenced that they would take part in the nonsense that I had just witnessed.

Another personal type of *nazr* most often seen in the vicinity of a shrine is a special form of begging, supposedly for the poor. The beggar carries a brass bowl in the center of which there is a brass replication of a human hand with the fingers extended upward. This represents the severed hand of Abbas, the man who, in Islamic legend, ran for water during the battle at Karbala. He was overtaken by a horseman of the opposing forces who slashed off the hand in which he was holding the water bag. Abbas transferred the bag to his other hand and the same thing happened. He then carried the water bag with his teeth, only to have the bag pierced by an arrow and the water lost on the ground. Abbas died, of course, but the supposedly true story of his heroic effort lives on in the preaching of the mullahs. Whoever puts money into this special bowl can participate in the *nazr*, but whether or not the money actually goes to help the poor is again a matter for speculation.

The Islamic Sunni sect have few shrines, the holiest being the Black Stone in the holy city of Mecca. This is a large meteorite that fell on that spot hundreds of years before Mohammed founded the Islamic religion. This stone had been a site of worship by polytheistic Arab tribes for centuries. The stone is covered by a structure called the Kaba, supposedly erected by Abraham. When Mohammed conquered the tribes controlling Mecca, he destroyed the idols and paintings that had accumulated around the Kaba and established it as a place of worship of the one true God, Allah.

The Islamic Shiites, on the other hand, have numerous shrines in Persia as well as in Baghdad and elsewhere. Any place that a descendant of Mohammed is purportedly or actually buried, or any object declared sacred by a grand *akhond* (mullah) may be declared a shrine. Some shrines are established out of expediency or to benefit a local mullah financially or politically. On the road between Tehran and Mashhad near the town of Nishabur there is a village called Ghadamgah, which many years ago was a tiny hamlet. In this village there is a tomb of a minor scholar. The courtyard adjacent to the tomb is paved with blocks of limestone, and on one of the blocks someone had carved an oversized left footstep pointing toward the holy city of Mashhad.

This footstep appeared miraculously one morning, but was probably carved during the night by a pilgrim on the way to Mashhad. It was no doubt intended as a directional sign similar to the footstep with a heart carved into the stones leading from the former waterfront of the ancient city of Ephesus that pointed the way to the local brothel for the convenience of newly arrived sailors. The local mullah did not enjoy a good income in this tiny village. He happened upon the idea of declaring the footstep to be a miraculous sign left by an invisible descendant of the Prophet who had visited the tomb and blessed the place. Henceforth the tomb would be designated a shrine and the village became known as Ghadamgah—The Footstep Place. The income of the local mullah thereafter increased considerably since travelers en route to worship at the Imam Reza shrine in Mashhad would stop to pray at the village shrine.

Another example illustrating how some shrines are established through political expediency is the story told about Shah Naseraldeen Qajar who had four legal wives and hundreds of concubines in his harem, most of the latter being young and beautiful. These girls insisted on frequent visits to the shrine in Rhay, a city south of Tehran, for worship. In those days the return trip took a whole day. The shah became suspicious of the excessive piety of the young girls and began to suspect that perhaps the time was spent indulging in some hanky-panky rather than in prayer. He could not openly forbid them permission to worship, so he called upon the head of the local mullahs for advice.

The mullah told him not to worry. He told the shah to announce one morning that he (the shah) had had a dream the previous night in which a tree growing near the *andarooney* (women's quarters) of the palace had appeared to him surrounded by a bright glowing light. The shah was then instructed to call upon the mullah to interpret the dream. The mullah's interpretation was that the tree must be growing over the site of a grave of one of the descendants of the Prophet, and therefore this was a sacred place just as suitable for worship as the shrine in Rhay. The shah erected an enclosure about the tree and henceforth the maidens all worshipped at home under the watchful eye of the shah.

Concubinage is an ancient custom believed to have started in China. The practice of keeping a concubine, in addition to a legal wife, was not only for sexual gratification but also a status symbol and, because of the expense involved, limited chiefly to the wealthy elite. In China, the concubine had certain legal rights. For example, her children were considered legal offspring of her master and belonged to his legal wife. The concubine became part of the household of her master and sometimes became a powerful influence in the household affairs. The practice of concubinage is permissible under Islamic law but, in contrast to the Chinese practice, the man bears no responsibility for any children born to his concubine.

In order to abet more temporary dalliances, the Moslems introduced a form of legalized (religiously speaking) prostitution. This is called *sigheh*, meaning "temporary marriage." The Sunni sect, for the most part, do not practice *sigheh*; but it is a common practice among the Shiites. The marriage may last one hour, several days, or even months, depending on the desires of the "john." The women willing to become *sigheh* are usually divorced or widowed without other means of support, and they are frequently found wandering around religious shrines. The

250

price and duration of the marriage is settled upon by the usual negotiation; and then a mullah (or any man who knows the Arabic words) asks the woman if she agrees to the marriage to which she replies, "*Baleh* [yes]," and the transaction is completed. The mullah deducts his percentage of the fee, and the balance goes to the woman. Obviously, the mullahs had a vested interest in the practice of *sigheh* and encouraged it.

Under Islamic law, a free man is entitled to have four wives[2] and a slave who embraces Islam is allowed two. Both classes may keep as many concubines as they can afford. An old Persian anecdote tells of a man, recently widowed, who was prevailed upon by his relatives to remarry. The man agreed but stipulated that any prospective bride must have four qualities: she must be a virgin; she must be beautiful; she must be rich; and she must have a good disposition. After much searching, his relatives reported that they could not find one woman with all of the attributes specified, but they had found four women each of whom had one of the necessary qualities. The widower then proceeded to marry all four of the women!

Under Islamic law, a man is entitled to divorce a wife with or without her permission merely by taking their marriage certificate to a notary public and, in the presence of one witness, state that he wishes to divorce his wife. The notary affixes his stamp to the certificate, and the divorce is done even though the wife is not present or even notified in advance. The man is then obliged to pay to his ex-wife whatever money and/or property that was specified in their marriage contract. It became customary over the years for the family of the wife-to-be to negotiate the marriage settlement so as to specify that any payment of money by the husband in the event of a divorce should be in a defined number of gold coins, thus protecting her from loss due to inflation.

Under Islamic law, women could not sue for divorce. The Mohammed Reza Shah gradually managed to do away with this inequitable treatment of women. First, he decreed that only a monogamous marriage would be legal. Then he forbade unilateral divorce and ordered that a divorce could only be obtained by mutual agreement of both parties and granted by a secular court of law. The man still had the right of custody over any children over age six, if he so desired.

Sometimes, especially if the man divorces his wife in a heat of anger, he may decide that he wants to remarry her. The woman usually agrees to this in order to preserve the unity of the family and have a means of support. This marriage and remarriage can happen three times; but a fourth marriage is not allowed unless the woman first marries another man, consummates the marriage, and then is divorced by him. This introduces a problem for the original husband. He must find someone whom he can trust to marry the woman for a short period and then divorce her after one or two days. This custom was inculcated in Islamic law as a punishment for the man, who has to go through the mental agony of realizing that his wife will be enjoyed by another man.

The temporary husband is called a *mohallel*. The Shiite mullahs decreed that the *mohallel* must be a mullah and usually an older mullah whom people believe they can trust. The *mohallel* is paid a fee for his services, as well as enjoying the one or two nights with the woman. This is probably why the mullahs created a monopoly by specifying that only they can serve as a *mohallel*. Many funny stories have been told about this practice of hiring a *mohallel*. Sometimes the mullah, especially if the woman is young and beautiful, will refuse to divorce her. The man then has no choice but to raise the ante until the mullah has been paid enough to carry out his original bargain. On the other hand, the woman may decide that she is better off married to the *mohallel* and plead with him not to divorce her. The woman may also decide, after being divorced from the *mohallel*, that she does not want to return to her original husband. Having savored a different sexual experience that may have been more satisfying than she had with her first husband, she might feel that it would be better to look for another fish in the pond!

Before the divorce reforms were instituted, I remember hearing a true story at a party I attended with some other ladies. It concerned a local businessman and his wife, who were going to go to the airport to see the man's boss off on a trip. Before leaving, the husband insisted that his wife put on all of her jewelry and her mink coat, ostensibly to create a good impression on his boss. After they left the airport, the man went to work and the wife returned home. She found that her house key did not open the lock on the front door. When she knocked, a servant answered, opening the door a crack because of a newly installed chain lock. The servant slipped his hand through the opening, handed her a paper, and said, "Your husband has divorced you and he told me to give you this and tell you that you are no longer to come to this house."

I had a European friend in Tehran who married a Persian man, whom she met while he was studying in Europe. Her husband's family were very religious, and in order that their marriage be legal in their eyes, they insisted that the couple be remarried in a Moslem ceremony. My friend had become fairly fluent in Farsi, but she could not understand a word of the incantations of the mullah during the ceremony. Her husband whispered to her not to worry. He told her that all she had to do was to say, "*Baleh* [yes]," when he nudged her. Although in order to be married in a Moslem ceremony, she had to become a nominal convert to Islam, she really did not know much about the Islamic religion.

Her female in-laws frequently attended *rowzeh*, both at the mosque and at the homes of friends. She was curious about the custom and asked them to take her along with them one time. They agreed to do so, providing that she wear a *chador*. She sat cross-legged on the floor along with the others and listened to the ravings of the mullah, watching with bewildered amazement the other women wailing and beating their breasts. A few days later she called me and asked me to have coffee with her at one of the elegant restaurants on Pahlavi Street. We sat together at one of the tables and she told me about her experience at the *rowzeh*.

She said, "I want to ask you to explain this ceremony to me. I didn't want to ask my husband or his family for fear of offending them. Why do these Persian people sit, crying and torturing themselves over an event that happened to some Arabs hundreds of years ago in another country? They were so intense that they appeared to me like a mother helplessly watching her child drown before her eyes."

"You are asking the right question from the wrong person," I said. "I don't go to *rowzehha* and I don't believe in the preaching of the mullahs. Thinking Persians for hundreds of years have questioned the stories told by the *akhondha*, and the only answer I can give you is that the custom was started by the mullahs over the years since the Arab conquest in order to keep their power over the minds and hearts of the illiterate masses.

"Since childhood, I have had a problem rationalizing some of the basic beliefs of Islam. For example, the Koran states that it is God's will that some people shall be guided to embrace Islam and others will not. Those that are not guided to Islam will burn in hell for eternity. If it is God's will that they not be converted in the first place, why should he punish them by eternal torture?

"Also, the mullahs teach that everyone's fate is inscribed on their forehead at the time of birth by the angel of God and nothing can alter it. If this is the case, then it makes no difference how I lead my life, because whatever I do has already been ordained. If I am evil, why should I be punished for something over which I have no control? Khayyam had difficulty rationalizing predestination and external damnation. One of his quatrains goes something like this:

'You, God, made me the way I am.
I love wine and I love revelry.
Since you decreed my way of life,
Why should you damn me for your creation?' "

Our conversation went on for hours, our coffeetime went on through lunch and into the afternoon. I explained to her, as best I could, the rich culture that had existed for hundreds of years in Persia before the Arab conquest. I told her about the ancient library in Ctesiphon (then a part of Persia) that was one of the most extensive in the world, containing millions of documents and manuscripts, all destroyed or pillaged by the Arabs. A similar fate befell the ancient library at Marvdasht. The largest university in the world at that time was in the city of Gundeshapur in the southern Persian province of Khuzistan. It was a center of learning specializing in medicine and philosophy. It was also destroyed by the Arabs.

I don't know if our conversation helped my friend understand the ceremonial wailing and breast-beating she had witnessed at the *rowzeh*, but I feel that she went home with a better understanding of Persian culture.

Persian scholars were in a state of shock following the Arab conquest. Despite the treachery of a few Persians who fervently embraced Islam and helped the conquerors and the efforts of the *akhondha* to brainwash the masses and keep their power over them, there were always patriotic Persian heroes who attempted to preserve Persian culture and showed their hatred of the Arabs in various ways. Persian artisans and architects learned Arabic and designed and constructed mosques of unsurpassed beauty throughout the Arabic empire. Persian poets, authors, and scientists published in Arabic works that became classics in their fields, surpassing anything ever done by the bedouin conquerors.

About one hundred years after the Arab conquest, the struggle to regain Persian autonomy became more overt. Poets began to produce masterpieces written in Farsi that were more and more satirical of the Arab mullahs' version of the Islamic religion. Pockets of armed resistance led by heroic figures such as Abumoslem Khorasani, Ya'qub Lace Saffari, and Babak Khorram-din deposed local Arab governors and replaced them with Persians. Various parts of the country became in essence feudal fiefs ruled by dynasties like the Ziarian, Deylamian, and Sarbedaran that persisted for several hundred years.

Some of the rebels gave vent to their feelings by attempting to establish new religions. One of these was Behafareed, who wrote his doctrine in Farsi. The basis of his religion was the belief in one God, but his religion was a combination of Zoroastrianism and Islam. Another person who began a religion was Eshagh. He believed that Abumoslem was not dead and would reappear soon. He raised an army that contained a mixture of Persian Christians, Moslems, Jews, and Zoroastrians, and conquered several provinces in the eastern part of Persia. He was eventually defeated by the Arabs and killed.

One of the most interesting of the religious movements that sprang up at that time was led by Hosham ibn Hakeem, nicknamed by his followers "al-Muqanna" (Masked Man), because of his habit of wearing a gold leaf mask to cover a facial disfigurement. He was born eighty-two years after the initial Arab invasion and, as a boy of twelve, had served in the army led by Abumoslem. At about age thirty, he was appointed lieutenant governor of Khorasan province. He was very learned, especially in the science of alchemy, and was an accomplished magician.

Despite the fact that he was appointed to his position by an Arab caliph, he hated their domination and continually sought a way to reestablish Persian sovereignty. He understood mass psychology and decided that the best way to gain a following would be to found a religious movement with himself as leader. He gathered together the remnants of the *Javanmardan,* veterans of Abumoslem's army, and proclaimed himself a prophet in whom the soul of Abumoslem had been reincarnated. He rationalized this by preaching that God, when he created Adam, inculcated in his creation a Divine Presence that was handed down over the years to Abraham, Moses, Jesus, Mohammed, Abumoslem, and finally to himself. His old army friends, including his father-in-law, spread the word; and gradually Hosham became so influential that the Arab caliph ordered his capture and jailed him in Baghdad. Khorasan at that time was not completely under Arab control and the caliph in Damascus was fearful that matters might get totally out of hand if a Persian became too powerful. The caliph died shortly thereafter, and his successor ordered the release of al-Muqanna.

Following his release, al-Muqanna returned to Khorasan and again gathered his followers. They moved north across the Oxus River to the town of Nakhshab. On top of a nearby mountain called Siam, they constructed a walled fortress in the center of which al-Muqanna built his castle. A second wall was built to enclose the mountain and provide a first line of defense. This enclosure was so large that thirty-five thousand men were able to pitch their tents there. The central enclosure about the palace housed the wives of some of the officers who had accompanied their husbands, about one hundred women. The followers of al-Muqanna were distinguished by the wearing of white clothing, which according to Zoroastrian belief symbolizes hope and cheer. It was at this time that al-Muqanna first began to wear the golden mask that hid his scarred face and led to his nickname.

Al-Muqanna is a famous figure in Persian legend because of an illusion that he contrived to attract converts and strengthen his image as a true prophet. He announced that every night for two months he would cause a moon to rise out of a well near the foot of Mount Siam and hang suspended for all to see. Accounts differ as to how he accomplished this, but there is general agreement that the moon was a large disk of light metal coated with mercury to reflect the light. How he managed to make it rise from the well remains a magician's secret, but it is said that it was visible for a distance of 6.24 *farsang*, about fifteen miles. The trick, however, served its purpose well and many supporters flocked to him.

Al-Muqanna ruled from his mountain fortress for a number of years. He defeated several armies sent by the caliph to capture him. Finally, the caliph himself led an army of Arabs from Baghdad to once and for all restore Arab rule in Khorasan and destroy al-Muqanna. A series of battles were fought across the province until the army of al-Muqanna was finally driven behind the outer wall of his mountain fortress. The Arabs laid siege to the fortress and over a period of four months finally breached the outer wall by tunneling beneath it.

A final battle was fought and all of al-Muqanna's commanders, including his father-in-law, were killed. When al-Muqanna saw that the end was inevitable, he prepared a poison and summoned all the women who remained behind the inner fortress wall. He told them that their husbands would all be killed and offered them the choice of falling into the hands of the Arabs or committing suicide with the poisoned wine he had prepared and rejoining their loved ones in the afterlife. All except one woman drank the poison. She managed to hide herself after pretending to drink. She later related that after all the other women died, al-Muqanna took off his golden mask and disposed of the bodies one by one by casting them into the roaring flames of the huge communal bakery. He then took off his clothes and leapt into the flames.

This period after the Arab conquest can be likened to the medieval period in Western history in many respects. After the reunification of Persia and especially after the founding of the Pahlavi dynasty by the Reza Shah, there began a period of enlightenment and modernization. I can only hope that the takeover by the *akhondha* after the revolution will not lead to another Dark Age. I hope and pray that this turn in the cycle of Persian history will soon end, and rationality and progress will be restored.

Notes

1. Avicenna (980–1037) was a Persian philosopher and physician who was a scholar-in-residence at several Islamic courts. His encyclopedia of philosophy was a compendious work that attempted to reconcile traditional philosophy with that of Islam. His famous Canon of Medicine was based on Greco-Roman studies and was later translated into Latin and used for over six hundred years as a basic textbook of medicine in the West.

2. The prophet Mohammed was, of course, exempt from this rule. He, at one time in his life, had many more than four legal wives and many concubines. At the time of his death, he had nine wives. The youngest one, Ayesheh, was engaged to him when she was seven years old and married him at age nine when he was fifty-four years old. When Mohammed died, she was seventeen years old. Mohammed decreed that none of his wives were to be allowed to remarry after his death.

Chapter Eighteen
Potpourri

A secret told to a dear friend is no longer a secret;
Dear friends also have dear friends.

—Sa'adi

Shahrbanoo, my father's oldest sister whom we called Grand Aunt, was born when Grandmother was about fourteen years old. Physically, she was a diminutive, thin person possessing a calm and serene disposition. She was one of the kindest and sweetest ladies whom I have ever known; and because she was so close in age to Grandmother, she seemed like another grandmother to me. She had a tragic first marriage: Her first husband died when she was only eighteen years old. Her second marriage was not very fulfilling because her second husband, a fanatical Moslem, became a mullah. He was not very well educated and was basically antisocial, becoming more and more so as time passed. We never saw him at any of the family gatherings or parties. However, Shahrbanoo always maintained a calm and pleasant demeanor despite whatever inner feelings she may have had. She was a sympathetic confidante to all of us, and whenever she came to visit, I followed her about the whole time, talking with her and listening to her many stories. One story in particular stands out in my memory, possibly because the heroine reminded me of Grand Aunt.

Once upon a time there was a young, beautiful girl, who married a man from a town some distance from her native village. In addition to her physical beauty, she had a cheerful, sunny disposition and always presented a calm, happy face.

After her marriage, she moved to her husband's hometown and took up residence with her husband. Her mother-in-law and her husband's spinster sister also lived in the same household. This girl had no friends or relatives in the town outside of her husband's family. When her husband's friends and relatives met the girl, they were struck with her beauty and personality, and at the same time, they all wondered how she could survive living with the other two women in the same house. The mother-in-law and sister were infamous for their ill natures and spiteful dispositions; the girl would be constantly subjected to verbal abuse.

As time went on, everyone was amazed that the girl still maintained her cheerful manner and seemed in no way affected by her domestic circumstances. Even the mother-in-law could not believe that anyone could be so detached and serene. The mother-in-law, after some months, noticed that the girl had a habit of disappearing for about an hour every day. She decided to find out what the girl was doing, and one day followed her closely but unobtrusively. She saw the girl disappear into a small room off the living room of the house and lock the door. The mother-in-law stood outside the door and listened intently. Soon she heard the girl crying and talking. She was describing all the bad things that had happened to her the day before, pouring out her heart with stories of the abuse that she had taken from her in-laws.

The mother-in-law was convinced that the girl had a lover, whom she somehow managed to meet every day, and she reported what she had seen and heard to her son. The husband at first did not believe his mother, but after she persisted that he should do something to stop this clandestine affair, he decided to investigate and determine whether or not his mother's suspicions were in fact true. Unbeknownst to his wife, he stayed home from work one day. After his wife had gone to her secret room, he stood outside and listened. He heard her sobbing and saying, "I know that you are my friend and that you will keep my secret. You have tried to teach me to be patient, but I cannot stand this any longer. I love my husband, but I hate living here and he pays no attention to me when I tell him about what I am going through. What do you think that I should do?"

The husband was convinced that she had someone inside

the room with her. He angrily unlocked the door and flung it open to confront the suspected lover. To his surprise, all he saw was his wife sitting at a little table in front of a tear-stained rock. He was overcome with shame and remorse. All these months his wife had been talking to her *sang-e-saboor* (pet rock) ! Within a few weeks, he found another house and he and his wife moved out of his mother's house and lived contentedly ever after. In later years, when I heard of people who went to psychiatrists weekly and poured out their troubles to a sympathetic ear, I was reminded of this sad story. When I moved to America, I learned that some enterprising entrepreneur had at one time created a fad for acquiring personal pet rocks and made a great deal of money selling them. Perhaps he had a Persian friend who told him this story!

A *gereh sheytan* (devil's knot) is an expression used by the illiterate peasant class to describe a method that they use to remind themselves to do something. The traditional head covering of the female servants is a large scarf folded into a triangle and fastened beneath the chin, leaving two ends dangling down over either breast. If they want to remind themselves to do a particular task the next day, they tie a knot in the end of one of the front folds. When they awaken the next day, they would see the knot and recall what they were to do. The men use a similar reminder, a short length of heavy twine that they carry in a pocket and knot as necessary.

For example, when Gholam made his daily visit to the market to pick up several items, he would tie a series of knots in his piece of twine, one for each item that he was to purchase. If the number of items bought corresponded to the number of knots, he then knew that he had not forgotten anything. Men also use a pocket handkerchief knotted in the corners for the same purpose. The term "devil's knot" came from the belief that the devil was the one who caused a lapse of memory, and the knot prevented the devil from entering the mind. Of course, the custom is really just a means of reminding oneself by association of ideas, used by a simple people who cannot read or write. I will sometimes do the same thing. For example, if I want to remind myself to make an important telephone call in the morning and do not want to take time to write myself a note, I might put a magazine on the floor by the phone the night before!

One day I noticed Naneh, Grandmother's cook, knotting one end of her scarf. That night, I decided to play a joke on her. After all the servants had gone to bed and were asleep, I crept into Naneh's room. All of her clothes were laid out on a bench near her bed ready to be donned the next morning. Her scarf was lying on top with one knot in one end. I tied another knot in the opposite side and slipped back to my bed. The next morning while Naneh was serving breakfast to Grandfather Khan, he noticed that she had a preoccupied look on her face and was mumbling to herself all the while. He asked her what was troubling her and Naneh replied, "I guess that I am getting old and forgetful. I remember what the knot on this end of my scarf is for, but for the life of me, I can't remember why I tied a knot on the other side!" Poor Naneh never did find out what she forgot to remember.

Another prank that I used to play without the help of my usual cohort in crime, Jamshid, had to do with two of my sisters. In the summertime, during the heat of the day after lunch, they often retired to their rooms and took a short siesta. I was supposed to be taking a nap as well, but usually I preferred to play and, in an effort to amuse myself, sometimes got into trouble, such as the time that I got trapped in the apricot tree in the orchard.

One afternoon, when my sisters were both fast asleep, I slipped into their rooms and sewed the ends of their skirts to the bedsheets. When they awoke and got up, as soon as they started to walk, the bedsheets trailed along behind them. They were very annoyed; and when they came out of their rooms after snipping away the sheets and found out that the same thing had happened to both of them, they instantly blamed Jamshid. Jamshid stood up to their berating in silence, but as soon as he could get away, he came to me and said, "I know you were the one who pulled that trick on Tooran and Azar. If you will help me with something that I want to do, I won't tell on you. If you don't help me, you will be in trouble!"

I agreed, of course, to his blackmail. It turned out that he needed a lookout so that he could work undetected on one of his pranks. Every spring, the cooks under Grandmother's supervision would prepare quantities of thick syrup *(sharbat)* flavored with herbs or the juice of various fruits from our orchard. These concentrates were storied in a pantry, and when guests called they would be served a cool drink made from the syrup diluted with water and iced. One of these syrups was called *serkangebeen* and was made by boiling a bag of mint leaves in water with sugar and a dash of vinegar. The resulting concoction had a yellowish color. One afternoon Jamshid stationed me as a lookout outside the pantry where the syrups were stored. He took one of the bottles of *serkangebeen* from the shelf and emptied about three-quarters of the syrup into a pot, then refilled the bottle with water and a little powdered tumeric. He shook it vigorously to dissolve the tumeric, corked the bottle, and replaced it first in line on the shelf.

A few days later, Grandmother had guests and ordered Naneh to prepare drinks for them. Naneh used the bottle that Jamshid had tampered with and served the guests. Grandmother noticed after her friends had gone that the glasses were still almost untouched. She tasted one of them and was appalled at the horrible flavor. The guests had been too polite to mention the taste, but at the same time they could not bring themselves to drink more than one sip. Grandmother took Naneh to task for serving such a foul-tasting concoction. Naneh was unable to explain why just one bottle out of all those that had been prepared had spoiled. Fortunately for Jamshid and me, they never did find out.

Grandmother had a friend who was several years older than she. This woman was a tall, skinny person who had been widowed for a number of years. She was quite prim and very old-fashioned. She even dressed in the same style as her mother had dressed years before. Her name was Bibi Afagh. One of the old customs that she observed was that no widowed woman should ever go out in public after two o'clock in the afternoon unless she were accompanied by a man. She used to come to visit Grandmother in the morning and usually departed before lunch. If, by chance, she did stay for lunch and could not get back home by

2:00 P.M., she always asked to have Gholam or Mashaallah walk her home.

One day, when she was visiting, she told Grandmother that she needed help with a problem. It seemed that she had been invited to the wedding of the daughter of one of her relatives who lived some distance away in a house that was located well into one of the large bazaars. The wedding was to take place in the afternoon and she had been invited to stay over that night. She asked Grandmother if she could come to our house the morning of the wedding, change her clothes there, and leave in the afternoon accompanied by Gholam. Since her relative's house was some distance from ours, she said that she would hire a horse along with a man to lead the animal so that she could ride as far as possible into the bazaar.

When I say "as far as possible," this calls for an explanation of the physical layout of the bazaar that she had to go through to reach her destination. In Persia, the streets of the bazaars are roofed over, and in the high ceilings there are a series of domes to provide light. The main streets are wide enough to allow a horse-drawn cart to enter for deliveries up to a certain distance, but the branching streets become progressively narrower until they are barely wide enough to allow four people to walk side by side. Also, at this point, the merchants install low beams between the shops on either side of the pathway to display goods such as fabrics, rugs, etc.; and at night, lamps are hung from the beams to illuminate the walkway. These beams make it impossible for anyone to ride down the pathway on horseback. If anyone happens to purchase a heavy, bulky article such as a large carpet, one of the numerous porters who hang around the bazaar is hired to carry it out to where it can be loaded into a *doroshkeh* or a waiting car. Bibi intended to ride as far as she could, then dismiss the horse and groom and walk the rest of the way with Gholam.

On the day of the wedding, she arrived at our house carrying a bundle containing the finery she intended to wear at the wedding. After lunch, she went to Grandmother's bedroom and dressed, emerging a short while later, ready to go. She slipped a long black *chador* over her fancy taffeta dress. The horse with his owner arrived and Bibi stepped on the stool provided and mounted, sitting prim and erect in the sidesaddle. The three walked off, Gholam on one side and the groom on the other. After a few hours, Gholam returned. He had a strange look on his face as if he could hardly contain himself from breaking out in laughter. Grandmother asked him if all went well. He told her that Bibi had been safely delivered, although she had been a little concerned when they got to the beamed part of the bazaar for fear that she might hit her head before they got her dismounted.

Later on that evening, he told Grandfather and my brothers what actually had happened. It seemed that as the entourage entered one of the narrow streets, the groom became momentarily distracted by one of his friends and stopped briefly to talk to him. At the same time, Gholam saw something on display in one of the shop windows and stopped to look at it. The horse and Bibi continued on unattended. Suddenly Gholam heard shouts of laughter from all around. He looked down the street and there was Bibi, a few yards away, hanging by her hands from one of the overhead beams and the horse was walking sedately along several yards ahead. Her *chador* had slipped off and she hung there in all her finery, screaming for Gholam. He and the groom rushed to her to help her down. Bibi shouted to them not to touch her—to be handled by a male would be a violation of her strict Moslem upbringing.

"Bring back the horse, you stupid asses!" she shouted. The groom retrieved the animal and positioned it with some difficulty beneath the beam from which Bibi was dangling. She managed to collapse onto the horse's back, and then stepped down to the stool and the ground. Gholam picked up her *chador* and dusted it off as best he could. She put it back on, dismissed the groom without giving him a tip, and proceeded the rest of the way on foot with Gholam. She did not come to our house to visit for a long time. Finally Grandmother, understanding how embarrassed she must be, went to see her. She told Bibi that she must not feel foolish over such a trivial accident. It could happen to anyone. Eventually, Bibi's embarrassment was mollified and she resumed her visitations. However, the story of "Bibi on the Beam" was told and retold privately among the family and servants for a long time.

It was one of those warm, sunny days in early autumn, a weekend day when the family gathered for the customary weekly lunch. The porch of the north wing of the house had been covered with carpets on which snow-white tablecloths were laid. I was about ten years old and had tarried too long in washing up after playing in the orchard, so I arrived late. The table was full—abut thirty relatives and a friend of one of my cousins were sitting cross-legged on the carpets around the periphery of the tablecloths and already eating. Grandmother usually sat in the very center of the long axis of the table with her back to the wall of the house. She always sat regally erect at these gatherings, smiling and beaming her matriarchal blessing on all the family and guests.

I glanced around looking for a place to squeeze in and saw, next to Grandmother, a narrow opening big enough to accommodate my thin frame. I made my way with some difficulty behind some of the guests and slipped into it. Someone passed me a plate of salad: cucumber, tomato, and onion. I began to eat the tomato and cucumber, but I pushed the onion to one side of the plate because I did not like it. Grandmother, while she was eating and talking with those seated around her, from time to time would glance down at me. She noticed that I was not eating my onion. Finally, she leaned over and whispered in my ear, "You should know how important it is for a girl your age to eat onion. If you eat plenty of onion now, when you grow up you will have beautiful large breasts."

I looked across at a recently married cousin who was sitting there dressed in a light summer dress, the décolletage showing her generous bosom. I decided then and there that I would like to be like that when I grew up. I managed to eat a few pieces of onion that day; and from then on I forced myself to eat it, even though sometimes it was so hot it brought tears to my eyes. Gradually over the months, I cultivated a taste for the vegetable and I still love to eat onion, both cooked and raw.

Years later, when I was visiting Grandmother in Mashhad one summer, we sat in her room one afternoon reminiscing. I reminded her of that day when she had advised me of the magical powers of the onion. I pointed to my less than ample bosom and said to her, "You were always very wise and gave me good advice when I was growing up except this one time when your advice didn't work."

Grandmother smiled her loving, wise smile and replied, "Yes it did. You like onions now, don't you?"

Another thing that I remember about that same luncheon party was a story told by a guest from Tehran, who was a friend of one of my cousins. Somehow, the conversation had gravitated to a discussion of ghosts, spirits, and *jinn*—those sometimes good and sometimes evil presences that now figure so prominently in Persian folklore after being introduced by the Islamic conquerors centuries ago. The belief in *jinn* predates Islam; the ancient Arabs believed that *jinn* were an invisible counterpart to man and, like man, were partly bad and partly good. In the Koran, there are many references to *jinn*; for example, Sura 72, 6, and 48. It is written that when Mohammed recited the Koran to the *jinn*, some were converted to Islam but others persisted as infidels. We didn't have any ghosts or spirits in our house except for the one that Gholam insisted he saw in the orchard late at night and those (my brothers) who repeatedly moved Mashaal-lah's bed one summer. The only *jinni* I had ever heard of was the one that was supposed to have appeared to Zivar in the depths of the stairwell of the public water reservoir.

The man from Tehran related a story about a house that was supposed to be haunted by *jinn*. His uncle owned a tailor shop on a street off Sepah Avenue, a main thoroughfare in down-town Tehran. Across from his shop there was an old two-story residence that the owner rented out. The uncle noticed that who-ever rented the house stayed there only a few months, then moved out. The house would remain empty for a while, but because the rent was cheap, sooner or later another family would move in only to leave after a short time. One of the residents became friendly with the tailor and told him about the mysteri-ous things that were happening in the house.

He said that late at night, especially on those nights when the moon was full, the family would hear from their second floor bedrooms the sounds of revelry and voices from the first floor. As soon as they got up and started downstairs to investigate, the noise would stop. One night, they heard sounds of laughing,

267

music, and dancing coming from the parlor. The man leapt out of bed, ran downstairs, and quickly turned on the lights. The rest of the family followed behind him. They found no one in the parlor, but the furniture had all been moved aside to the walls and the large carpet was rolled up to one end of the room. They checked all the windows and doors and all were locked just as they had been when they retired. The family was shocked and mystified by the rearrangement of the furniture, but satisfied that no one was in the house, they decided to set things to right in the morning and went back to bed. The next morning, to their surprise, they found the carpet unrolled and all the furniture back in place. The only thing unusual was marks of henna paste on some of the furniture and walls as if someone had pressed a henna-painted hand there. The family soon moved out and the tailor said that, even though the house was empty, late passersby reported hearing sounds of partying and music coming from the house during the night.

Years later, when I was living in Tehran, I remembered this story and decided to seek out the house. I found the tailor shop by its sign in front and looked across the street. There the house stood. The windows had no draperies, and the walls of the house were overgrown with ivy. It had obviously been empty and unattended for a long time. A few months later there was a short article in the newspaper that stated that the *"jinn*-occupied house has been sold to a nearby fire company and is to be torn down to make a parking lot for fire-fighting equipment."

The belief in *jinn* by the Arabs is an amusing superstition. However, there is a basic tenet in the Islamic religion that is taken most seriously by devout Moslems. This is the belief that when one dies, the first night after burial the deceased is visited by two angels, *Nakeer* and *Monkar*, who question the departed regarding his or her behavior during life. If the deceased has led a good and pious life, he is able to answer freely and clearly. If the opposite is the case, the dead one will be unable to speak intelligibly; and as a consequence, when the Day of Judgment arrives and the dead all are resurrected, the scroll kept by the interrogating angels will reflect no redeeming acts and the unfortunate ones who could not speak will be consigned to hell.

An illustration how seriously this belief influences the thinking of devout Moslems is found in the story told of Fath Ali Shah, the king mentioned in chapter 13 who launched the ill-fated invasion of Russia in 1804. The mullahs, who had gained great power and influence under this king, were really responsible for instigating hostilities. They prevailed upon Fath Ali to go to war in order to bring the Moslem population of the Russian Caucasus under the rule of a Moslem nation (Persia).

The shah did not want to fight the Russians but the leader of the mullah faction, Seyed Mohammed, persisted in his demands that the shah declare war. Finally, Fath Ali agreed to do so, but only on the condition that Seyed Mohammed write a scroll on which the mullah acknowledged his responsibility for the war. This scroll was to be placed on the chest of Fath Ali and buried with him at the time of his death so that it could be shown to *Nakeer* and *Monkar* when they came to question him and thus absolve him of blame for any harm that might result to the country because of the war.

Another story concerning this superstition is a personal recollection that has to do with a woman whom I knew by reputation only, although I did have a passing acquaintance with her daughter. This woman was a believer in black magic and was, on the whole, a devious and unsavory character. Her daughter told me that her mother had a piece of agate on which was inscribed in Arabic a prayer for her salvation. She instructed her daughter to insert the agate in her (the mother's) mouth at the time of her death so that she might speak clearly to the visiting angels and impress them with her piety. The daughter related to me, with some pride, how she kept vigil beside her mother as she lay on her deathbed and, at the critical moment of death, she slipped the agate into her mother's mouth! I could not help but think how stupid can one be to believe that all the harm done during life could be erased by a fragment of agate engraved with a few Arabic words, probably purchased from an enterprising mullah.

In Persia, unlike the strict Sunni country of Saudi Arabia where punishment is swift and severe, thievery and burglary are about as common as they are in the West. Some of the stories that I have heard about and know to be true are amusing. A neighbor of a friend of our family in Mashhad awoke one morning and looked out her bedroom window to their courtyard to find that the wooden double door between the courtyard and the street was missing. She rushed to awaken her husband who reacted in disbelief. "Whoever heard of an old door being stolen?" he asked. When he got up and saw that his wife was not pulling his leg, he made the rounds of the neighborhood asking if any of the neighbors had heard or seen anything unusual the night before. No one could help him.

Suddenly he remembered that, several months before, he had been approached by two men who offered to replace his door with a new steel door in exchange for the old one and a small sum of money. He refused the offer, telling them that he had lived in that house since childhood and was used to things just as they were and did not want to change anything. He did not realize that the old wooden door had become an antique of considerable value, and it had become fashionable to incorporate antique pieces in new construction. He went to the police and reported the theft, describing what he could remember of the two men although he did not know their names. The police investigated as best they could, but the door was never recovered. The man finally was forced to install a new and supposedly theft proof steel door.

Another story in the same vein is told about the drunk who was staggering home along a deserted street early one morning when he came upon two men who were sawing at the door frame of a courtyard gate belonging to one of his neighbors. The drunk stopped and asked the men what they were doing.

"We are playing the violin," one of the men replied.

"I can't hear any music," said the drunk.

"Go on home," answered the thief. "You will hear it tomorrow morning!"

Another incident that happened to a couple who were acquaintances of our family concerned an attempted burglary that was foiled in a most unusual manner. The husband of the family, possibly undergoing what is now called the male midlife crisis, had begun to play around, and almost every night he would be out pursuing his philandering until the early morning hours. When he came home, he would quietly enter and try to slip into bed in the hope that his wife would be fast asleep and unaware of when he came in. She was not fooled for one minute; but when she confronted him about his suspicious nocturnal habits, he denied that he ever stayed out late. He insisted that he always came home around midnight.

"What if a thief breaks in while you are out?" she asked him. "I am all alone and afraid almost every night."

The man laughed and said, "You are a strong woman—if anyone tries to break in, beat him."

The wife was unhappy with his offhand manner and decided to take his advice and at the same time teach him a lesson. She armed herself with a stout cudgel and waited in the dark beside the front door for her husband to come home. Shortly after 2:00 A.M., she heard the sound of someone fumbling with the lock on the door. She decided that her husband was very drunk and having trouble getting his key in the lock. Finally, the door opened and a figure slipped into the house. She immediately began to beat him as hard as she could on the head and shoulders. The man cried out in pain and yelled for mercy.

She suddenly realized that it was not her husband's voice and turned on the light. There on the floor was a bleeding, cowering stranger, a real burglar. He leapt up, fled out the door, and went to the police to lodge a complaint of assault against the woman. He told the police, "I admit that I am a thief; and if I am caught, I should get a striped suntan [slang for being put behind bars]. Look at me—I have a broken nose, a broken collarbone, and a cut up head! I should not be attacked like this!"

The police came to investigate, and the woman explained that she thought that the burglar was her wayward husband. "If I had known that it was a real burglar, I would have been terrified and hid!" she said. When the husband heard about the incident and the damage done to the poor thief, he mended his ways and never chanced coming home late again.

Grandfather told me a story of another capture of a would-be burglar by a man who owned a very upscale antique shop near his clock shop in Arg Avenue. This shop had a large display-sales area fronting on Arg Avenue with the usual steel shutters in front that were lowered each night to prevent thieves from breaking in. Behind the main shop there was a small stockroom with a rear door opening onto an alley that was used for deliveries and as a exit and entrance for employees. This door had been repeatedly forced over a period of years by thieves who made off with whatever they could carry. It got so bad that, at one point, the owner purchased a large bear trap that he set every night just inside the back door before leaving. This was not very effective, because one morning he arrived to find the door had been forced open and the trap missing, apparently dragged off by a frightened thief! Nothing was stolen that night.

One night, the owner was working alone in the store after he had closed up and lowered the steel shutters over the front of the store. Around midnight, he heard some noise coming from the back room. He extinguished the small light that he had been working by, and holding a screwdriver in hand, he noiselessly opened the connecting door and saw the back of a man who was rummaging through some goods stored on a shelf. He pressed the screwdriver against the man's back and told him that he had a knife, which he would use if the man tried to resist. He marched the burglar into the front room and then quickly slipped back into the rear room, locking the connecting door. The thief was unable to leave because of the locked and shuttered front entrance, and remained there until the police arrived and took him away. Grandfather ended his story with one of his proverbs: "There are two people who are frightened of an empty gun: the one who knows that it is empty and the one who does not know that it is."

Repressed as they may be in the Islamic culture, women have found ways of asserting themselves, as we saw in a previous anecdote. Another story, which was widely reported in all of the Tehran newspapers, concerned a middle-aged woman whose husband had divorced her in order to marry a younger girl. The girl had insisted upon the divorce because she didn't want to become a second wife. The first wife was infuriated by the treatment she had received but hid her anger and tried to maintain contact and friendly relations with her ex-husband. They would frequently meet for lunch or tea, and appeared to be the best of friends.

One afternoon, after they had lunched together, the former wife suggested that they go to see a new movie that was playing at the Homa Cinema; and the man agreed to take her. It was a hot summer afternoon, but it was cool and pleasant inside the theater and not very crowded. The woman chose to sit in the last row in the back of the theater and her ex-husband settled down in the seat next to her. After a little while, the woman began to caress her husband in areas that she knew from long experience would result in his arousal. The man responded with a fine erection, and thereupon the woman whipped out a sharp knife she had concealed in her chador and swiftly amputated the tumescent member.

The poor man leapt to his feet and ran screaming from the theater with blood running down his front. Someone called an ambulance, and the man was rushed to the Sina Hospital where, after a long operation, the severed member was supposedly successfully reattached. The woman made her escape in the confusion; but after a few days, she was tracked down by a newspaper reporter who asked her why she had done such a terrible thing to her ex-husband.

She replied, "I really didn't mean to cut off the whole thing. I meant to cut just a piece from the tip to teach him a lesson and also punish the young girl he married. Just as I started to cut, he plunged forward in his excitement and lost much more than I intended to take!"

During the days that the story made headlines in the newspapers, men would jokingly caution each other not to take their wives to the Homa Cinema. Recently I read a newspaper account about a man in the Washington, D.C., area who had the same misfortune. His amputated part had been discarded by his wife along a roadside. It was found by the police after a several-hour search and successfully reattached. I was instantly reminded of the poor man from Tehran.

Another, but less traumatic, story illustrating the increasing independence of women under the Mohammed Reza Shah has to do with the wife of a wealthy manufacturer of medical supplies. The man was well educated and held a Ph.D. from a French university. His wife was a refined lady from a good family and pos-

273

sessed a strong-willed, forceful personality. The husband spent much time away from home, ostensibly working late and traveling on business.

One day, while the husband was away on one of his trips, the wife met a friend in the street who stopped her and told her how sorry she was to learn about her husband's accident.

"What accident are you talking about?" the wife asked. "My husband has been away on a business trip and I expect him home tomorrow."

The friend replied, "I was visiting a friend in the hospital and happened to glance into another room and saw your husband lying in bed with his leg in the air in traction and a cast on one of his arms. I thought that you must certainly know about it!"

The wife excused herself and hastened to the hospital. She asked the receptionist the location of Mr. Anvari's room and the girl replied, "He is in room 101, and his wife is in the room next to him!"

The wife went to her husband's room and told him how shocked she was to hear of his accident and how sorry she was for his pain and suffering. After she had visited with him for a while, she left his room and went into the next room where she found a young lady lying in bed, also with a cast on her arm. She asked her, "Are you Mr. Anvari's wife?" When the young lady replied in the affirmative, she continued, "I am his wife also. How long have you been married to him?"

"Nine years," replied the patient.

Now the first wife understood why her husband worked so late at night and why he took so many trips on business. She did not say anything to her husband while he was in the hospital, but on the day he was discharged and came home, he found that all of his clothing and personal possessions had been packed in suitcases that were lined up in the hallway just inside the front door.

"Here are your things," said the wife. "Take them and never come back here again. I thought that I had married an intelligent, well-educated man who would be faithful to me, and now I find that you have been betraying me for over nine years. You are no better than a common Arab who marries more than one wife, and I never want to see you again."

This incident happened before the shah decreed that monogamy was to be the law of the land. However, the better class of educated women were already emerging from the subjugation of Islamic tradition!

Auto theft is common in Tehran, especially the theft of one make of automobile, the Peykan, that was manufactured in Persia except for the motor, which is made by the Hillman Company in England. The reason that the Peykan is an easy target for thieves is that the ignition-door key of a given model will often work on any other car of the same model.

One morning, a neighbor of ours in Tehran went out to go to work and found that his Peykan, which he had parked in the street the evening before, was gone. He reported the missing and presumably stolen car to the police and took a taxi to work. The next morning, as he was leaving for work, he was amazed to find his car in front of his courtyard door. He looked over the exterior and there was not a scratch or any other damage. Upon opening the door, he found on the front seat a lovely bouquet of flowers with a note.

He opened the note and read, "Thank you for the use of your car. I did not use it for any illegal purpose or damage it in any way. The night before last, my wife went into labor and I could not start my car to take her to the hospital. I tried to call a taxi, but I could not get through to the taxi company. [The telephone service in Tehran at that time was notoriously erratic.] I went out into the streets to see if I could find a passing taxi; and then I saw your car, the same model as my own. I borrowed it and got my wife to the hospital just in time. I am sorry for any inconvenience this may have caused you. Please accept these flowers as a token of my gratitude."

The neighbor was happy to get his car back in perfect condition and notified the police that he had recovered it. However, he found a garage for rent nearby and never left it out on the street again. If his car were to disappear again, it might not just be borrowed.

When I was a young adult living in Tehran, I became friendly with a lady in our neighborhood who was married to the assistant chief of police. This colonel of police traveled frequently to Europe and the United States for training courses in various police academies. He would usually be away for four to six weeks at a time. One trip, which lasted about six weeks, took him to several police departments in the United States. He wrote to his wife frequently, and in one of his letters, he informed his wife that he had purchased two beautiful sets of china for her as well as a large screen TV set. He described the china patterns in detail, especially one that was decorated with twenty-four karat gold paint.

About two weeks before the colonel was to return home, the wife was visited by an elegantly dressed young man who informed the servant who answered the door that he had just returned from the U.S. and had a message from the colonel to his wife. The wife received the young man in her parlor and was most impressed with his polite manner and educated speech. The young man informed her that the colonel had asked him to bring the TV set, which the colonel had bought, back to Tehran for him. He also casually mentioned that he had been with her husband when he shopped for china and described how lovely the gold design was on one set. He then told her that the TV set was in customs at the airport, and four hundred *touman* in duty was owed. He volunteered to return to the airport with her driver to pick up the TV set if she would kindly advance him the money to pay the duty.

The lady was happy to have the services of such an obliging young man to relieve her of the hassle of customs. She gave him four hundred *touman* in cash and instructed her chauffeur to drive him to the airport. On the way, the driver passed in front of the large Bank Bazargani in Sepah Square. The man asked him to stop while he went inside to cash a check. He told the driver to double park and wait for him, promising to be back in a few minutes. After over an hour had passed and the man had not returned, the driver found a parking place and called his mistress to tell her what had happened. She instructed him to go into the bank and look for the young man. If he could not be found, the driver was to return home. Needless to say, there was no trace of the man in the bank; he had left by another entrance and was long gone.

276

The wife called her husband's colleagues in the police department and reported what had happened. The police told her that her experience was but one of many similar ones, all of which happened to various wealthy families around the city who had a family member traveling abroad. Apparently the confidence man had an informant in the passport office who reported to him whenever a well-to-do citizen left the country. The con man would then watch the mail delivery to that person's house and when he saw the distinctive foreign airmail envelope, he would somehow intercept it, read the mail, reseal the envelope, and deliver it the next day. Armed with the information obtained, he would then work his con game, as he had with the colonel's wife.

When the colonel returned and found out what had happened, he exploded with rage at the effrontery of a man who would dare to rob the assistant chief of police. He vowed that the man would be caught and brought to justice. Unfortunately, the thief was never apprehended. Apparently he left the city, because no more complaints were received by the police regarding a thief with his *modus operandi*.

There are some stories that are told when the older ladies get together for a morning coffee klatch or afternoon tea that are never repeated in the presence of male members of the family. Some people might justifiably classify these as gossip. They might be about clandestine romances, women's hygiene, wayward husbands, or any other private topic.

One of these stories I overheard Grant Aunt tell Grandmother. It had to do with a couple who had been married for a few years but were never able to conceive a baby. They consulted with the local doctors in Mashhad who assured them that everything was normal, and the only thing that they could do was to keep trying and be patient.

The husband was a businessman who made frequent trips to Tehran, sometimes accompanied by his wife who went along to visit with her aunt who lived there. After one trip with his wife, he returned alone. He informed everyone that his wife had become pregnant and that the doctor in Tehran had advised that his wife not travel until the pregnancy became more advanced.

Over the following nine months, he made a number of trips to Tehran, but each time when he returned, he said that his wife still had been advised not to travel and would continue to stay with her aunt. After about eight months, he told his family that he was going to Tehran and stay there until the baby was born, then return with her and the new baby. Several weeks later the couple came back to Mashhad, the wife proudly carrying a fine baby boy in her arms.

Great Aunt said to Grandmother, "Everyone thinks that Mr. Afrookteh's wife finally was able to conceive and give birth; but I'll tell you the real story. I learned it from her aunt in Tehran. The husband, on one of his trips to Tehran, found a poor widow in one of the villages who had a teenage daughter. He took them to Tehran and rented a house for them. He made the girl his *sigheh* [temporary wife] and promised the mother and her daughter that he would buy them a house in the city and give them money if the girl produced a baby by him. When and if a baby was born, he told them that he would take the infant and they should never contact him again. The girl conceived and delivered a healthy baby. She kept her bargain and no one in the family, other than his wife and her aunt, knows about it. As the child grew older, everyone could see that he looked very much like his father, so no one suspected that there was a mother other than the wife!"

Recently, my sister Tooran told me a story about Grandmother that I had never heard before. When Sheereen Banoo (Grandmother) was a young married girl of about twenty, she lived in Mashhad next door to a widow who supported herself by matchmaking. One day this widow came to Sheereen Banoo who was in the appropriate age group to be plausibly seeking a husband and, in addition, quite beautiful.

The widow said to her, "I want to ask a favor of you. My matchmaking business has not been doing well recently and the cost of living keeps going up, so I need every cent that I can earn. I have a client, a very wealthy woman in her early thirties, who wants to find a husband. The only problem is she is not very good-looking. In fact, she is quite ugly; but she does have a good figure. I have shown her to various men in the past few weeks but no one wants her. I also have a male client who is middle-aged and he promised to pay me well if I found him a second younger wife. I am worried that if I show her to him, he will turn her down. The favor I want from you is this. Next Tuesday morning, around ten o'clock, will you walk in your courtyard and dally around checking your garden or whatever for about ten minutes? Don't look up at my roof, because I will be there with this man and I will show him you instead of my woman client!"

Sheereen Banoo may have felt a passing guilt about being part of such a deception; but she was young and adventurous and felt sorry for the matchmaker, so she agreed. In addition, Sheereen Banoo was a firm believer in monogamy, and since the man was looking for a second wife, the plan appealed to her as a form of poetic justice. The appointed morning she paraded around her courtyard as instructed, and the man was smitten instantly. He agreed to the marriage, and the contract was drawn up and signed by both parties.

The reader will remember that in the old days, in accordance with the traditional Moslem custom, the groom does not see his intended wife until the veil is lifted after the ceremony of marriage has been performed, unless a distant preview is arranged by someone such as the matchmaker. The marriage went off without a hitch. When the man found out that he had not married the girl whom he had seen from the matchmaker's rooftop, it was too late. On the other hand, the woman was much younger than his first wife and quite rich, so he resigned himself to the situation. He did not want to advertise the fact that he had to resort to a matchmaker to find another wife and said nothing about the deception to anyone. Probably, when he slept with his new wife, he fantasized about the beautiful girl whom he had seen in the courtyard; remember, all cats are gray in the dark!

Chapter Nineteen
Farewell to Mashhad

The sea of life is filled with waves;
You must be the captain of your own ship.

—Kamalpoor

In the spring of the year that I was in the fifth grade, a few weeks after Now Ruz, two of my brothers, Kayvan and Jahan, announced that they were going to move to Tehran to attend one of the several colleges in that city. They intended to work to help support themselves while in school, and they thought that the work opportunities would be better in the capital. Kayvan wanted to study at the college of history and geography, and Jahan intended to pursue a career in accounting and business at another school. My oldest brother, Kaveh, was already living in Tehran where he had taken up residence after his return from his graduate studies in London. He was married and had one child at that time. Kayvan and Jahan intended to live with cousin Saleemeh. She was the one who had briefly nursed me as an infant, and she now lived in Tehran with her husband and three sons.

With the departure of my brothers, it seemed that our house was somewhat empty; but this feeling did not last long. Shortly after they left, my father announced that our old family friend from Torbat, Mrs. Noor, would be coming to stay with us, along with her son and two daughters, until she could find a suitable house in the city. Mrs. Noor had a large house in Mashhad, but this had been rented to the Russians, who still lingered on in Mashhad in the aftermath of World War II. My father, because of his fluency in Russian acquired on visits to that country on government business, had acted as rental agent for Mrs. Noor and represented her interests in dealing with the Russians. The south wing of our house was prepared for the Noors: woodwork was freshly painted, furniture polished, draperies and carpets cleaned, etc. Because of this additional work, Grandmother had to hire another maid to help out. This new maid was named Talaat. She was a widow in her late twenties and a hard worker who learned quickly.

Mrs. Noor arrived with her children in late spring, as soon as the schools had closed for the summer. Suddenly our house became a beehive of activity. Again it was always full of people who came to visit because, in addition to my family's many friends, Mrs. Noor had a wide circle of family and friends in Mashhad. The house seemed crowded since she had brought a quantity of beautiful antique furniture with her that she intended to sell rather than use in her new home. This furniture was stored wherever room could be found; most of it was on the porch of the south wing.

For several days, there was a continual stream of antique dealers in and out until it was finally all sold. I remember a number of the pieces were upholstered in a silver and gold filigree fabric decorated with seed pearls. I asked her if I could snip off some of the pearls to make necklaces for my dolls. She agreed but cautioned me to only take the pearls from the bottom of the backs of the chairs and sofas where their absence would not be obvious. I took full advantage of her generosity, and before the furniture disappeared to the antique dealers' shops, most of my rag dolls were wearing real pearl necklaces!

That summer seemed to pass much quicker than any previous summer in my memory. Although we did not go to the country for our usual summer stay, we had many picnics, both in the day and by moonlight. Jamshid, Genoos, and I missed our hiking and play in the country, but there were plenty of activities around our house to fill our days. During that summer, Mrs. Noor's only son was making his preparations to move to the United States to begin his medical studies at The Johns Hopkins University, following in the footsteps of his father and six preceding generations of physicians. Incidentally, his oldest daughter is now the ninth generation of physicians and the only female one. Mrs. Noor's eldest daughter became engaged to a law student, the son of a prominent businessman in Mashhad. The younger daughter was enrolled in the fourth grade of the same school that Genoos and I attended.

My sisters, Tooran and Azar, had graduated from the twelfth grade several years before and were now teaching in primary schools. They were on summer holiday and taking classes in music and foreign languages. My oldest sister, Katayoon, was the principal of Hefdaheday, the public coeducational elementary school, and was occupied with administrative duties during the summer holiday. In addition, she spent a lot of time working for a charitable organization called Anjoman-e-Parvin (named for a famous female classical poetess), which she and the daughter of the minister of education for Khorasan had started several years before. The Anjoman-e-Parvin was devoted to helping the poor of the city by organizing fund-raising activities and doing volunteer work for families in need. That summer to raise money they put on a variety show, which was a great success both financially and in recruiting additional volunteer workers.

Jamshid went to the school gymnasium to work out for a couple of hours three days a week. While he was gone, I spent that time studying for the upcoming school year, as I usually did every summer. We still had a lot of time for play, and Jamshid now had a larger number of victims on which to play the tricks his fertile imagination contrived. In addition to Genoos and me, he now had Mrs. Noor's youngest daughter.

Jamshid invented one trick that summer with, as usual, me as his accomplice. I think that he got the idea for this game from the stories about Aladdin and the lamp, an old Persian fable. Aladdin got his magic lamp from an underground cave, but Jamshid's version involved the pool in our courtyard. He would line up us three girls, and any other young children who happened to be visiting, along the side of the pool. He told us that there was a secret door in the bottom of the pool that no one could see when the pool was empty; but when it was full, the door appeared to only Jamshid and to no one else. This door opened into a small chamber and another door at one end opened to a second chamber. This went on and on until a final seventh chamber was reached. This chamber contained all sorts of treasure, gold, jewels, silks, and other valuables beyond measure. He said that he had never been able to get beyond the second chamber; but in the first chamber, there was a good *jinni* who would give him whatever he asked as long as it was of little value.

Then Jamshid would jump in the pool, and while swimming around call out to his audience to name some object they wanted. We would all huddle together to decide what to ask for, and I would make a suggestion that I finally got everyone to agree upon. "Let's ask for a magnifying glass," I would say. "That should be hard to find even for a *jinni*." Jamshid and I had agreed beforehand on the objects that he would retrieve that day, and I had secreted them in my skirt pockets. As he swam by the edge of the pool, I would slip the appropriate object into his hand. Jamshid would do a surface dive to the bottom of the pool and disappear into the somewhat murky depths. He stayed underwater as long as he could, then would emerge to the surface carrying exactly what had been ordered, to the amazement of all. This game went on at intervals all summer. Occasionally, Mrs. Noor's older daughter would stop by and watch. She never spoiled the fun by saying that Jamshid's story could not be true, but she never did figure out how he did it!

That summer was also marked by an amusing incident that happened to me. For several years, I had had a lovely white Persian cat that I raised from a kitten. She was one of a litter born to our family cat, and this kitten was my special pet. She followed me about whenever I was home; and every afternoon when I came home from school, she would be waiting for me at the door. She slept on the foot of my bed every night; and sometimes, when the temperature dropped near morning, she would come to the head of the bed and burrow beneath the covers to keep warm next to me. One night we were all sleeping outdoors on our wooden beds scattered about the courtyard and around the pool. I was in my favorite place beneath the willow tree.

During the night I felt my cat come next to my cheek and slip beneath the sheet and thin blanket. I did not really awaken fully, but rolled a little to one side to give her room. The next morning when I got up, I saw that she was still in the bed beneath the covers. This was unusual because she invariably got up before I awakened. I pulled off the bedcovers; and to my surprise there was my cat with five kittens sucking greedily on her nipples and a wet mess in the foot of the bed. I covered her and her litter and ran to find Grandmother. I pulled her by the hand to my bed and unveiled the new feline family. She laughed and exclaimed, "You must sleep like a stone. How could your cat have five kittens right next to you and you sleep through the whole thing?"

Soon all the family and servants gathered around, laughing and making fun of me. The maids were giggling and one of them said, "This is a good omen!" Naneh found a cardboard carton and lined it with an old blanket. I put my cat and her kittens in it, and Naneh carried it to a corner of the pantry behind Grandmother's kitchen. I followed along and on the way I asked Naneh, "Why did the maids say that this is a good omen?"

Naneh replied, "If you were an older girl, it would mean that you would soon get married." Then she smiled knowingly and added, "Since you are not old enough, it means that there will soon be a marriage in the family. Just you wait and see!"

Toward the end of the summer, Mrs. Noor's son left for Tehran to complete the paperwork at the U.S. Embassy to allow his entry into the United States for his postgraduate education. A few days later, Mrs. Noor and her daughters went there to see him off. After he left, they stayed on there with relatives. About a week later, my father announced that he had to go to Tehran on business. He had been gone only a couple days when we received a telegram addressed to the whole family. Father and Mrs. Noor had married in a quiet ceremony in Tehran! The maid's prophesy had come true. I was still not sure that my cat's birthing in my bed brought about Father's marriage, but I was happy that he had married Mrs. Noor. I had loved this pretty lady from the first time that I met her in Torbat years before, the night that the moon was swallowed by the dragon.

Grandmother and Grandfather were not surprised at the news of Father's marriage. They knew all along that Father and Mrs. Noor were attracted to each other; and my father, of course, in the old-fashioned tradition, consulted with his mother before taking such an important step. My sisters did not comment one way or the other but accepted the news gracefully. They had been much closer to my mother than I, and it was difficult for them to wholeheartedly accept a replacement for her; but they knew that Father was still relatively young and, sooner or later, would remarry. Little Aunt, who had been visiting when the telegram arrived, remarked that her brother had been a widower for almost seven years and was close to fifty years old. It was time that he found someone with whom to share the rest of his life.

The telegram was followed a few days later by a long letter from Father. He informed us that he and his new wife would be coming back to Mashhad within two weeks and would be staying with us for a while until they found a suitable house. He then planned to move out to live with his new wife and her two daughters, because it would be difficult for three families along with their servants to crowd into one house permanently. I remember the weekend when they finally arrived. It was early fall and the trees in the orchard and gardens had once more assumed their beautiful autumnal colors. The servants had cleaned the house from top to bottom, and Grandmother had finished all of her usual fall chores—making pickles, preserves, drying herbs, etc.

Father and his bride entered by the east gate. The brick pathway through the orchard was strewn with red, yellow, and russet leaves as if someone had laid down a carpet of colorful flowers to welcome them home. We met them in the courtyard. My sisters, Jamshid, Genoos, Grandmother, Grandfather Khan, and all the servants crowded around to embrace and congratulate the newlyweds. Naneh had brought out a brazier full of hot coals into which she dropped a pinch of *esffand* to burn for good luck. The fragrant smoke filled the air and Father promptly rewarded her with a few coins. My father announced to the assembly, "You all know my new wife. From now on you will call her *Khanom* [lady]." She deserved the name for she was a beautiful, intelligent, kind lady with an air of dignity and breeding.

Khanom brought a gift for everyone in the household; not even a single servant had been forgotten. This gracious act made me feel that she had been thinking about all of us while she was away and wanted to show her friendship with everyone on her return. My father and Khanom were much in love, and they enjoyed a mutual respect for each other that lasted throughout the twenty-two years they had together. I don't believe that they ever had any disagreements; and when Khanom suddenly died at age fifty-eight following a heart attack, my father was heartbroken.

About a month after Father and Khanom returned, a very exciting thing happened. The family were all sitting at dinner in the north wing of the house one night when someone glanced out a window across the courtyard and saw that all of the lights were on in the south wing. We all jumped up from the table and rushed to the south wing. When we got there, we saw that the door to the *beerooney* courtyard was wide open as well as the double wooden doors between the courtyard and the street. Obviously, we had been visited by a thief! Everyone looked about and nothing appeared to be missing until Khanom went into a closet in her bedroom where she kept a small metal safe in which she stored a small fortune in jewelry. It was gone!

Father called the police, and within a few minutes, a small army of policemen descended on the house. The officer in charge surveyed the premises and pronounced that this was obviously an inside job. No casual thief would turn on all the lights and leave the doors wide open. Two police officers gathered all the servants in one room for questioning while the rest of the men went out and searched the grounds. Grandfather told the officers that Gholam, Naneh, and the rest of the servants had been with us for many years and were completely trustworthy. The only new servant was Talaat, the girl whom Grandmother had hired in the spring.

The servants were all dismissed save for Talaat. The police began to interrogate her, and soon she broke down in tears and shook like a leaf in the wind. She confessed that she had taken the safe and hid it in the corner of the orchard where the stream exited through the wall. Her boyfriend was to come later, slip through the culvert, and retrieve it. The police, Father, and Talaat went out to the spot where Talaat had carried the heavy metal box and there it was in the water. The police had arrived before the boyfriend had a chance to run off with it. The police brought the safe back to the house and asked Khanom to open it and check to be sure that nothing was missing. She did and, thankfully, nothing appeared to be missing. By this time it was close to midnight. The police took Talaat off to jail to further question her about the identity of her boyfriend and her past.

The next morning a policemen returned. He told Father that Talaat had confessed to taking other things from the house and suggested that her room be searched. Grandmother and two of my sisters did so and found, in a wooden chest, various articles that had been missing for several months. Almost everyone in the family found one or more of their belongings there—a scarf, silk stockings, costume jewelry, and so forth. The only articles that did not belong to our family were several sterling silver spoons and two silver tea glass holders. Grandmother remembered that, several months before, she had taken Genoos to a wedding at a friend's house and Talaat had accompanied them to look after Genoos. She sent a message to the family inquiring if they had lost the silverware. They replied that it had been missing since the wedding. Grandmother returned the spoons and tea holders, along with a letter of explanation and apology, to the proper owners by return messenger.

Talaat was kept in jail for two nights until her boyfriend was found. Father did not press charges against Talaat, and she was released. When she returned to our house to pick up her clothing, Grandmother asked her why she had stolen the silverware from her friend. Talaat answered that she was only "stealing the bride's wisdom." She was referring to an old Persian custom, a joke played by the groom's family on the bride's family during the wedding celebration. The groom's family will "steal" some worthless article such as a safety pin, an ashtray, or some other trinket and by doing so they say they are stealing the bride's wisdom so she will not be able to connive against the groom or his family.

Father and my stepmother found their new house during the winter and moved into it along with Khanom's daughters. It was only a ten-minute walk from our house and Father visited us every day, sometimes alone and sometimes with Khanom. Nothing really changed in our manner of living; our grandparents were living as usual in the north wing and our old familiar servants remained as before. The only difference was Father's library gradually became smaller as he from time to time carried various volumes to his new home. Khanom was busy preparing for her older daughter's wedding; furniture, silverware, carpets, and other necessities for her new home had to be bought and a bridal gown made.

I was in the sixth grade that winter. In the spring I would be taking the standardized national examination prepared by the Ministry of Education that I had to pass in order to go on to high school. This exam is given on the same day in every school in the country. In addition to this final examination, there were three other examinations given quarterly during the year that one had to pass in order to qualify to take the national examination. As usual, due to my summertime preparation, I was at the top of my class, receiving perfect twenties in almost all my courses. My best subjects were sewing, art, and mathematics. My sewing teacher was so impressed with my work that she asked me one day if I ever did sewing at home. I told her about the doll dresses that I had made, and she asked me to bring them to school to show her. I brought a large carton full of dresses the next day, and she was so amazed at the detail that she asked me if she could keep them for a few days to show them to her friends and the other teachers. This kind praise was a source of great encouragement to me to excel.

There was one particular problem that arose that year. My sister Azar had been transferred to my school to teach hygiene to the fifth and sixth grades. As a consequence, I found myself being taught for a few hours a week by my own sister. I knew the subject well and answered every question on the quarterly examinations correctly, but Azar never gave me a perfect twenty. The first quarter I was mad and upset but said nothing. When the same thing happened on the second exam, I exploded. I stormed out of the class clutching my textbook and went to the principal's office. I knocked on the door, and after being told to enter, I said to the principal, "I want you to examine me in this subject, not my sister. She never gives me the marks that I deserve!"

The principal replied, "I will talk to her about this."

"Talk will do no good," I answered. "I have talked with her at home and told everyone in the family what she was doing, but nothing helps. I want you, not her, to examine me!"

"Calm down," she said. "Wait outside the door until the morning break, and I will send for your sister and talk to her."

When the bell rang at the end of the period, Azar came to the office. As she passed me, she gave me a dirty look because I had left the class in such an impolite manner, but said nothing to me. I stood outside until the principal called for me to come in. I entered with my textbook and handed it to her. She opened the book and asked me all the questions that had been on the examination. I answered each perfectly while Azar looked on in silence. The principal finished her questioning, smiled, and said to me, "You have your twenty on this examination." Azar did not speak to me for several days, but I didn't care; I had gotten what I deserved. On the third quarterly examination, I earned and received a perfect twenty. Azar was not going to risk another embarrassing scene!

My oldest sister, Katayoon, was a devoted educator. She never married, and all of the love and dedication that characterized her life seemed to be poured into her duties as principal of the only public coeducational elementary school in Mashhad. She also gave much of her time to the Girl Scout movement in Tehran after we moved to that city.

I took the national qualifying examination at the end of the sixth grade that spring and passed with flying colors, which meant that I was able to enter a high school the next school year that took only honor students. That same examination was taken by the sixth graders in Katayoon's school. Her students achieved the highest average test scores of all of the schools in the province of Khorasan for the second consecutive year. For this achievement, Katayoon received a certificate of excellence presented by the provincial minister of education at the commencement ceremony.

Later on Katayoon became the assistant principal of a large public high school in Tehran. She finally left the field of education to devote herself full time to the Girl Scout organization, where she worked in an administrative capacity at the national level until a few years before her death at age seventy-three. I, by that time, was living in the U.S. and was not able to attend her funeral, but Tooran told me that there was a moving tribute paid to her by her former Scouts. They made a large placard showing pictures of her in uniform over the years and telling of her numerous contributions to the Scouting movement. This was displayed at her funeral ceremony in Tehran.

Late that spring, after I had graduated from the sixth grade, my sisters decided to reveal a plan that they had been formulating for many months. Katayoon, Tooran, and Azar called Father and asked him to meet with them to hear their plan. The next day when Father arrived for his daily visit, he called out to us that he would be in the library and ready to talk any time. My sisters and I went to the library, and Katayoon began to talk of their plan which was as much a surprise to me as it was to Father.

Katayoon started the discussion something like this: "For some months Tooran, Azar, and I have been thinking of making a major change in our lives—we want to move to Tehran. We all have teaching jobs and can easily transfer to the school system in Tehran. We feel that the opportunities for postgraduate education are better there. Since three of our brothers are living in the city, we will not be alone. We propose to take Mehry with us so she can enter high school there. Jamshid will be going into his last year of high school here in Mashhad, so he will stay here until he graduates, then he can join us next year.

"Our cousin Saleemeh and her husband, Mirza Kamal, have agreed that we can stay with them until we can find a place of our own to rent. What we want to ask of you is, first, your blessing and permission to do this; and, second, will you help us financially after we move? We will need some extra money for rent and to pay for a maid and servant. We will pack up some of the furniture and carpets from here, along with some china and utensils, and would like you to send them to us after we find a house."

Father sat silently for several minutes as he thought over the proposal, and we four girls waited patiently while he made up his mind. Finally he said, "You three are all grown women and intelligent enough to know what is best for you. You certainly can look after Mehry, because you have been doing that for years since your mother died. So, you have my blessing and I will help you just as you asked. If you ever need anything else, you just have to let me know and I will help."

I left the library after our talk with Father in a high state of excitement. I, who had never been farther than thirty miles from

Mashhad, was going to Tehran! Moreover, I was going to live there! The reactions of the other members of the family varied when they heard the news. Grandmother and Grandfather were saddened that they would no longer have our company, but they realized that my sisters were adults and entitled to lead their own lives as they thought fit. Jamshid was not unhappy at all, because he knew that he would be joining us in a year. Aunt Ozra also was not upset because she often visited her two married children who lived in Tehran (we were going to stay temporarily with one of them) and would see us frequently. The only reason that she had not moved to Tehran herself was because her father, Agha Bozorg, was 105 years old by that time and in too fragile health to move.

The servants were all unhappy to see us leave. Katayoon asked Gholam and Soltan if they wanted to join us after we found a place to live but they refused, saying that they were happy in Mashhad where they had lived for many years and had many friends. The one who was most affected by the news was my little cousin Genoos. She and I had grown so close over the years that I suppose she felt the same sort of loss she had felt when her mother died. For days, she moped about the house and she would burst into tears whenever anyone asked her what was troubling her. Finally, in an effort to cheer her up, I told her that I intended to give her all of the dolls I had made, except for a couple that I wanted to give to friends. At first she reacted with anger and again began to cry, but after a few minutes, I could see her anger gradually fade away. The prospect of acquiring all those dolls was too great a temptation. She finally smiled a sad sort of smile and accepted the inevitable.

Because of his advanced years, Grandfather Agha Bozorg had not been able to come to see us for a couple of years. My sisters visited him frequently, but I had not seen him for over a year. One day we heard through Aunt Ozra that he was ill and confined to bed. My sisters decided to go visit him and took me along. I will never forget the sight of that wonderful old man lying there in his bed. His hair and beard were the same color as the snow-white sheets on his bed, and his hands were so pale and so fragile-looking. I sat on a chair beside his bed.

His bedroom was not very large and was simply furnished

with a brass bed and a small bedside table on which there was a pitcher of water, a glass, and his reading glasses. One wall was covered with shelves of books. Sunlight was shining through two small multicolored stain-glass windows in the opposite wall, casting spots of color that danced across the bedsheets and over Agha Bozorg's face and beard. The colors, contrasted with the stark white of the bed and beard, were a lovely sight; and I was reminded of the colorful stories that he used to tell us when he came to visit our house years before. As the sun moved slowly higher in the sky and the colors gradually disappeared, I thought that this somehow symbolized the fading of this old gentleman's life. My fears were groundless at that time because Agha Bozorg went on to recover from his illness and lived on for almost five more years.

Over the next few weeks, my sisters and I busied ourselves with packing the things that we wanted to have delivered to Tehran when we found a house there. The largest item that we were to take was a few carpets, rolled and tied. We decided not to bother with furniture; the chairs and sofas imported years before by Aunt Ozra's first husband would have been nice to have, even though the original rich brocade had been replaced by green velvet, but moving bulky furniture over a distance was too difficult in those days. Most of this furniture is still in my late uncle's house. There is no way to describe the deep emotion that the whole family felt during the last few days before our departure. That secure invisible bond that had held the family tightly together in the protective circle, which Persians value so much and which we had been accustomed to all our lives, was about to be loosened. We were still a family, of course, but the day-to-day contact and camaraderie that we so loved was to be no more. Nevertheless, the decision had been made and we went on with it, looking forward to new adventures but at the same time looking back with sadness at leaving our loved ones.

Chapter Twenty
Emerald Valley

A loved one said to her lover,
"O youth, thou hast seen many cities abroad.
Which of them, then, is the fairest?"
He replied,
"The city where my sweetheart dwells."

—Mathnawi

Finally the day of our departure from Mashhad arrived, a day to which I had been impatiently looking forward, the day of a new beginning, new adventures, new sights and sounds, and another way of life. However, my excitement was tempered somewhat when I remembered that I would be far from the loving arms of Grandmother, Grandfather Khan, and my father. It was before dawn when Father's chauffeur arrived to drive my three sisters and me to the bus depot. The depot was on Arg Avenue within walking distance from our house but we had heavy carry-on valises containing some necessities for our trip, since it would take us about four days the way we planned to go. Our large suitcases had been delivered the day before to the bus terminal so that they could be loaded onto the roof of the bus. Luggage was loaded in the order in which it would be unloaded at each stop along the way as the passengers disembarked. Since we were going to Tehran, the last stop, our luggage would be at the very front of the roof.

When we arrived at the bus depot, I saw my Nanny-jon standing there waiting to see us off. Soon Aunt Ozra arrived, then Grandfather Khan came, holding Genoos by the hand, followed by Jamshid, Gholam, Soltan, and Naneh. A number of cousins, some with wives and children, came also. Soon the courtyard was filled with people—the passengers on the three busses scheduled to leave at 7:30 A.M. and their families and friends to see them off. About seven o'clock, much to our surprise, Father and our stepmother arrived. The reason we were surprised was because Grandmother had given a farewell dinner party in our honor the night before, and Father had kissed and hugged each of us girls good-bye. We assumed that he would not come to the bus station but would be busy at work. However, he could not resist coming to see us for the last time and wish us Godspeed. A few minutes before 7:30, we kissed everyone good-bye, and at the last possible minute, we got on the bus.

For me, the most difficult part was saying good-bye to Nanny-jon and Genoos. I sat next to the window beside Tooran in the seat behind Katayoon and Azar. Through the window I could see Genoos standing with Grandfather and chewing on one of her hair braids, a habit she had whenever she was upset. Her face was sad but gradually became resigned as she clutched Grandfather's comforting arm. The bus moved out exactly on time, and I watched all those familiar, loving faces slide backwards and disappear one after the other. For a minute I felt my heart sink; I was actually leaving all those people I loved so much and all the familiar places I had known throughout my childhood for an unknown city where I knew no one other than my family.

A fleeting thought went through my mind: If I could make the bus stop, I could jump out and run back home. Then I closed my eyes, took a deep breath, and said to myself, "Don't be so childish." I glanced at my sisters and saw that they too were staring out with somber expressions on their faces. I thought at the time they were having the same feelings that I was; but now I realize they were probably thinking of the responsibilities they were assuming, not only for their own lives but for mine as well.

Ordinarily, the journey by bus from Mashhad to Tehran was a two-day journey with an overnight stop in the town of Shahrood. However, we were in no hurry, and my father encouraged my sisters to take the bus that detoured north at Shahrood to the towns along the Caspian Sea, then swung back south to Tehran. This would give us a chance to see a part of the country that we had never visited. Another reason that Father wanted us to take that route was that we would be in the company of a newly married cousin, with his wife and some male members of her family. They were taking the same bus to their new home in Babol, a city near the Caspian seacoast, where the bus was scheduled to make an overnight stop. The busses in those days did not run after dark; travelers were still not completely safe from molestation by roving bands of brigands. This was graphically illustrated by an adventure we had later on during our journey.

As the bus passed through the familiar streets of Mashhad, our depression after the tearful parting from our family and friends gradually lightened. The mood of our fellow passengers also became gayer, reflecting the beautiful spring day that was just beginning. The air was cool but soft and the sky clear and bright. I could see the full moon still visible ahead in the blue western sky, hovering like a huge silver tray above the horizon, while behind us the sun began its upward climb. The passengers who knew each other began to converse, happy to have such congenial company on the long trip ahead. We began to get acquainted with the few people whom we did not already know.

All ages, except for the very elderly, were represented. There was even one boy younger than I traveling with his family. In the very last seat, four young men were traveling together to spend a holiday at the seaside; they seemed inseparable and the other passengers soon began to call them "the quadruplets." The driver was a friendly man in his early forties; and he had an assistant, a young man in his twenties, who sat next to him and whose chief function seemed to be to keep up a running conversation with the driver to keep him awake. Of course, he also was the baggage smasher and took care of minor repairs to the bus as necessary.

Four or five rows behind us there was an older lady traveling with her daughter. The daughter was a friend of Tooran's and Tooran asked me to change seats with her so that they could talk together for a while. I became petulant and said that I didn't want to go to the back of the bus. "Why not?" answered Tooran. "The back of the bus is going the same place as the front and will get there the same time!" When I remained adamant, Tooran finally put her foot down. "Young lady," she said, "we are going to be close together for a long trip, and if you are not going to listen to me, you will be in trouble!"

Katayoon and Azar overheard our argument, and they both turned in their seats and laughed at us. I was somewhat chagrined when I saw their good humor, so I got up and moved back to change seats with Tooran's friend. I noticed that a number of the other passengers were exchanging their assigned seats to visit with various friends. I sat down beside the mother, and she was a pleasant and entertaining companion for the short time we sat together. After about an hour, the high Beenalood mountain chain came into view in the distance and then the green city of Nishabur nestled in the southern foothills of the mountains gradually appeared. The city is only about fifty miles north of the Dasht-e-Kavir (Salt Desert), but because it is twelve hundred meters above sea level and receives abundant water from the melting mountain snows, it is a lovely green city.

We arrived at the bus station in Nishabur a little before eleven o'clock. The driver announced that we would be leaving at 12:30 and the passengers would have time to have lunch, take a cab to visit the tombs of Omar Khayyam and Attar, or walk around on a short tour of the city. Our Uncle Nishaburi was waiting for us at the depot. He told us that lunch was being prepared and his wife and children were anxiously waiting to see us. We all walked to his house and had a delightful luncheon and family reunion. After lunch, Uncle Nishaburi filled a basket with fruit from his orchard and gave it to us to eat on our journey. Of course, we later shared the fruit with the other passengers and the drivers.

We left Nishabur at 12:30 and drove straight through, except for two brief rest stops, to our next stop, Shahrood, where we would stay overnight. The road between Nishabur and Shahrood skirts the northern border of Dasht-e-Kavir, and the countryside is gently rolling but monotonous. To the left the desert stretched to the horizon; on the right, to the north beyond the desert, one could see mountains in the distance. The desert was a patchy white and brown, and here and there one could see the clustered yellow umbrellas of the spring-blooming giant fennel plants. These plants *(ferula galbaniflua)* grow to the height of two to three feet and in Persia are only found in the Dasht-e-Kavir. The local chemists extract a resin *(galbanum)* from the stem of this plant that is used as an antispasmodic for stomach disorders as well as a stimulant.

At intervals we would see ruins of old caravanserai,[1] because this road was part of the ancient silk route from China and India to the West. These were built, probably beginning over a thousand years ago, by rich philanthropists or the government to provide shelter and water to travelers at no cost. The caravanserai were large walled structures providing protection, as well as that essence of life to the desert traveler—water. Each one had a well that was usually within the walls. The ruins of an old caravanserai not far from Mashhad contain a well that still provides potable water after hundreds of years. The enclosed courtyards of the caravanserai have to be large to accommodate the many camels, mules, and other animals that made up the caravans in ancient times. It is said that one caravan bringing silks, spices, and other goods from the east to the seaports of Turkey and Persia for transshipment to Europe contained five thousand camels!

The caravanserai were built in various shapes; some were octagonal, others simply rectangular or square. They usually were two-storied to provide maximum protection from marauders; and high-ceilinged rooms surround the central courtyard, which had a single entrance for better defense. The rooms, of course, were sleeping accommodations for the travelers; the animals were bedded down in the courtyard. Because travelers from the East would meet those from the West at these havens of rest, the caravanserai served as places for the intermingling of diverse cultures. Marco Polo traveled this route on his historic journeys of exploration. It was also the road traveled by the Mongol and Turkoman invaders from the East.

The weather in the barren desert that spring afternoon was warm and the only air-conditioning was the breeze from the open windows. The bus plodded along at about forty miles an hour, and it was quite boring just sitting there looking out at the unvarying scenery. Fortunately, one of the four quadruplets in the back of the bus had brought along his accordion and, with the encouragement of his three friends, began to play. Soon everybody was singing along and clapping time to the music, and we cheerily passed away the afternoon hours across the desert. Near sunset, the landscape gradually began to show signs of greenery as we neared Shahrood. It was about an hour after sunset before we safely arrived in that city, much to the relief of the drivers as well as the passengers.

Our quarters, for that first of our overnight stops, were in an old caravanserai, now in the center of the city, that had been converted to resemble what is now known as a motel. A second entrance opening out to a large paved parking lot for busses and cars had been made in one of the old walls. After alighting from our bus, we all filed through it to find the rooms that had been reserved for us by the bus company. The motel was a two-story rectangular structure with the rooms lining the large central courtyard on four sides. Although they had been refurbished, the rooms retained the original high ceilings and were larger than those found in the modern motels. A covered wide brick walkway-patio ran around the courtyard in front of the first-floor rooms. Overhead, there was a covered balcony to provide access to the second-story rooms. There were two small windows in each room looking out onto the central courtyard, but there were no windows in the outside wall. In two corners on each floor, diagonally opposite each other, there were bathrooms for each sex next to the stairway that connected the two floors.

The passengers on our bus almost filled two floors of one wing. Our room was on the ground floor and contained a double bed and two single beds. It was next to the room occupied by our cousin Safa and his wife, and he invited us to have dinner with them in their room. All meals were served in the rooms by one of the many waiters employed by the motel. After we found our room and deposited our carry-on bags in it, we went to the next room to dine with our cousin. I detoured to the bathroom at the end of the building to wash my hands.

After I finished, I saw a huge scorpion crawling out of one corner of the bathroom. I was terrified; I had overhead one of the people on the bus telling that a particular venomous variety of scorpion was common in Shahrood. They were almost as deadly as those found in the city of Kashan, where the people had to sleep with each leg of their bed in a can of water to keep scorpions from crawling in with them. I dashed out of the bathroom and ran to my cousin's room. On the way, I suddenly had the thought that perhaps the scorpion might be clinging to one of my shoes. I was too afraid to look so I just kicked off my shoes outside the door and burst into the room in my stocking feet.

My sisters, Safa, and his bride were all sitting, waiting for me before starting to eat. They all looked concerned on seeing my distraught face. After hearing what had happened, they reassured me that there were no scorpions in that room, and we all sat down to eat. After dinner there was little conversation because we were all tired, so my sisters and I excused ourselves and started to go to our room to get ready for bed. Then I realized that I was still in my stocking feet. Someone asked me what had happened to my shoes, and I told them where I had left them and why.

My sisters and Safa went out to look for them and came back to tell me that they were nowhere to be found. I was heartbroken. They had been my very best shoes and were special to me because they were the first shoes I owned that had heels. My sister Azar had them made for herself a year or so before, and after she wore them once or twice, she found that they were a little too narrow for her feet. She gave them to me knowing that I would soon grow into them. They were lovely black suede open-toed shoes with a one-inch heel and an adjustable leather strap, which buckled over the top of my foot to hold them on. The strap was still a little too loose, which was why I so easily kicked them off. It was the first time that I had worn them, and I felt so elegant and grown up with them on.

My cousin went out and asked several of the passing waiters if they had seen my shoes, but no one had. Finally, he called the manager of the motel, who came to our room. The manager could offer no help, but he did say that there were still some shoe stores open in the bazaar and he would call a cab for us if we wanted to go buy a new pair. We had no choice. My other shoes were packed in the luggage stored on the roof of the bus, and there was no way to get to them without unloading all the other luggage stored behind ours. My sister Katayoon had the smallest feet of all my sisters so she brought her shoes for me to wear; and Tooran, Safa, and I started across the courtyard to the entrance to pick

299

up the cab. On the way to the gate, one of the waiters came running toward us, shouting, "I've found them!" A number of the waiters had gotten together and decided that one particular one of their number was a likely candidate for petty thievery. They confronted him, and he admitted that he had found the shoes and thought someone had thrown them away!

After all this excitement, we were even more ready for bed. We went back to our room and undressed. My sisters were making fun of me; Tooran, with whom I was going to share the double bed said to me, "I hope that you didn't put your shoes under your pillow!"

Katayoon interjected, "No, she is going to hang them around her neck from now on!"

In the meantime, Azar was carefully inspecting the single bed that she was going to sleep in. She pulled down the blanket and looked at the sheets, then picked up the pillow and looked inside the pillowcase.

Tooran watched her with amusement and said, "If you are looking for scorpions, there are none in the room. If you are looking for lice, you will not find them now; they will find you later!"

Azar gave her a dirty look but did not reply. Instead, she opened her overnight bag and withdrew a sheet. She had packed one of her own sheets from home along with her towel! She wrapped the sheet around herself, covering herself from head to toe, and lay down on the bed to sleep, confident that she would be protected from any contamination. She was and still is a most fastidious person. Everyone, except me, had brought along a towel because amenities such as clean towels were not always supplied in lodgings in the outlying areas of the country. Tooran had told me, while we were packing the night before we left Mashhad, that I did not need to bring my own towel. She said that she would pack an extra large one and I could share it with her, providing I promised I would not blow my nose on it!

We all slept like logs that night. The next morning we were awakened by a knock on the door at six o'clock. There were no telephones in the rooms for wake-up calls; and one or two of the waiters were assigned to make the rounds of the rooms and awaken the occupants at the proper time for them to prepare for the departure of their bus. Thirty minutes later, our simple breakfast arrived—tea, hard-cooked eggs, bread, butter, honey, and feta cheese. Our bus was scheduled to leave at eight o'clock on the next leg of our journey, which would take us over the nearby Alborz mountains to Babol. All of the passengers arrived promptly, looking cheerful and well rested; and as soon as we found our seats, we were on the road again.

Shahrood is a city with a plentiful water supply, and the streets are lined with trees and flowers. Many orchards growing a variety of fruits surround the city proper, and the place is also well known for producing seventy-odd varieties of grapes. The wines produced from these grapes are some of the best to be found in Persia. The road passed by some of these orchards, and we could see the trees heavy with ripening fruit on that early June morning. Soon the road began to ascend, winding upward to the north through a mountain pass. The scenery was beautiful, and the pure fresh air seemed to sparkle in the sunlight. I had always loved the mountains since my first visit to Shandeez on summer holiday years before. There was something majestic and timeless about the rugged peaks that appealed to my imagination. In my mind, I likened them to a huge giant, chained to the earth looking patiently down into the valleys, inscrutable and secretly brooding.

The bus groaned along slowly with the driver shifting through a range of gears as the road leveled off somewhat on a switchback then resumed its upward course again. After about two hours, we were through the mountains, and the road became more straight and level as it turned to the west. To the right, we caught an occasional glimpse of the Caspian Sea in the far distance and to the left vivid green terraces of rice paddies rose in steps along the foothills of the mountains we had just crossed. Streams of water, some small and some the width of a small river, flowed down from the mountains finding their way to the sea. We crossed them over numerous bridges. At one point, we caught a glimpse of the peak of Damavand Mountain, some seventy miles away on the left, looming over the other lesser peaks.

Damavand Mountain (the famous logo of Paramount Pictures) is the highest mountain in Persia; it is 5,771 meters (18,934 feet) high, and the peak is snow covered the year round. The peak is usually obscured by clouds, but on that day we were lucky and the glistening summit shone forth in full glory. Damavand figures prominently in Persian mythology, chiefly due to the writings of Ferdosi. In his epic poem "Shahnameh," Ferdosi tells of Zahak, the evil tyrant, being chained in a cave in the mountain by Feraydun, the heroic protagonist. The villagers who live in the village of Damavand (now a thriving resort town) at the foot of the mountain believe that if ever Zahak manages to free himself, Damavand will become an active volcano again and erupt with disastrous results to the town.

The Persian coastline along the Caspian Sea extends for four hundred miles. The Alborz mountain chain stands like a wall between the sea and the rest of Persia, blocking the moisture of the seacoast from the arid areas to the south. However, the land between sea and the mountains is fertile and green, and crops such as rice, tea, and citrus fruits usually associated with subtropical regions flourish there. The drive from east to west through this area is through the most magnificent picture-postcard scenery in all of Persia. We passed little villages along the way and saw many country folk. The women wore long colorful skirts and were bareheaded, many blonde and blue-eyed. In their multicolored garb, these women, bent over working in the rice paddies in the far distance, looked like flowers springing up among the rice. We stopped in one village for lunch. The restaurant tables were outside; we sat together with Safa and his wife and her family at one long table. The sun was shining brightly overhead, but the air was pleasantly cool. When we had almost finished our simple but tasty lunch, the driver came to our table and placed a basketful of figs in front of my cousin.

"This village has excellent figs," he said. "Please be my guest and have these for dessert." He blushed as he stood there, and everyone knew why because we had noticed that all during the trip he could hardly keep his eyes off of Tooran. The poor man had become smitten with my sister, but in the proper Persian manner, he politely addressed all his conversation to my male cousin. Safa replied, "Thank you very much. Please sit down and have some tea with us."

The driver sat down next to my cousin, and the menfolk chatted until it was time to go. During the course of the conversation, my cousin mentioned that he intended to rent a car when we arrived at Babol and take my sisters and me to Babolsar, a resort town on the seacoast, to see the Caspian Sea.

The driver then said, "I have a better idea. Why don't you tell me the address of your house in Babol, and I will pick you up in my bus early in the morning and take you to the seashore to see the sunrise? I will have plenty of time to get the bus back to Babol, because we are not scheduled to leave until 8:30. Don't mention this to any of the other passengers. I prefer to take just your family group."

We were delighted at the prospect of seeing the sunrise at the sea and accepted his offer with thanks. The lunch break was now over, so we all got back on the bus for the final leg of the trip before Babol that turned out to be more eventful than anyone could have imagined. I mentioned before that travel was not without danger in those early postwar times. The young shah was gradually subduing the militant communist cells left behind in the north by the Russians; but there were still rebellious tribal factions, some of which were no more than bands of thieves.

We had a narrow escape from two highwaymen who were foiled in their attempt to rob us only by the quick thinking of our driver. It happened that afternoon on the road to Babol. At one point, the two-lane road passed through a stretch of woods. As we approached the woods, the driver saw in the distance two men emerge from the trees and stand on either side of the road. They wore turbans, with one end masking their faces, and waved as if they wanted the bus to stop and pick them up. The driver's assistant turned and shouted to the passengers, "Brace your-selves!" Everyone stopped talking and their attention became riveted on the road ahead. Then the driver slowed the bus as if he were going to stop to pick the men up.

When the bus came to within about thirty meters of the men, the driver floored the accelerator and the bus shot by the two men who were forced to leap backwards to avoid being run over. The bus plunged on as fast as it could go, and we heard sev-eral shots from behind us. Turning back, we saw the men stand-ing in the middle of the road with their rifles pointed at the bus. Later, the driver explained that he had seen the guns that the highwaymen had tried to conceal by holding them behind their bodies. He knew that they intended to shoot out the tires to immobilize the bus and then rob the passengers. When we arrived in Babol, the driver reported the incident to the police, but no one could give an accurate description of the bandits since their faces had been hidden.

Those passengers whose end destination was Babol retrieved their luggage from the roof of the bus and bade farewell to the rest of us. Others left to look around the city or go to the lodgings reserved for them. That night we were to stay at our cousin's house. For dinner we were invited, along with Safa, his wife, and her relatives, to the house of a friend with whom Safa worked. After we had made a brief tour of the city on foot, we went to wash up; and then we all walked to the house where we were to dine. We were nine in all; and when we got to the house, my cousin's friend and his wife greeted us warmly and showed us into their parlor where we had tea with them along with their two teenage daughters and Safa's friend's mother-in-law.

After we got acquainted and exchanged a few pleasantries, the hostess announced that dinner was ready. She showed us to the dining room where a large white tablecloth was spread out on the carpet. It was covered with an abundance of food; there was enough for at least thirty people. There were several different rice dishes, various kinds of *khoresht* (stews), fish, poultry, pickles, herbs—everything but dessert. The nine of us and the two young daughters sat down around the edges of the tablecloth, and our hostess went back to the door, smiled, and said, "Please enjoy your dinner." With that, she left, closing the door behind her. We sisters sat there in surprise but Safa soon enlightened us.

"It is an old custom in this part of the country," he said. "The hosts never join their guests for the main meal. They will join us later for dessert in the parlor." In later years, when I thought back on that night, I realized that this custom reflected a delicate sensitivity on the part of the hosts. They would not be present during the meal so their guests could eat as much as they liked without feeling embarrassed. After we finished our meal, one of the daughters went out and told her mother that we were ready for dessert. Our hostess returned and invited us to be seated in the parlor. A maid, helped by the daughters, served everyone a bowl containing a variety of sweet dishes and a glass of tea.

Our host was a jolly, witty man, and he kept up a running conversation interspersed with amusing jokes and stories. His mother-in-law did not join us, so he felt free to tell one anecdote that I remember in particular. "My mother-in-law has not spoken to my wife for the last several days," he said. "She is quite religious and goes to the mosque every week. My wife never goes, because she does not believe in the preaching of the mullahs. However, last week my mother-in-law told her that a famous old mullah was going to be preaching and begged my wife to go with her to hear him. My wife didn't want to hurt her feelings, so she agreed to go. When they came back home, my mother-in-law was seething mad and my wife was trying to keep a straight face. When we were alone, I asked my wife what had happened to make her mother so angry.

"She told me, 'We were sitting on the floor of the mosque along with the rest of the women listening to this old man preach. When he got to the part about the story of Karbala, he was beating his left leg in time to his chanting and waving his right arm in the air when suddenly his false teeth popped out of his mouth. One plate he caught in the air with his waving right hand but the other one fell on the carpet. He put the one he caught back in his mouth, stepped down from the pulpit, picked up the other one, and after wiping it on his shirt, put that one back, too. All the while he kept up his chanting and beating himself. I couldn't help myself—I burst out laughing and soon everyone else except Mother and a few other old ladies were laughing, too. The mullah got mad and left in the middle of his sermon. Now she won't speak to me because she is so mad at my disrespect.'"

Our host went on to say, "There is one other thing that you must understand. When my wife laughs, she really laughs. You can hear her a block away! I told my wife that this was a blessing in disguise for her. Her mother will soon get over her anger but she certainly won't be after her to go to the mosque again!"

Our host asked us where we were going after we left Babol. We told him that we would be going to Chalus and then south to Tehran. He told us that it was a pity that we were not going farther west along the coast to the town of Ramsar, where the Reza Shah had built a fine modern hotel near the hot mineral springs that came out of the mountain near the city. We could not change our itinerary to go there on that trip, but many years later I did go and took the waters. Then I understood why it was so famous. It was a delightful experience. The hot water from the springs was piped into a bathhouse where there were separate baths for men and women. Each bathing pool was about five feet deep, and the sides and floor were smooth and slick from the mineral deposits over the years. When I stood in the warm water, it felt like my skin was covered with bubbles due to the natural effervescence of the water. It was like bathing in hot champagne!

After the evening of pleasant company and splendid dining, we all trooped back to my cousin's house and promptly retired because we had to get up very early in the morning for our trip to Babolsar. We four sisters were all put up in one room where my cousin had laid a large mattress on the floor for us to sleep on. We began to talk about our morning excursion to Babolsar. Katayoon and Azar began to tease Tooran, telling her that it was only because of her that the driver had made his generous offer to take us to the seashore. Finally, Tooran could take no more. "You two shut up," she said. "I can't help it if, of all the people in the world, it had to be a bus driver who falls in love with me!" I'm sure that she was thinking of the several offers of marriage into good families, which she had had, that had been aborted through the malicious machinations of Little Aunt who wanted her to marry one of her sons.

The next morning, as promised, the bus and driver were waiting for us in the street in front of our cousin's house. It was 5 A.M. and pitch-dark. The driver's assistant opened the door of the bus and our party of nine boarded; we four sisters had our carry-on luggage with us because we would not be returning to the house. The bus left Babol and we drove north. We reached Babolsar just as the false dawn was starting to chase away the night. Babolsar, at that time, was a small town with one main street. There were side streets on both sides, and those on the north side of the street all led to the seashore. The driver turned down one of these streets and drove to the end of the paved portion, about a quarter-mile from the beach,. He turned the bus around and parked.

We all got off and started to walk to the sea. No one was up and about at that early hour in that area, and we had the sandy road to ourselves. Because of the darkness, we could not see the water at first but could hear the rhythmic pounding of the surf and the cries of the seagulls and other shore birds. I breathed the fresh salty air from a light sea breeze that caressed our cheeks. We soon reached the beach; and as we stood there next to the wet sand left by the receding tide, the eastern sky was becoming brighter and brighter and streaked with red. We were able to see now, in the distance, a few fishing boats. I was not able to resist the temptation; I took off my shoes and stockings and waded in the edge of the surf where the spent waves gently lapped my feet. To my surprise, the water was not cold and I wished that I had my bathing suit with me so that I could plunge in. I thought to myself, *Jamshid would love this.* By now, the sky in the east was completely red, and the rim of the sun began to show above the horizon. As it gradually rose, it looked like a monstrous red plate from which a shimmering reddish-gold road extended across the sea to us. To my eleven-year-old mind, it was the most beautiful sight that I had ever seen and it is still etched in my memory.

We were no longer alone on the beach. About a half-mile away, there was a pier where several fishing boats were tied up. The crews were walking on board and making ready to put to sea and set their huge nets to harvest the sturgeon. The best caviar in the world comes from the Persian side of the Caspian Sea, because in this part of the sea, the water is highly saline and the sturgeon feed on a particular variety of anchovy found in the sea near the coast. The natives call this caviar "the black pearl of Persia." We had to leave to get the bus back to Babol before 8:30, so we did not have time to watch the fishermen.

A number of years later, I did have the opportunity to see how the fishermen worked and it was fascinating to watch. A boat with a folded net on the deck at the stern would leave the dock at dawn. One end of the net was secured to the shore and the boat slowly moved out to sea, paying out the weighted net in a huge arc. When the net was fully deployed, the boat would anchor at the one end of the arc until about eleven o'clock. Then a large number of men would gather on the shore at each end of the arced net. A small boat would bring a rope attached to the end of the net on the boat ashore to the men gathered at that end, and the men at the other end of the net would pull in concert with their counterparts. As the two groups pulled the net to shore, they walked toward each other until the fish caught in the net were confined in a relatively small area and almost on the beach. The net seemed to have a life of its own as it pulsated under the pressure of the teeming fish. The men would then quickly wade into the water, and working with lightning speed, they would toss the smaller fish back into the water and the large fish onto the shore. The net would then be carefully refolded to be carried back to the dock and the kept fish were loaded onto a truck for transport to one of the processing plants.

We arrived back in Babol a little before eight o'clock. The driver dropped off my cousin and his family, and Safa gave him a generous tip. At the bus station, we greeted the passengers with whom we had been traveling from Mashhad and met some of the new passengers who were boarding in Babol. Tooran's friend and her mother were still on the bus, so I knew that I would be moving back and forth between two seats again. By this time, I had become acquainted with the mother and enjoyed her company so I really didn't mind.

The road to Chalus was very scenic. We passed through many small villages with tea plantations and rice paddies on their outskirts. We saw many women working in the rice paddies with their long, colorful, floral-patterned skirts gathered up around their waists as they waded barefoot along the rows of rice plants. They all looked cheerful, and smiled and waved to us as we passed. In the villages, we would see their men sitting in front of tea houses, smoking cigarettes or hookahs, and drinking tea. Apparently, in this part of the country, the women were expected to do all the work. The houses, in this area of abundant rainfall, had gabled roofs covered with terra cotta tiles in contrast to the flat-roofed houses seen in the rest of the country.

We stopped in one of the villages for lunch at a small restaurant. Tooran's friend and her mother sat with us at one of the outdoor tables. After we finished eating, they got back on the bus, and Katayoon and Azar excused themselves to go to the rest room. Tooran and I walked slowly around waiting for them to rejoin us before getting aboard.

As we stood there near the bus, the driver came up to us and blushing shyly said, "How are you enjoying your trip so far, Miss Tooran?"

I saw an opportunity to create some mischief by leaving Tooran alone with the driver. I started to go to the bus, but quick as a flash, Tooran grabbed my hand and held it tightly so that I could not leave.

"We are enjoying the trip very much, thank you," she replied. "The scenery has been beautiful."

"It is even more lovely after we leave Chalus and go through the mountains to Tehran," the driver answered.

Just then Katayoon and Azar joined us and we all got on the bus with Tooran still clutching my hand tightly. My fingers hurt, and after we were seated, I grumbled to Tooran, "Why did you have to hold my hand so tightly? You complain that I stick to you like a leech sometimes, but you wouldn't let me go when I wanted to get on the bus."

"Just be quiet," she said.

Katayoon and Azar turned in their seats and laughed at us. "You two are at it again," Azar said.

"You shut up, too," Tooran snapped. She buried her nose in a book and didn't talk to any of us until we reached Chalus. We got to Chalus in the midafternoon, and after we deposited our bags in our hotel room, we went for a walk to see the town and especially to visit the Harir Chalus, a famous silk factory that is one of the oldest in the country. We walked in and wandered around looking at the long tables filled with silkworms gorging on fresh mulberry leaves. We watched the women as they pulled the filaments from four or more cocoons at once and twisted them into one thread. They knew exactly where to find the end of the filament in each cocoon so that it came out in one long fine thread hundreds of feet in length. The cocoons had been dipped in boiling water to kill the larvae before they matured to the point where they would begin to eat their way out and destroy the cocoon. The threads were then combined with other threads to form a yarn on a reel from which the silk fabric would be woven.

That night after dinner we were all sitting in our room talking and reading when we heard a knock on our door. Katayoon opened the door and there was the mother of Tooran's friend. We invited her in and she said, "I must talk to you because I don't know what to do. The bus driver talked to me after we arrived and he is much taken with Tooran. He wants to call on her after you reach Tehran and is too shy to ask himself. He asked me if I would speak to her for him."

"Tell him to go to hell!" Azar exploded. "Who does he think he is to even think of calling on one of the daughters in our family?"

"Calm down," Katayoon said. "We still have another day to travel with him; and the road through the mountains is dangerous, I have heard. We don't want to do anything to upset him."

The mother thought for a moment then said, "Why don't I tell him that Tooran is already spoken for and that her engagement will be announced soon after you arrive in Tehran?"

My sisters all agreed that this was the most diplomatic approach, and so the problem was solved. Now I knew why Tooran would not let go of my hand that afternoon at the lunch stop.

The next morning we left on the last leg of our trip, south through the Alborz mountains to Tehran. Most of the passengers who had started out with us in Mashhad had disembarked in either Babol or Chalus. Tooran's friend and her mother were still on board, along with two other couples. The road from Chalus to Tehran passes through some of the most beautiful mountain scenery in Persia. Soon after we left Chalus, the road entered a valley. On both sides, there were terraces of rice paddies extending up the mountainsides. To our left the sun was shining brightly and reflecting off the water of the rice paddies full of the spring growth of rice. The green plants shone so brightly that I was reminded of the emerald in the ring that Grandmother always wore.

I turned to Tooran and said, "Look at those fields. They look like emeralds!"

"They certainly do," she answered. "This place is so beautiful that it should be called Emerald Valley."

The farther we drove, the narrower the valley became, and there were fewer and fewer rice terraces. Here and there one could see smoke rising from charcoal kilns clinging precariously to the high cliffs. Small and large waterfalls spilled down from the mountains on both sides of the road, and as we began our ascent the road began to twist and turn like a giant serpent. As the bus climbed higher and higher, the valleys between the mountain peaks became smaller and narrower, and wisps of clouds began to gather in the blue sky. Finally, we were completely immersed in the clouds and approaching the mouth of the Kandovan tunnel. This tunnel, built by the Reza Shah, is about two kilometers long and was bored through solid rock. When we were inside, there was no light except for the headlights of the bus. Large drops of water from the melting snow on the mountain peak fell from the roof of the tunnel, and the water was drained off by ditches on both sides of the road. The seeping water was so extensive that the driver had to use his windshield wipers most of the way through the tunnel.

When we finally emerged, we were greeted by a clear and sunny sky; there was not a cloud in sight. People used to say that when one entered the Kandovan tunnel, one never knew what sort of weather would be at the other end. This was certainly true that day. The road now began to descend the mountain, winding down in a series of switchbacks. After a while, we passed by the Veresk railroad bridge, a towering engineering marvel built between two mountain peaks with a tunnel entrance at either end. It was part of the railroad system built from 1927 to 1939 under the short sixteen-year reign of the Reza Shah and one of his greatest achievements. This system connected the south of Persia to the north and had more than 4,100 bridges and 224 bored tunnels.

I often wonder what Persia would be like today if the Reza Shah had not been deposed from his throne by the foreign occupying forces during World War II. He achieved so much in the way of modernization of the country with so little (there was no significant oil revenue at that time) that, if he had been able to continue his progressive programs, the country today would not be in the shape it is under the rule of the Islamic fundamentalists. We didn't see a train that day, but I have seen one crossing the bridge on other occasions. From the road below, it always reminded me of a black snake emerging from one hole and disappearing into another one.

The road now ran along the mountain on one side of the Karaj river valley. In later years, this valley was almost completely inundated by a lake formed by a large dam that supplied a hydroelectric plant built by Mohammed Reza Shah. This plant generated electricity for the city of Tehran. At the time of our trip, there was a small dam; and the lake behind it was a popular place in summer for boating and water-skiing. This area also abounds in ski resorts, and we saw signs along the way pointing directions to some of them. About a half hour after we passed the dam, we were out of the mountains and passing through the town of Karaj where the Karaj Agricultural College is located. The bus did not stop in Karaj, but we did glimpse the lovely campus of the college with its many shade trees and flowerbeds.

Soon after we passed Karaj, we entered the outskirts of Tehran. It took the bus another hour to reach the bus terminal in the center of the city. When we finally arrived, our cousin Saleemeh and her oldest son were waiting to meet us and take us to their home where we would stay until my sisters found a suitable house. Our adventurous trip, one that I would never forget, was over; now we would begin our new life.

Note

1. A place for rest, from the Farsi *caravan*, meaning "army or group of people," plus *serai*, meaning "house or place of rest."

Chapter Twenty-one
Crystal Palace

My feelings are like the wind-tossed surf
That crashes on the shore, then retreats to the sea.
—Nazemi Shirazi (Grandfather Agha Bozorg)

We lived in Cousin Saleemeh's house in Tehran for about two months, during which time my sisters were tied up almost every morning at various government offices completing the paperwork necessary to transfer as teachers from the public school system in Mashhad to that in Tehran. The afternoons they spent house hunting for a place for us to live permanently. Azar registered in the College of Foreign Languages where she would study at night for the next four years while teaching in one of the elementary schools during the day. When school started in the fall, Tooran would be teaching at a boys' elementary school and Katayoon at a school for girls. I was registered in the seventh grade at one of the best lycées for girls in the city. It, by coincidence, was named Shahdokht, the same name as the elementary school that I had attended in Mashhad. I had no trouble being accepted to this excellent school because of my good grades in one of the most reputable schools in Mashhad. That summer marked my twelfth birthday, and I celebrated it at a family gathering with my two of my brothers, my sisters, and Cousin Saleemeh, along with her husband and three sons.

Cousin Saleemeh's house was on a dead-end street near Jaleh Avenue and close to the parliament building. Her house was one of the older ones in the area. At that time, it was one of the best neighborhoods in the city. Many ranking government

313

officials and military personnel as well as foreign embassy officials lived there. Over the next decade, this neighborhood changed completely as the wealthier people moved north to the foothills of the Alborz mountains, where the weather is cooler in the summer and the scenery greener. Less affluent people from south Tehran moved in, and town houses and apartment buildings were built on land that had formerly been devoted to spacious orchards and gardens.

Her husband, Mirza Kamal, was the only offspring of a wealthy merchant family who had spoiled him outrageously as a child. In his youth, he was taught by a succession of private tutors who schooled him well in the classics and philosophy but did little to prepare him for the practical things in life, such as earning a living. Both of his parents died when he was seventeen years old, and he had almost depleted the fortune they had left him when he married my cousin at age twenty-two. One of the first things she did after they were married was to talk him into buying their house with what money was left.

The property consisted of two buildings separated by a brick-paved courtyard with a central reflecting pool surrounded by four flowerbeds filled with beautiful flowers and a number of mature trees, which provided wonderful shade in the summer. A two-story building on the side of the courtyard next to the street functioned as a guest house, and this is where we stayed while house hunting. Saleemeh rented the rooms in this building to college students when it was not being used as a guest house. On the opposite side of the courtyard, there was a single-story building that was occupied by the family.

Since it was summertime, we spent a lot of time in the courtyard, especially in the late afternoon and evening when we would all gather and sit on a slightly elevated terrace that ran along one side. High brick walls separated our courtyard from those of the neighbors on either side. The walls were of little help in shielding us from the noise generated by the teenage sons of the neighbor on one side. These boys would bring out a gramophone almost every evening and play popular records at full volume while singing along with the music. Saleemeh had discreetly complained of the disturbance to their mother but it did no good. After one particularly noisy night that lasted well past midnight, I mentioned to Saleemeh that it must be terrible to have to put up with this every summer.

She replied, "They do not realize how annoying they are. They have to go through the same experience someday, just like the story of the fox and the crane that I'm sure you remember reading in school."

Saleemeh was referring to a fable that told of a fox and a crane who lived in the same wood. In an effort to become better acquainted, they decided to invite each other to lunch. The crane was the first host, and he served soup in a container with a long narrow neck that only he, with his long bill, could reach. The fox sat and watched his host eat, but said nothing. The fox then invited the crane to his house for lunch, and he also served soup. However, he served it in a shallow saucer from which the crane was unable to eat. Now the shoe was on the other foot, and the crane realized his thoughtlessness. He learned his lesson, and from that time on, he considered his neighbor's needs before his own.

The neighbors on the other side were a middle-aged man and his young wife who were childless. They often quarreled bitterly and loudly, and from time to time we could hear the sound of a slap of a hand. Whenever we heard this, my cousin would remark that "this man too often speaks with his fist instead of his tongue." However, whenever we chanced to meet the young wife in passing, she always had a cheerful countenance and never complained of any maltreatment.

Cousin Saleemeh was a tall, slim woman who was strong both mentally and physically. She was very kindhearted and went out of her way to help anyone who needed her assistance. She was a volunteer aide qualified to administer intramuscular injections, and she worked at one of the local clinics several mornings each week. In addition, if any neighbor needed her services, she would go to them any time of the day or night. She handled all of the family finances, in addition to running the household with the help of only one maid. Her husband would hand over his monthly paycheck to her willingly. He often remarked that he did not know how she managed to get along so well, and he did not want to know! He was happy to let Saleemeh manage things for him.

Their three sons were tall and strong like their mother. They were all in high school, and during summer vacation they all had part-time jobs during the day. The middle son was an exercise fanatic; he had set up a bar in one corner of the courtyard where he would chin himself every day and work out with barbells until he was drenched with sweat. He also was a judo student and had won several prizes in competition. After he finished high school, he joined the paratroop division of the army and rose to the rank of colonel before he was forced into retirement by the revolutionary fundamentalists.

During that summer, I was almost constantly with Saleemeh, since my sisters were either working their way through the governmental red tape or house hunting. She took me on long walks around the neighborhood and nearby downtown streets. The first thing that she showed me was how to find my way to Shahabad Street and the school that I would be attending in the fall. On the way to the school, we had to walk across the large Baharestan Square in front of the *Majles* (lower house of parliament) building. Here is where many demonstrations and celebrations had taken place over the years. It was in this square that, for the first time, Persian Christians, Jews, Zoroastrians, and Moslems all got together in harmony to celebrate the first anniversary of the Persian constitution that was adopted during the Qajar dynasty.

The *Majles* building is fronted by an expanse of lawn and flowerbeds along with several decorative pools. Separating this area from the street is a low marble wall surmounted by a high wrought iron fence. In the center, there are two tall marble gate pillars, each topped by a sculpture of a rearing male lion holding a sword in his right paw while his left paw rests on a globe. The semicircle of a shining rising sun rests on his back. This is the same logo that appears in the center of the Persian flag. The lion symbolizes courage and strength; the sword, power for defense; and the sun, divine light. Between the gate pillars, spanning the massive gates, there is a marble arch with a large green, white, and red Persian flag flying from a mast in the center. In elementary school, the children are taught that the green symbolizes the fertile greenery so cherished by the Persian people; the white stands for peace and friendship; and the red for courage.

Walking farther west beyond my school, Saleemeh and I came to what was then the center of the city. We saw Laleh Zar Street with its many cinemas and theaters. *Laleh zar* means "tulip filled," and this area, in the nineteenth century, was a park with many flowerbeds, all planted with tulips. Centered in the park, there was a building that was used by government officials to meet with foreign emissaries. The park also had a bridle path for public use. Now, the former park is a business district; and the only reminder of its former existence is the street named Laleh Zar. We window-shopped the stores on Shahabad, Estanbol, and Nadery streets; and I felt, for the first time, the different atmosphere of a big city as opposed to the friendly atmosphere of Mashhad. Here, no one seemed to know anyone else; and the people, well dressed in Western style, bustled about on their business without greeting or stopping to talk. In addition, there were many foreigners on the streets: friendly Americans, aloof English, wooden-faced Russian soldiers, and even Poles left over from the refugees relocated in Persia by the Russians during the war. Many of these Poles had intermarried with Persians, and those married to Persian women almost invariably stayed on to live in their adopted country,.

As I mentioned before, Saleemeh had only one all-purpose servant. She therefore was involved with preparing dinner every day, the one meal when everyone was home. It was not an easy job to cook for twelve people, and soon I was pressed into service as her helper. Saleemeh taught me much about cooking, and I enjoyed learning from her. This was the beginning of my lifelong interest in cooking. Many of the recipes that I learned from her are incorporated in a cookbook that I wrote many years later.

One day Saleemeh said to me, "I'm going to show you something that I'm sure you never saw before. We will make some rock candy, and I know that you will find it very interesting."

She put a saucepan half-full of water on the stove. After the water came to a boil, she began to add sugar, stirring all the time, until no more sugar would dissolve. Then she took a pencil, tied a length of cotton string to it, and placed the pencil across the top of a widemouthed jar so that the string dangled inside down the length of the jar. Saleemeh removed the syrup from the

317

stove and, still stirring, allowed it to cool slightly. Then she poured the syrup into the glass jar and I watched in amazement as the cooling syrup crystallized around the string until finally there was a central clump of crystals of various shapes hanging down the length of the string. The candy was slightly yellow in color, and Saleemeh explained to me that if one added a pinch of *zaj* (aluminum sulfate) to the water before adding the sugar, the candy would be as clear as ice.

While Saleemeh was the moving force and the doer in the family, her husband, Mirza Kamal, was the direct opposite. He was a thin, frail little man at least two inches shorter than his wife. He was active in his movements and very talkative, especially when he was drinking his evening vodka. He would sometimes go into such irrelevant detail that he would forget the main subject he had started to discuss. He was such a warm and friendly person that no one minded listening to his chatter. He had the habit of prefacing most of his remarks with the Farsi expression *arz konam* which roughly translates to "I have the honor to present." His two great passions in life were gardening and caring for his two pet canaries. He kept his canaries out of sight of each other in cages suspended from various metal bars scattered about the courtyard, changing the location of the birds depending on the time of day. The bars projected several feet from the walls of the house and from some of the trees so that any wandering cat would not be able to get near enough to frighten the birds. The canaries were not allowed to see each other because this encouraged them to sing back and forth, each answering the other.

Early every morning he would feed and water his pets, and the first thing he did when he came home from work shortly before four o'clock was to clean their cages and feed them again. All the while he did this, he would talk to them and they would chirp in response. No one except Mirza could get a sound from the birds, no matter how hard we tried. Twice a week he would feed them a sprig of parsley, and once a week he would mash the yolk of a hard-cooked egg and divide it between them. They loved the egg yolk and would devour it to the last crumb.

Saleemeh often said, as she watched him fussing over his pets, that she didn't know whom he liked more, his children or his birds. Mirza would always reply, "To those helpless canaries in their cages, I am everything. My children have you, as well as me and the rest of the family!"

As soon as Mirza Kamal finished his afternoon care of the canaries, he would turn his attention to the flowerbeds and the potted plants that were scattered about the courtyard. This is when the canaries would start their loudest and most melodious singing, calling to each other back and forth until sunset. After sunset, Mirza covered their cages with a thin, light cloth, and they went to sleep for the night. It was strange to me to see him working so hard in the flowerbeds because, in Mashhad, every-one who I knew had a gardener to do this work. Later on, I learned that gardening was a popular hobby in Tehran. Virtually every house in the better areas had at least a small garden with a decorative pool where the family could relax at the end of the day and enjoy the cool air and greenery beloved by every Persian.

After Mirza had finished his gardening, Saleemeh would bring him a small tray on which there would be a little bowl of chopped cucumber with yogurt, a few fresh herbs, a piece of bread, and a glass. Then Mirza would bring out his unique bottle of vodka, and this was the time he relaxed and looked for some-one to listen to his real or fabricated stories.

I say "unique" bottle of vodka because, although it was an ordinary quart bottle with a long narrow neck and no brand label, inside the bottle there was a large yellow lemon with a short stem of branch still attached. Whenever anyone saw this for the first time, they were amazed and curious as to how he could have gotten a fully ripe and intact lemon inside the bottle. The answer was very simple. One of the potted plants in the courtyard was a lemon tree. When the first tiny fruit appeared in the spring, Mirza would take an empty bottle and, after prun-ing away any leaves, insert a branch bearing a budding fruit into the bottle. The bottle was supported by a wooden prop and the fruit allowed to mature inside. When it was fully ripe, he would pull the branch as far as he could to the opening and snip it off. Then he would fill the bottle with vodka and cork it. As he con-sumed the liquor, he would add more so that the lemon was always immersed and preserved. Two bottles so prepared would last him through the summer and winter until the next growing season. This was Mirza's version of vodka with a twist!

Mirza Kamal had a close friend who was the father of a six-teen-year-old boy. Once or twice a month, on a weekend, he would invite the two of them for dinner. The father played the *tar* and the son, Abi, was a virtuoso on the *santoor* (a percussion stringed instrument), having taken lessons from an early age as well as being blessed with a natural musical talent. After dinner, we would all sit on the carpet in the living room and listen to Mirza's friend and his son as they played and sang to their own accompaniment. Mirza would bring out his famous vodka bottle and keep his and his friend's glass full the entire evening. It seemed that the more they drank, the better they sang! All of us marveled at the boy's talent and justly so, because years later he became a well-known composer and performer and made many appearances on local Tehran television.

Whenever we gathered for one of these musical evenings, I noticed that Abi would from time to tie glance at me. It was vaguely disturbing to me, because none of the boys that I had known in school back in Mashhad had ever looked at me in quite the same way.

One night, after Abi and his father had left for home, Saleemeh's maid whispered to me, "Come to my room. I have something for you." I went to her room and she handed me a piece of paper, folded many times so that it could be easily held in the palm of her hand. "Abi gave me this and asked me to give it to you," she said. I took the paper and went to my room to open it in private. It was a love letter and to this day I remember exactly what he wrote: "Dear Mehry, You are the loveliest, most beautiful person in the world. There is no one on this earth I love more. I love just to sit and look into your sparkling eyes. Abi."

I was so surprised and confused. This was the first time that I had ever received such a letter! I did not know how to han-dle the situation and was too embarrassed to ask one of my sis-ters. I stormed back to the maid's room and said to her, "What do you think I am that you should give me a letter from a boy? How dare he write this to me? Who does he think he is, another Mar-ius? If he ever does this again and you give it to me, I will tell my brothers and my cousin!" The poor maid could not understand my anger and certainly did not know what I meant by comparing

Abi to Marius. I have to admit that I, too, didn't know exactly what I was trying to say, but I knew that I had to pretend to be mad.

I had blurted out the reference to Marius because of another incident that had happened when I was in the sixth grade in Mashhad. One of the Golkani girls, Lila, who lived across the street from us, was in high school and the good friend of a girl in her class who was in love with a boy who lived in a house just behind the Golkanis' orchard.

One day, while I was playing in the orchard with Iran Golkani, we noticed her sister Lila putting a piece of paper under a stone on top of the wall between the two properties. We asked her if she was writing love letters to the neighbor's boy.

"Oh, no!" she answered. "This is not from me but from my friend Parvin. I carry letters between them. Please don't ever tell my mother."

We kept her secret, but from then on Iran and I would watch for the telltale stone on top of the wall. Whenever we saw it, we would sneak over and read the letters. Soon we began to call the boy Marius and the girl Cozet after the two lovers in Hugo's *Les Miserables* who had corresponded in a similar way.

The summer passed quickly. By early August, my sisters had settled their business with the Ministry of Education and were all set to begin teaching in different schools in the fall. The only unresolved problem was that of finding a suitable house large enough to accommodate my sisters, my two brothers, and me. We wanted to live within walking distance of Cousin Saleemeh, and my eldest brother and his wife who lived on Jaleh Avenue. My sisters could not find a large house to rent, so they decided to rent a smaller newly built house on a street off Jaleh Avenue. It was similar to what today we call a town house, or row house. It had a small walled courtyard with a decorative pool in front, a basement with two rooms, which we intended to use as maids' quarters, and two more stories. The second floor had three bedrooms that, by doubling up, would accommodate the six of us. My sisters signed a lease for one year and planned to look for a better place the next summer.

A telegram was dispatched to Father in Mashhad asking him to send the carpets, kitchen utensils, and small items of furniture we had previously packed for shipment. Grandmother found two maids for us, a mother and daughter combination; and they were sent off to us by bus. Fortunately, they arrived before the furniture, so they were there to help us move in as soon as it arrived. The carpets, which we had selected to be sent, had been neatly folded and securely wrapped in canvas for shipment. While we were unpacking the carpets, we noticed that the canvas wrapper on one carpet was torn in one corner. When we took off the canvas, we were shocked and horrified to find a whole stick of opium and a number of crumbs of the drug inside. We were all terrified at the thought that this contraband might be traced to our house.

Fortunately, my brother Jahan was home and he soon deduced that some drug smuggler had seized the opportunity to transport a shipment of drugs to Tehran in our baggage; and he or one of his cohorts had hurriedly removed the drugs when the carpet arrived at the Tehran terminal, leaving a small amount behind. Smuggling of opium from Afghanistan and Pakistan by way of Mashhad was common at that time, and the penalty was severe. We were all afraid to report the drugs to the police for fear of becoming involved in an exhaustive investigation, so Jahan cleaned up the crumbs and flushed them, along with the intact stick of opium, down the toilet. The contraband apparently was never traced to our shipment by any of the authorities, because we never were questioned about the incident.

My sisters bought a dining room table and chairs, and six inexpensive beds. Our stepmother contributed some fine living room furniture that she had in temporary storage with some of her friends in Tehran. A week before the schools opened for the fall semester, we were all comfortably ensconced in our new home.

The first day of school I walked to my school on Shahabad Street. A high brick wall with a central gate ran along the front of the school property. Just inside of the wide iron fence gate, there was a small area with another short segment of wall behind the gate. This wall shielded the students of this all-girls school, when they were outside playing at sports in the large central blacktop courtyard, from the ogling of any passersby. On the north, east, and west sides of the courtyard, there were long two-story buildings; those on the east and west sides housed classrooms, and the one on the north side was devoted to administrative offices and an auditorium.

As I entered the courtyard, I saw that it was filled with students from all of the grades seven through twelve. Soon the headmistress and one of her assistants appeared at the north end. The assistant had a megaphone through which she shouted out directions as to where each class was to assemble outside which classroom. My seventh grade class was divided into two sections of about forty students each, and my section was assigned to the first classroom nearest the street on the right as you entered the courtyard and the other section to the adjoining one.

When my section was all assembled, we filed into our classroom, where we were greeted by our history teacher who proceeded to assign us to our seats. The seats were a table with two drawers and an attached bench designed to accommodate two students. These double seats were arranged in two rows of ten facing a large blackboard on the north wall. The teacher assigned the seats based on the height of the student, the shorter ones being seated in the front rows. I got the very last seat in the first row next to the three large windows that overlooked the courtyard. On one side of the blackboard, there was a desk for the teacher; and on the other side, there was a large coal-burning stove with a curved stovepipe that disappeared into the wall. Behind the teacher's desk, there was a bulletin board on which was posted the schedule of classes for each day of the week by subject and hour for the forthcoming year. One of our first assignments was to copy the schedule into our notebook.

The subject the first hour that day was history. Before the lesson began, the teacher asked everyone to stand in turn and state their name and what elementary school they had attended. Our history teacher was a short, pale woman in her late thirties with long, lank black hair that looked as if it had never been styled. She had a large hooked nose and spoke with a nasal tang. Her name was Mrs. Aghakhani; but we students in private called her Mrs. History, not only because she taught history, but also because she dressed in an old-fashioned manner with high-necked, long-sleeved dresses.

That first day Mrs. Aghakhani laid down the ground rules

that applied to all the subjects we would be studying. The school year was divided into three trimesters, and at the end of each there would be an examination. The minimum passing average was ten (the Persian marking system is on a scale of one to twenty); and if one received a grade less than seven in one subject, the student was allowed to take a reexamination after the summer vacation. If a passing grade was then achieved, she advanced to the next grade when school reconvened.

Mrs. Aghakhani also emphasized that the faculty of the school all had either a college degree, master's degree, or doctorates, unlike our teachers in elementary school, and that we were expected to work hard at our studies. She told us that Dr. Mosahab, the headmistress of the school, was one of the best-educated women scholars in the country. It turned out that we students had little contact with Dr. Mosahab since the day-to-day running of the school was handled by her two assistants. Also, Dr. Mosahab resigned after my first year to accept a high post in the Ministry of Education. Later on, she was appointed to the Senate and served there many years until forced out of office by the fundamentalists after the revolution.

My seatmate in the last row was a girl named Parvaneh. She, of course, was as tall as I but more buxom. She had short, curly, black hair and large, black eyes; and while not what one would call very pretty, she was an attractive girl. She was very talkative and mischievous and to me she was almost a replacement for my brother Jamshid, my partner in so many childhood pranks. We soon became fast friends, so much so that Mrs. Aghakhani finally separated us because we were always whispering in class.

Parvaneh, like Jamshid, was fond of playing pranks. One day, she brought a live mouse to school in a matchbox and set it free during a class in Farsi composition while we were all sitting in dead silence concentrating on our essays. This completely disrupted the whole period because as soon as the first girl to see it scampering around shouted "mouse" and jumped on her desk, the whole class soon followed suit. The teacher finally called the janitor who chased the poor animal around the classroom with a broom until, finally, he dispatched it and carried the body away. By this time, the forty-five minute period was up. Needless to say, no one completed a composition that day.

We had a male teacher for chemistry and physics who was a most severe and tyrannical person. He had a haughty Prussian-like bearing and never sat at his desk during class, but rather would stand in front of it and from time to time lean his rump on the front edge. One day, when he was scheduled to teach, Parvaneh brought a dark red lipstick to school, and during the break before his class, she smeared an inconspicuous spot over the front edge of the desk. The teacher, wearing the light gray suit that he always wore, assumed his usual stance and began his lecture. True to habit, he eased his rear on the edge of the desk and sat right down on the spot of lipstick. When he turned to write something on the blackboard, there was a red stain in the middle of the seat of his trousers. The entire class began to giggle. We whispered to each other, "The teacher must be having his monthly period." He turned around, frowned severely, and demanded silence. When he resumed his writing, the class still could not control themselves, and the man left us at the end of the period in a state of fury, puzzled by our behavior. When he got back to the faculty lounge and one of his colleagues told him what his rear end looked like, he was even more furious but unable to lay the blame on anyone.

Another of Parvaneh's mischievous pranks, which reminded me so of Jamshid, happened one winter day. There is a type of firecracker made in Persia called *taraghgheh* that is in the form of a long double strip of paper. Between the strips, there are pellets of gunpowder about the size of a lentil bean spaced about an inch apart. When one lights the end of the strip, the pellets explode in rapid sequence. Parvaneh brought several strips of these firecrackers to school one day. During the break between classes, when everyone was out in the courtyard for a short exercise period, she stationed me as a lookout by the door and then proceeded to arrange the strips of firecrackers on the unburned coals around the periphery of the fire in the stove. When class resumed, the fire spread to the coal around the edge and the firecrackers began to explode. The sound was amplified by the metal stovepipe, and in an instant the classroom was emptied by the students and teacher who fled out into the courtyard. The commotion brought the janitor and assistant principal on the run. Soon all of the firecrackers had exploded and the janitor cautiously entered the room. He could find nothing out of the ordinary except for a little soot that had escaped from a seam in the stovepipe.

All this carrying on in one classroom finally attracted the attention of the school authorities and one of the assistant principals began an investigation. Every student knew or suspected that Parvaneh and I were responsible for most of the tricks and pranks and someone, I don't know who, pointed the finger at us. We received a severe dressing-down, but it did not end there. From that time on, any mischief that occurred in our class was blamed on us; and we were threatened with expulsion if we could not learn to behave.

When Mrs. Aghakhani separated Parvaneh and me, my new seatmate was a girl named Pooran. She had been sitting in the seat just in front of me and exchanged seats with Parvaneh. Pooran was a recent émigré from Persian Azerbaijan and spoke Farsi with a strong Turkish accent. She had long golden blonde hair that she wore in braids and a very fair complexion with red cheeks and hazel eyes. She was very shy and quiet and blushed whenever she was addressed by a teacher. She was a lovely girl, and although Parvaneh and I joked and kidded her about her accent, we were close friends throughout our school years. Later on, in the tenth grade, we had a teacher of Arabic who was a plump middle-aged man. He became completely smitten with Pooran and hardly ever took his eyes off her during the time that he was teaching. This infatuation I was able to turn to my advantage in a manner that I still laugh about whenever I think back to those years.

My academic achievements in the seventh grade were nowhere near the level at which I had performed in elementary school. I still managed to pass all the subjects, but only with average grades. This was because I did little or no studying. My grades improved the next year and continued to do so until by the ninth grade my average placed me first in the class. However, there was one subject that I hated and in which I never managed to get a grade higher than ten or eleven. That was Arabic. Because the Koran is written in Arabic, it was a compulsory subject for at least two hours every week during high school. At the end of the third trimester in the tenth grade, we took our final exam in Arabic that would determine our mark for the year. The Arabic teacher told us that he would examine us orally, two by two, and the examination would consist of reading a page from our Arabic textbook, chosen by him at random, and translating it. On hearing this, I was suddenly struck with an idea. I said to Pooran, "Let's you and I go in together for the examination." She, of course, readily agreed.

The night before the examination, I picked out one page in the textbook and literally memorized it. Let's say that it was page forty-five. The next morning, when it became our turn, Pooran and I filed into the classroom where the teacher was conducting the examination. We stood together in front of his desk and, as usual, he could not take his eyes off of Pooran. He said to me, "Mehry, you go first. Read page twenty-six and then translate the first two paragraphs." I opened my book to page forty-five and began to reel off the words that I had so laboriously memorized the night before. The teacher did not bother to open his copy of the textbook but sat there listening and occasionally murmured, "Beautiful, beautiful." I was not sure if he was talking about my reading or Pooran. When I had finished, he told me that I could leave and I dashed from the room without further ado. I waited outside the door until Pooran was finished. She eventually emerged, blushing furiously.

"How did you do?" I asked her. She said nothing but walked as fast as she could away from the classroom. I followed her, repeating my question and begging her to speak until finally, she turned to me and asked, "Why did you leave me alone in there?"

"I had to," I replied. "He told me to leave, but I stayed just outside the door waiting for you."

Pooran said, "I guess I did well in the exam. When I had finished he said to me, 'I so admire the flower that has grown from the seed planted by your father.' I got out of there as fast as I could after hearing that!"

The end result was that both Pooran and I got a grade of twenty in Arabic. When my sister Katayoon looked at my report card for the year and saw the grade, she said, "You must really have been working hard on your Arabic this year. This is the first time you managed to get above eleven since starting high school."

I could tell by the way that she looked at me that she was suspicious that I had not obtained my twenty grade by legitimate means. She started to question me further but I merely replied, "I just read it right" and left the room.

The other girl who sat in the seat in front of me, next to my erstwhile seatmate Parvaneh, was named Maneejeh. She was two years older than the rest of the girls in the class. She explained this discrepancy in age by saying that she started elementary school a year later than the usual age of six and had lost another year because she failed to pass the second grade and had to repeat that grade. While the rest of the class was just beginning to pass through the hormonal changes and other throes of puberty, Maneejeh was already a woman of fourteen and therefore, by old-fashioned Persian standards, eligible for marriage. She was a very beautiful girl with long blonde hair and blue eyes, but her beauty was marred slightly by one of her eyes being walleyed. In those days, operative correction of this condition was not available in the country. She hid her deformity by always wearing dark sunglasses outside the classroom.

Maneejeh was a very sensitive and compassionate girl. Whenever any of us was punished for some infraction of the rules or other misbehavior, she would be moved to tears in sympathy. She also had a romantic nature. She had a notebook in which she had copied poems and some literary passages. She asked me one day if I would do a few paintings for her notebook to illustrate some of the works she had collected. I was flattered to be asked and happy to oblige. When we had nearly completed the eighth grade, she announced that she would be ending her education at the end of that year. When I asked her why she was not going to continue, she said that she was needed at home to care for her younger brother because her mother was unable to cope with him. I later found out that her father, who had been the mayor of a small city in the northwest part of the country prior to moving to Tehran, was an opium addict and I suspect that her mother shared his addiction. This explained some of the selections of verse that I had read in her notebook while I was illustrating it for her; one in particular I remember dealt with the feelings of a bird trapped in a cage.

We all noticed that Maneejeh spent a lot more time on her personal toilet than the rest of us; she was always meticulous about the appearance of her nails, her hair, and her clothing. One of my classmates told me that if I followed Maneejeh home after school, I would see a line of boys walking behind her. Despite the differences in our age and backgrounds, Maneejeh and I became fairly close friends in the two years we were together in school although we never visited each other at home. After she left at the end of the eighth grade, I did not see her again until after I was married. I ran into her one day as I was walking down the street carrying my baby home after a routine checkup by our pediatrician.

She stopped and admired the baby and we began to exchange reminiscences about our school days. I asked her if she was married and when she said that she was not, a tear escaped from below her sunglasses. Then I noticed that there was a subtle difference in her appearance from the girl whom I had known. She still wore her large dark sunglasses, but her makeup was heavier than good taste would dictate and I noticed that men who passed by eyed her with some speculation. Suddenly, she broke off our conversation, saying with some confused embarrassment, "We shouldn't be standing here alone talking in the street." With that, she hurried off and I never saw her again. Then it suddenly occurred to me: Poor Maneejeh had become a woman of the streets!

Our physical education classes were held in the large central courtyard of the school. The two sections of our grade were combined into one class for physical education and we competed with each other in such sports as basketball, volleyball, and footracing, in addition to group calisthenics. Our phys-ed teacher, Mrs. Motamed, was a short, rotund woman; but she was in excellent physical condition and she invariably beat all of her students in footracing. I had taught Parvaneh a language that was the Farsi version of pig Latin. I had learned this from my stepsisters back in Mashhad who used to converse in that tongue frequently, especially whenever a servant was present and they wanted to keep their conversation private. Parvaneh and I used to talk back and forth in this language during our phys-ed classes and Mrs. Motamed, who didn't understand it, became very annoyed with us.

I enjoyed the phys-ed classes, especially basketball and volleyball. I usually earned a mark of twenty, but in an effort to further impress Mrs. Motamed, I volunteered to bring my roller skates to school and give an exhibition of skating. I had learned to skate in Mashhad on the area behind Mr. Golkani's house that he had blacktopped for his daughter's use for skating. I should note parenthetically that, when I was growing up, proper young girls and even boys of good families never played in the streets. Mrs. Motamed agreed to my proposal, and one day I brought my skates and performed for the class. Mrs. Motamed was very pleased and told me that, since I had no place at home to skate, I was welcome to bring my skates to class whenever I wished and could skate during free intervals in the phys-ed class.

I continued to get twenty in phys-ed, sewing, and art; but my overall average at the end of the seventh grade was close to failure. Parvaneh's average was even worse and there were two subjects in which she had to be reexamined at the end of the summer. Pooran had a good average, and Maneejee was also well above passing. That year was particularly difficult for me for several reasons. The transition from the small classes and few teachers and subjects that I had enjoyed in Mashhad to the large class with many teachers and many subjects was harder than I had anticipated. In addition, I had not studied during the summer in preparation for the coming year as I had in elementary school.

I was lonely much of the time. Whenever I came home to our small house from school, there was no one there but the two maids and I never became very friendly or close to them as I had been with the servants back in Mashhad. I desperately missed the activity and constant companionship that I had enjoyed at home in Mashhad. Sometimes I would stop off on the way home and visit with Saleemeh or stop in my oldest brother's house and play with his young daughters. Even after my sisters and brothers came home between six and seven o'clock, they were busy with their own studying or working. The only time we had together was at the dinner table. Also, I was going through the throes of early adolescence with its attendant identity confusion. Nothing I did seemed to be appropriate. If I ran about the house playing with the cat, someone would say, "Stop that childish behavior!" If I sat in front of a mirror fussing with my hair for a long time, one of my sisters would say, "You are not old enough to worry so much about your coiffure!"

The maids whom Grandmother had sent from Mashhad were good workers. The mother, a widow in her fifties, we called Naneh; and her twenty-six-year-old daughter was named Tahereh. Naneh did the cooking and some cleaning. Tahereh did the marketing, cleaning, washing, and ironing. The house was kept spotless and the dinner was always ready on time. They were a perfect couple to take care of our needs, because they appeared to be trustworthy and could work without supervision, a necessary attribute since no one was home during the day. I was always the first one home in the afternoon. I usually came home around four o'clock, and the rest of the family didn't arrive until six-thirty or seven.

One day, when I came home from school and rang the bell at the door in the outer wall of our small courtyard, it, to my surprise, was opened immediately by Naneh. "That was quick" I said. "You must have been standing there waiting for me."

"I just happened to be outside in the courtyard," she replied. I went into the house and up to my room on the second floor. After I had hung up my coat and returned downstairs to the living room, I happened to glance out of the window that overlooked the courtyard and saw that Naneh was still standing just inside the courtyard door. I watched her from behind the curtains, curious as to what she might be doing. From time to time, she would open the door and look up and down the street, then shut it again. Finally, after about fifteen minutes of this, she opened the door and in walked a well-dressed lady. Suddenly I realized that this was not a guest but was Tahereh. The first thing that I noticed was that Tahereh was not wearing her usual kerchief over her head. Then I saw that she was made up with rouge and lipstick and clad in my sister Azar's black woolen coat with the fur-trimmed collar that she only wore on dress-up occasions. On her feet were suede shoes that I recognized as belonging to my sister Katayoon. Tahereh ran into the house and down to her

331

basement room. After a few minutes, I heard her going up the stairs to the second floor. I knew that she must be putting back the coat and shoes in my sister's closets.

That evening, after dinner when the maids had finished clearing and cleaning up, and had retired to their rooms in the basement, I told my sisters what I had seen. My meticulous sister Azar blanched when she heard the story and was furious that her coat had been on the back of a servant girl.

"Don't worry," Tooran said. "All you have to do is take your coat to the dry cleaners. What do you suppose that she borrowed from me and was wearing underneath your coat? Do you think that she wore her own dress and underwear? Now I have to take all my dresses to the cleaners. I am sure that she has been doing this for a long time and just happened to come home late today when Mehry caught her."

Azar was all for firing the couple on the spot, but Katayoon calmly told her to quiet down. "We can't get along without them," she said, "but we can plan to let them go in the spring after the school year ends and write to Grandmother now to ask her to find someone to replace them. Tahereh is probably looking for a husband and had a date to go to the movies with someone she met while marketing, probably that young butcher down the street."

Tooran interjected in her usual teasing way, "She is not a bad girl and I am sure that she did no more than give him a little kiss." The thought of her coat being touched by a butcher made Azar all the more furious, but Katayoon and Tooran finally managed to calm her down and it was decided that nothing would be said to the servants about the matter. In the future, everyone would lock their closets before leaving in the morning. From that time on, we noticed that Naneh and Tahereh were spending a good portion of their salaries on clothes for Tahereh. In early spring, before my sisters had a chance to tell the maids that their services would not be required after early June, Naneh announced that they would be leaving us in June. Tahereh was going to be married and they were going to move to her husband's house and not work for anyone again. Their investment in new clothing had paid off!

One Thursday afternoon I was home alone; the schools close

at noon on Thursdays for the weekend, which ends Saturday morning, the first day of the new week. The house was so still and I felt stifled with the lack of activity. A strong feeling of homesickness for the bustling atmosphere of our house in Mash-had came over me. I missed my grandparents, Genoos, Jamshid, Gholam, Soltan, Nanny-jon; even my dolls and my cat. I wanted to go back to what I still considered my home, the house in Mash-had that I had left; but now that fondly remembered haven seemed a thousand miles away and completely out of reach. I didn't feel like doing my homework, because I knew that there was plenty of time to finish it the next day. I had to do something for amusement. Then I remembered the day that Cousin Saleemeh had taught me how to make rock candy. I decided to try to make some myself.

I went to the kitchen and found an empty jar of the right size. I took one of my pencils, attached the proper length of string and placed it in readiness on one counter by the stove. I prepared the syrup and after it had cooled slightly, poured it into the jar. Then I took the jar to the living room and put it on a table to wait for the candy to form. It was taking a long time, so I transferred the jar to a stack of a few books on the floor and arranged a pillow next to it. I lay down on the carpet on my belly and rested my elbows on the pillow, holding my head in both hands to watch the candy form.

Inside that glass jar there was another world in my imagination. Small and then larger blocks of crystal began to slowly build up along the string. Some looked to me like miniatures of house furniture: crystal sofas, table, chairs, and chandeliers. All this crystal furniture furnished a huge room. I was walking in the room and saw that all the walls, windows, and ceiling were crystal.

I walked between pillars and arches of crystal that supported the ceiling. The sun, shining through crystal windows on huge chandeliers, refracted into colors that danced on the floor like a carpet of flowers. My feet seemed to float along rather than walk on any solid surface and, as I wandered about, my shoes caught the changing hues of the dancing colors. I felt as if I were walking in heaven. I looked through a window and saw a garden full of crystal trees with the sun shining through their crystal branches. I wanted to go out and walk among those beautiful trees, but there was no door in sight. I ran around looking for one in vain: I was trapped in my crystal palace. I became panicked and frantically continued my search, running round and around. Then I heard my sister Tooran's voice asking, "Why are you sleeping on the floor?" I opened my eyes in surprise: It was all a dream, a reflection, no doubt, of the feeling of entrapment that I had been experiencing.

As soon as the school year was finished, Naneh and Tahereh left us to begin their new life of ease. About one week later, their replacements arrived from Mashhad. Grandmother had found a man and a woman, the latter a widow named Zari who had a five-year-old son. The man, coincidentally, was named Gholam. He was a bachelor about thirty years old and had a sixth grade education. While he worked for us, he attended night school in order to get the equivalent of a high school degree. After a few years, he left us to take a clerical job, but Zari continued in our employ for a good number of years while her son attended a nearby public school. Zari was a friendly, cheerful, and sincere person; and we all loved her and her son. She was a great help in preparing for my wedding some years later. About the same time that Gholam and Zari came to us, we had a marvelous stroke of luck.

Father had a good friend who worked in the Ministry of Education in Tehran. He owned a fine, spacious house on Jaleh Avenue with a large courtyard filled with trees and flowerbeds and a good-sized pool. He was transferred by the ministry to take over as Superintendent of Schools in another province and would be in this position for at least three years. He did not want to rent out his house to a perfect stranger because he wanted to keep some of his furniture stored in one large room pending his eventual return and also he wanted to be sure that the house would not be damaged. He offered to rent us his house for only a little more than the rent that we were now paying, with the proviso that we would look after it and keep up the gardens and grounds. He did not want to sign a lease, but he promised that if and when he were transferred back to Tehran, he would give us at least six months' notice so that we could find another place.

We, of course, were delighted to move out of our cramped town house and into a place that approximated what we had been used to when we were in Mashhad. The rooms were large and numerous. We all had our own room and the servants' quarters were comfortable for Gholam and Zari and her son. Katayoon started to learn gardening and soon came to love working in the gardens. The tending of the flowerbeds and grounds was no problem with the help of Gholam. Within a few days, we were moved into our new home and, with the help of Gholam and Zari, soon settled in. As soon as this was accomplished, Azar and I packed our bags in preparation for our trip to Mashhad for a six-week summer visit. How I looked forward to again seeing Grandmother and Grandfather, Genoos, Father, Nanny-jon, and all the friends I had missed so much!

Chapter Twenty-two
Moon in Scorpio

If I had the Divine power to create
First I would annihilate, then
Re-mold the universe and re-create
A world wherein we could design our fate.

—Omar Khayyam

The day before Azar and I left for our summer holiday in Mashhad, Katayoon brought home several books. She sat down next to me on the sofa in the parlour and, giving me a severe, serious look, said, "These are all eighth-grade textbooks and I want you to take them with you to Mashhad. While you are there, you are to study them at least two hours every day. If you have any problems, ask Azar or Jamshid for help. You will be back here a few weeks before school opens in the fall and I will test you. You did a terrible job last year and you are never going to do poorly again!" I was shocked by the number of books, but I knew that I had not done my best in the seventh grade and I was too embarrassed to argue with her. I did take Azar aside and begged her not to tell anyone in Mashhad about my poor performance in school. She promised that she would not if I studied during the summer as instructed by Katayoon.

One morning, a few days later, we boarded the bus for Mashhad and arrived there the next day in the late afternoon. We took a taxi from the bus station, and soon we were reunited with our grandparents, Genoos, and Jamshid. Within the hour, Father and my stepmother arrived. There was much excitement and chatter. It was so good to see their loving, familiar faces again.

Genoos was taller and slimmer, but still wore her long hair in two braids. She had the same adoring look on her face when she looked at me, and we had so much to talk about after our long separation.

The place was not the same. The stream of water that had flowed through our property continuously and provided such a pleasant background sound, as well as beauty and life to the orchard and gardens, was no longer running. Now water filled the streambed for only a few hours once a week to allow people in the neighborhood who did not have their own wells to fill their cisterns. The dry streambed seemed like a dead snake coiled around the property. The government was in the process of installing a citywide piped water system, and they had curtailed the use of streams such as ours for private use. However, the new water system had not yet been extended to our neighborhood, and the trees in the orchard were beginning to die for lack of water. Our well did not produce enough water to irrigate the orchard although there was enough for family use, to water the flowerbeds in the courtyard, and to fill the pool. The rose gardens were lifeless as were the jasmine and climbing roses that had covered the gazebo. The wooden skeleton of trellises remained, but, unadorned, the gazebo appeared so forlorn and abandoned.

This was not the only change. My father's younger sister, Little Aunt, whom I despised for her treatment of my mother, had moved into the south wing of the house with two of her unmarried sons as soon as we sisters had moved to Tehran. Azar and I, of course, stayed in the north wing with Grandmother; but we were effectively cut off from free access to the whole house. As I hinted in a previous chapter, our relationship with Little Aunt, while civil, was not what one could call cordial. We all knew that she and her children had coveted our house for years; now they had moved in and we felt dispossessed. In years past, Little Aunt had tried to marry off her oldest son to Tooran and another son to Azar. She had asked her sister, Grand Aunt, to approach my sisters and broach the subject to them. Azar, whose temper was always on a short fuse, responded in her typical manner: "If you were to put Akbar on one side of a scale and his weight in the finest jewels on the other and say to me, 'If you will have him, you can have the jewels also,' I would say to you a hundred times that amount could not buy me for him!" Tooran, in her usual laconic fashion, merely said, "Forget it."

I was angry and resentful to see Little Aunt and her sons occupying the rooms that I had always considered my own. The room in which I had been born, my mother's bedroom, was now off-limits to me. I noticed that Little Aunt and her sons did not come to see Grandmother or even say hello from across the courtyard. When I mentioned this to Grandmother, a troubled look came over her face and she replied, "If I say anything bad about them, it looks as if I am spitting in my own face for they are, after all, my own flesh and blood. However, I have to admit that they are like the time when the moon is in Scorpio. Yes, they are always moon in Scorpio."

She was referring to the old Persian superstition that says that anytime the moon is superimposed on the constellation of Scorpio, people get nasty and quarrelsome. No one should make any serious decision or attempt any major undertaking during those few days. Fortunately, this juxtaposition does not occur very often. Grandmother was too gentle a person to tell me, but I later found out that Little Aunt and her family did not speak to her for a whole year. The reason for the falling out remains a mystery to today.

Also, my cat, which I had missed so much, was missing. When I asked Grandmother where she was, she told me that Akbar, one of Little Aunt's sons, did not like cats and he had taken my cat away. Later on, Grandmother's maid told me what really happened. She said that she had seen Akbar put my poor cat in a sack and beat it to death with a club, then he carried the body away and disposed of it somehow. He certainly had inherited a sadistic nature from his mother. I never forgave him. There was nothing that I or my sister could do to change the way things were around the house. The only thing I could do was to avoid contact with my aunt and her sons as much as possible. That summer, I made frequent visits to my father's house, where I would stay one or two nights at a time.

Early in the morning of the day after we had arrived in Mashhad, I set out for Nanny's house. I walked through the familiar streets and narrow alleyways until I reached the double wooden door that I knew so well. On either side of the entrance door was a small window. These provided light and ventilation for two tiny rooms that were the living quarters for Nanny's mother-in-law. As I stood outside the door, I felt an overwhelming nostalgia for those happy days when as a tiny tot I came here to play while Nanny took care of her own household chores. I visualized the brick pathway that led from the entrance door to the small courtyard with its miniature reflecting pool surrounded by a little bed of flowers and, on the other side of the courtyard, the small single-story building containing three rooms that housed Nanny and her family. To the right would be the low storage shed with its roof covered with melon rinds put there to dry in the hot summer sun. These would be used for kindling during the coming winter, a common practice among the thrifty poorer classes. There was always a plentiful supply since everyone ate melon for lunch during the long growing season.

I was so excited at the prospect of seeing my beloved Nanny-jon again. How I had missed her and the afterschool talks that we used to have. I knocked, using the "women's knocker" on the right door. In the older Persian houses, the double wooden doors leading from the street into the courtyard had two brass knockers. The one on the right side was the smaller and made for a woman's hand. The one on the left door was used by male callers. It was larger and made a louder booming noise. When any woman inside heard it, she was warned that a man was knocking and knew that she should don her *chador* or other head covering before opening the door.

I felt a fleeting moment of dismay and disappointment when there was no immediate answer. *Maybe she is not home.* I thought that perhaps I should use the left knocker to be sure that she heard me, but decided to try again with the proper knocker, banging it as hard as I could. This time I heard her voice calling, "I'm coming, I'm coming." Finally the door opened and, for a brief instant, we stared at each other, then we fell into each other's arms. She hugged me and kissed me all over, my cheeks, my eyes, my hair, and with our arms about each other, we walked across her tiny courtyard and into her house. We sat on the edge of her bed and began to talk. She remarked on how tall I had become in just one year and that my figure was now beginning to mature.

Then she asked me to tell her all about my sisters and brothers and about school and the new friends I had made. I told her how different the school was from the one in Mashhad. There were no boys in the school, and it was so large and full of older girls all the way up to the age of eighteen or more. The academic subjects were so many and so difficult that there was no way to compare it with elementary school. Then I did something that I had asked Azar not to do: I confessed to Nanny about how poorly I had done in the seventh grade. I was no longer the first in my class.

She regarded me gravely for a minute, then she smiled and put her arms around me saying, "Don't worry. I'm sure that you will do much better next year. This could happen to anyone who moves to a strange city and has to start out in a new school." I felt as if a great load had been lifted from my shoulders. She was the first one who didn't blame me for my poor work. How I missed this love and understanding! Then she told me that her oldest daughter and her family had moved to Tehran and that she would be going to visit them at least once a year and we would be able to see more of each other.

The next morning I went to see Gholam and Soltan. Father had discharged them after we girls moved to Tehran; there were no longer any orchards or flower gardens for Gholam to tend. They had been employed immediately after they left our family by a neighbor who lived only a few blocks away. The neighbor had installed them in a two-room house at the end of his orchard. Around ten o'clock, without disturbing our neighbor, I slipped through the orchard gate and knocked on their door. Soltan opened the door and stood there looking at me in surprise. Then she gathered me into her arms and hugged and kissed me. "Come in, come in," she said. "Let me call Gholam. He is working in the orchard. Then I will fix some tea and we can talk." She called for her husband, and within a few minutes, he appeared. He also was surprised and overjoyed to see me. He shook and kissed my hand, and inquired about each of my brothers and sisters, one by one. I realized that these two faithful old servants missed our family just as much as I had missed them.

The first thing that I noticed about Gholam was that he was wearing spectacles, which he had never done before. Then I noticed that both he and Soltan had acquired a few wrinkles at the corners of their eyes. This could not have happened in only one year; I just hadn't noticed them before! Gholam, after a few minutes, excused himself to go back to work, and Soltan and I sat down and began to chat over a glass of tea. I asked her how she liked working for her new employer.

"I don't work too hard," she said. "I only do the laundry twice a week, and they have another maid who does the cooking and cleaning. Gholam takes care of the orchard and does the marketing, but now that water in the neighborhood is cut off, the trees are beginning to die and probably by next year no shrubbery will be left and he will be out of a job. Then we are going to move back to our village and open a little grocery store with what we have managed to save over the years."

"Do you remember how we used to sit in Grandmother's kitchen after dinner and tell stories?" I asked. "Does Gholam still see ghosts in the orchard at night?"

"I remember those good times well," she replied. "It was not so long ago, but I think of them as the good old days. Gholam has not seen any ghosts since we moved here. It is not very far from your house, and if there were ghosts in your garden, there surely must be some here. Sometimes I think that he never really saw a ghost at all!"

"There is another thing that I am curious about," I said.

Soltan smiled as if she knew what I was going to ask. "Go on," she said.

"Do you still wear your snake's marble charm and does it help to keep Gholam in love with you?"

Soltan laughed and replied, "Yes, I still wear it. Gholam doesn't fool around with the neighborhood maids anymore. I don't know whether it is because of my snake's marble or because he is getting old. In either case, I wouldn't part with my charm. But enough of that; will you stay and have lunch with us?"

I glanced up at the little windup clock that sat on a shelf and saw that it was twelve noon. How the time had flown. We had been talking steadily for two hours, reminiscing about the good old days, recalling the tricks that Jamshid used to play, the good times we had making rosewater, the winter evenings around the table in Grandmother's kitchen, and many other fond memories. I declined her invitation for lunch since I was expected back home by Grandmother, but I promised to return to see her again before leaving for Tehran and made her promise to come to say good-bye to me if they left for their village before my summer holiday was over. However, I never did see them again. I was so busy that summer that I did not go back and the following year when I came back to Mashhad for the summer holiday, they had returned to their village. I hope that they found peace and prosperity in their retirement.

That summer was a continuous round of visiting and receiving visitors. My classmate, Parvaneh, came to Mashhad with her parents to make a pilgrimage to the Shrine of Imam Reza. They stayed for a week in one of the hotels, and Parvaneh came to see me. We spent one whole day together. I still have a few pictures of Parvaneh and me taken in our garden that day. I, of course, had to do my two hours of studying every day, but I still found time to visit with most of the girls whom I had known in elementary school as well as numerous relatives. Lila Golkani was married, and no longer living across the street in her parents' house. Her sister, Iran, was preparing to go to London that fall to complete the last two years of high school and then remain there to study medicine.

One morning, a few days after we had arrived in Mashhad, Azar and I went to see Grandfather Agha Bozorg. We arrived about eleven o'clock, and when we entered the courtyard we saw him out walking around with the familiar walking stick in one hand and holding to his son's arm with the other. He looked so tiny and frail, but his shoulder-length snow-white hair and full, long beard still gave him an imposing appearance. He was a 107 years old at that time, but he recognized us immediately. The same old twinkle was in his eyes and his smile was as benign and loving as ever.

Unfortunately, his deafness had progressed to the point where conversation with him was difficult and his second wife, Shareehe, had to repeat many of our words in a loud voice next to his ear. Shareehe invited us to stay for lunch and for this we repaired to Grandfather's bedroom. He had difficulty in sitting in a chair and was more comfortable on the floor with his back leaning on a cushion against the wall and his legs stretched out. Shareehe had put a small mattress with a large cushion next to one wall and after Agha Bozorg was helped into position on it, she spread a tablecloth in front of him on the carpet and we all sat around it to eat. I thought to myself that my grandfather now seemed like a helpless baby, unable to do anything for himself anymore. Even his speech was slightly slurred and he tended to mumble. We had a pleasant lunch, and shortly afterward, Azar and I left so that Agha Bozorg could take his afternoon nap.

I could not help but contrast his present state to the man I had known who used to regale us with his wonderful stories and poetry. The following summer when I went to visit him, Agha Bozorg was completely bedridden but still in possession of his mental faculties. The year after that, I did not go back to Mashhad for the summer. Before I again visited my hometown, he had passed away a few weeks before his 110th birthday.

The summer passed quickly and soon it was time to return to Tehran. Jamshid had finished the twelfth grade, and he was to come to Tehran with us and enter the University of Tehran that fall. He was the last of us children to leave the nest, and our farewell this time was even more painful than the one the year before because Jamshid was the most favored of all the grandchildren. The morning we left, Grandmother and Grandfather hugged and kissed Jamshid and showered him with their blessings. For the first time in my life, I saw Jamshid in tears as he put his head on Grandmother's breast to say good-bye. Genoos was mournfully standing by, trying to contain herself because she had grown very close to Jamshid after I left. Finally, she could not stand to watch any longer, so she turned and ran sobbing into the house. Poor girl: That had been the story of her young life. Everyone whom she loved sooner or later left her; first her mother, then her nanny, her father, me, and finally, Jamshid. Unfortunately, there was no time for me to run after her to try to comfort her.

Azar, Jamshid, and I arrived back in Tehran the later part of August. Katayoon and Tooran had spent a rather uneventful summer working. One of the first things Katayoon did when we got back to Tehran was to quiz me on the subjects that I had been studying the past two months. She was satisfied that I had been working as promised, but she warned me that she was going to keep a close eye on me from now on to make sure that I did not have another scholastically disastrous year. I didn't. I settled down in the eighth grade as did Parvaneh. We both gave up the childish pranks and behavior that had been part of my downfall in the seventh grade. By the end of that year, I ranked second in my class and Katayoon was finally proud and satisfied with my work.

In the spring of that school year, Grandfather Khan came to Tehran to visit us for a month. After school was out, he took me with him back to Mashhad for the summer holiday. None of my sisters went with us, and he promised them that he would find someone to accompany me back after the summer was over. Grandfather decided that we would go to Shahrood by train, stay there two nights with an old friend of his, and then go on to Mashhad by bus. We boarded the train early one morning, and as usual, I carried an armful of books to study in preparation for the ninth grade. We arrived in Shahrood shortly after lunch. Grandfather's friend, a dentist who had practiced in Mashhad before retiring to Shahrood, met us at the station and took us to his house.

That night, after dinner, we were all sitting on the verandah of his house overlooking his orchard when suddenly there was a power failure. We waited and waited for the power to come back on to no avail. I had to go to the bathroom and could no longer hold myself. I whispered my problem to Grandfather who told his friend. Our host gave me one of the lanterns they had lit when the power went off and directed me to a nearby outdoor privy in the orchard that was there for the convenience of the workers. I went to the privy, put the lantern on the floor, and sat down. Suddenly, in midstream, I spied a huge scorpion, large tail erect and ready, in the corner. I jumped up screaming, snatched the lantern, and ran to the verandah. I told everyone what had happened and how the same thing had happened to me before in Shahrood. Grandfather laughed and said, "Perhaps you had best not go to the bathroom when you are in Shahrood."

344

Two days later we went to the bus station and got on the bus for Mashhad. The bus was not full, and we had seats in the first row directly behind the driver. There are a number of small villages between Shahrood and the stretch of desert outside Mashhad. As we were passing through one of them, we saw a mullah waving his arms for the driver to stop and pick him up. The driver ignored him and sped past. Grandfather, who never liked the mullahs but who nonetheless was sorry to see any man standing alone along the roadside in the sun, asked the driver why he didn't stop.

The driver replied, "Mullahs never pay and they are a bad omen. If I had picked him up, probably we would have an accident due to the bad luck he brings!"

As we approached another village, the bus was flagged down by a pretty bareheaded young woman. She boarded and the driver's assistant gave her his jump seat beside the driver and stood behind her. They were soon laughing and bantering back and forth. I could see Grandfather becoming more and more angry. His face became flushed and his lips compressed. Finally, he leaned forward and whispered something in the driver's ear. At the next village, the driver told the woman that this is where she should get off and she cheerfully obliged. I did not know at the time what was going on but in reflecting on this in later years, I realized that grandfather had recognized the woman as a prostitute and had told the driver to get rid of her so that the children of the families traveling on the bus would not see her unseemly behavior with his assistant.

When we arrived in Mashhad, I was again shocked to see further change in my old home. The orchard was no longer there and a high wall had replaced the row of hedges that had separated it from the house and inner courtyard. Father had sold off the land where I had played as a child, and now there was a large hospital under construction on the site. Little Aunt and her family still occupied the south wing. One of her sons had married, and he and his wife and baby were living in several rooms in the central wing. The house was crowded with new servants, and there was a constant stream of visitors who were friends of Little Aunt and her sons. However, it was not the pleasant and convivial place that I had known. The east gate was gone and we all used the *beerooney* courtyard entrance. A paved pathway next to the new wall allowed access to the north wing where Grandmother and Grandfather lived. All day long that summer we lived with the din of construction in our ears as the hospital gradually rose to tower over the wall that was now the eastern limit of the property. With all these changes, I finally accepted the fact that the house that I had known and loved as a child was no longer home to me, and I was just another family visitor from Tehran.

Grandfather, as promised, found a middle-aged couple, friends of a friend, to accompany me back to Tehran at the end of the summer. I had, voluntarily this time, studied the subjects that I would be taking in the ninth grade all summer long, and I was ready to begin what corresponds to the first year of high school in the U.S. In addition, I decided to enroll in an art class after school, two days a week. The art school was located between our house and Shahdokht school, near the parliament building. The class that I attended began at 4 P.M. and lasted an hour and fifteen minutes. I would dash out of school as soon as the final bell rang and hurry to the art academy that was known as Kamalalmolk. From 8 A.M. to 2 P.M., this school held formal classes for students pursuing a degree in art. At 4 P.M., a noncredit class open to people of all ages, who wanted to learn the rudiments of painting, was held. Our art instructor was a young man named Mr. Katoozian, now a famous artist in Persia.

I was the youngest of the twenty-five students, both male and female, in my class. Some were as old as fifty. The class was held in a large atelier with a table in the center upon which the teacher placed the basket of fruit, a vase of flowers, or whatever other subject we were to paint. We students stood behind our easels in a circle around the table and painted the subject. Of course, each student saw the subject from a different angle and painted what he or she saw. Mr. Katoozian would circulate among us, offering suggestions and criticism of our work. I enjoyed the class very much and attended it for two years. All of my family, except for Tooran, were amateur painters of varying skill. The men of the family, including my father, his father, and his grandfather were better, in general, than the women of the family. My eldest brother, the economist, long since retired, now spends his days painting and has sold a good number of canvases.

One of my fondest memories of the art class was the day that Mr. Katoozian took us on a field trip instead of painting. We went to a gallery where the paintings of Hossein Behzad were on display, and we all met the renowned artist. None of his miniature works, for which he was famous, were hung in this exhibit; but there were at least fifty full-sized canvases. One in particular caught my eye. It was a painting of an old man leaning against the trunk of a tree, the leaves of which, bright with the colors of autumn, littered the ground about his feet. The symbolism of a man in his declining years was beautifully expressed.

I was now fourteen years old and the first stirrings of my hormones were becoming manifest. I no longer looked at boys as classmates, as I had in elementary school, but rather as members of the opposite sex. I took the city bus to school in the morning, but Parvaneh and I used to walk home together on those days when I didn't go to art class. She lived a few blocks closer to the school than I but in the same direction. All along our route we would pass groups of boys who used to loiter about after school to look the girls over. It was all quite innocent compared to the behavior of some of the teenagers of today. There would be a lingering glance or a covert smile, and once in a while we would see a note being passed from one hand to another.

One afternoon, we noticed a young man staring at the two of us as he approached from the opposite direction. We passed him without giving him any apparent attention, but once we were out of his sight we broke out in giggling speculation as to which of us he was interested in. The same young man soon began to haunt our footsteps every day. Finally, one afternoon, he stopped in front of us, and while briefly shaking my hand, said, "My name is Mehrdad." He then turned to Parvaneh and gave her a lingering handshake. "I live close to you and I would like to give you this letter. I wrote all about myself in it!" With that, he thrust a folded note in between the textbooks that Parvaneh was holding next to her chest and hurried off before she could say anything.

Parvaneh and I continued quietly on our way; and when we reached the place where we normally parted, Parvaneh asked me to come with her to her house to read the letter with her. I enthusiastically agreed. We arrived somewhat breathless and giggling with excitement. We went right up to Parvaneh's room and she unfolded the note. The first thing we noticed was his fine handwriting. "Oh, my God," exclaimed Parvaneh, "his writing is as beautiful as he is!" She read aloud from the letter. " 'Next week will be the fifth month from when I first saw you. I admired you from the first glance. You probably did not notice me that day, but I will never forget it. That day was the day that changed my life and gave meaning to it. The more I see you, the more I see your perfection and the more I love you.' " The rest of the letter detailed his age, education, and work; and it finished by his asking if he could continue to write to her.

This correspondence continued throughout the ninth grade. Mehrdad would approach us a couple of times a week as we walked arm in arm home from school. After glancing about to make sure no one was watching, he would quickly thrust his letter into her books and extract her letter to him which was projecting out of another book. By the end of that school year, they knew a lot about each other; and it appeared that they were falling in love, even though their only contact had been by the surreptitiously exchanged letters.

After school was out for the summer, Mehrdad's family sent a message to Parvaneh's family asking permission to visit. This, of course, was granted; but when they arrived and asked for Parvaneh's hand in marriage to their son, her parents exploded with anger. "Our daughter is only fifteen years old and hasn't finished school. Also, our families have nothing in common and any marriage is out of the question!" Mehrdad's family departed feeling, understandably so, rather insulted. Parvaneh's parents did not know about the correspondence between her and Mehrdad, but they saw that she was unhappy about their rejection of the marriage proposal. They decided that she had best be away from Tehran for a while, so they sent her to her oldest brother's home far in the southwest part of the country. Parvaneh told me what had happened before she left for the summer.

"Perhaps it is for the best," I told her. "If Mehrdad really loves you, he will be here when you come back." So the two were parted for three months; but when school began again in the fall, their correspondence resumed and became more and more frequent throughout the tenth grade. About four months into the school year, Mehrdad persuaded his parents to again call upon Parvaneh's family and ask for her hand. This time, however, they made a big mistake. They told Parvaneh's parents that the two were in love and had been exchanging letters for almost two years. Nonetheless, the proposal was again summarily rejected. Mehrdad's parents tried to reason with him, pointing out that there were other girls who would be glad to marry him and that he was foolish to want to marry into a family who thought so little of his family. He could not be dissuaded.

Parvaneh's mother reacted to the news of their correspondence by announcing to Parvaneh that henceforth she would accompany her to school in the morning and again walk her home after school to make sure that no exchange of letters took place. Parvaneh was shocked by her mother's pronouncement and pointed out to her that it would be very embarrassing to her to be seen walking to school with her mother at her age. Her mother assured her that she would follow at a distance, but she would be watching to be sure that Parvaneh did not contact Mehrdad. I was sorry for Parvaneh. It dawned on me that all love stories were not straightforward and uncomplicated as those in the stories that Zivar used to tell me as a child. I decided to do what I could to help Parvaneh keep up her contact with Mehrdad.

We concocted a scheme whereby we would walk home together from school to a certain point, then we would part our ways. Parvaneh would continue on Jaleh Avenue with her mother following along. I would turn left onto a little-traveled byway called Fakhrabad Street. Then Mehrdad would intercept me, and we would exchange Parvaneh's and his letters. I would give his letter to her the next day. This continued throughout the tenth grade. I never learned how her family found out about our subterfuge, but the following summer Parvaneh was again dispatched to her brother's house for the summer months.

All through the tenth grade while I was acting as a mail carrier for Parvaneh and Mehrdad, Parvaneh and I talked, as all teenage girls do, of love. She told me how happy she was now that she had found Mehrdad and urged me to find a boy for myself. I was not attracted to any boy in particular the first part of the school year. Some of the boys I passed on the street on the way home gave me suggestive glances, but I gave them no encouragement. Two older boys in art school also tried to get my attention, but I felt no attraction to either one. Another young man who was a friend of our family and lived in Mashhad used to frequently send small gifts to us in Tehran—baskets of fruit, candy, etc.—and I knew that these gifts really were directed at me. I felt nothing for him.

However, one morning in the second trimester, I was standing at the bus stop waiting for the bus to school when I noticed a tall, fair young man standing beside me. I got on the bus and he followed, taking the seat next to me. When he sat down, we both turned our heads to look at each other and then we did a double take. I felt the spark of a sensation unlike anything I had ever felt before. The next morning we again met at the bus stop. He glanced at his watch and I looked at mine. It seemed that there was some unspoken agreement between us. During this week, I told Parvaneh that I thought that I was falling in love.

"Tell me all about it," she said excitedly. "Who is he, where does he live, what is his name?"

"I don't know his name or anything about him," I answered, "but I saw him on the bus and I feel that he is the one for me and I'm sure that he is attracted to me."

Several mornings later, the bus was more crowded than usual and the only unoccupied seats together were in the rear. I could have sat with someone else further forward, but I made a beeline for the empty seat and he followed. We sat together and finally he spoke to me. "My name is Shahriyar. I noticed that you get off at the Shahdokht school. You must be a student there. What is your name and what grade are you in?"

I replied, "Yes, I am. My name is Mehry and I am in the tenth grade."

"I finished the twelfth grade a year ago," he said.

That was the extent of our conversation that morning. There was no school over the weekend, and I spent a good deal of time thinking about my new friend. The morning of the next school day I looked for Shahriyar in vain. The following morning, I found him again waiting for me at the bus stop.

He came up to me and said, "I went to your school yesterday afternoon to meet you when you came out, but you dashed off before I had a chance to talk to you. I haven't been on the bus in the morning, because I am a student at the American Institute and all last week I was late for class because I wanted to ride with you. The first day I saw you, I was late for class and just happened to take the same bus as you. All week long, I took the same bus but now the school will not tolerate my late arrival anymore; and I must remain in school to improve my English so that I can study abroad. Which way do you walk home in the afternoon? I will walk with you, if you don't mind."

"I go to art school twice a week and that starts at four o'clock, the same time that classes are over in Shahdokht school. That's why I was in such a hurry yesterday. When I don't go to art class, I usually walk home with my friend Parvaneh down Jaleh Avenue," I said. "Then sometimes I cut over to Fakhrabad Street. [I didn't mention my role as postmaster.] I don't like to go down Fakhrabad Street alone when I come home late from art school because it is usually so deserted."

When I came out from art school the next afternoon, he was waiting for me. "Let me walk with you down Fakhrabad Street," he replied. "Then you will not be alone and we can talk without anyone seeing us." I agreed and for almost the entire remainder of the school year, Shahriyar met me every day that I had art class and we walked together. Fakhrabad Street at that time had a number of large properties situated behind the usual high wall fronting the street. Some foreign embassies were located on that quiet thoroughfare. One property, which appeared to be unoccupied at the time, had a concrete bench on either side of the front gate. Shahriyar and I used to sit on one of these benches and talk for fifteen or thirty minutes. It was relatively safe to do so, because there was very little traffic on that street. No one from either of our families or any of my fellow students ever saw us. Parvaneh promised to cover for me in case anyone asked where I was. She said that she would tell them I was studying with her at her house.

However, one day, Afsar, the woman that my eldest brother employed as a nanny for his children, happened to walk by and saw me sitting on the bench talking to a boy. What a scandal this would cause if it got out! I told Shahriyar who she was, and he urged me to run after her and ask her to keep her mouth shut. I ran after Afsar and begged her not to mention to my brother or his wife that she had seen me with a boy unchaperoned. I told her that all we were doing was talking, and there was no harm in that. After she extracted a promise from me that the talking would progress no further, she agreed to keep my secret.

During those few months before the time that Shahriyar had to leave for America and college, we learned all about each other. We discovered a common interest in poetry, music, and art. We discussed our families until I felt that I knew every member of his, and he knew everyone in mine. We talked about everything but never mentioned love. We both knew that he would soon be far away and that we probably would not see each other again. One day I told him about Parvaneh and Mehrdad and how I had been acting as go-between for them. He didn't comment at the time, but a few days later, he said to me, "I am not as good as your classmate's friend Mehrdad is at writing letters, but I am collecting an anthology of Persian poetry for you and I will give it to you before I leave to remember me by. Today I brought you a poem from the Divan Shams Tabrizy. To me, one good poem says more than a hundred letters."

This is the poem he gave me that day; the translation is by Reynold A. Nicholson (1868–1945).

Happy the moment when we are seated in the palace, thou and I.
With two forms and two figures but with one soul, thou and I.
The colors of the grove and the voice of the birds will bestow
    immortality.
    At the time when we come into the garden, thou and I,
      The stars of heaven will come to gaze upon us;
    We shall show them the moon itself, thou and I.
Thou and I, individuals no more, shall be mingled in ecstasy,
    Joyful and secure from foolish babble, thou and I.
    All the bright-plumed birds of heaven
    Will devour their hearts with envy.
In the place we shall laugh in such a fashion, thou and I.
    This is the greatest wonder, that thou and I,
    Are sitting here in the same nook.

Shahriyar left for America shortly before the end of my school year. The day before he was to leave was on a day when I had art class. I skipped art class that day, and we sat and talked for two hours in the early spring sunshine until the sun began to set in a bloodred sky. It seemed that the red sky was a symbol of our bleeding hearts, and the few puffy clouds scattering before the wind high overhead were like the parting of the two of us. When we bade farewell to each other, I received my first kiss—a quick, chaste brushing of the lips! That was my first and only experience with sex before my marriage.

Just before the summer vacation between the tenth and eleventh grade, an amusing incident occurred in which Afsar, the nanny who cared for my eldest brother's children, played the star role. The reader may recall that this brother, after his education in London, returned briefly to Mashhad and then moved to Tehran where he was employed as an economist by the government. Shortly thereafter, he married and his wife, Maheen, who was employed by another government agency, continued to work.

When their first child was born, Maheen hired Afsar to care for her; and she continued in the same capacity following the birth of their second daughter. Both my brother and Maheen continued to work full time, and the burden of care of the children fell upon Afsar. She was a cut above the usual maidservant and might better be characterized as a governess. She did not wear a *chador* and was always stylishly dressed in the Western fashion. She was very fond of the children and lavished them with little presents, such as ice cream, dolls, etc., until Maheen at times felt guilty that this servant spent so much of her salary on the children. She tried to make it up to her by buying Asfar clothes and slipping her a little extra cash now and then.

One day Afsar announced that she wanted to take the whole family, including my sisters and brothers and me, to lunch at Darband, a fashionable resort area north of Tehran. Let me digress for a moment and describe a little geography for those unfamiliar with the area north of Tehran. The Alborz mountains form a majestic backdrop to the city to the north. Most of the year, the craggy peaks are crowned with snow, and skiers are able to find good skiing until early summer. The foothills were a favorite place for the city dwellers to picnic and hike, because the temperature during the hot summers was at least twenty degrees cooler than the city. There were a number of passes through the mountains: Colakchal, Toochal, Haft Howz,

Darakeh, Evin, Darband, and Pasghaleh.

Darband was the most popular area and it was reached by taking a car or bus to the small city of Tajreesh. From there, a wide paved road, lined on both sides with trees and streams of water, wound past several royal palaces on up to the series of terraces leading to the elegant Hotel Darband. The road ended at a large parking lot just south of the tiny village of Darband. No busses or trucks were allowed on this road, but cars were available for hire in Tajreesh,.

Just beyond the parking lot and the village, donkeys and mules were available for hire for those who did not care to walk along the narrow dirt path that led into the Darband pass and up into the mountains. As one walked or rode along this path, climbing all the while, one could see picnic tables scattered along the path; and occasionally there may be found a small restaurant with outdoor tables that catered to those picnickers who didn't want to bring their own food. Once in a while we passed a teenage boy who had set up a small table by the side of the path from which he sold mulberries, blackberries, or shelled fresh walnuts, which he had picked from the trees in the mountains early that morning.

The scenery along the path is magnificent: On one side there is the rocky face of a mountain, and on the other side a deep gorge through which flows the Darband River. The path is a favorite of hikers, who can follow the river gorge as far as their stamina permits. The more hearty who persist for several hours and climb to Pasghaleh will be rewarded with the sight of Twin Falls, a waterfall, divided in the center by an outcropping of rock, that plunges from a height of about fifty feet. The river, of course, is fed by the continuously melting snows on the mountain peaks and the water is ice cold, clear, and delicious.

On the appointed day, we all set out, a total of ten or twelve people, including my brother's family, Afsar, and I along with my sisters and one of my brothers, as well as two of Maheen's lady friends. We walked up the path until we began to tire, then stopped in one of the restaurants for a lunch of *chelow kabab*, the national dish of Persia. This is broiled lamb kabob served with a steaming mound of rice *(chelow)* with a raw egg yolk in the center and spices. Over the objections of my brother and Maheen,

354

Afsar insisted on picking up the check for the entire feast. We passed a very pleasant afternoon in the cool fresh air beneath the trees beside the murmuring river, the adults talking and the children playing along the bank of the river. About four o'clock, we made our way down the mountain.

On the way, Afsar walked beside me and, when no one was looking, whispered in my ear, "Do you still see that boy?" I told her that he had left the country and when she saw my eyes start to brim with tears, she patted my shoulder and said, "There are many other fish in the sea."

Maheen had a chest stored in a walk-in closet in their house; and in the chest, under a pile of clothing and linens, she kept a small box in which she stored forty or fifty gold coins of various denominations that she had accumulated over the years, mostly from the traditional coins given by the bride at her wedding to her relatives and guests. A few weeks after our outing, she went to the chest to retrieve some article of clothing and by chance opened her coin box. To her horror and surprise, there were only two coins in the box. Obviously, it could not have been the work of a casual thief since the box was not entirely empty and there was no evidence of any disorder.

The only guilty one could be Afsar. Now it was apparent where the funding for Afsar's generosity came from. Maheen was in a terrible rage and confronted Afsar with her accusations. At first Afsar denied any knowledge, but as it became more and more apparent that she was guilty, finally broke down and confessed that she had taken a couple of the coins. She was immediately dismissed.

Maheen now found herself with no one to take care of the children so she took a week off from work to care for them herself while she looked for a new nanny. While walking with the children one day, she encountered one of her neighbors whom she had never formally met or even seen before. However, the neighbor recognized the children and stopped to chat.

"Where is the children's mother?" she asked.

Maheen was dumfounded. "I am their mother," she replied.

"Really?" said the neighbor. "Afsar told me that she was the doctor's wife." Afsar's elegant clothing and reputation for generosity, funded by Maheen's gold coins, had certainly elevated her status in the neighborhood! Afsar continued to come back to visit occasionally, because she truly loved the children and wanted to see them. Years later, when she was very sick, she asked someone to send for Maheen. Then she made her deathbed confession: She owned up to the theft of all the missing coins!

When school reconvened for the eleventh grade, I dropped out for the first three months to attend a school of nursing. I soon determined that a nursing career was not for me and after about three months decided to return to my class in Shahdokht school. Since I had missed the first three months of the school year, it took considerable persuasion to be allowed to come back into the eleventh grade, but finally I was allowed to reregister. By this time, Parvaneh had worn down her parents and her mother no longer accompanied her to and from school. She openly corresponded with Mehrdad, so my services as a go-between were not needed that school year.

The persistence of the two lovers finally broke down Parvaneh's family, and they, with much reluctance, consented to the marriage of their daughter to Mehrdad. This took place the summer after we finished the eleventh grade. However, the ceremony did not take palce in the bride's home as is the custom. They were married in Mehrdad's parents' house. Parvaneh's father and mother attended the wedding ceremony, but they did not invite any of her relatives. I went to the wedding and Parvaneh looked beautiful. Her face shone with happiness, and I was so glad for these two lovebirds who had finally made their own nest.

Parvaneh's parents sat apart from the rest of the guests with impassive expressions on their faces. They showed no happiness that their only daughter was getting married. Somehow their attitude reminded me of the old saying told to me by Grandmother: They were moon in Scorpio. Despite all the trouble with Parvaneh's parents, the groom's parents were very fond and proud of their new daughter-in-law. As years went by and grandchildren began to arrive, Parvaneh's parents gradually began to soften their feelings toward Mehrdad and his family. Parvaneh and I continued our friendship even after I married, but over the years we gradually drifted apart. The last time I saw Parvaneh, some years later, she was still happily married to Mehrdad and the mother of four children.

356

Chapter Twenty-three
The City of Roses
and Nightingales

Joy be to Shiraz and its unrivaled borders,
Oh, heaven! Preserve it from decay.

—Hafiz

The summer holiday between the ninth and tenth grades brought a new and exciting adventure. For the first time I was to visit the "City of Roses and Nightingales," Shiraz, the city where my mother's family had lived for generations. I had dreamed of seeing this city all my life; and whenever I was with Aunt Ozra and she talked of the orange and lemon groves, the beautiful gardens, and the warm friendly people of her birthplace, my desire to go there became more inflamed. Early one morning in the first week of June, a hired *doroshkeh* pulled up to the east gate of the courtyard and, with the help of Gholam, Katayoon and I loaded our suitcases and set out for the bus depot. We would be gone for two whole weeks and I planned to savor every minute of it, because we rarely had an opportunity to visit with Uncle Shirazy and his family. As the bus left the Tehran depot, I was beside myself with excitement. The nine-hour journey seemed interminable and when the bus made a halfway stop in Isfahan, I could hardly wait to reboard and be on our way.

When the city of Shiraz began to appear in the distance, my heart beat faster and faster in anticipation. At last I was going to see the city where my mother had been born and see at firsthand the sights that I had been hearing about all my life! I felt a sense of fulfillment such as I had never felt before. It seemed as if a void in my life that I had felt subconsciously since the death of my mother was about to be filled. Whenever Aunt Ozra talked of Shiraz, she made it appear like a paradise on earth and now, as the bus passed through the city, I could see why. The warm, soft afternoon breezes brought the perfume of oranges and lemon blossoms blended with the fragrance of a multitude of roses. Everywhere one looked, there were roses climbing over the walls that separated the courtyards from the sidewalks. Bed after bed of roses marched in colorful array down the centers of the divided streets.

Uncle Shirazy and his wife were waiting in the bus depot to meet us. He opened his arms, embraced us, and welcomed us with a line of poetry from Hafiz, "My eyes are your abode and I welcome your footsteps thereon."[1] The warmth and joy in my uncle's eyes made me feel that seeing us was the most important event in his whole life. When we arrived at his house, the rest of his family, five sons and a daughter, were waiting to greet us. The tradition of hospitality for which Shirazians are justly famed was exemplified by Uncle Shirazy and his family. Everyone was prepared to go out of their way to ensure that our visit would be enjoyable. His eldest son had hurried home from his studies at the College of Pharmacy to be sure to be there when we arrived. His wife's sister had brought her husband. The second son, who was serving his compulsory military service, had obtained leave for the day. The other three sons and the daughter were still living at home and were on summer holiday from high school.

This was the first time that I had met my cousins from Shiraz. Whenever Uncle Shirazy came to Mashhad to visit his father, Agha Bozorg, he never brought his family because his visits had to be brief due to the pressures of his veterinary practice. As my uncle introduced me to my cousins one by one, he told them that although they had never known their aunt, I was the living image of her. Then, as he turned to me, he said, "Your mother was greatly loved and my heart still pains at her loss."

That evening we had a wonderful family dinner. Uncle Shirazy's family, during the summer, dined outdoors in a gazebo that was open on two sides, one of which looked out on a decorative pool with the opposite side facing the house. The other two sides were trellises that supported a multitude of climbing roses that completely covered these two sides and the roof of the gazebo. At dinnertime every evening during the summer, the servants laid a carpet on the floor of the gazebo and spread a tablecloth over it. That night we all sat on the carpet around the tablecloth and ate a huge variety of dishes, some of which were specialties of the Shirazian area such as *Shirazy polo*, a rice dish containing lamb, eggplant, tomato, and spices. This particular dish is so colorful that some people call it *javaher polo* (jewel rice). All the cooking and serving was supervised by a middle-aged servant, named Laleh, who had been with the family many years and had been nanny to all six of my uncle's children.

After the dinner was over and the dishes cleared, we all sat around talking for hours. All the time we were talking, we were entertained by the antics of Uncle Shirazy's two pet ferrets who continually climbed up his arms and around his neck and shoulders. Uncle Shirazy and his family described the many things that we must see in the city that had once been the capital of all Persia during the Zandieh dynasty in the eighteenth century. At that time, it was a walled city surrounded by a deep moat. Fragments of the ten-meter-high and four-meter-wide stone wall can still be seen in various parts of the city. Shiraz was the birthplace of two of the most renowned poets in the country, Hafiz and Sa'adi, as well as many less well-known literati. These minstrels are the "nightingales" in the expression "the City of Roses and Nightingales." One of my cousins said that our sight-seeing must include a visit to Persepolis, fifty kilometers northeast of Shiraz; and he promised to take us there one day during our visit. We decided that the next day we would go to see the tomb of Hafiz in the gardens of Hafiziyyeh and then go to Sa'adiyyeh, the tomb of Sa'adi. Mahnaz, Uncle's daughter, volunteered to accompany us there in the morning.

Right after breakfast the next morning, Mahnaz, Katayoon, and I set out by cab and, after a ride of about fifteen minutes, arrived at the gardens of Hafiziyyeh in the center of which stood the tomb of Hafiz. There were numerous shade trees with benches where people could sit and meditate, or simply enjoy the sight of the beautiful flowerbeds and reflecting pools. Some go there to seek an augury in the *Divan*, the chief work of Hafiz, which is a collection of about seven hundred of his poems. They would sit in the garden and open a copy of the *Divan* at random in an attempt to find a verse that they could interpret as applying to their particular problem or question. For example, if one opened the *Divan* to the page containing the following verses, one could find comfort and/or advice for a variety of circumstances.

From Canaan Joseph shall return, whose face
A little time was hidden: weep no more—
Oh, weep no more! In sorrow's dwelling place
The roses yet shall spring from the bare floor!
And heart bowed down beneath a secret pain—
Oh, stricken heart! Joy shall return again
Peace to the love-tossed brain—oh, weep no more!
Today may pass, tomorrow pass, before
The turning wheel gives me my heart's desire;
Heaven's self shall change and turn not evermore
The universal wheel of fate in ire.
Oh, Pilgrim nearing Mecca's holy fame,
The thorny bush shall wound thee in vain,
The desert blooms again. Oh, weep no more!
                    —from a translation of the *Divan* by Gertrude L. Bell

Persians throughout history have had a love of poetry; and hundreds of Persian poets over the ages have written their thoughts on love, politics, religion, or whatever came to mind. Thus their writings are a kind of historical record since they reflect the contemporary thinking of their time. No Persian poet is more revered than Hafiz. His *Divan (Collection of Odes)* is found in every literate household in Persia, and many Persians have memorized hundreds of his verses and quote them often. My grandmother knew so many that she was able to hold her own with anyone in a *moshaereh* (poetry contest).

Little is known about the life of Hafiz. He was born into a poor family in Shiraz about 1325 and died around 1390. His father died during his infancy, and Hafiz is said to have earned his living as a youth in various ways before the beauty and brilliance of his odes came to the attention of several kings and princes who became his patrons.

360

During Hafiz's lifetime, Persia was in the throes of insurrection and conflict, and Hafiz was witness to the slaying of kings, attempted coups, and the devastation of war; yet he seemed to view these events as mere ripples in the surface of the great lake of time as he sought for tranquillity of the heart in the midst of a tumultuous world. Some historians have said that he was a member of the monastic Sufi sect, but while he may have been a member for a brief time, his many derogatory references to the hypocrisy of Sufi in some of his verse make it appear unlikely that he embraced Sufism for any length of time.

> Keep away from me, O Sufi, keep away;
> Because I have vowed to avoid thy law!
> My heart fled from the cloister and chant of monkish hymn,
> What can avail me sainthood, fasting and punctual prayer?

It would appear more likely that his mysticism was derived from Mithraism, the ancient Persian religion that antedated Zoroaster, and worshipped Mithra, the god of sun and light. This religion was a spiritual path that progressed through seven ascending stages, the last of which was that of the Magian Master, or Elder. Hafiz refers to the Master frequently under various names such as the Tavern Keeper, the Rose-Colored Master, or the Wine Seller. All of these references are to a single real person, a Magian Elder, whose disciple Hafiz had become. Many attempts have been made to translate Hafiz's works into English, beginning almost two hundred years before Fitzgerald made his famous translation of Omar Khayyam; but much of his work does not lend itself easily to translation; many of his subtle nuances are lost in the process. He has been ranked along with Shakespeare, Goethe, and Dante as one of the greatest poets of all time. He will live in the hearts of Persians forever.

After we had explored the gardens and viewed the tomb of Hafiz, we walked a kilometer or so farther north to the Sa'adiyyeh, the garden tomb of Sa'adi. His tomb had fallen into disrepair over the years and had been completely renovated in 1948; the exterior is now faced with marble of various colors and turquoise-colored tiles. Like that of Hafiz, the tomb of Sa'adi is in the center of a beautiful garden, about two acres in size, that is enclosed by a high brick wall. Above the entrance gate there is a row of tiles inscribed with an epitaph composed by Sa'adi himself. It translates something like this: "The scent of love shall arise from the soil of the grave of Sa'adi of Shiraz for eternity." A unique feature of the garden is the Pool of Fishes. Beneath the garden there is an underground spring-fed lake. Adjacent to the northwest corner of the tomb, there is an excavated area about twelve feet square with a flight of steps leading down to the water surface. When one looks into the crystal clear water, the pool is seen to teem with hundreds of fish apparently attracted by the light and the opportunity to feed on insects that land on the surface of the water.

Sheykh Moslehoddin Sa'adi was born in Shiraz around the close of the twelfth century and lived for about one hundred years. He came from a well-to-do family and had an extensive education. His life can be described as having three periods: his education, his travels, and his literary period. After his initial education in Shiraz, which lasted twelve years, he went to Baghdad, at that time the center of learning for the Islamic world, for his higher education. He studied there for about twenty years, then he began to travel extensively throughout the Middle East and Asia Minor, visiting Mecca, India, and cities in North Africa. He lived as a hermit for a period of time in Jerusalem, where he was captured and imprisoned by the Crusaders. Eventually, he secured his release and returned to Shiraz, the city of his birth, where he lived out the rest of his days and produced his best-known works of literature and poetry.

He wrote at least twenty-two books, the most important of which are the *Bustan (Garden of Fragrance),* written in 1257, and the *Golestan (Flower Garden),* written in 1258. The *Bustan* is a collection of moral stories written in prose. Ralph Waldo Emerson, in describing Sa'adi's works, declared, "He speaks to all nations and, like Homer, Shakespeare, Cervantes and Montaigne, is perpetually modern." To Emerson, Sa'adi's *Golestan* is "one of the Bibles of the world" and in it he found "the universality of moral Law." Voltaire, Benjamin Franklin, and other savants of enlightenment also held Sa'adi's *Golestan* and *Bustan* in high regard. Sa'adi viewed humanity as being an internal state of the soul and, by the suppression of its ego, capable of attaining to the Divine. The following excerpts from one of his odes expresses his philosophy.

> The body of man is noble
> Because of his soul.
> To wear beautiful clothes alone
> Is not a sign of humanity.
>
> Eating and sleeping, rage and lust
> Are tumult, ignorance and darkness;
> The beast has no knowledge
> Of the world of humanity.
>
> If from your nature
> This viciousness dies
> You will be alive forever more
> In the spirit of humanity.
>
> Man reaches a plane
> Where he sees nothing but God.
> Behold at what heights
> Is the dignity of humanity!

During the duration of our stay in Shiraz, we saw many beautiful places, chiefly gardens that were built during the Zandieh dynasty in the early eighteenth century. Of all the gardens we saw, the Bagh-e-Eram (Garden of Paradise) was the loveliest. This garden, in the north of Shiraz, was designed by a tribal chieftain in the early 1700s and patterned after gardens built centuries before during the Sassanid dynasty. In it, he planted numerous cypress, pine, orange, and persimmon trees interspersed beside walkways lined with flowerbeds. The gardens were bought about seventy-five years later by a wealthy man named Nasir al-Molk who hired a famous Shirazian architect, Mohammed Hasan, to design a pavilion for the garden. This pavilion is unique in that part of the tiled first floor is partially underground and cooled by a stream of water that runs through the building then passes out into the garden, cascading through it in a series of pools and small waterfalls.

While the Bagh-e-Eram is probably the most famous and

beautiful garden in Shiraz, there are numerous other lovely gardens scattered throughout the city. Among these are the Golshan, Delgosha, and Jahan Nama gardens; we visited all of them. A favorite picnic area of the people of Shiraz lies to the north of the city on the terraced slopes of a mountain called Baba-Koohi. About two kilometers up the mountain, there is a spring-fed pool in a large terraced area. From here, one can look out over the whole city of Shiraz and truly appreciate its beauty, an oasis of greenery surrounded by mountains. Near the top of the mountain, there is a tomb containing the remains of a poet named Abooabdolah Shirazi, who died in A.D. 1050 at the age of one hundred. He wrote under the pen name of Baba-Koohi and lived near where he is entombed, hence the name given to the mountain.

Toward the end of the first week of our visit, Cousin Mahnaz told me that a friend and classmate of hers had invited us to spend an afternoon in her house along with a few other friends. I was delighted at the prospect of meeting some girls close to my own age. I really enjoyed meeting and talking with the people of Shiraz; they were exceptionally warm and friendly and had a certain *joie de vivre*, which probably came from living in such a lovely city. Mahnaz and I arrived at her friend's house about 2 P.M., and Mahnaz introduced me to our hostess whose name was Mithra. Mithra escorted us to the *hozkhaneh* in the basement and introduced me to three other girls who had been invited to meet me. They were all classic Persian beauties with long shining black hair, flashing black eyes; and they had the effervescent personality typical of Shirazians.

I had seen only one other *hozkhaneh* before, the one in my Aunt Ozra's house in Mashhad. This one was much larger and more beautifully decorated than Aunt Ozra's. The decorative pool was at one end of a room, the floor and walls of which were covered with beautiful tiles, all with a turquoise background and painted in a variety of designs in white, green, and gold. A large brass chandelier with colorful ceramic shades was centered over a sitting area next to the pool furnished with sofas, chairs, and coffee tables. Potted lemon trees, gardenias, and jasmine were scattered about, and even though it was midafternoon, the room was delightfully cool and refreshing.

We girls sat and talked for hours, all the while munching on nuts, fruit, and cookies and drinking tea. None of the girls had ever been to Tehran and their curiosity about the city, the schools, and the people was insatiable. They asked me all sorts of questions, including the relationships between the sexes. I told them that I did not have much experience, but I knew that teenage boys and girls did exchange love letters. They marveled at the apparent progressiveness in the capital and explained that they could never think of writing a letter to a boy in Shiraz. Everyone knew everyone else, and it would be impossible to hide such a daring moral digression. A girl's reputation could be ruined forever!

One of the girls mentioned that she knew that the summer sun was very hot in Tehran. She told me, "Our grandmothers here in Shiraz always warn us not to walk in the sun when your shadow is shorter than you are or your skin will be ruined."

Another girl giggled and said, "Why don't you tell Mehry our grandmothers' other advice?"

Everyone laughed and Mithra said that I didn't need to hear it. I became curious and persisted in hearing the secret. Finally, one of the girls broke down and said, "I'll tell you and you can tell it to the other girls back in Tehran. Our grandmothers say that in order to keep a happy marriage, a woman must keep two ovens warm—one in the kitchen and one in the bedroom!"

At one point, during a rare lag in the conversation, Mithra turned to me and said, "Mehry, did you know that your name and my name have the same meaning? *Mithra* means the 'sun or light' and *Mehr* means the same thing, as well as 'kindness.' If you tell me a story that has your name in it, I'll tell you one with my name in it."

I confessed that I did not know any story in which my name figured, but along with the other girls, I begged Mithra to tell her story.

"Very well," she said; and with that she began: "Once, long ago, there lived a young couple on a plain near the Zagros mountains. In those days, there was perpetual summer, and there was no snow on the mountaintops. The husband, Firooz, was a farmer who, in addition to growing grain, raised all sorts of farm animals and tended a large fruit orchard. The second year they were married, Soroosh, the wife, bore her first child, a pretty girl. Although Firooz was hoping for a boy, he welcomed his new daughter and was thankful that she was a healthy baby.

"Over the next four years, Soroosh had four more children, all girls, and each one prettier than the previous. During this time, the couple seemed to prosper more and more with the birth of each child. Their crops were bountiful, their animals bore healthy and thrifty young, and the fruits of the orchard were large and sweet. Firooz accepted his lack of a son philosophically and loved and cherished all his daughters. The girls were so pretty and well mannered that each one was married by the time she was fifteen, and Firooz and Soroosh were left all alone. They decided that it was still not too late to try for a boy, and Soroosh soon became pregnant.

"The couple anxiously awaited the birth of the baby; and when it finally arrived, it was another girl! But such a lovely girl that all the friends and relatives marveled at her beauty and said that she shone like the sun. Firooz and Soroosh decided to name her Mithra after the ancient god of sun and light. Mithra grew more and more beautiful with each passing year. She loved the outdoors and was always playing outside. One day, when she was six years old, she was playing in the meadow near their house. Her mother watched her through a window. Suddenly, there was a loud rumbling sound and a huge black cloud in the shape of a giant appeared over the head of the little girl. She looked up in fear and began to run for the house. She was not quick enough; before she had run but a few steps, the giant swept her up into the cloud and she disappeared.

"Her parents were stricken with grief. For months, they wandered from place to place hoping that the giant had dropped their lovely child somewhere. The farm did not prosper as before; the fields became brown and dead, the trees leafless, and even the earth itself froze. After some months, Firooz and Soroosh gave up their search and returned home. They locked themselves in the house and continued to grieve. Six months had passed since their daughter had disappeared. Suddenly, one day while they were sitting together trying to comfort each other, they heard the loud rumbling noise that they had heard before their daughter vanished. They ran outside and saw a huge black cloud hovering overhead. There was a loud clap of thunder and Mithra appeared standing before them in the meadow. Where she stood, the dead grass suddenly turned green; and as she walked toward them, violets and buttercups sprang up in her footsteps; the air became soft and fresh and the songs of birds were heard. They rushed together and clasped their daughter between them, showering her with kisses and tears of joy. With Mithra's arrival came the first spring. Since that day, the date she first disappeared has signaled the time when all nature goes to sleep, and the date she reappeared has heralded the rebirth of all things."

The afternoon passed quickly and soon it was time to thank our hostess and leave. Mahnaz and I lingered after the other girls had left. I commented to Mithra on how beautiful the *hozkhaneh* was and how it must be a wonderful place to have a party. She agreed and said that often her father would have a group of his friends in on a weekend evening, and they would sit and talk and recite poetry for hours. "My father is not a poet," she said, "but he has a number of friends who are and he loves poetry."

In later years, I read a book written by an English diplomat, Sir Austin Henry Layard, telling of his travels in Persia during the nineteenth century. He relates that he was entertained in many of the best Persian homes throughout the country. In describing one particular evening in Isfahan, he comments that "the food was of the best and, although there were no alcoholic beverages served, listening to the verses of Hafiz and Sa'adi being recited by trained professionals accompanied by music seemed to have the same intoxicating effect on my Persian hosts as the wine of Shiraz."

During the second week of our visit to Shiraz, Cousin Shaheen made good his promise to take us to Persepolis. A friend of his had a car, and one morning he came to take us to visit the ruins of the old capital of the Persian Empire. Shaheen and his friend sat in the front and Katayoon, Mahnaz, and I sat in the backseat for the fifty-kilometer ride to the northeast. The road was paved and well maintained by the government, because Persepolis is a tourist attraction and has been for hundreds of years. The trip did not take long and we soon arrived at the site of the city built by the Emperor Darius I in 515 B.C.

The magnificent columns and portions of the walls of the palaces and buildings stood as they had for almost twenty-five hundred years. We wandered about through the city admiring the bas-relief carvings on the walls of the stairways leading up to the hundred-column audience hall. The sixty-five-foot columns are surmounted by carved figures of lions' heads, bulls, and horned lions and originally supported a ceiling of cedar wood imported from Lebanon. Signs identified the palaces built by Darius and, later on, by his son Xerxes, as well as the site of the treasury and the throne hall of Xerxes. After about two hours of walking about in the sun, we were all ready to return home. We piled back into the car and by early afternoon were back in Shiraz.

To any Persian, the sight of the ruins of Persepolis recalls the glories of the Achaemenid dynasty founded by Cyrus the Great and continued by Darius and his son Xerxes. The precepts introduced by Cyrus the Great in the sixth century before Christ are often described as the first charter of human rights. In 1971, a memorial plaque to Cyrus the Great was dedicated in the United Nations building in New York City.

The last day of our visit we went to the Vakil Bazaar to do a little shopping. The Vakil Bazaar is one of the most beautiful roofed bazaars in the country; all the ceilings and walls are made of yellow brick set in intricate designs. It was well lit by sunlight, because in addition to the usual skylights set at intervals in the ceilings, there are windows high up in the walls. The bazaar was built in the eighteenth century during the Zandieh dynasty when Shiraz was the capital of Persia for a short time. Katayoon and I wandered through the bazaar and made a few purchases to take back to Tehran as gifts for our sisters and our maid's little boy. We were both sad at the thought that our visit to Shiraz was over. We had had such a delightful time with Uncle Shirazy and his family, and enjoyed seeing the beautiful city.

Shortly after dawn the next morning, our bus left the Shiraz depot and headed north to the city of Isfahan, about five hundred kilometers away. The day was sunny, the sky cloudless, and the road smooth. We gradually ascended through the mountains, enjoying the lovely scenery, and shortly after twelve noon we arrived in Isfahan. It is said that Isfahan, the second-largest city in Persia, is the most beautiful city in the country. There is an old Persian saying, *Esfahan nesf-e-jahan*, meaning "Isfahan is half the world."

Isfahan is located on a wide green plain, bounded on the west and the south by high mountains rising two to three thousand meters. The river Zayandeh, which arises in the Bakhtiary mountains to the west, winds eastward for a distance of about 480 kilometers and, about halfway along its path, flows through the city of Isfahan. It supplies abundant water to the city and its environs before disappearing into the sandy ground in a swamp, called the Govkhooney, southeast of Isfahan. Since Isfahan is located at an altitude of almost a mile, the climate is quite temperate.

The driver stopped the bus close to the main square, Maydan Naghsh-e-Jahan (Image of the World). He announced that we could get lunch and look around a bit, but we shouldn't wander too far since the bus would be leaving at 2 P.M. sharp. We still had another four hundred kilometers to go to reach Tehran. Katayoon and I filed off the bus along with the other passengers and entered the Qaysariyya Bazaar at the north end of the square. Here we had lunch at a small cafe and watched the crowds passing by. Something was happening everywhere around us. People were bargaining with the various merchants, criticizing the merchandise offered for sale, arguing, and joking, all in their strong Isfahanian accents.

After lunch, we left the bazaar and walked around the square for a short time admiring the buildings surrounding the square and marveling at its size. We didn't even have time to completely walk around the huge square before it was time to reboard the bus. We left Isfahan promptly at 2 P.M. and arrived back in Tehran about 9 P.M. On the way back, Katayoon and I talked a lot about Isfahan, and we both vowed that we would return to that lovely city one day and explore it more thoroughly. A few years later, after I had married, I did return to Isfahan and the first place I went was to the Maydan Naghsh-e-Jahan.

The Maydan was originally laid out as a polo field before the Safavid dynasty but now is more like a park with many flowerbeds, decorative pools, trees, and pedestrian walkways. It is 500 meters long, 150 meters wide, and oriented north-south.

Shah Abbas I, during the Safavid dynasty in the early years of the seventeenth century, redesigned the area and built his most important buildings around the square, buildings that have retained their beauty after four hundred years and are still a major tourist attraction. On the west side of the square is the Ali Qapu, the sixth-story gatehouse built in 1609 in front of one of the palaces of Shah Abbas I. This building was the seat of authority where Shah Abbas held court and received visiting dignitaries. It housed a guardroom on the first floor, and a spiral staircase on one side leads to the upper floors. The uppermost story consists of a central room surrounded by a group of smaller rooms and is known as the Music Room.

The ceilings and walls of the Ali Qapu are all elaborately decorated with carved wood and painted plaster in a multitude of designs and colors. Behind the Ali Qapu is the palace area that is really a series of pavilions in a garden area rather than the traditional European palace. Only one of these pavilions survives in anything like its original state, the Chehel Sutun, or "Forty Columns." This is a relatively small building with a magnificent loggia supported by twenty columns that in turn are reflected in a great pool in front of the building, so it appears to have forty columns. This building was redecorated during the reign of Shah Abbas II who ruled from 1642 to 1666 and has many fine wall and ceiling paintings.

On the north side there is the Qaysariyya, the magnificent two-story covered bazaar where Katayoon and I had lunched on our way back to Tehran after our visit to Shiraz. The four-hundred-year-old Qaysariyya is a continuous warren of shops and caravanserai linked by high-ceilinged tunnels with domes at intervals to let in light. Because of the high ceilings, too much heat is prevented from entering in the summer or escaping in the winter, and thus a fairly even temperature is maintained throughout the year. On one wall at the entrance to the Qaysariyya, there is a tile mosaic depicting the satyr archer Sagittarius, the symbol for the year in which construction of the bazaar was begun by Shah Abbas. Abbas was a frequent visitor to the bazaar and often entertained ambassadors and other dignitaries in one of the many cafes.

A seventeenth-century memoir of Don Garcia, the Spanish

ambassador to the court of Shah Abbas I, describes one such evening. After viewing a fireworks display in the Maydan, the ambassadors from India, Spain, England, and Portugal along with several Portuguese priests retired with Shah Abbas to a sumptuous cafe in the Qaysariyya where they ate and drank for several hours. Other contemporary accounts describe how on certain evenings Shah Abbas would order the Maydan and Qaysariyya to be cleared of all males. Male merchants and shop-keepers would have to leave their shops in the care of a female relative. Then the Shah would bring his harem to the bazaar and allow them to shop and wander about. The area was open to any other female in the city who wished to shop unobserved by any male except for the eunuchs of the harem.

On the east side of the Maydan is the Lutfallah mosque built in 1603 by Shah Abbas I in honor of his father-in-law. This mosque was one of the first buildings to be erected around the square and is an exquisite example of Islamic architecture. It is unique in that the dome of the mosque is made of unglazed *café au lait*-colored tile with a series of glazed dark blue and white arabesques winding over its surface. When the sun strikes the surface of the dome, the glazed tiles reflect the sunlight whereas the unglazed background does not. This effect lends an air of serenity and repose that is unmatched and in contrast to the usual glittering blue domes seen on most mosques. On the south side of the square there is the huge Royal Mosque.

Both of these mosques posed problems in design due to the fact that, according to Moslem law, they had to be oriented to face Mecca, which lies to the southwest of Isfahan. In the case of the smaller Lutfallah mosque, the problem was solved by con-struction of an entrance corridor that curved upon itself before entering the dome chamber of the mosque proper. The dome therefore appears from outside the facade to be slightly off to one side. In the case of the Royal Mosque, the entrance portal is in the center of the outer facade but, inside the facade, the archi-tects rotated the entire mosque forty-five degrees. Thus, instead of the mosque lying immediately behind the entrance portal, where in fact the domes would have been partially obscured, it all lies to one side and can be seen in total as viewed from the Maydan. An interesting acoustic phenomenon is found in the

Royal Mosque. If one stands beneath the main big dome and claps once, the sound is echoed repeatedly twelve to fourteen times. In the southwest courtyard there is a gnomon installed by the Persian mathematician and scholar Sheykh Bahaie that determines the exact instant of noon regardless of the season of the year.

A famous tourist attraction in Isfahan are the Allahvardi Khan and Khwaju bridges over the river Zayandeh. Over the centuries, many bridges have been built over the Zayandeh to connect the east bank to the west. Today there are fourteen in use; but the two mentioned above are the most famous, and although four hundred years old, they are still in use except for truck traffic. The Allahvardi is also known as the Bridge of the Thirty-three Arches. It is three hundred meters long and fourteen meters wide and constructed of brick. A covered pedestrian walkway is on both sides of the central roadway.

The Khwaju Bridge is even more elegant. It is constructed of stone and brick and supported by a series of twenty-four arches spanning sluiceways that can be closed so that the river becomes a shallow lake temporarily. It is two-stories high with the main roadway on top and pedestrian walkways and pavilions on the first story, where one can sit and enjoy the view. The bridge is 133 meters long and 12 meters wide. Shah Abbas used to enjoy viewing from this bridge fireworks displays on the lake.

About six kilometers to the west of Isfahan in the village of Karladan, there is an interesting building called Menar Jonban (Moving Minarets) that houses the tomb of an ancient scholar named Abdolah. The building predates the reign of Shah Abbas the Great by about two hundred years, according to the date inscribed on the tomb. Two minarets about eighteen feet in circumference are located on either side of the building. When one puts one's arms around one of the minarets and shakes it, the opposite minaret moves in harmony. If a bowl of water is placed on the tomb before shaking a minaret, the surface of the water can be seen to move as well.

Another tourist attraction in Isfahan is the district in the southern part of the city called Jolfa. It is famous because of the number of Christian churches built in this area during the reign of Shah Abbas the Great and his successors in the Safavid dynasty. Shah Abbas the Great was a very open-minded ruler who wanted to maintain good relationships with the Western countries. There was a small Christian population in Isfahan, and he encouraged them to build their own houses of worship, stipulating only that he approve the design. Other Christians from other parts of Persia, on hearing of the shah's tolerance of their religion, flocked to Isfahan until the population reached close to one hundred thousand at one time. Over the years, the twelve churches were constructed, and they are famous for their beauty. They combine a blend of Western architecture with the beautiful tile mosaic work and painting for which Persian artisans are renowned. Libraries and museums housing valuable manuscripts written in Armenian as well as beautiful paintings have been built next to some of the churches.

All of the beautiful buildings mentioned above plus many more were built during the 225-year rule of the Safavid dynasty, at which time Isfahan was the capital of the Persia united by Shah Abbas I (the Great). In 1722, the country was invaded by the Afghani, and Isfahan was captured and sacked. Beautiful palaces and other public buildings were destroyed or converted to stables and caravanserai. The city languished in relative obscurity for the next two hundred years. The Afghans were defeated and driven out of Persia by Nader Shah Afshar, who made Mashhad the capital. The Zandieh dynasty that succeeded Nader moved the capital to Shiraz; and finally, the Qajar dynasty made Tehran the capital in the early nineteenth century.

When the Reza Shah Pahlavi came to power in the 1920s, he established a Ministry of Archeology and work began throughout the country to restore and preserve the ancient archeological treasures. Isfahan, in particular, benefited from this revival. Restoration of the buildings around the Maydan and elsewhere was begun and industries, which provided employment for the people, were established. This program was continued and expanded under the rule of Mohammed Reza Shah, who also began to publicize the city internationally by means of motion pictures and books describing its attractions in various languages. As a result, Isfahan has become a tourist attraction for visitors from around the world as well as a shoppers paradise. Some of the finest carpets made in Persia are woven in Isfahan;

and lovers of tile work, engraving, decorative enameling, and inlaying find many wonderful buys.

The farmlands around the city produce some of the best melons and pomegranates in the country. A common sight around the city and countryside is the pigeon towers built over the centuries to house flocks of pigeons. Once a year, the pigeon droppings are collected and used to fertilize the ground where the melons are grown. These melons are shaped like a watermelon but longer than the average watermelon; ivory or light yellow in color; and sweet, juicy, and crunchy in texture. The sweet, juicy pomegranates are as large as a large grapefruit. When they ripen on the tree, the pomegranates split open and offer their ruby treasures to the wild birds. The shining red seeds revealed accounts for the nickname "ruby tree."

During my last visit to Isfahan, I stayed with an old school chum in the luxurious Shah Abbas Hotel; and on that occasion, the king of Sweden was visiting Isfahan and staying in the same hotel. While sitting in the lobby, my friend and I caught frequent glimpses of the royal entourage. Many foreign dignitaries who were guests of the Persian government were housed in this hotel while they toured the historical landmarks of the city. The Shah Abbas Hotel is a converted caravanserai that was originally built during the Safavid dynasty.

Shah Abbas the Great built a beautiful wide avenue called Chahar Bagh (Avenue of Four Gardens). His successor, Shah Sultan Hussein, ordered a theological college to be built at the end of this avenue. His mother, who was a very practical person, commissioned the building of a huge caravanserai adjacent to the seminary with the intent that the profits from its operation be used to support the college.

The central camel courtyard is now the vast garden of the hotel, and the surrounding camel stalls and the rooms on the second story are now the hotel. Just inside the main entrance, there is a large lobby and adjacent bar, both with lovely hand-painted ceilings. Several restaurants serving the best of Persian cuisine as well as international dishes are scattered about the building. The guest rooms are spacious and have the high ceilings found in all caravanserai and originally designed to allow a laden camel to enter.

In Isfahan, the architectural masterpieces created from mud bricks and tile reflect the creativity of man over the centuries. One can see in them the Persian love for beauty, harmony of colors and purity of form. The gardens in Shiraz are, to me, a visual representation of Paradise. They are a less tangible, but nonetheless as powerful, expression of the same emotions.

I'll close this chapter with a story that I heard on one visit to Isfahan. The Isfahani have a reputation for a tricky cleverness. One time a merchant came from Tehran to trade with a merchant in Isfahan. They concluded their business over a period of several days and, in the process, became quite friendly. The evening before he was to return to Tehran, the merchant said to his new friend, "You Isfahani are supposed to be so clever, but I don't think that you are any more clever than I or any other Tehrani."

The Isfahan merchant replied, "You are mistaken, my friend. If you would care to make a wager, I can prove to you that we Isfahani know all the right questions and all the right answers." The Tehran merchant agreed, so the Isfahani continued, "Let us place two gold coins on the table between us. This will be the reward for whoever asks the best question. I will ask you a question; and if you do not know the answer, you will pay me a gold coin. Then you can ask me a question; and if I cannot answer it correctly, I will pay you a gold coin. Here is my question: What animal has four legs, three horns, and no wings, but can jump and fly?"

The Tehrani thought for a long while, then he confessed that he did not know the answer and gave a gold coin to the Isfahani. Then he said to the Isfahani, "I will not ask you a question of my own, but answer for me the question that you asked. What is that animal?"

The Isfahani answered, "I don't know. Here is your coin." Then he pocketed the two coins on the table saying, "You must agree that I asked the most difficult question!"

Note

1. To the Persian, an invitation to tread upon his eye, a most precious organ, symbolizes a warm and loving greeting similar to saying, "I would give up my life for you."

Chapter Twenty-four
My Childhood Ends

Don't hurt my heart; it is like a wild bird.
If it flies from the rooftop, it will never come back.
If a thorn is in my foot, I can easily pull it out,
But what can I do with a thorn that pierces my heart?
—Tabid Esfahani

The summer after I finished the tenth grade I was very anxious to go to Mashhad. The previous summer I had visited Shiraz, so I had not been to Mashhad for two years and I missed Grandmother very much. My father and grandfather as well as other members of the family made frequent trips to Tehran to visit with us and other relatives but Grandmother, as usual, refused to travel. Her trip to Qandehar (now part of Afghanistan) when she was very young had soured her for life on travel. None of my sisters or brothers planned to go to Mashhad that summer, so I had to find some other relative to accompany me. During the previous few years, a number of cousins had moved to Tehran from Mashhad, and I thought that surely one of them would be going back for a visit. However, I could find no one. Finally, a friend of one of my brothers sent word that he and his family were going to Mashhad for three weeks, and I was welcome to go and return with them.

I was happy to accept their offer because somehow it seemed important to me to get away from Tehran and return to the scenes of my childhood. I had been working hard the past academic year and felt drained both physically and emotionally. The recent departure of my friend Shahriyar for America still weighed heavily on my mind.

376

When I arrived at my former home, I was relieved to find that Little Aunt and her sons had moved out of the house. My uncle from Torbat had moved his medical practice to Mashhad and was now living with his family in a newly constructed house built on the site of what had been the north wing of our house. The former connecting center wing had been torn down and the south wing was now being used as a guest house. Grandmother and Grandfather lived in two rooms in a wing of the new house.

Even though my father visited often, it was good that my uncle was living in the same house and looking after Grandmother because, although she was in good health, she was now over ninety years old. Naneh, her longtime cook and maid, no longer worked for her. She had retired and now lived with her son, Mashaallah, and his wife. The hospital beyond the new wall had been completed and now loomed over it.

The porch that Grandfather used to sleep on in the summertime was gone. Since he still insisted on sleeping outdoors, he now slept in the courtyard on the same old wooden bed. I slept inside in my grandparents' bedroom along with Grandmother when I was not staying at Father's house. After the lights were out, we talked back and forth every night, reminiscing about the old house, the former servants, and the good times we had.

One night, after Grandmother had fallen asleep, I got out of bed and sat on the sill of the open window looking out on the moonlit courtyard. I thought to myself, *The house, gazebo, gardens, and orchards that I knew so well from every angle and every corner are gone. Only the ground beneath my feet and the stars overhead are the same.* I could still feel the joys and sorrows of the past in the air around me, almost palpably brushing my body and whispering in my ears, but there was nothing physically left.

Even my childhood companion, Genoos, seemed different. She was now a girl of twelve. She didn't follow me around as she did as a little child, and somehow seemed withdrawn whenever we conversed. I thought that she would be happier now that her father was living with her rather than in Torbat, but somehow she seemed depressed. The only reason that I could think of for her change in personality was that she now had to share her father's affections with a stepmother and two stepbrothers. We never went into her problems, because I sensed that she was too shy to talk about them. I was content just to see her again, and I knew that our love for each other was just as strong as ever.

The three weeks in Mashhad passed quickly. I returned to Tehran refreshed and in a better frame of mind after seeing Grandmother, Genoos, Nanny-jon, and the rest of my friends and family in Mashhad. Then I made a momentous decision: I decided that I would enter nursing school in the fall instead of returning to Shahdokht school. I had heard some of the girls talking about Shams Nursing School in the city of Rhay, south of Tehran. This was a boarding school, and most of the students came from cities other than Tehran. This school accepted students who had completed nine or more grades of school. The course of study was for four years, including a final year of supervised work in a hospital. Although it was rather late to apply for acceptance and not many students from Tehran were admitted, I had a cousin in Tehran who knew the physician who was head of the Persian Red Cross, which supported the school, and he managed to get me accepted to the fall class. When I announced my decision to enter nursing, my brothers and sisters were surprised; but they offered no comment and did not attempt to dissuade me. In retrospect, I believed that they knew that nursing was not for me, but they wisely decided that I should find this out for myself.

In the fall I moved into the nursing school. It was a modern two-story building with a basement. The second story was the living quarters for the students, who lived six to a room. The rooms were very spacious and pleasant with central heating and air-conditioning. The first floor contained classrooms, a laboratory, a small auditorium, and a library. In the basement there was a kitchen and dining room along with several apartments, where the headmistress and some of the lady teachers lived. The headmistress and the lady teachers were French, and all instruction was in French except for the Persian physicians who came in the mornings to teach anatomy, physiology, and other medical subjects.

My nursing career lasted three months! After the first month, I decided that nursing was not for me. After a good deal of negotiating and pulling of strings by my sisters, I managed to get readmitted to Shahdokht school. I had to work very hard to catch up with the rest of my eleventh grade class.

As the end of the academic year drew to a close, I studied even harder to prepare for the final examinations. Even though I was concentrating very hard on my schoolwork, I had a sense that something was going on in the family that would affect me. This sensation was heightened by my brother Jamshid, who was now living with us while he attended the University of Tehran. He no longer played elaborate pranks on the servants and family but was still an inveterate tease. Almost every afternoon when I came home from school, he would say to me, "Mehry, if you only knew what is happening!" No amount of pleading would get any more information out of him. Finally, I went to my sister Katayoon and asked her what Jamshid was talking about. She told me to pay no attention to him but to concentrate on getting ready for the final exams.

I managed to pass the final examinations for the eleventh grade despite my late start. A few days after the school year ended, I enrolled in the art school for a four-week course, which would be over before my annual visit to Mashhad.

When I came home that afternoon after signing up for the art course, I found Katayoon and my brother Jahan talking to a man whom I knew. He was a friend and classmate of Jahan's from Mashhad, now living in Tehran, and a frequent visitor to our house. I joined them for tea; and during the course of the conversation, I announced that I had just enrolled in the art school.

The gentleman, whose name was Tahmasb, said to me, "Before you came, your brother and sister and I were talking about how artistic you are. Have you ever seen the crown jewel display in the Central Bank jewel museum? Some of the pieces are really beautiful creations."

When I told him that I never been there, he continued, "How would you like to visit it with me next Tuesday afternoon?"

I was somewhat taken back and didn't know what to say; I had never been asked to go out alone with a man before. I glanced at my brother and sister. Both of them gave me an almost imperceptible nod indicating their approval, so I accepted Tahmasb's offer.

The next Tuesday, he called for me right after lunch and we

379

drove in his car to the Central Bank and went down to the basement vault where the jewels were on display. We saw the jeweled globe, eighteen inches in diameter, commissioned by the Qajar Shah Naseraldeen in 1874, who wanted to find a use for 51,366 loose gems that were lying around in his treasury. The globe is made of gold with the equator defined by a row of diamonds. The oceans of the world are shown by emeralds and the continents by rubies. The famous gem-studded Peacock Throne brought from India by Nader Shah in 1739 was on display in all its massive glory, as was the huge diamond known as the Ocean of Light. I never would have believed so many jewels existed in the whole world if I had not seen them with my own eyes. One entire wall was covered with pearls in all sizes, strung in necklaces and bracelets and set in earrings and rings. The coronation robe and gold crown used by the Reza Shah glittered in one glass case. After an hour or so, we had seen all that was to be seen and Tahmasb took me home.

I thanked him for the afternoon excursion and assumed that he would leave. However, Tooran saw us pull up to the door and invited him in for a cup of tea with the family. After a few minutes of polite conversation, he turned to me and asked, "Would you like to go to an art show that is on display in one of the galleries? I would like to take you there on Thursday afternoon, then we could have dinner at the Cafe Shahrdary that evening." Again I was overcome with shyness and didn't know what to say. I had enjoyed the visit to the crown jewel museum and Tahmasb seemed like a mature well-mannered gentleman, but to go out at night to a public restaurant with a man! What to say? Again I glanced at Katayoon and Jahan and was surprised to see them give a slight nod of approval. I accepted.

Thursday afternoon, Tahmasb presented himself to pick me up about three o'clock. He was most elegantly dressed in a dove gray suit and looked very handsome. We drove to the gallery and walked all around looking at each picture. Tahmasb listened respectfully to my comments on the artworks and was a most agreeable companion. I felt like an adult for the first time in my life. After we had spent several hours in the art gallery, we drove to the Cafe Shahrdary for dinner. It was an elegant restaurant with outdoor dining in a lovely garden with a small stage at one end where musicians played for the diners' entertainment. We sat opposite each other at a secluded table and dined sumptuously, all the while talking about art, music, and my studies at Shahdokht school.

After a few hours, I glanced at my watch and saw that it was ten o'clock. It would take us another thirty minutes to get home. I had never been out this late in my whole life and never with a man who was not a relative. I began to panic; but Tahmasb put his hand on mine and said, "Mehry, it is all right. Your sisters and brothers know that we will be late. You don't know what has been going on. My family approached your father several months ago and asked for your hand in marriage to me. No one wanted to tell you because you were busy with your final exams, and we didn't want to distract you from your studies. I want us to get to know each other better and to know if you yourself want to marry me. The first time that I saw you in Mashhad, you were about nine years old and I remember you bringing a basket of nectarines from the orchard. When you saw your grandmother and me sitting and talking on the porch, you asked if we would care for some, and when we said yes, you washed the fruit and brought it to us on a tray. As you have grown older, those nectarines have tasted sweeter and sweeter to me and I want you to be my wife! Your father will be coming to Tehran in a week or so, and I would like to make the final arrangements for our marriage if you want me."

I didn't know what to say. Now I knew what Jamshid had known and had been teasing me about that spring. Now I knew why my sister and brother allowed me to go out with this man without a chaperone. I felt that I could not say yes or no at that time. I was somewhat attracted to him; he was an accomplished conversationalist and came from a good family. But I had not finished school and I wanted to go on to higher education. On the other hand, several of my lady relatives had frequently told me in private that if I had a chance to marry well, I should take it before it was too late. We left the Cafe Shahrdary without any commitment from me, and he took me home.

The next day I went to see my school chum and confidante, Parvaneh. She and Mehrdad had finally worn down their parents' opposition and were to be married shortly. I told her what

381

had happened to me, and her first question was, "Do you love him?" I could not say that I did in the way that she and Mehrdad loved each other. After all, I had always thought of this man as a family friend and my sister Azar's suitor. I knew that he had asked for her hand in marriage two years before, and she had turned him down. I told her that our families approved our marriage and that I was excited at the prospect of donning a beautiful white dress, being the focal point of my wedding party, and then becoming the mistress of my own home with my own servants and probably a baby. I didn't tell Parvaneh, but in the back of my mind there was the thought that I had three older sisters who were not married and that I should follow the advice of some of my female relatives and snap up this opportunity.

Parvaneh and I talked for a long time about her forthcoming wedding and about my own prospective engagement. She did not encourage me in any way, but when I left her house, I knew that I was going to accept the proposal. As I walked home, I reflected on the plans and dreams that I had had for the future. Marriage had never been a consideration; I planned to pursue an artistic career in design or painting, with perhaps a bit of writing on the side. Now that I had made up my mind, within the fifteen minutes that it took me to walk home, I put aside all these aspirations for a career and decided to devote all my attention to becoming a good wife.

When I got home at dinnertime, Jamshid was still teasing me, but now that I knew what he was talking about, it didn't bother me. Katayoon took me aside after dinner and told me what I already knew—that Tahmasb had asked for my hand in marriage. She said that my father would be coming to Tehran in about a week to talk to me about it.

After my father arrived from Mashhad, he took me aside one day and told me that he wanted to talk to me alone. We went upstairs to a sitting room and sat opposite each other. I felt so shy, because I knew what he was going to say. He must have sensed this because he opened the conversation by saying, "I guess you know what I am going to talk with you about." I nodded in the affirmative and he continued, "Tahmasb's father and grandparents have come to me and asked for your hand in marriage to Tahmasb. I have known this family for many years and

Tahmasb grew up with Jahan. He appears to be a warm and understanding person, but I want you to know that the decision is yours and yours alone to make. I am not going to encourage you or discourage you, nor will anyone else in the family."

I thought for a few minutes in silence, then I said to him, "If you think that he will make a good husband for me, I agree."

Two days later, Father sent for Tahmasb and took him up to the same parlor. They talked for a long time and when they were done, Father came to me and said, "I made him agree to two conditions in order to marry you. First, he must allow you to continue your studies for as long as you wish; and second, he must never associate himself in any way with the Tudeh [communist party]."

At that time, it was considered fashionable by some people to be *rowshanfekr*, or open-minded, to the communist party, especially by the better-educated young people, similar to the attitude prevalent in Cambridge among such as Maclean and Philby, the British communist spies who eventually defected to Russia. The country was torn between the proselytizing of Mossadegh, the policies of the young shah, and the clandestine but resurgent Tudeh. Father was a staunch supporter of the shah and wanted no part of the communists. He believed, in view of the diversity of language and religion in Persia, that only a monarchy could keep the country united, strong, and progressive.

The rest of that spring and summer, I had no time for my art class. I was busy making my trousseau with the help of my sisters, Cousin Saleemeh, and Aunt Ozra. Since it is the custom in Persia for the bride's family to furnish the newlyweds' house, we were also busy shopping for carpets, furniture, and appliances. The wedding took place in late summer. A large number of relatives from both our families came from Mashhad for the ceremony. Grandmother, of course, did not make the trip.

In fact, the first and last time that I saw Grandmother after my marriage was three years later when I made a brief one-week visit to Mashhad. The thing that stands out in my memory of that last visit was one sunny morning when Grandmother and I were sitting in her bedroom talking together, as we had so many times in the past. She asked me to comb her hair, because she was having difficulty raising her arm due to arthritis in her shoulder. She sat on the floor and I sat behind her. Her hair was still long, reaching almost to her waist, and it was a beautiful pure white color. As the sunlight streamed in the window and fell upon her head, it looked like a shimmering silken cloth. I remarked on how lovely it looked and how wonderful it was that she still had such a full, long head of hair. She turned to me and smiling her old loving smile, said to me, "Mehry, when I was young, no respectable woman ever had short hair. The only ones who wore their hair short were the *gisoo bori-deh*, the women who were caught having affairs and their family cut off their hair as a punishment!"

My husband kept the two promises that he had made to my father before we married. Even though I was soon pregnant, I continued my studies at home under private tutelage and was able to take and pass the final examinations for the twelfth grade and graduate. Later on, I attended college in England and in the United States. However, I soon found that marriage is not always the idyll that Zivar used to describe in her stories. In real life, people do not always live happily ever after. Fundamental differences in philosophy soon cropped up and worsened over the years. Finally after twenty-two years, I was able to obtain a divorce under the laws enacted under the Mohammed Reza Shah that allowed a woman to petition for divorce. Although my first marriage was not a happy one, it did result in the birth of my beautiful daughter, Mojdeh, who in turn has presented me with my first grandson and, hopefully, will have many more. Mojdeh was studying in the United States at the time of my divorce and she never returned to Persia.

In the early spring of 1976, three months after my divorce, I left Persia. Except for my sisters and brothers, no one knew that I was leaving. We had a dinner together the night before I departed, and I told them that I didn't want anyone to come to the airport with me the next day. I remember that day very well: It was a dull, cloudy day with intermittent rain. This was not the first time that I was flying out of Persia for a foreign country, but it was the last time. I was leaving behind my native country where I had lived most of my life. It was not easy to put aside my former life, like a snake shedding its skin, but I thought to myself, *This is no time for regrets or second thoughts.*

A few minutes after the plane took off, it burst through the clouds into the bright sunshine under a clear blue sky. The change was quick and my spirits rose.

I thought to myself, *This is the way my life will change and I will come out of the darkness into the sun. There will always be a tomorrow, a new day offering new opportunities to grow. The whole future lies before me; I have to accept that the past is gone forever and I am flying into the future.*

I leaned back in my seat and closed my eyes. A quatrain from Khayyam came to mind:

> Ah, fill the Cup: what boots it repeat
> How time is slipping underneath our feet:
> Unborn Tomorrow, and dead Yesterday,
> Why fret about them if Today be sweet!

Epilogue

The reader may be curious as to what happened to the various members of my family to whom I have introduced you in this book. The generation from whom I learned so much and who guided me on the path to adulthood are gone in part—those people whose sincere devotion was endless and whose hearts were full of love. Growing up with them was an experience of learning by example. How short was that time that I had with them, although as a child I thought it would last forever. The house, the courtyards, the gardens, and the orchards that I so loved as a child are all gone; this book of memories is all that remains to remind me of those idyllic days.

Grandmother died in 1963. She was over one hundred years old and refused to go to any hospital. My physician uncle along with a number of his colleagues attended her at home to the end. Grandfather Khan, although fifteen years younger than she, after sixty-odd years of marriage was completely devastated by her death and lost his will to live. He died within six months of her passing, although he appeared to enjoy robust health to the end. Agha Bozorg, my maternal grandfather, died a few years after I and my sisters moved to Tehran. He was almost 110 years old, the longest-lived person on my mother's side of the family.

Shortly after Agha Bozorg's death, Aunt Ozra moved to Tehran to live with her daughter Saleemeh. In 1961, Aunt Ozra died at age seventy-six of a heart attack while saying her evening prayers. Father's sister, Little Aunt, died in Mashhad at age seventy-five, a few years following a stroke. Her sister, Grand Aunt, died several years after I had moved to the United States. She had lived to be one hundred years old. Her eldest son, Hameed, died in 1993 at age 103, to date the longest-lived on the paternal side of the family.

My father retired and, within a year after his mother's death, moved to Tehran with his wife. His marriage to my stepmother lasted twenty-two years before she succumbed to a stroke. After her death, Father lived with Katayoon until his sudden death from a heart attack in 1975 at age eighty-six. His brother, Uncle Ardesheer, after the death of Grandmother and Grandfather, built another house and moved out of the one he had built on the site of the north wing of our old house. This became a maternity hospital, and the south wing of our old house was remodeled and became an out-patient clinic for the hospital that had been built in our orchard. Uncle Ardesheer died with his boots on in 1977 at age seventy-six of a heart attack while attending a patient in his office.

Mother's brother Uncle Nishaburi died in Nishabur in his eighties after a brief illness. At the time of his death, he had over thirty children, grandchildren, and great-grandchildren. His brother, Uncle Shirazy, followed a few years later, dying in the City of Roses and Nightingales that he loved so much. Most of his numerous descendants still live in Shiraz. Cousin Saleemeh and her husband, Mirza Kamal, who grew lemons in his vodka bottle and loved his canaries, died within a year of each other in 1982–83. I regret that I was not able to see my uncles, Saleemeh, or her husband before they died, but I was out of the country during their last years. My Nanny-jon died in her sixties in Mashhad. Fortunately, she visited Tehran a few months before her death and we had a long visit together.

Jahan married a couple of weeks after I did and became the father of three children. Azar left Persia after I married and went to the United States to study for one year. When she returned, she married after about one year and bore one fine, brilliant son. Tooran married a few months later. She never had any children but has been happily married for almost forty years. Katayoon never married but devoted her life to her work and her family. I last saw her two years before her death in 1992 when she made a visit to the United States. Jamshid, after Azar and Tooran married, moved to the United States for graduate study and never returned to Persia to live. He married, fathered two children, and is now retired. Kaveh, my oldest brother, still enjoys good health at age eighty and climbs every weekend in the mountains. He and his wife had four daughters, all of whom are married, have children, and live in Europe or the United States. Kayvan, my second eldest brother, died of a heart attack at the young age of sixty-three in 1989. He is survived by two sons.

Three years after I married, my cousin Genoos married and eventually became the mother of two beautiful daughters. I have other first and distant cousins scattered all over the world, from Australia to Canada to the West and East Coasts of the U.S. to Europe. If ever we could have a family reunion, I am sure that the living members would number over three hundred. God keep them all!